THE GENTRIFICATION PLOT

LITERATURE NOW

LITERATURE NOW

Matthew Hart, David James, and Rebecca L. Walkowitz, Series Editors

Literature Now offers a distinct vision of late-twentieth- and early-twenty-first-century literary culture. Addressing contemporary literature and the ways we understand its meaning, the series includes books that are comparative and transnational in scope as well as those that focus on national and regional literary cultures.

Caren Irr, *Toward the Geopolitical Novel: U.S. Fiction in the Twenty-First Century*

Heather Houser, *Ecosickness in Contemporary U.S. Fiction: Environment and Affect*

Mrinalini Chakravorty, *In Stereotype: South Asia in the Global Literary Imaginary*

Héctor Hoyos, *Beyond Bolaño: The Global Latin American Novel*

Rebecca L. Walkowitz, *Born Translated: The Contemporary Novel in an Age of World Literature*

Carol Jacobs, *Sebald's Vision*

Sarah Phillips Casteel, *Calypso Jews: Jewishness in the Caribbean Literary Imagination*

Jeremy Rosen, *Minor Characters Have Their Day: Genre and the Contemporary Literary Marketplace*

Jesse Matz, *Lasting Impressions: The Legacies of Impressionism in Contemporary Culture*

Ashley T. Shelden, *Unmaking Love: The Contemporary Novel and the Impossibility of Union*

Theodore Martin, *Contemporary Drift: Genre, Historicism, and the Problem of the Present*

Zara Dinnen, *The Digital Banal: New Media and American Literature and Culture*

Gloria Fisk, *Orhan Pamuk and the Good of World Literature*

Peter Morey, *Islamophobia and the Novel*

Sarah Chihaya, Merve Emre, Katherine Hill, and Jill Richards, *The Ferrante Letters: An Experiment in Collective Criticism*

Christy Wampole, *Degenerative Realism: Novel and Nation in Twenty-First-Century France*

Heather Houser, *Infowhelm: Environmental Art and Literature in an Age of Data*

Jessica Pressman, *Bookishness: Loving Books in a Digital Age*

Sunny Xiang, *Tonal Intelligence: The Aesthetics of Asian Inscrutability During the Long Cold War*

The Gentrification Plot

NEW YORK AND THE
POSTINDUSTRIAL CRIME NOVEL

Thomas Heise

Columbia University Press
New York

Columbia University Press
Publishers Since 1893
New York   Chichester, West Sussex
cup.columbia.edu
Copyright © 2022 Columbia University Press

Library of Congress Cataloging-in-Publication Data
Names: Heise, Thomas, 1971– author.
Title: The gentrification plot : New York and the postindustrial crime novel / Thomas Heise.
Description: New York : Columbia University Press, [2022] | Series: Literature now |
Includes bibliographical references and index.
Identifiers: LCCN 2021027450 (print) | LCCN 2021027451 (ebook) | ISBN 9780231200189
(hardback ; acid-free paper) | ISBN 9780231200196 (trade paperback ; acid-free paper) |
ISBN 9780231553483 (ebook)
Subjects: LCSH: Detective and mystery stories, American—History and criticism. |
American fiction—21st century—History and criticism. | Gentrification in literature. |
New York (N.Y.)—In literature.
Classification: LCC PS374.D4 H45 2022 (print) | LCC PS374.D4 (ebook) |
DDC 813/.0872093587471043—dc23
LC record available at https://lccn.loc.gov/2021027450
LC ebook record available at https://lccn.loc.gov/2021027451

Columbia University Press books are printed on permanent and durable acid-free paper.
Printed in the United States of America

Cover design: Elliott S. Cairns
Cover image: © Michael Ver Sprill / Dreamstime.com

for my love, Allison Akiko Hiroto

CONTENTS

DEATH AND LIFE IN
POSTINDUSTRIAL NEW YORK

What should a crime novelist write about when there is not much crime to write about anymore? This question weighed on the minds of the crime writers Lee Child, Reggie Nadelson, and George Dawes Green during a discussion in 2009 on New York Public Radio's *The Leonard Lopate Show*. Invited to chat about "New York City Thrillers," the three novelists found themselves instead musing about how the city had become less thrilling over the years. "It's a very benevolent, peaceful place," Child noted with a touch of sadness.[1] "New York has changed, I think, in terms of crime. It's relatively crime free," he went on to say, adding, "It feels like a different city." Nadelson, who grew up during the rough-and-tumble 1970s in Greenwich Village, when it was known as much for its muggings and derelict buildings as for its rich social and cultural history, quipped in her gravelly voice, "It's hard to find a crime these days." "The problem with New York now is that it's become such a sweet city," Green chimed in, offering the most back-handed compliment one could give New York. When Nadelson was interviewed a year later by Salman Rushdie, she echoed Green's sentiments, calling New York "sweet,. . . safer, more welcoming and polite."[2] Cleaned up by the law-and-order mayoralty of Rudolph Giuliani (1994–2001) and then rebranded as a "luxury product" by the developer-friendly administration of Michael Bloomberg (2002–2013) that followed, the new New York posed and continues to pose a problem for crime writers.[3] *The Gentrification Plot* investigates this problem.

By many measures, it is a good problem to have. And it is a problem that social scientists in the early 2000s measured and remeasured to assure themselves that their numbers were really right and that New York really was the safest big city in the country. By 2009, reported crimes were well into their second decade of an unprecedented free fall. Homicides had dropped 82 percent from their grisly peak in 1990, when the city witnessed a staggering 2,245 killings, earning it the title of the murder capital of America.[4] Crime in all major categories fell off a cliff. The reported number of sexual assaults declined 52 percent between 1990 and 2000 and another 51 percent over the following nine years. Robberies plummeted 70 percent in a decade, then another 46 percent on top of that by 2009.[5] Auto thefts were down 94 percent in the nineteen-year period. Burglaries, 86 percent. While the saying goes that "crime can happen anywhere in New York," it increasingly seemed to be happening nowhere. The sudden, sharp, and sustained plunge left not only crime novelists looking for crime but also sociologists and criminologists searching for the right words to capture its disappearance. "A miracle," "an astonishing turnaround," a "momentous reversal," claimed the sociologist Andrew Karmen. "Never before had double-digit declines, year after year, taken place in a major metropolitan area," he remarked with astonishment. "No appropriate expression" exists for the drop, he wrote, before settling on the phrase "crime crash" as a way to "describe an unanticipated plunge of this magnitude and importance."[6] New York City's "continuous decline" in crime from 1990 to 2009, the criminologist Franklin Zimring observed, "is twice the length of the national downward trend and the longest big-city decline that has yet been documented with reliable crime statistics."[7] The writer Pete Hamill had predicted in 1990 that "as this dreadful century comes to an end, poor New York will slide deeper into decay, becoming a violent American Calcutta. . . . If there are two thousand murders this year, get ready for four thousand. New York is dying."[8] Hamill, who had spent the better part of five decades observing and writing about New York, could not have been more wrong in his prognostication.

The unprecedented "crime crash" is one of the major unforeseen developments that shifted the ground of crime fiction. More foreseeable developments are development and gentrification. Or put another way, if

Giuliani's zero-tolerance policing was the billy club of gentrification that changed the city for New York crime writers, Bloomberg's efforts to incite more luxury growth by private developers was the carrot. When Bloomberg was elected mayor in 2001, his administration took advantage of the previous decade's steep decline in crime to launch a building bonanza. What transpired over the next twelve years was a sustained surge of rezoning, demolition, and rebuilding that would profoundly alter the built space and social life of twenty-first-century New York, creating a new supergentrified city powered by finance, real estate, and information services that was fitting for a founder of the global financial services and media company that bears his name. Mayors Lindsay, Koch, Dinkins, and Giuliani all left their physical mark on New York, but none went as far to remake it as Bloomberg. As Julian Brash argues in *Bloomberg's New York: Class and Governance in the Luxury City* (2011), the mayor's policies, what he calls "the Bloomberg Way," "constituted an effort to establish the dominance of the ascendant postindustrial elite"—the transnational capitalist class and the professional managerial class, in particular—"vis-à-vis other social groupings in New York City. . . . In the arena of urban development," Brash posits, "the Bloomberg Way reached its apotheosis, subjecting the very urbanism of the city itself to its corporate logic."[9] "To capitalize on [our] strength[s], we'll continue to transform New York physically . . . to make it even more attractive to the world's most talented people," Bloomberg declared in his 2003 State of the City address.[10] It was a promise he largely kept by prioritizing the creation of new office towers in Manhattan to entice companies to relocate to the city and upscale residential areas all across the boroughs to house the financial, media, and business-services professionals who would follow. It was a *Field of Dreams* logic writ large: if you build it, they will come. And come they did. During the time Bloomberg was in office, the city's population swelled by 400,000, the equivalent of incorporating all of New Orleans into New York. With the newest arrivals, waves of gentrification soon washed across the city.

The gentrification of the city during Bloomberg's three terms was not the result of a market unrestrained by the guardrails of governmental regulation. Quite the opposite. The Bloomberg administration actively facilitated gentrification through a number of tactics, including private-public partnerships, generous 421a tax subsidies for the construction of upmarket buildings in underused areas, J-51 subsidies to landlords to renovate their properties, the creation of empowerment zones in poorer neighborhoods, and wide-scale alterations in zoning laws to spur development. Before Bloomberg left City Hall, "nearly one hundred rezoning changes . . . more than the previous six administrations combined," were enacted, affecting more than a third of the city's land area.[11] Hundreds of blocks of Harlem, East Harlem, Williamsburg, Greenpoint, and downtown Brooklyn; swaths of Coney Island, Hell's Kitchen, West Chelsea, TriBeCa, and Bedford-Stuyvesant; sections of the Bronx; and over 2,400 blocks in Queens alone were rezoned by his Department of City Planning.[12] In the process, 40,000 buildings were constructed; another 25,000 buildings across the city were pulled down.[13] To give context to this last number, "the number of buildings demolished between 2005 and 2007 alone was almost triple the number demolished in all the years from 1990 to 1999 combined."[14] The back-to-the-city movement that had been slowly underway since the 1980s accelerated after 2000, a dramatic U-turn that reversed decades of white flight to the suburbs in remarkably little time. With crime crashing across the city, developers cashed in on neighborhoods—from Harlem to Red Hook, Brooklyn—that for generations had been redlined into poverty and left behind as too dangerous, too Black, too Latinx, and too poor for investment. Researchers associated with New York University's Furman Center on housing and urban policy asked by the decade's end the obvious question in a study titled "Has Falling Crime Invited Gentrification?" (2019). The equally obvious answer—obvious to anyone watching New York change before their eyes—was "yes." The researchers concluded that as "violent crime" fell "dramatically,. . . growing proportions of high-income, college-educated, and white households mov[ed] into central city neighborhoods, a process referred to as gentrification."[15]

I take it as axiomatic that literature emerges out of, responds to, and reshapes the material conditions of its production. *The Gentrification Plot* proposes that for recent crime fiction these conditions are the city and the crimes that occur within it. In spite of all their murky complexity, shady dealings, and labyrinthine subterfuge, in the estimation of the scholar Dennis Porter, crime novels boil down to one thing: the relationship "between site and event."[16] So what happens to the genre when the city (the site) and the crimes of the city (the event) have been radically altered? How do crime writers reimagine and reposition the genre when "Fear City" (as the New York Police Department labeled New York in 1975) becomes "Sweet City," or, as Reggie Nadelson writes, what happens to the genre when the "old industrial city" of crumbling tenements, graffitied subways, and decaying piers is rebuilt as "a brand new city" of live-work lofts, Uber drivers, and cruise ships?[17] How does the genre of crime fiction change when its underlying material conditions have been upended by the "crime crash" of the 1990s and the "development boom" of the 2000s? The story of these changes—to a city and to a genre—is the story of this book.

Lee Child's remark that early twenty-first-century New York was "relatively crime free" seemed to imply that the city had less crime compared to earlier decades, especially the 1970s, the apex of the city's decline, when it was an international symbol of urban dysfunction and violence. Yet another way of looking at his assessment is to understand the nature of crime as always relative. Crime is always a matter of perspective, its definition always an act of politics and power. Child went on to comment that today "the crime doesn't happen when you step out of the bank. . . . The crime happens while you're in the bank."[18] In other words, the fundamental crimes of the new New York are not the crimes of passion, grievance, and desperation, which of course still occur, but the crimes of the financial sector and the other major sectors—real estate, tech, services, and culture—of the new economy. He was not suggesting, of course, that crime novelists write stories about abstract flows of capital or transformations in the mode of production. Aside from a smattering of academics, who would want to read such stories? He was, instead, implying that they write stories about how such abstractions are felt personally by "you" when "you" are in the bank and when "you" step out of it and back into your life and your neighborhood. If while staring bug-eyed at your direct-deposit slip or the outstanding balance on your underwater mortgage you felt you had been robbed, you needed to do what any good detective had always done, Child suggested. You needed to follow the money.

In a 2018 article in *Harper's* titled "The Death of a Once Great City," the journalist Kevin Baker reflected on the irony of New York's being a victim of its own successes. "New York today—in the aggregate—is probably a wealthier, healthier, cleaner, safer, less corrupt, and better-run city than it has ever been," he wrote. Yet Baker went on to claim that "for the first time in its history, New York is, well, *boring.*" The boredom Baker laments is a racial and class privilege, as is, conversely, the aestheticization of violence or urban decay as "thrilling," but what is more important to recognize is that the new urban narrative of New York as the safest big city in the country has been underpinned by socioeconomic and spatial transformations that have precipitated new urban crises or, one might say, new crimes. The subtitle of Baker's postmortem underscores the point: "The Fall of New York and the Urban Crisis of Affluence." "For all of New York's shiny new skin and shiny new numbers," he writes, "what's most amazing is how little of its social dysfunction the city has managed to eliminate over the past four decades."[19] New York at the end of the second decade of the twenty-first century is a city of greater inequality, increased homelessness, more and more bankrupt mom-and-pop stores, increased cultural homogenization, and greater levels of racial, ethnic, and class displacement. Baker goes on to cite statistics that both startle and numb. In 2016, the city with the greatest number of billionaires in the world had a poverty rate of 19.5 percent, higher than it was in 1970. Almost half the city lives at "near poverty . . . one paycheck away from disaster." Thirty percent of the city spends 50 percent of its income solely on rent. Having doubled in just the past ten years, the homeless population has reached a historic high. In the 1970s, the Bronx was home to the nation's poorest congressional district. In the 2010s, the Bronx was still home to the nation's poorest congressional district. The "brand-new," "sweet city" of New York is sour in old and new ways.

Despite these numbers, the boosterish narrative of urban revitalization and rebirth has been *the* narrative of New York since the 1990s, repeated ad nauseam by politicians, pundits, and police commissioners at the bully pulpit. "As we move toward the new millennium, we as New Yorkers can take pride in the fact our great city has regained its true stature as the Capital of the World. Our crime rate is at levels not witnessed since the 1960s," Giuliani boasted in 1997. "Four years ago, few would have dreamed, much less believed that these strides were possible," he said, looking back to the date he was first elected.[20] Versions of this narrative are also told indirectly in popular culture. In TV series such as *Seinfeld*, *Sex and the City*, and *Girls*, to name only a few, the absence of everyday crime in New York is the very precondition for plotlines about the anodyne and amusing foibles of bourgeois life and the personal and professional fulfillment of middle-class women. *Sex and the City* could not exist in the 1970s, or if it could, it would be a drama about prostitution and sexual assault. In other words, it would be something like David Simon's TV series *The Deuce*, about crime and the sex industry in the pre-Giuliani-era Times Square, but without Simon's early twenty-first-century wistfulness for a grittier, grimier, and purport-edly more authentic city. The crime crash of the 1990s and the development boom of the 2000s have spawned countless versions of a triumphalist urban narrative from all corners of the culture.

Yet the self-congratulatory narratives of urban revitalization are just one of the storylines of the new city. Recent crime fiction tells a different and darker, and certainly more ambivalent, set of stories. It tells stories of urban displacement, racial conflict, class grievance, community erosion, and cul-tural erasure, stories that are traceable in one form or another to the socio-economic transformations of the city. In recent crime fiction, many of these storylines are braided together into what I discern as a new development in the genre: the *gentrification plot*. Throughout this book, the word "plot" resonates with multiple meanings, all of them entangled. Plot refers, of course, to a parcel of land and the property associated with it, but also to the meaningful arrangement of events in a story, as well as to a secret scheme or criminal plan, which in recent crime fiction has meant machinations, frauds, and murderous plots involving real estate. The real estate industry comprises a complex set of interactive forces that remake the social and built spaces of cities, forces that include changes in tax policy, policing, popula-tion flows, the regional decline of industries and the emergence of new ones, and the global reorganization of capital and labor relations that have ushered forth neoliberal urbanism and the literature arising in response to it. Every one of the novelists in *The Gentrification Plot* has singled out the indus-try's disruptive affects for close scrutiny. "This whole neighborhood, I mean, it's all what the realtors want it to be anyhow," remarks Richard Price's protagonist about New York's Lower East Side in *Lush Life*.[21] In each of the novels in this study, the physical and social churning of urban geog-raphy by development and the real estate industry enables and elicits nar-ratives about the right to the neighborhood and the city. These appeal to writers because such narratives place human actors and human environ-ments, rather than abstract economic processes, at the forefront. Or as the protagonist of Wil Medearis's thriller *Restoration Heights* (2019) puts it about gentrifying Bedford-Stuyvesant, "This isn't theory, this is real fucking life," not "a fucking textbook."[22] In the hands of the writers in *The Gentrifica-tion Plot*, the crime novel stages conflicts over territory and real estate, using them to mediate, refract, and reimagine fights over culture and language by which we represent the city and make it meaningful. Real estate agents and real estate developers, well-heeled gentrifiers, older residents, and cops violently clash in these books. It is the "reality of realty," states the crime novelist Henry Chang.[23] As we will see, the writers in this study interrogate how apartments, streets, and neighborhoods shape, sustain, and materially encode different articulations of life, and they investigate the cultural practices and memories that, having been built up over time, are lost if not passed down as stories. In short, these are books about place making and policing space, and they tell the stories that arise when one is uprooted from one's place, forced off of one's plot and compelled to plot another course for one's life. At the radio roundtable in 2009, Reggie Nadelson remarked that "what's interesting about there not being so much outright crime" is that "it has opened the door for a lot of us to do more interesting things." It has made possible more interesting stories. *The Gentrification Plot* is about those stories.

New York City's profound sociospatial changes in the past quarter-century have been manifestations of regional, national, and global processes that have been variously labeled as postindustrialism, post-Fordism, neoliberalism, or, for the more optimistically minded, late capitalism, though capitalism shows no sign of being slow to arrive, almost over, or dead. In *The Gentrification Plot*, the catchall terms I employ most frequently are "postindustrialization" and the "postindustrial city"—the latter the city shape coextensive with and expressive of the latest mode of capitalism. The postindustrial city, as Michael Katz describes it, is an "urban form unlike any other in history." "Suburbanization; heightened segregation; increased concentrations of poverty; the revitalization of downtowns and the decay of neighborhoods; the balkanization of districts through the location of freeways and public housing; and gentrification": these are the spatial transformations, Katz argues, that have created the postindustrial city.[24] Postindustrial, as I use it, will refer not only to this spatial form but also to the changes in the economy, from the decline of blue-collar manufacturing to the rise of the finance, real estate, information technology, and service sectors as the engines of growth. In New York, these economic transformations happened slowly and then seemingly all at once. A million people worked in manufacturing in the city in 1950. By 2000, the number was under 175,000; by 2015, it was down to 76,000. "New York City should not waste its time with manufacturing," Bloomberg told the *Financial Times* in 2003. It was a lost cause, and under his watch the losses mounted, totaling

nearly 100,000 manufacturing jobs. Deindustrialization and the restructuring that followed have upended the class and racial composition of New
York and have reorganized its built environment—from the street to the
skyline—in ways that facilitate capital accumulation and suit the needs of
a largely white professional managerial class of new residents.

The Gentrification Plot is a work of microgeographical contextualiza-
tions. It analyzes how large-scale postindustrial changes, which are hastened by policing, real estate development, tax policy, and zoning ordinances at the local level, are given form in literary narratives anchored in
specific urban environments. In particular, this book maps the gentrification plot across five iconic yet highly distinctive New York City neighborhoods: the Lower East Side (chapter 1), Chinatown (chapter 2), Red Hook
(chapter 3), Harlem (chapter 4), and Bedford-Stuyvesant (chapter 5), neighborhoods of singular importance to working-class, immigrant, Latinx, and
African American life in the city. Given their different immigration histories, demographic compositions, built environments, and statuses in the
urban imagination, these five neighborhoods have experienced policing and
gentrification in different ways, even as commonalities can be found among
them. Many of these neighborhoods are highly racialized spaces, meaning
that they are not just home to different racial groups but also the creations
of decades-old racialized urban practices and policies, such as "urban
renewal, redlining, discriminatory mortgage lending, exclusionary zoning,
and empowerment zone designation," to say nothing of the warehousing
of the poor in underfunded public housing complexes.[25] At the same time
that the Federal Housing Administration underwrote the construction of
white suburbs in the early and mid-twentieth century, frequently mandat-
ing that developers include restrictive covenants prohibiting the sale of
property to African Americans, banks drew red borders around the maps
of poor and African American neighborhoods and refused to lend to would-
be homeowners or businessowners inside them. Economically cordoned
off from loans to start small businesses or buy an apartment, redlined neighborhoods in New York City withered. The redlined areas of the Home
Owners' Loan Corporation's maps from the late 1930s include "large chunks
of the South Bronx and almost all of north Brooklyn, along with the Lower
East Side, Chelsea, Hell's Kitchen, and Harlem," neighborhoods fenced in
and walled off with the mark of a pen.[26] Yet today, in a reversal of historic
proportions, these neighborhoods and others considered in this book have

been targeted for new development. Rather than redlined into the ground, they are now subprimed into the air, pumped up with the steroids of highly leveraged cheap capital. Flush with cash, these neighborhoods by the early 2000s were filled with refurbished rowhouses and sparkling apartment towers and were experiencing a demographic sea change from an influx of whites comparable to the mass, midcentury exodus to the suburban promised land a generation or two ago by the parents and grandparents of the same newcomers. These poor, working-class, African American, and ethnic neighborhoods, long associated with high rates of crime, blocks of abandoned buildings, blight, and intractable poverty, have been so fundamentally altered that they are nearly unrecognizable to many. As *The Gentrification Plot* shows, since the early 2000s these same five locations have also been the site of new struggles over territory and identity; over who has the right to tell the stories of the city's past, present, and future; and over what kind of stories get told.

The set of diverse neighborhoods that this book maps is matched by its set of diverse writers—Richard Price, Henry Chang, Gabriel Cohen, Reggie Nadelson, Ivy Pochoda, Grace Edwards, Ernesto Quiñonez, Wil Medearis, and Brian Platzer. As Jewish, Chinese American, African American, Latinx, and white writers, they exemplify the diversity of crime literature too. In the chapters to follow, I will turn to Price's *Lush Life* (2008), Chang's Jack Yu series (2006–), Cohen's Jack Leightner series (2001–), Nadelson's *Red Hook* (2005), Pochoda's *Visitation Street* (2013), Edwards's *If I Should Die* (1997), Quiñonez's *Bodega Dreams* (2000) and *Chango's Fire* (2004), Medearis's *Restoration Heights* (2019), and Platzer's *Bed-Stuy Is Burning* (2017). Each of these novels is inextricably embedded in the tumultuous world of the five historically important and rapidly upscaling locales that are the beating heart of this study, and, as such, they interrogate matters of class, ethnicity, and race that are inseparable from crime, policing, and urban development. The crimes that we will discover in this book are the crimes incited by gentrification. They range from a mugging gone horribly wrong in a so-called transitional neighborhood to the intentional defrauding of homeowners by rich developers in the Black community. With this focus on crime at the local level, these novels exemplify what I see as the other related development in the genre: the *neighborhood turn* in crime fiction. This claim I will elaborate on in what follows, but here I want to note that a fixation on the urban neighborhood signifies the primary way crime literature has reoriented itself around questions of urban space in the contemporary city. "Place is arguably the most important feature in crime fiction," posits Stewart King. And Alfred Bendixen remarks that "the power of most effective crime fiction in the United States depends as much on the creation of carefully rendered communities in specific locales as it does on the vivid characterization of detectives and criminals." Eva Erdmann concurs, adding that in the genre "the main focus is not on the crime itself, but on the setting, the place where the detective and the victim live and to which they are bound by ties of attachment." In recent crime fiction, that place is the urban neighborhood. That intimate geography one level out from one's house or apartment is where the social and spatial upheavals of the postindustrial city are most poignantly and painfully felt. As David Harvey attests, the local level is "for most people the terrain of sensuous experience and of affective social relations," the level where our consciousness is formed, our political action is exercised, and our bodies are embedded.[27] Fittingly, the postindustrial city's neighborhoods are where the writers in this book stake their claim.

THE TURN TO GENRE AND THE FORMS OF CRIME FICTION

Genres are messy. They are analytic categories meant to create clarity and bring order to the untidy, cluttered, and shambolic world of literature, yet as soon as we try to place a text in one box rather than another, we find so many exceptions to the taxonomic structure, so many texts that are hybrids or blurry at the edges, so many texts that refuse to play by the rules, that the exercise can feel fruitless.

Given this messiness, I will try to be clear. *The Gentrification Plot* is not a book solely about hardboiled detective fiction, the subgenre most people think of when they think about crime literature. "Detective stories," Bendixen rightly points out, "represent only a relatively small part of the larger genre of crime fiction, which encompasses a remarkably wide range of narrative possibilities."[28] Under the umbrella of "crime fiction" are numerous subgenres, including genteel, locked-room mysteries; detective novels; crime thrillers; true-crime stories; police procedurals; and literary crime novels. So what is crime fiction, you might ask? The answer is surprisingly elusive. When editors of companion guides to crime fiction and scholars of single-authored monographs attempt an answer, they usually give up in frustration or end up embracing the genre's multiplicity and respecting its seemingly borderless nature. For instance, in the introduction to Blackwell's *A Companion to Crime Fiction* (2010), Charles Rzepka starts by acknowledging a definitional cul-de-sac—"To say that crime fiction is fiction about crime is not only tautological, it also raises a host of problems, beginning with the definitions of 'crime' and 'fiction'"—and ultimately concludes that the "term 'crime fiction' is a bit vague" and "seems to straddle some gaping generic divides."[29] In *The Contemporary American Crime Novel: Race, Ethnicity, Gender, Class* (2000), Andrew Pepper calls for a "genuinely elastic conception of genre" in recognition of "the dizzying range of texts that constitute the genre of American crime fiction."[30] For their part, Jesper Gulddal and Stewart King in *The Routledge Companion to Crime Fiction* (2020), in a chapter titled "Genre," nearly throw in the towel at the outset: "The aim of the chapter is not to *define* the crime genre," they write, noting that "genre is an ambiguous term in crime fiction studies." However, they go on to state that they "see crime fiction as a field, characterised internally by a multiplicity of formats, styles and themes, and externally by porous borders to the wider field of literature, especially the realm of (elite) Literature. As such, any attempt at a definition would be provisional and run counter to the mobile understanding of genre that we develop here."[31] Generic categories, Gulddal and King imply, are only as useful as the work they perform. To this end, they understand crime fiction as "not just a form of popular entertainment, characterised by its constant recycling of commercially successful conventions," but as "an *interface* that links specific narrative forms to particular sociocultural questions and concerns." In their words, crime fiction is "a narrative vector for exploring a range of wider social, political, cultural or philosophical issues that do not necessarily have anything to do with crime in themselves."[32]

The Gentrification Plot, too, understands "crime fiction" as an elastic, fluid, and heterogeneous genre. When Bendixen contends that crime fiction evinces "a remarkably wide range of narrative possibilities," he is noting that work in the genre often deploys narrative procedures other than a formal criminal investigation led by a police officer, private eye, or amateur sleuth.[33] In this study, many of the books do indeed take that form, including the novels by Price, Chang, Cohen, Nadelson, Edwards, and Medearis. But others, such as the novels by Pochoda, Quiñonez, and Platzer, do not. Instead, these writers tell the story of crime not from the point of view of cops and investigators but from the perspective of its perpetrators, victims, or the community at large in which crime occurs. These crime novels are also varied in where they sit on a spectrum anchored at one end by genre fiction and at the other end by literary narratives. Some of these writers (Henry Chang, Reggie Nadelson, and Gabriel Cohen) work within the formulas of the genre, others (Richard Price and Wil Medearis) aspire to what we might see as literary crime novels that push the genre in new directions, while still others write literary novels (Ivy Pochoda, Ernesto Quiñonez, and Brian Platzer) that harness the inherent dramas of crime to explore the emotional territories traditionally associated with serious fiction. In the latter, we see how the themes of literary fiction—personal fulfillment and the knowable pleasures of domestic life—are disrupted and made immeasurably more complicated by policing, crime, and gentrification. Regardless of the narrative angle, what unites the novels in *The Gentrification Plot* is that they explore crime—"its causes, its consequences, and its social, moral, and political implications"—in order to pursue a "deeper inquiry" into the state, the economy, the judicial system, and other areas and institutions bound up with ethics and law.[34] In doing so, these texts pursue large questions about how crime is defined and what constitutes criminal behavior. They interrogate what is technically legal but socially a crime, and they question what is illegal but socially justified. Ultimately, I am less interested in policing the genre's borders than I am in understanding how different kinds of texts deploy crime as a way of understanding the human costs of gentrification and postindustrialization. To borrow from Gulddal and King, the postindustrial crime novels of *The Gentrification Plot* are dialectical "interfaces" between literature and a low-crime city that is being redeveloped as the capacious genre of crime fiction itself is remade too. In these novels, crime brings to the forefront the anxieties and precarities of neoliberal urbanism, the desperation and anger of life lived on a knife's edge.

As the scholarly perspectives I have already cited attest, crime-fiction studies have rapidly emerged and matured as a field of serious academic attention after years of being relegated to a critical backwater. Three recent edited volumes on the topic—*Globalization and the State in Contemporary Crime Fiction* (2016), *The Centrality of Crime Fiction in American Literary Culture* (2018), and the aforementioned *The Routledge Companion to Crime Fiction* (2020)—are evidence that the field has, on the one hand, flourished to a degree that it accommodates dozens of scholars and, on the other, has begun to organize itself around major issues and topics. A further sign of the growth of the field can be seen in the sheer number of monographs on crime fiction published since 2000. To name only a few, one might cite Sean McCann's *Gumshoe America: Hard-Boiled Crime Fiction and the Rise and Fall of New Deal Liberalism* (2000), Gill Plain's *Twentieth-Century Crime Fiction: Gender, Sexuality, and the Body* (2001), Leonard Cassuto's *Hard-Boiled Sentimentality: The Secret History of American Crime Stories* (2008), Andrew Pepper's *Unwilling Executioner: Crime Fiction and the State* (2016), and Fredric Jameson's *Raymond Chandler: The Detections of Totality* (2016). When I first proposed teaching a crime-fiction course as a new assistant professor, a senior colleague, at the time director of undergraduate studies, could barely conceal his derision but still managed to politely suggest, "Perhaps you could teach something a little more canonical." Thankfully, such dismissive opinions are increasingly in the minority.

As part of an expanding body of work on crime fiction, *The Gentrification Plot* also participates in a broader turn to genre—from crime fiction to sci-fi—by scholars and novelists. A brief consideration of two recent interventions in genre criticism by Jeremy Rosen and Theodore Martin highlights some of the latest thinking in the field. In "Literary Fictions and the Genres of Genre Fiction" (2018), Rosen articulates a set of helpful distinctions between genre as a category and genre fiction as a practice. The former designates "an existing literary framework or recipe that writers may adapt and vary according to their needs," while the latter refers to work that is treated as subliterary, "formulaic, commercial, and low quality."[35] Though genres are "generative and malleable," their "patterns" in certain contexts can produce "a considerable degree of formal regularity," such as in commercial publishing, leading to familiar and derivative novels. For their part, "'genre fiction' and 'literary fiction'" in Rosen's estimation name "relatively coherent and meaningfully distinct subsets of the literary field," even as the borders between them fluctuate and evolve. The differences between literary fiction and genre fiction are less formally constituted than, he argues, "determined institutionally" by "agents, readerships, and reviewers."[36] Rosen goes on to analyze "a highly visible phenomenon in contemporary fiction" whereby literary writers—such as Colson Whitehead, Gary Shteyngart, Jonathan Lethem, and Ursula Le Guin—adopt and remodel genres of all stripes. Leveraging their "generative capacity and plasticity," such authors deploy and remake the frameworks of genre for "serious purpose[s]" but at the same time reaffirm, rather than blur, hierarchical distinctions between literary and genre writing through their use of metaphorical language, self-reflexivity, and ironic distancing. They eagerly play in the sandbox of genre fiction but do not want their reputations to be sullied by being associated with lowbrow mass culture. Ultimately, Rosen has little to say about genre fiction itself. However, in my opinion, writing that scholars or readers devalue as putatively "formulaic, commercial, and low quality," a charge one might level at some novels in *The Gentrification Plot*, is some of the most interesting work to subject to critical analysis. The ideological dispositions in such writing come unselfconsciously prepackaged within forms that are worth unpacking to show how they operate, to show how their lack of critical self-awareness is actually a sign of their cultural power. Other writers in this study who are firmly associated with the genre of crime fiction but aspire to move beyond its formulas express what I term *genre anxiety*, a frustrated wish to work in a higher literary mode (or be recognized for doing so) while feeling trapped within a form policed by publishing houses, readers, reviewers, and academic scholars.

In *Contemporary Drift: Genre, Historicism, and the Problem of the Present* (2017), Theodore Martin approaches the subject of genre criticism from a different angle and with a different purpose. He grapples with the question of how to historicize contemporary fiction in the "absence of historical distance." His short answer is through genre. "Genres lead distinctly double lives," he asserts, "with one foot in the past and the other in the present; they contain the entire abridged history of an aesthetic form while also staking a claim to the form's contemporary relevance." Put another way, they are simultaneously old and new, containing residual and emergent manifestations. Their "formal change over time," Martin argues, "makes the process of becoming contemporary uniquely visible." Building on this insight, he proposes that contemporary genre fiction registers through evolving forms the problems of the present: "the global triumph of consumer society, the pervasion of geopolitical and environmental risk, and the precarious conditions of postindustrial work." Since forms are always historical and history is the measure of changing processes, one does wonder how a genre could ever even avoid "conceptualizing the contemporary."[37] After all, everything is historical, especially those things that claim they are not. But when Martin abstracts five key organizing terms from genre fiction—decade, revival, waiting, weather, and survival—he shows something new about how this fiction provides figures for a present that often feels inchoate and difficult to limn.

This brief reflection on recent scholarship about genre and genre fiction helps us foreground some of the reasons why crime fiction marks an important site for interrogating the postindustrial city. Foremost among them is that crime fiction is relentlessly urban, more urban in fact than any other genre. Lucy Andrew and Catherine Phelps, for instance, posit that crime narratives are fundamentally about "reconstructing, remapping and, hence, recreating the city." Despite that, crime fictions are not city fictions merely because they take place in urban environments. They are part of a class of urban fictions because they are centered around "the conflicting relations and struggles over the meaning and function of space," as Catalina Neculai has argued about city literature in general. In crime fiction, "the city is a problem that needs to be solved," David Schmid asserts. With observations like these as a starting point, *The Gentrification Plot* argues that another reason we might turn to fiction about crime to understand the changing neighborhoods of a city is that crime and one's fear of it have a nearly unique ability to aggregate, condense, and dramatize (as well as obfuscate) manifold issues. Carlo Rotella observes that "talking about almost any neighborhood-related subject can take the form of talking about crime." Thus "talking about muggings, murders, and burglaries" is one way of accessing the "larger complex of problems" that ails a city. Crime fiction is about crime, of course, but it is always about something else too: racial tensions, feelings of economic precarity, the unspooling of one's familiar way of life. Addressing a related point, Andrew Pepper comments that plots in crime novels are often a "Trojan Horse" smuggling other subject matters into the work. Crime, the writer Richard Price explains, is "an excuse to get into the world."[38] Writing about crime is a way of writing about (and also sometimes not writing about) changing racial demographics, the ethnic and class succession of neighborhoods, immigration, growing income inequality, perceptions of moral decline, or the sense that a city has spun out of control.

Crime fiction does not proffer any secret solutions to the "larger complex of problems" about the postindustrial city. This "most politically minded of all the literary genres" dramatizes—rather than solves—urban problems by focusing, as Pepper maintains, "on the ways in which individual lives are shaped by the push and pull of larger social, political, and economic forces."[39] While intensely political, the politics of the genre are not easily categorized; nor are the politics of individual novels within the genre. In fact, the texts examined in *The Gentrification Plot* are themselves contested terrains much like the neighborhoods they represent. They are riddled with omissions, blindnesses, and competing ideological positions. These novels can be sappy and nostalgic. Some of them are racially obtuse, while others do antiracist work to demystify the racialization of space, expose the racism of urban policing practices, and complexify racial subjectivity. Some evince little awareness of their class privilege, while others champion the life of the working class. Many of them are animated by unreconciled structuring tensions, pulled in more than one direction by opposing loyalties to individual self-determination, professional and institutional identity, and racial or ethnic allegiances. Indeed, the varied politics of this literature can be uncomfortable, surprisingly nuanced, and sometimes cringeworthy. Despite the genre's reputation for formulaic plots, there is no formula to its politics. If you are looking for a clear takeaway, an easy message or moral, good luck. You will not find it in these books.

Yet another reason that crime fiction is a critical site for interrogating the postindustrial city is that its distinctive formal features—especially in its hardboiled detective variants—make it particularly adept at reading space. Principal among these features is the way that the genre structures narrative. One of the great pleasures and frustrations, or pleasurable irritations, of reading crime fiction is the inevitable delay that bulks up the middle of these books. Red herrings, detours, false starts, dead ends, and subplots are trademarks of detective fiction. Sandwiched between the initial shock of a crime and the eventual closure or abandonment of a case is where the narratologist Peter Brooks locates the story's "dilatory space," the space created by "partial unveiling" and "temporary blockage" in a game of peek-a-boo and keep-away from the reader. Brooks remarks that these narrative delays engender suspense, "the play of desire in time that makes us turn pages."[40] A crime, usually a murder, launches a narrative of investigation that, on the one hand, pursues the questions of the case and, on the other, ironically works to defer as long as possible the inevitable and ultimate resolution. This extension of time is, in effect, an extension of language. Raymond Chandler once remarked about his own meandering and cluttered novels that "with me a plot, if you could call it that, is an organic thing. It grows and often it overgrows. . . . So that my plot problem invariably ends up as a desperate attempt to justify a lot of material that, for me at least, has come alive and insists on staying alive."[41] In a genre preoccupied with mortality, what awaits readers at the end is not just the exposition and resolution of the crime but the death of narrative desire itself, extinguished by the final period like a tiny bullet hole, if you will, on the last page. Crime novels forestall this death as long as possible.

Building upon Brooks's insight, Martin understands the genre's notable delays as freighted with new meanings in recent crime fiction. They force readers to "wait," keeping them suspended in the "unresolved political crises that structure the novels." For Martin, the wait "redirects our attention to the complexity of a present in crisis," leaving us to feel and think through the unsettling social and political paradoxes of contemporary life.[42] While this is an important insight, one that builds on a critical tradition that understands crime fiction as thrusting readers into the whirlwind of ambiguities and contradictions of modernity, I understand these delays, false starts, and digressions differently. The genre's circumambulatory structures and scopic point of view—embodied in the frequent scenes of the gumshoe hustling along the sidewalk or the cop cruising in a patrol car—are the pathways by which the branching and weaving narrative investigates myriad social spaces of the city that it calls into being, from the rarified milieu of the rich to the underbelly of the poor. The "real content of these books," concludes Fredric Jameson, "is an almost scenic one."[43] As the circumambulatory narrative roves over the urban neighborhoods, the crime novel sucks up as much local detail as it can hold. In the process, the narrative experiences a "thickening of the verbal texture" akin to a Geertzian thick description of the capitalist city. The narrative produces a socially recognizable reality for readers, immersing them in the city's architectures, streets, sartorial styles, commodities, languages, and class and racial hierarchies. The novels in *The Gentrification Plot* recreate the city in words with geographically verifiable precision, naming not just streets and specific addresses but noting distinctive landmarks, real shops and restaurants that exist off the page, and real people from mayors to police commissioners to urban developers who have left their stamp on the city. More than proffering this superficial realism, these texts endeavor to semiotically reconstruct the urban neighborhood's kaleidoscopic, conflictual, and chaotic social life, what Quiñonez describes as the "neighborhood ready to boil." David Schmid labels this distinctive urban fecundity a "semantic overload," the city's "riotous signification."[44] The background moves into the foreground in these novels. The setting—the city and its neighborhoods—becomes the subject.

The first action the literary detective takes when appearing on the scene is to map space and scrutinize every gesture, every article of clothing, and every object for latent meaning. When Dashiell Hammett's detective disembarks in Personville in *Red Harvest* (1929), the novel that set the template for the hardboiled genre, he immediately heads out "to look at the city," walking through Personville's streets, surveying "men from the mines and smelters," "gaudy boys from pool rooms and dance halls, sleek men with slick pale faces, men with the dull look of respectable husbands, a few just as respectable and dull women, and some ladies of the night."[45] From the city's blue-collar workers to middle-class husbands, from young delinquents playing pool to prostitutes plying their trade—the novel surveys the whole urban menagerie at the outset in an effort to figure out later what holds it all together. The answer for Hammett is power, corruption, and lies—and, of course, capital in the form of the dirty industrialist who rules the town. Perhaps the most extreme example of this narrative feature that we can find is in Paul Auster's literary detective novel *City of Glass* (1985), where a walk by the accidental PI Daniel Quinn is a street-by-street tour of Manhattan that stretching over several pages flatly lists right and left turns, intersections, notable pieces of architecture, and so on. It turns out mapping is a prerequisite for the discovery of a social reality that Quinn, isolated and depressed, has failed to notice. He feels an "urge to record certain facts" after his long walk, and when he writes these down suddenly the poor, as a symbol and lived reality of injustice that is ubiquitous yet invisible in New York City, surfaces in a novel that had heretofore paid them no mind. In an eyeblink, Auster populates the novel with "the down-and-outs, the shopping-bag ladies, the drifters and drunks."[46] Mapping scenes like Auster's are rife in more recent crime fiction. In *The Gentrification Plot* we will find them in Price's work, where cops continuously circle the Lower East Side in their cars; in Chang's novels, where his protagonist drives the entire length of Manhattan at night; and in Edwards's text, where her sleuth strolls around Harlem, nothing escaping her eyes.

Mapping is a precursor to the act of sewing together what Medearis calls the "web of connected actions," an elucidating narrative revealing deep links between disparate social lives (the rich and the poor) and disparate

spaces (white neighborhoods and Black ones) in the city that are on the surface compartmentalized and segregated for the purposes of maintaining
the socioeconomic and political order.[47] Hence, what we see here in crime
narratives is that the layered accumulation of detail sets the stage for an
eventual decoding, as the genre promises an interpretation, not just a
recording, of the crimes of the contemporary city. More than other literature, crime fiction (detective novels in particular) performs reading and
exegesis, the act of piecing together bits of information and figuring out
what it means. In fact for Brooks, the detective serves as an allegorical figure for the reader and the literary sleuth searching for clues, "reconstruct[ing]
intentions and connections."[48] This work is performed by the genre's hermeneutics of suspicion—another of its signature features—that accepts nothing at face value. My intention is not to suggest that crime fiction actually
pierces through the urban veil, which it itself has created on the page, to a
foundational truth, which it itself has posited. What drives the narrative,
however, is the desire to do so. The genre recreates the city in words, then
purports to see through the verbal construction to another reality composed of criminal conspiracies and nefarious economic forces that lurk
beneath the surface. Franco Moretti proposes that this tendency in the genre
evinces a desire for "a *transparent* society," which he aligns with a Foucaul-
dian project of social control through surveillance.[49] Conversely, one
could see it as an effort, however heavily stylized and formally distorted it
might be by the genre's linguistic codes, to peer through the reified surface
of bourgeois life and contemporary capitalism to ascertain underlying
structures and processes—from gentrification to globalization—that project the chimeras of reality.

What makes crime fiction particularly adept at narrating stories of urban
change, generally, and gentrification, specifically, is the genre's preoccupa-
tion with the puzzle of time and its relentless focus on fundamentally historical questions: "what happened" and "why." This is another reason why this
literature is an important site for thinking through questions of gentrification. The question of "who did it," if even asked, is more often than not rather
trivial and the answer rather obvious. The question crime fiction implicitly
raises, Pepper suggests, is not who but "*what* is to blame: what has caused
this problem called 'crime' in the first place?"[50] Crime is always a shatter-
ing event that ruptures a neighborhood into a "before" and an "after,"
shaking up those immediately affected but also the community at large. In

this fiction, crime "always occurs in a community," Dennis Porter argues, and given this fact, it indexes a larger system that has gone septic or, as people used to say, has gone down the tubes.[51] While the rupturing happens in a flash—the muzzle flash of a pistol in Price, the flash when a lit match lands on a gasoline-soaked floor in Quiñonez—it exposes something deeper: the slow, nearly invisible erosion of a community, a neighborhood, a way of life over time that gentrification causes. Stated differently, in this literature crime signifies the latest endpoint of a set of economic processes— urban disinvestment and decline that are followed by the neighborhood's rebirth for a different set of residents—that have broken down a shared sense of place, changes that happen incrementally over years so that one hardly notices until one day the familiar world has vanished. "It used to be different," Gabriel Cohen's Detective Jack Leightner claims when driving through the potholed streets of Red Hook, his former stomping grounds that are just beginning to gentrify. Cohen proposes that the literary detective's fundamental work is less solving a crime than narrating why it happened. "The essence of the job was to go back in time," he writes, "to project yourself through the still eye of the storm, and to come out into another whirl of activity, the one that had put the body there in the first place."[52] Importantly, crime fiction reads the city not just at a moment in time but understands each moment as the culmination of histories and forces that have preceded it and then tries to weave together a story of how and why it changed.

The rupturing event of a crime incites a need for narration. "The detective," Porter argues, "encounters effects without apparent causes, events in a jumbled chronological order, significant clues hidden among the insignificant. And his role is to reestablish sequence and causality."[53] Nadelson's novel—which tells the story of the transition from the old industrial city to the brand-new city from the perspective of one impacted neighborhood where the dead bodies are piling up—offers a metacommentary upon this process that sounds an awful lot like the author herself reflecting on her compositional method. "I built a scenario. I made connections, I introduced characters, I erected a plot and pieced it together and embroidered it and gave it conviction," her protagonist states.[54] The work of the narrative is to sew the broken strands of time together again and disclose the intricacy of its knots in the "big reveal," those moments of semantic excess we find in the genre's deathbed scenes, gunpoint confessions, or postinvestigation summaries that claim to reveal a meaning to what otherwise appears as disorder, confusion, and randomness. Even in novels in this study that do not fall into the hardboiled-detective subgenre, we still find acts of urban mapping followed by the familiar gesture of summing up and explaining the nature of the crime in the final pages. These concluding disclosures and summaries attempt to restore narrative wholeness and order to life in the changing neighborhood before time and space were thrown out of whack when someone was, well, whacked.

But a note of caution is in order. How trustworthy is the tale crime fiction tells of the city, and how trustworthy is its teller? We should be skeptical of the skepticism, suspicious of the hermeneutics. Like the detective, we should trust no one, not even the detective. Yet this is a reason to read crime fiction, rather than avoid it. Carlo Rotella reminds us that "we should never settle on treating literature as merely a window on material reality."[55] I agree, yet I am also not convinced that we should see literature as a window *into* material reality either. If it is a window into anything, it is into how we see, not what we see. Some, though certainly not all, of the literature in *The Gentrification Plot* is saturated with a sense of loss for a prelapsarian city that in truth never existed but is nevertheless mourned over. Or put another way, what is mourned over is the death of an idea of a city and its neighborhoods. Crime literature is, at times, structured by the myth of a unified organic community that has putatively undergone disruption only with the influx of other races, classes, and cultures. "El Barrio was no longer my barrio," mourns the protagonist of Quiñonez's *Chango's Fire*, his novel of arson, insurance fraud, and gentrification in East Harlem. Other texts, such as Medearis's *Restoration Heights*, offer non-nostalgic understandings of a neighborhood's struggles against gentrification: "We're not fighting . . . because we want to preserve a moment. That's just another kind of conservatism, another kind of looking backward. . . . We're fighting because we want to control our own change. We want to *direct* it." What the literature in the genre often fails to acknowledge is that neighborhood communities are constituted by internal differences, diversities, and divisions, not by the absence of them. In a city as palimpsestically layered as New York, crisscrossed by voluntary and involuntary flows of people for centuries, the act of laying claim to a neighborhood, whether by ontological privilege or chronological priority, is always an act of denying someone else's claim. When a character in *Lush Life*, Price's novel about the hypergentrifying Lower East Side (the neighborhood with more immigration traffic than any other), asserts "I was here *first*," the claim is absurd.[56] This literature is most honest when it recognizes that the right to the city is a struggle against another person's right to occupy the same space, a scarce resource in a city as dense and expensive as New York.

GENTRIFICATION AND THE PROBLEM WITH FLORIDA

As the forms of crime fiction allow for purchase on the changing city, they permit us to think about gentrification as a spatial and narrative process. Put another way, gentrification is itself a story about the city and its neighborhoods, a story of their past, present, and future. It thus makes sense to turn to fiction to see how this story is told. Investigating gentrification through a genre specifically dedicated to crime and policing makes sense for another reason: gentrification requires cops. As Steve Herbert in *Policing Space* (1997) remarks, "territoriality is a basic strategy that officers employ to secure public order," adding that "control of space is a fundament of overall police efforts at social control."[57] "Quality-of-life" policing, also known as "broken-windows" policing—which James Wilson and George Kelling formulated in 1982 and New York Police Commissioner William Bratton implemented in 1994 under Giuliani—has been a primary lever of gentrification in New York. As its very name suggests, quality-of-life policing served to establish normative orders in the city—good neighborhoods and bad ones—at the same time that it served to "construct [police] as valuable moral agents" or, at the very least, as enforcers of retributive justice against the immoral criminal classes, the loiterers, prostitutes, squeegee men, the drug addicted who were held responsible for urban decline. I will return to Wilson and Kelling's writings, but here I note that this globally influential and controversial strategy has served as a means to forcibly pacify marginal or blighted neighborhoods and render them "safer" for upper-middle-class homeownership and future development by the private sector. By the 1980s and 1990s in New York, Julian Brash argues, "there was a sense (mostly among whites) that an overly generous and permissive liberal state had led to urban 'disorder' and that retrenchment was required," retrenchment that would come swiftly and violently through police crackdowns on public behavior that offended heteronormative, middle-class values and, perhaps more importantly, affected the resale value of middle-class homes.[58] From a wider angle we can see, with Brash's comment in mind about the "permissive liberal state," that battles over gentrification are not solely battles over the fate of one neighborhood or another. More broadly, they are battles over different conceptualizations of the state itself—the welfare state or the neoliberal one—and its administration of law; its responsibility, or lack of, for promoting social justice; and its role in an economy whose mid-century industrial foundations have been crowbarred apart over the last thirty years. This point is key. Policing and gentrification cannot be disaggregated and should be seen for what they are: instruments of state power and private capital that have been conjoined to remake New York into a twenty-first-century neoliberal postindustrial city.

Of late, scholarly work on gentrification has grown into something of a cottage industry in the fields of urban history, urban sociology, and urban ethnography.[59] Yet the literary implications *of* gentrification and the contribution of literature *to* an understanding of gentrification is still an emerging area with much territory to explore and many gaps to fill. My book's contribution to this new field is predicated on a theorization of human spatiality that is indebted to the work of a number of writers and thinkers, including Henri Lefebvre, Edward Soja, Manuel Castells, Neil Smith, and David Harvey. To properly understand gentrification, we first have to understand how space is a social product. Setting aside the nuanced differences between the aforementioned thinkers, these critical spatial theorists are united in their efforts to complicate the notion that space is a primordial category—the idea that it is something always already there, a divine attribute like the ether, "an order immanent to the totality of what existed." Lefebvre underscores that space is conceptually difficult to theorize because of its illusions of transparency and natural simplicity. When it comes to space, it seems there is no there there to theorize, and if there is, there is nothing really to be said or done about it, except to positivistically measure it, describe it, and catalogue what it contains. The initial step of critical spatial studies is dispelling these two illusions by recognizing that space is something made. "Space is not a 'reflection of society,' it *is* society," Manuel Castells contends. "Spatial forms," he declares, "at least on our planet, will be produced by human action, as all other objects are."[60]

If spatial forms are constituted by human actions, they also shape them. "Space and the politics of space 'express' social relationships but also react against them," Lefebvre argues in *The Urban Revolution* (1970). Or as Edward Soja, in a similar effort to avoid reifying space, would later phrase it, "social and spatial relations are dialectically inter-reactive [and] interdependent."[61] To take an example of a sociospatial dialectic, we might think about how the spatial relations of racism, which are instituted by segregation, redlining, and zoning ordinances and lived daily in myriad ways, divide a city's regions into unequal areas, such as the so-called inner city and the suburbs or the wrong side of the tracks and the right side, and how this arrangement reinforces white privilege and Black disempowerment in ways that are social, psychic, and economic. Or we might consider how the relations of gender are constituted in the bifurcated construction of public space and private domesticity and how these spaces have obviously constrained and reinforced normative gender identities that are unequal, polarized, and interdependent. Or we might see how the moral rectitude of middle-class white neighborhoods is articulated against the moral dissoluteness of ungentrified areas that house the poor, the queer, or residents of color, even as these neighborhoods have long served as markets for middle-class whites searching for drugs, prostitutes, pornography, and so on, the very vices they would never permit in their own backyards. The point that cannot be stressed enough is that the social relations of race as well as of ethnicity, gender, sexuality, and class are always expressed spatially. There is always a geography to identity. And geography—as an arena of social struggle—is always historical and always mutable.

Edward Soja's work, which has been instrumental to my thinking, historicizes the spatial specificity of capitalism across different modes of production to highlight a "broad patterning" that then allows for an analysis of the "particularities and complexities" of urban and regional development that varies from place to place depending upon existing landforms, histories of migration, structures of governance, and the like. His central idea is that the evolution of capitalism transforms the city's spatiality over time. Each new mode of production (e.g., mercantilism, Fordism, postindustrialism) borne out of the socioeconomic and political crises that are the result of the inherent contradictions in capitalism itself remakes urban space over again. The small-shop mercantilism of the early nineteenth century has a different spatiality than the globalized information services–driven postindustrialism of the early twenty-first. As a result of capital's evolving spatiality and spatial requirements over the long term, new geographies for natural resources, goods, and cheap labor are opened up; new consumption habits are generated; new spheres of life are commodified and incorporated into capitalist production, all fueled by an insatiable need for surplus value. "Under capitalism," David Harvey writes, "there is then a perpetual struggle in which capital builds a physical landscape appropriate to its own condition at a particular moment in time, only to have to destroy it, usually in the course of crises, at a subsequent point in time."[62]

However, it is not all destruction, not even capitalist creative destruction, but rather a slow, uneven process of development and redevelopment. This process occurs in fits and starts as an "evolving sequence of partial and selective restructurings" that over decades reshapes how and where people work, live, and socialize and culminates in a new urban morphology, a new kind of city.[63] Zoned by class, the densely packed industrial city of the late nineteenth and early twentieth centuries, with factories concentrated around the city center and tightly ringed by residential housing, gives way, in time, to its successor, the mid-twentieth-century Fordist city. This later urban form sprawls outward to the suburbs designed for corporate managers and other white-collar professionals who leave behind a depopulated downtown of hotels, state agencies, and a smattering of corporate headquarters. They leave behind, too, a city whose residential districts are now increasingly divvied up by race. This decentralized urban form, in turn, is succeeded by the postindustrial city of today, which is networked as never before to global flows of capital and national and global flows of high-wage labor in finance, information technology, and the knowledge and creative industries. The new economy is both dispersive and agglomerating, its whirlwinds centrifugal and centripetal. It has led to the managerial classes pouring back into the revitalized inner cores and gentrified enclaves of cities, while poor and working-class residents, who tenaciously held on during decades of decline, are shoved closer to the urban cliff. This overview paints with a broad brush, but the point, simply put, is that the shape of the city changes not because change is natural or inevitable but because underlying socioeconomic structures and policy choices push and pull it in one direction or another or in many directions at once.

When it comes to recent transformations of the city, *gentrification* is the word often cited as an explanation or cause. The term, however, must be historicized; otherwise we fail to understand that the upscaling of city neighborhoods today is qualitatively different from their rehabilitation in the past. From its first printed appearance in 1964, the word, coined by the sociologist Ruth Glass in *London: Aspects of Change*, has been defined by the tumultuous politics of urban class succession. Setting a context for her use of the term, Glass wrote:

> One by one, many of the working-class quarters of London have been invaded by the middle classes—upper and lower. Shabby, modest mews and cottages—two rooms up and two down—have been taken over, when their leases have expired, and have become elegant, expensive residences. . . . Once this process of "gentrification" starts in a district it goes on rapidly until all or most of the original working-class occupiers are displaced and the whole social character of the district has changed.[64]

The first cited usage of "gentrification" in the *Oxford English Dictionary*, mistakenly pinpointed to 1973, also carries the same implicit class critique. In the cited article, a September 26 exposé by John Plender in the *Times* of London, the dealings of two relatively unknown real estate speculators, Timothy Gwyn-Jones and John Chalk, are uncovered. Operating through upward of 150 companies and with financing from City of London banks, they had quietly purchased thousands of flats on the cheap in Islington, Camden, Fulham, and other boroughs, many of which they refused to repair, letting them fall into intolerable decline as a strategy for inducing tenants to leave. Then the owners would rehab the properties and rent them out at higher rates. In a lengthy follow-up piece by Plender the next day, titled "Baffled Tenants in Search of Their Landlords in London's Flat-land," gentrification's capacity to create social disorientation, uncertainty, and bewilderment was on full display. "The old landlord used to repair and replace things," an elderly tenant fretted. "These people don't. We're old age pensioners, we can't afford to do up the outside of the building. The tenants here are living in fear. They don't dare to complain in case the rents go up."

From its early uses, then, the word "gentrification" has been inseparable from the urban politics of class, geography, speculation and profiteering, and the fears, desires, personal crises, and life trajectories of individual city residents. Gentrification is and has always been about class, as *gentry*, a reference to those of high social position in the United Kingdom or the upper-middle and upper classes in the United States, makes evident. To soften gentrification's embarrassingly frank class implications, some prefer the more "anodyne terminology" of " 'neighborhood recycling,' 'upgrading,' 'renaissance,' and the like," remarks the sociologist Neil Smith. But when we define gentrification as "renewal" or the "process of transition," as a natural or evolutionary outcome of unhistoricized urbanization dynamics, we lose sight of its politics. Martha Rosler argues that "urban cycles of decline, decay, and abandonment followed by rebirth through rehabilitation, renovation, and reconstruction may appear to be natural processes. In fact, the fall and rise of cities are consequences not only of financial and productive cycles and state fiscal crises but also of deliberate social policy" that benefit some urban residents at a great cost to others.[65] Ghettoization, redlining, and segregation severely restricted the neighborhoods African Americans, Chinese immigrants, and Puerto Ricans could live in for much of the twentieth century. The recent gentrification, in turn, of these same neighborhoods is also the outcome of development tax subsidies, zero-tolerance policing, and rezoning that have attracted young upper-middle- and upper-class professionals to fringe areas once considered inhospitable at best, dangerous at worst. When discussing "urban change," we would do well to keep asking basic questions, rather than accepting change as natural or inevitable: who benefits and who does not; whose interests are served and whose are not?

In fact, what needs to be made clear is how much, as the writer Jeremiah Moss puts it, "the nature of urban change has changed." One of the truisms of urban life, perhaps expressed more frequently in New York than anywhere else, is that "cities change," usually followed by some version of "that's just the way it is," delivered with a shrug, said in resigned exasperation, or, conversely, celebrated as evidence of a city's inexhaustible vitality. For example, the urban scholar Richard Florida, whose work I will return to shortly, champions the urban ecological model that Rosler critiques. Florida claims that if we adopt a longer historical view regarding U.S. cities, especially New York, "it becomes clear how neighborhoods continuously shift and change. . . . This process of neighborhood transformation is a natural, if wrenching, feature of cities, which are perpetual works in progress. As they grow and change, their demography and class structure shift."[66] What this view misses entirely, even as it gives the briefest of head nods to the "wrenching" quality of the process, is that the historical succession of populations in New York City neighborhoods—southern Italians and Jews replacing Irish and German immigrants in the Lower East Side, Puerto Ricans replacing Italians in East Harlem, African Americans replacing Germans and Norwegians in Bedford-Stuyvesant, to cite just a few examples—is not gentrification. If anything, it is the opposite. Until recently, the historical pattern has been for the poor and marginalized to move into the spaces vacated, willingly and often not so willingly, by the slightly less poor and less marginalized, not the other way around. Before the mid-1960s, selected parts of cities experienced gentrification avant la lettre, but they did so primarily as spot rehabilitation in small, isolated pockets of redevelopment that resulted from targeted civic initiatives or the investment of a single actor in the private sector. Even into the 1960s, the term "gentrification" continued to carry quaint connotations of neighborhood rehabilitation through the sprucing up of streets and homes, some of which can be heard in Glass's original usage. A fresh coat of paint on the exterior, begonias in the window boxes, a café on the corner—these are the still-familiar images of the gentrifying neighborhood from when the word first appeared in print. They continue to inform how many people envision gentrification in the twenty-first century. This nice view gives a false impression.

The gentrification of fifty years ago is not the gentrification of today. Late twentieth- and early twenty-first-century gentrification cannot be understood as the outcome of the choices of individual homeowners remaking a neighborhood one brownstone or Craftsman-style house at a time. If in the 1960s gentrification could still be thought of as a byproduct of a handful of industrious homeowners and landlords fixing up the block, it needs to be seen now for what it is: "the class remake of the central urban landscape" through global capital's penetration to the local level.[67] Rather than a selective process with one or two streets singled out for redevelopment, gentrification has become multipronged, sustained, widespread. As Smith has argued, it has become "generalized," metastasizing into an expression of capital's power to restructure entire cities. If the class dynamics of gentrification are inescapable, so too are its unsightly racial politics. Paula Johnson contends that "the infusion of global capital into local neighborhoods on a large, systematized scale . . . facilitates Whites' exercise of economic, legal, and political prerogatives to occupy whatever spaces—including previously devalued racialized spaces—for their greater security and greater wealth accumulation and for the greater disadvantage and insecurity of Blacks."[68] Gentrification is, in short, a neoliberal structure of racial and class violence. As it has aided and abetted the birth of postindustrial New York, to say nothing of numerous other cities from Boston to San Francisco, gentrification has created local spaces for globally restructured and increasingly unequal relationships between capital and labor, as well as between races, ethnicities, and classes of every strata. Not coincidentally, such changes have coincided with ongoing attacks on every remaining facet of 1960s liberalism. The welfare state, Brash asserts, had "aimed to reconcile conflicts among various racial, economic, and political constituencies via support for working-class consumption and social-welfarist redistribution as well as real estate development and corporate investment." But as the liberal state has been systematically taken apart, these conflicts increasingly have been adjudicated (unsuccessfully) in the private marketplace, have spilled into the streets as new social and economic justice movements, and have sparked the interpersonal violence and counterviolence of gentrification and its resistance.

For the urban scholar and business consultant Richard Florida, the gentrification of North American cities since 2000 is less a crisis than an opportunity.[69] More than anyone, Florida has been the loudest cheerleader of the urban-renaissance narrative, in which the formerly moribund cities of blight and high crime are now hip, bustling "cauldrons of creativity" and "vehicles for mobilizing, concentrating, and channeling human creative energy." The central contention repeated across his numerous books is that the main driver and source of wealth creation in the early twenty-first-century economy are members of the "creative class" who work in the "creative sector" and "technology-based industries." Florida's rhetoric maintains its class connotations, while softening it with the fuzzy concept of "creativity," which could conceivably include well nigh anyone but in practice is exclusionary and elitist. Case in point: "Mayor Michael Bloomberg is a classic example of a creative person," Florida asserts, praising him both as the CEO of a global finance and media company and as the steward of New York's transition to a postindustrial economy oriented around these same sectors. What is imperative to note is that the lionized risk takers of the creative class—the largely white, college-educated, young professionals—not only fuel the sectoral restructuring of the postindustrial city; they also, in Florida's view, fuel gentrification by flowing back into city centers, recolonizing spaces that had in the 1960s and 1970s suffered from the racist urban policies of abandonment and planned shrinkage. Florida has little to say about the deeper economic structures that have historically directed and managed these population flows, and he is even more silent on racial and class privileges that make his creative class's risks and rewards possible in the first place. What spurs creative-class gentrification, he concludes, is primarily personal choice. This is, I would counter, a simplistic reduction of complex, overdetermined socioeconomic phenomena to the neoliberal mantra of individualized and privatized decision making and responsibility. The creative class, Florida posits, prefers to live not in the gated suburban communities of their parents but in cities with a mix of people, languages, and ideas, that frisson of urbanity, that feeling that makes you want to be in a place that is dense, dynamic, and diverse. Because of this, he concludes, they are attracted to places that are "open to immigrants, artists, gays, and racial integration."[70] This notion that "immigrants, artists, gays," and people of other races are relegated to an interesting backdrop—an exciting bit of local color—for the lifestyle enrichment of white professionals passes without comment by Florida. The idea that the creative class actually might be attracted to undervalued neighborhoods because they can buy property and make a killing there also does not factor into his thinking.

For Florida, cities should be grateful to count the creative class among their citizenry, especially those cities seeking to revitalize stagnant economies through property development after the social and fiscal crises of the 1960s and 1970s. No longer sites of urban decay, resistant cultures, and radical democratic politics, downtowns are transformed with the creative-class influx into "idea generator[s]" and "incubators."[71] To appeal to data-driven politicians and C-suite executives, Florida and his collaborators have helpfully developed a "Bohemian Index" and a "Gay Index" to measure the relationship between diversity, human capital, and high-technology industries and to map "a geography of bohemia" and a geography of social openness as a predictor of which cities are likely to entice creative types into their folds.[72] New York ranks third in the Bohemian Index and fourteenth on the gay scale, less gay than one might expect (Rochester is statistically gayer) but still gay enough to attract creative-class workers to the "new city," which is "defined more and more as a city of consumption, experiences, lifestyle, and entertainment."[73] These indexes locate "the kinds of places," writes Florida, "that by allowing people to be themselves and to validate their distinct identities, mobilize and attract the creative energy that bubbles up naturally from all walks of life" and in the process greenhouses fresh ideas and unleashes human potential that once monetized becomes *creative capital*."[74] In this formulation, the life and cultures of immigrants, gays and lesbians, and people of color exist to be repurposed by those better off. It is a starkly instrumentalist view of culture in which the value of marginal communities is alchemically transmuted into the gold of capital without the benefit accruing to its source. Most of those who inspire the creative class to create are locked out of the new economy or service it through low-wage, low-status jobs, a fact also largely unacknowledged by Florida. The further irony is that the very qualities of diversity and difference that attract upscaling newcomers to a neighborhood are usually the first that disappear upon their arrival. The original producers of culture are displaced out of the area, and what is left behind are their commodified symbols of urban authenticity, which are marketed to the next wave of colonizing residents seeking a neighborhood with a storied past that, because of gentrification, is now history.

The point I wish to underscore—one fundamental to my analysis of literature—is that gentrification is a spatial and economic phenomenon that also produces "cultural meanings and practices related to the constitution of proper personhood, markets, and the state," selectively validating and valorizing some identities while devaluing or erasing others from sight.[75] Given gentrification's processual nature, it remakes the city and its neighborhoods into spaces of contestation where different "identities, imaginaries, and meanings" are continually constituted, mobilized, and resisted. As Brash observes, New York's formerly gritty and newly gentrifying neighborhoods "have become centers of class formation for upper professionals." Places like the Lower East Side or Williamsburg, and more recently the formerly unforgiving streets of Bushwick and the waterside desolation of Red Hook, are surprising centers in the new economy. In such bohemian areas, not in autonomous office parks or corporate campuses, we find many of the essential ingredients in the postindustrial economy: innovative tech start-ups, short-term contracted but highly skilled labor, and lifestyle consumption. In neighborhoods such as these, "shared habits of consumption, aesthetics, architecture, dress, household structure, socialization, and so on embod[y] class distinctions" and provide "a sense of mutual recognition among the city's ascendant" professional managerial class.[76] These "shared habits," and the scornful resistance to them by others, are narrativized into stories of daily life and one's place and position in a city. These stories take many forms: advertising and branding campaigns, urban planning discourse, the stories of everyday life that residents tell themselves and one another, and, yes, stories in the form of crime novels, as *The Gentrification Plot* will show.

If gentrification is frequently misunderstood as the result of pioneering, entrepreneurial individuals, it is also frequently misrepresented as a transition to a new and better phase. Or as Florida puts it, gentrifying cities are "works in progress." The most common story of gentrification is the story of a neighborhood's initial development giving way to its decline, assumed to be part of a neighborhood's natural aging process, which in turn is the grounds for eventual renewal. However, "the language of revitalization, recycling, upgrading and renaissance" that Neil Smith finds mobilized in real estate advertising and civic planning discourse and that we find in contemporary literature of the city "suggests that affected neighborhoods were somehow devitalized or culturally moribund prior to gentrification." Such a view fails to recognize that those things dismissed as a public nuisance and an unruly obstacle to renewal by one faction of a community, such as socializing on stoops, in streets, and in parks, are the very signs of everyday life and cultural vitality for another faction of the same community. How we define gentrification, historicize its operations, and explain its logics are thoroughly politicized subjects that have constituted, as Smith states, "an intense ideological as well as theoretical battlefield."[77] The language of "revitalization" and "renewal" is ideologically freighted with the notion that gentrified spaces are improvements on what came before. This view presupposes a telos in which the inevitable endpoint of gentrification is the material regeneration of the land, culture, and people, all of which carries unmistakable spiritual overtones, heard clearly enough in the wellness spas and reiki healing centers that have bloomed in one gentrified neighborhood after another. If gentrification makes a neighborhood better for the postindustrial elite, what made the neighborhood worse to begin with—redlining, earlier urban renewal projects, systemic racism, capital flight—is rarely accounted for. The rhetoric of pioneering itself, derived from the language of settlement and Manifest Destiny, is conveniently structured on historical amnesia, assuming as it does that the land is virginal and that either no one had been or is living on it before the gentrifiers arrive or, if they have, they are temporary stewards before the rightful heirs show up. This sense of the timelessness of one's existence is the essence of racial and class privilege, the feeling, as Sarah Schulman describes it, that one need not "be aware of [one's] power or of the ways in which it was constructed," a blissful lack of self-consciousness that is, in effect, "the gentrification of the mind."[78] It is that peaceful feeling, which only money can buy, that one can live freely in the city.

To understand gentrification solely as a *sequential* process that culminates in a neighborhood free of conflict is highly problematic and inaccurate. Gentrification and urban development are dialectical *seesawing* processes characterized, as Smith observes, by "the successive development, underdevelopment, and redevelopment of given areas as capital jumps from one place to another, then back again, both creating and destroying its own opportunities for development."[79] For Smith, what makes an area ripe for gentrification is its rent gap, or the difference between the current value of a property and what it might be worth if rehabilitated. Properties with wide rent gaps, as a result of historical disinvestment, reattract capital in due time, provided the area is reasonably safe. Capital flees a neighborhood, such as it did the Lower East Side or Harlem in the 1970s, leaving behind a tatterdemalion landscape of dilapidated buildings, razor-wired lots, and bankrupt businesses, only to return when crime trends downward and the opportunities for profiteering trend up, leading to the displacement of those who have had the wherewithal to hang on through the downturn or have moved in in the meantime. Disinvestment followed by the retilling of the land was official housing policy in New York. Roger Starr, the head of New York's Housing and Public Development agency in the 1970s, called for planned shrinkage in "deteriorating areas" to hasten "internal resettlement" of populations: "stretches of empty blocks may then be knocked down," he avowed. "Services can be stopped, subway stations closed, and the land left to lie fallow until a change in economic and demographic assumptions makes the land useful once again."[80] Useful for whom, one wonders. Understanding gentrification as part of a seesawing dynamic of geographical differentiation and equalization underscores two important aspects of it that are otherwise easier to occlude: first, it is a historical process, and, second, it is "a perpetual struggle," never reaching a final terminus.

So what does crime fiction help us grasp about gentrification? As I have been arguing, the official rhetoric of gentrification often depicts it as something that just "happens" if people and money are allowed to flow unimpeded. In contradistinction, crime fiction stages gentrification as a problem. It is a problem for people competing for the same space. Writ large, it is a problem or struggle between the old vestiges of the liberal welfare state, and its stakeholders, and the new mandates of neoliberal urban governance, and its stakeholders. In contemporary crime fiction, gentrification is a highly disruptive process both hastened and resisted by the choices of politicians, police, developers, homeowners, and people living in government-subsidized apartments. To be sure, this literature does not always depict gentrification negatively. It does, however, always portray it as a source of intense conflict. "Real estate is violence," Richard Price has insisted in interviews.[81] "The history of all countries is the battle over land," Quiñonez has remarked, paraphrasing Emiliano Zapata's claim that "all revolutions are based on land." "In New York City," Quiñonez adds, "it's always been a battle over the slums."[82] Gentrification shakes up geographies, judders the city. It piles people on top of one another. It manifests tensely overlapping social orders of race, class, and ethnicity in ways that make the articulation of place-bound identities more, not less, urgent. Resentment, displacement, and exploitation all come with the territory being torn up and rebuilt in the pages of contemporary crime fiction. The putative telos of gentrification may be rehabilitation, regeneration, and redemption, but in crime fiction someone almost always dies in the process of a neighborhood's rebirth. As we will see, crime fiction narrates the countertendencies, resistances, and impasses of gentrification to show it is anything but natural. Simply put, it is urban political economy etched into the neighborhood, though as we will see, it is never simple in this complicated art of murder.

The contemporary battles of gentrification that are at the heart of recent crime fiction are part of long-wave sectoral transformations of the postindustrial city. This is the historical and spatial context of *The Gentrification Plot*. These changes, of course, require time and often feel more like a slow erosion than a wildfire. Yet we should also note that moments arise when an immediate crisis is pounced upon to accelerate the process. Brash, for instance, remarks that the fiscal crisis of 1975, which led to the near bankruptcy of New York City, "was quickly seized upon by an alliance of New York City elites"—bankers, corporate executives, real estate powerbrokers, and politicians—"as an opportunity to reorient municipal policy and the city's political economy, as well as to restructure the city's ruling coalition by drastically reducing the power of labor and minorities."[83] Similarly, the AIDS crisis, the September 11 terrorist attacks, the Great Recession of 2008, and Superstorm Sandy in 2012, which battered New York City's coastal areas, have hastened gentrification in neighborhoods depopulated and damaged. Postcrisis or postdisaster rebuilding efforts create opportunities for well-positioned individuals looking to invest in a neighborhood and lead to landgrabs by large private and public-private entities, such as the post-9/11 Lower Manhattan Development Corporation, that alter the character of a place faster than otherwise possible. This idea of disaster capitalism meets gentrification, this capitalization upon human suffering through new capital projects in the unfolding shock and disorientation of a collapsing world, this idea that one should "never let a good crisis go to waste," as Churchill is credited with saying, haunts the edges of recent crime novels. It is rarely commented on directly but is obliquely suggested by writers in this book and is inescapably part of the historical context out of which this literature emerges. We will sense it, among other places, in the empty figural space in the skyline where the Twin Towers in Price's *Lush Life* stood and in the roiling waters off Red Hook that swallow people alive in Pochoda's *Visitation Street*.

You will have undoubtedly noticed that I have returned to the level of the neighborhood again and again, even as I reflect upon postindustrial New York at large. The reason is that gentrification today, though a global urban phenomenon, is always expressed locally and up close in one's neighborhood. Sure, we can conceptualize it in the abstractions of theory, but we see it every day in the neighborhood hardware store that goes bust and in the Citibank branch that opens in its place. At the neighborhood level we see most clearly the decline of the state's investment in social housing, the prioritization of a different set of citizens, and the elevation of privatized commerce over the maintenance of the public sphere. These too are hallmarks of gentrification and postindustrialization. At the neighborhood level we espy the layered histories of a city, its demographic turnover, its modes of production becoming outmoded, the nuts-and-bolts factory that shuts down and reopens as live-work condos or a hive of WeWorkers clicking away at desks rented by the hour. To see gentrification in action, look at the neighborhood. That's where contemporary crime writers look. Ultimately what this book reads for are the narratives that Price, Chang, Cohen, Nadelson, Pochoda, Edwards, Quiñonez, Medearis, and Platzer create out of gentrification's disruption to the neighborhood. Their novels tell the stories of gentrification through narratives of cultural loss and nostalgia, narratives of opportunity, narratives of invasion, and narratives of moving on and moving out of the neighborhood. *The Gentrification Plot* recognizes that all narratives are selective (one story of the neighborhood as opposed to another), shaped by the pressures of literary form and freighted with biases that see the city through the lens of racial resentment, or the operations of class power, or the privileges of heteronormativity.

What *The Gentrification Plot* also reads for are the smaller units that make up these narratives. I allude here to synecdochic signifiers in these texts that help periodize capitalist urban development, such as images of dilapidated housing projects in Harlem, rehabbed brownstones in Bedford-Stuyvesant, rotten piers in Red Hook, and synagogues converted into multimillion-dollar lofts in the Lower East Side. These are not just stage dressing but a form of literary materialism, images of time architecturally and textually materialized, sedimented, and reified. They are images of always flowing historical processes concretized but mutable. In the pages that follow, I will pause over such images so we can see the urban transformations they signify. When we see in this fiction rundown, high-rise public-housing projects looming over renovated row houses, we discern in one Janus-faced glance the decay of the mid-twentieth-century liberal state and the dominance of late twentieth- and early twenty-first-century do-it-yourself entrepreneurialism. When we see in one sweeping gesture, as we do in an aerial shot from a Lower East Side balcony in Price's *Lush Life*, the demolition and rehabilitation of the old ethnic neighborhood and the canyons of Wall Street in the distance, we can sense an inchoate attempt by the novel to systematize the city, the start of an effort to limn the latent connections between the influx of new money into a historic immigrant area and the hegemony of finance capitalism that remakes the world in its own likeness. Moments like these—when we are lifted in the air through the abstractions of theory—we experience what Michel de Certeau from atop the World Trade Center once called the "pleasure of 'seeing the whole'" that comes with "totalizing the most immoderate of human texts," by which he meant New York City.[84] From this vantage point, we attempt to not only see the city, but we try to apprehend it. At heart, the novels in *The Gentrification Plot* are about how someone—a cop, a detective, a new homeowner, or a displaced resident—tries to decode the puzzling world around them, about how they struggle to piece together a coherent account of a changed and changing place. In this sense, they are novels about us, about how we too read, interpret, and narrativize the city and its neighborhoods.

FROM BROKEN WINDOWS TO GLASS CONDOS

To fully appreciate developments in crime fiction of the postindustrial city, we need to understand corresponding developments in policing and how they have contributed to neighborhood gentrification, the central formal and thematic problem in this literature. By far, the single most important change has been the implementation of the racialized quality-of-life policing formulated by James Wilson and George Kelling in "Broken Windows: The Police and Neighborhood Safety," published in the March 1982 issue of *Atlantic Monthly*. Their prescriptions were not immediately adopted but were eventually put in place in New York City in 1994 by Giuliani, who rode an anticrime mayoral campaign to victory against New York's first Black mayor. The vicious irony of Giuliani's law-and-order platform was that in 1992, shortly before his election, he had helped incite a police riot against Mayor Dinkins, a riot that saw ten thousand off-duty NYPD officers storming City Hall and shutting down the Brooklyn Bridge, many of them hurling racial slurs and drinking in public, the latter the most common quality-of-life offense during his two terms in office. As we will see, this incident is alluded to in Grace Edwards's work and is critical for understanding her depiction of the underlying racism of broken-windows policing. In spite of this racist origin story, once Wilson and Kelling's ideas were adopted by Giuliani's police commissioner, William Bratton, their ideas spread to other cities in the United States and internationally, revolutionizing policing practices. In 1998, to take just one year, police officials from 150 countries met with the NYPD to study its zero-tolerance crime-control tactics. New York's style of "strict enforcement" was subsequently adopted as "the new official policy of police forces in countries as different as Britain, Norway, the Netherlands, Switzerland, Germany, Hungary, Italy, Portugal, Israel, Japan, Brazil, and China."[85]

Wilson and Kelling proposed a radical shift in policing: from solving major crimes to maintaining public order. Persuasive in its apparent commonsensical simplicity, their theory was that the failure to aggressively police minor offenses—ranging from public drunkenness to littering—created a lax atmosphere in which fear could insidiously take hold and major crimes could eventually flourish. "At the community level," they argued, "disorder and crime are usually inextricably linked, in a kind of developmental sequence." Disorder for Wilson and Kelling was concretized in the image of a broken window, which became a shorthand for a set of police tactics that they advocated. When we step back from the image we can see it for what it is: a synecdoche for violence against private property and a signifier for the fragile nature of public order in the minds of the authors. "One unrepaired window" in a neighborhood, they worried, "is a signal that no one cares, and so breaking more windows costs nothing."[86] To illustrate their point, Wilson and Kelling referenced (and misconstrued) a 1969 experiment by the Stanford psychologist Philip Zimbardo in which he parked an Oldsmobile with its hood up and its license plate removed on a street in a low-crime neighborhood of Palo Alto and did the same with an Olds in the South Bronx.[87] Within ten minutes, the Olds in the Bronx was stripped of its parts and then destroyed, but the car in Palo Alto "sat untouched for more than a week." Yet once Zimbardo and his research assistants smashed all its windows with a sledgehammer and gleefully stomped in the roof of the car, it was "within a few hours . . . turned upside down and utterly destroyed" by people who had before given the car scant notice. From this single piece of evidence, Wilson and Kelling strongly implied that when people believe "no one cares," all hell breaks loose. Even "respectable whites" in middle-class Palo Alto turn into " 'vandals.' " "People who ordinarily would not dream of doing such things and who probably consider themselves law-abiding" were suddenly out for "plunder."[88]

Wilson and Kelling wanted to underscore that Palo Alto or any other "respectable," "white" neighborhood, town, or city could descend into the Bronx—a national symbol of arson, blight, and crime, the ground zero of every suburban dweller's worst urban nightmare—seemingly within hours if law and order were not enforced 24/7. But Zimbardo's conclusion was really the opposite. For Zimbardo, the experiment was evidence that the Bronx and Palo Alto were different, not the same as Wilson and Kelling had suggested, and the difference was the result of structural inequalities that led residents of the Bronx to opportunistically dismantle the car and repurpose its parts (which is different from just destroying it) and residents in Palo Alto to let it sit untouched. As Bench Ansfield has shown in a critique of Wilson and Kelling, they refused to fully acknowledge, too, that the car in California was not "utterly destroyed" by a community that suddenly laid waste to it at the slightest provocation. It was first destroyed by Zimbardo and his assistants, who tore it to pieces in plain view. The piling on occurred only after their act of vandalism was witnessed publicly. Wilson and Kelling left out Zimbardo's conclusion in their summary because it did not comport with their Hobbesian view of urban American life, in which a "sense of mutual regard and the obligations of civility" are the delicate bulwarks that keep a neighborhood from descending into chaos. "A stable neighborhood of families who care for their homes, mind each other's children, and confidently frown on unwanted intruders can change," they asserted, "in a few years or even a few months, to an inhospitable and frightening jungle."[89] Following Wilson and Kelling, Commissioner Bratton strongly echoed this declension narrative in "Reclaiming the Public Spaces of New York" (1994): "New Yorkers have for years felt that the quality of life in their city has been in decline, that their city is moving away from, rather than towards the reality of a decent society." Bratton, whose earlier beat was cleaning up New York's filthy and crime-ridden subway system, pledged to work "systematically and assertively to reduce the level of disorder in the city." This was the best strategy, he thought, to prevent serious crimes from ever taking root.[90]

Wilson and Kelling's panicked view of city life was not just of a hellscape of crime but of a crumbling racial and sexual order that needed propping up and reinforcing by aggressive policing. If even "respectable whites" can turn into " 'vandals,' " the not-so subtle innuendo was that nonrespectable nonwhites were like this all the time. A student of the archconservative urban theorist Edward Banefield, Wilson had previously written that "the patrolman believes with considerable justification that teenagers, Negroes, and lower-income persons commit a disproportionate share of all reported crimes," a sweeping claim that failed to acknowledge glaring racial and class inequities which prompted forms of policing that effectively produced higher reported crimes in communities of color and working-class neighborhoods.[91] Among the warning signs of urban disorder, or as Wilson called them, "impropriety," that should raise an officer's suspicions was the mere presence of African Americans and queers, or, as he put it, "a Negro wearing a 'conk rag,' " "boys in long hair," and "interracial couples." "All of these are seen by many police officers as persons displaying unconventional and improper behavior."[92] As its subtitle, "The Police and Neighborhood Safety," indicated, Wilson and Kelling's broken-windows policing was about putatively broken communities and how to restore them to an ideal of white heteronormative homeownership where residents take pride in their homes, watch over children in the neighborhood, and keep their eyes peeled for "unwanted intruders."[93] Theirs was an invasion narrative in which public urban space—the neighborhoods and streets of the city that are in theory open to all—belong to middle- and upper-class whites who own property. Part of the rhetorical power of their vision is the implicit contrast it draws between the racially and ethnically diverse concrete "jungle" of the 1970s and early 1980s and the supposedly tight-knit urban villages and insular suburban communities of yesteryear. Theirs was also a "before" and "after" narrative that privileged the former term, the urban neighborhoods of America before they racially degenerated in Wilson and Kelling's view. Only aggressive policing of incivility and disorder could reverse urban decline and restore such neighborhoods to what they once were. Wilson and Kelling wanted to make cities safe; however, the impression one comes away with is that they hated the very qualities—diversity, mixture, openness, a sense of serendipity—that make a city a city in the first place.

For Wilson and Kelling, the tactics needed to restore the urban neighborhood required strenuously clamping down on activities that were not strictly speaking criminal, like blasting music from a boombox, loitering in a group on a sidewalk, or panhandling at an intersection. Wilson and Kelling recognized that such activities may not be illegal and that cracking down on them may not be legal either, but they nonetheless arrogated to the police extralegal powers to quash what was permissible, if undesirable, under the law. Reading their article, one sees them wringing their hands over the troublesome issues of "individual rights" and "universal standards" that prohibit or impede the police from taking actions they deem as necessary. As to how to prevent police from becoming "the agents of neighborhood bigotry" in their effort to clean up "disorder," they confessed they could "offer no wholly satisfactory answer." All they could offer was "hope" that the police would have "a clear sense of the outer limit of their discretionary authority" and realize that their duty was not to "maintain the racial and ethnic purity of a neighborhood."[94] The history of the NYPD's fatal abuses from Abner Louima to Eric Garner has proved this "hope" to be tragically misguided.

Put into action by Bratton, broken-windows tactics would install the police on the frontlines of gentrification in the years to come. The point not to be missed is that the shift in policing toward the maintenance of public order was illustrative of a shift in how the state managed urban space. The utopian vision of urban renewal by the midcentury liberal state was that it could produce "orderly individuals and communities through interventions in the built environment."[95] Better housing and better neighborhoods on a massive scale made better people. Title 1 of the Housing Act of 1949 had greenlit federally subsidized urban redevelopment projects in nearly a thousand cities and municipalities, reshaping urban America during the heyday of industrial Fordism. The racial and class inequities of the Housing Act and its myriad failures are well known. Before it was suspended in 1974, it had authorized urban renewal projects that displaced over a million people, mostly poor, Black, and Latinx, and hastened the decline of the neighborhoods that renewal ostensibly was designed to help. Locally funded urban redevelopment continued on a smaller scale after the Housing Act was suspended, but for all intents and purposes, renewal as a state project was dead by 1975, no longer economically feasible or politically desirable. In New York and other cities, what replaced it was a neoliberal paradigm for *managing* urban space, rather than *constructing* it, by the state, at scale. "After the fiscal crisis of 1975," Themis Chronopoulos argues, "neoliberalism and neoconservatism became the dominant ideologies of governance in New York City and their prescriptions of ordering space prevailed." He adds, "Left without an efficient spatial ordering strategy, neoliberals embraced neoconservative prescriptions such as the 'broken windows' theory and order-maintenance policing. Instead of seeking to produce orderly individuals like the liberals, neoliberals and neoconservatives sought to banish 'disorderly' ones."[96]

For Wilson and Kelling, and later Bratton, disorderly spaces and disorderly people were indistinguishable. "The panhandler is, in effect, the first broken window," Wilson and Kelling wrote.[97] Removing a panhandler was akin to repairing a window. This neoconservative turn in policing and governance was an ideological reorientation that had its basis in risk reduction. As Marianne Maeckelbergh explains, with the federal government's cessation of support for urban renewal, withdrawal from public housing, and shrinking financial support to cities overall, "local governments have become economically dependent on gentrification," which they have facilitated "through land assembly, tax incentives, property condemnation and the adjustment of zoning laws." Gentrification signaled to would-be residents, real estate developers, and corporate elites that the city was a safe investment. To limit "investment risks," which fell on the shoulders of local governments in the absence of federal support, cities adopted more repressive police measures, such as "Giuliani's 'zero tolerance tactics.' "[98] The first step was to secure urban space. Then cities could secure the plinth of capital to be plunked down in new urban development designed for upper-class whites.

The structural reasons why a neighborhood staggers into decline, from the loss of living-wage jobs to the breakdown of a sense of community, can be difficult to grasp and more difficult to solve. But the immediate threats—real or perceived—in a neighborhood, like young men loitering and blasting music in front of a boarded-up rowhouse that you have to hurry past each day, are never so abstract. Agents of broken-windows policing understood this and played upon racial fears without naming them as such. For them, cleaning up the city did not require tackling what liberal governance had taken as the root causes of crime—poverty, low-achieving schools, or lack of access to mental health services—but merely required harassing (what the police call dislocation tactics) or arresting homeless people, sex workers, and public drunkards who made life a daily trial for families and business owners.

In the final analysis, Wilson and Kelling's theory not only changed how policing was done; it also changed what people believed made a city work (or not work). In other words, it changed the story of the city. Their theory, Chronopoulos contends, "laid the groundwork for a reinterpretation of the decline of U.S. cities in the postwar period. . . . Instead of focusing on economic structuring, deindustrialization, suburbanization, and shrinking government budgets as indicators of urban decline," Chronopoulos explains, "Wilson and Kelling argued that the behavior of 'disorderly' people in urban space affected the desirability of cities in profound ways and that the urban centers had become undesirable because city officials had not adequately dealt with this problem."[99] One might reasonably expect that gutting the social safety net would result in more urban disorder, not less. Even if it did, conservatives argued it freed up funds for additional police, making the tradeoff worthwhile. Liberal social programs were not only a waste of money, they reasoned, but were counterproductive, since they created cultures of dependency that contributed to the erosion of neighborhoods and resulted in more crime. While city services shrank in almost every area in New York under Giuliani, the police force ballooned, expanding from 27,000 in 1993 to 41,000 in 2001.[100] Quality-of-life citations and misdemeanor arrests skyrocketed. The NYPD would endeavor to rescue the city by "reclaiming the public spaces of New York," to quote the title of Bratton's policing strategy, as though those spaces had been stolen. The police would take them back one street at a time, one park at a time, one neighborhood at a time. Doing so pacified parts of the city that had been off-limits to capital investment for years, if not decades. Giuliani's broken-windows policing helped create the spatial conditions for gentrification that would pick up speed through the 1990s and then race across the city under Bloomberg. The urban planners and activists Brad Lander and Laura Wolf-Powers note that "while observers of urban economies have been debating about the emergence of the post-industrial city for decades, the administration of Mayor Michael Bloomberg is the first to focus its economic development and urban planning policy around it."[101] He did so while continuing Giuliani's policing tactics, and, in time, the broken windows in neighborhoods from Harlem to Red Hook were replaced with the sparkling glass condos of a gentrified city.

So was quality-of-life policing successful in lowering major crimes in New York? A months-long NYPD inspector general's report in 2016 on the practice concluded there was "no empirical evidence demonstrating a clear and direct link between an increase in summons and misdemeanor arrest activity and a related drop in felony crime."[102] Wilson and Kelling had warned that if small infractions were not stamped out, then serious crimes in the city would flourish. This was the central contention of their theory. It turned out not to be true.

What is inarguably true is that quality-of-life policing laid the groundwork for the city's gentrification, a fact that crime novelists recognized. We find on the pages of Giuliani- and Bloomberg-era crime novels brokenwindows policing, rising rents, the refurbishing of working-class and ethnic neighborhoods, and the displacement (and resistance to displacement) of communities of color. But how this literature represents these transformations and the narratives it fashions out of them varies from text to text. In some of these novels, the broken-windows policing strategy operates methodically in the background, the low hum of the police work of handing out citations, while the foreground is devoted to the higher-order work of homicide investigations. Some of the cops in this body of literature openly advocate for the revitalizing miracle of gentrification, which promises to restore the antediluvian neighborhoods of their youth. In other novels, the cops find the latest arriving cohort of gentrifying hipsters to be an annoying demographic that they have to protect from being robbed or worse in the transitional neighborhood. Still others find themselves caught in impossible double binds, such as the ethnic cops forced to police ethnic identity. And in those more literary novels that place front and center the lives of everyday residents, rather than cops, the police are viewed as safeguarding the investments of white, upper-class homeowners in ways that drive working-class residents and residents of color to the margins of postindustrial New York's gentrifying neighborhoods.

CRIME FICTION'S NEIGHBORHOODS

The *neighborhood turn* in contemporary crime fiction, as I have been suggesting, is a reaction to the accelerated pace of gentrification from the 1990s onward that has put the (police) spotlight on so-called transitional areas. This narrower focus on a neighborhood, as opposed to the city at large, is often advertised in the titles of these books—*Chinatown Beat, Red Hook, Visitation Street, Bed-Stuy Is Burning*—informing readers upfront that these are investigations first and foremost of a specific place and the lifeworlds it contains. With the careful construction of geographical borders and the filling in of life within them, the crime narratives in *The Gentrification Plot* can be seen as an iteration of what Carlo Rotella labels the "neighborhood novel," which assembles a neighborhood's ethnic, racial, and working-class residents and its "pieces of urban terrain" in a "flexible structure that can encompass corollary matters . . . intersecting with urbanism." The neighborhood novel uses the neighborhood to condense the city to a smaller format. It simultaneously captures a neighborhood singularity and deploys it as a canvas to "generaliz[e] outward . . . to broader notions of place, peoplehood, politics, history, and so on."[103]

Limiting the narrative to single neighborhoods brings the abstract and widescale into greater relief and amplifies the drama in the process. But the neighborhood focus of recent crime literature can be seen as an acknowledgment, too, of the bewildering nature of the neoliberal urbanism and globalization that make cities as a whole increasingly difficult to cognitively map. "The physical transformation of the city and the sociological diversification of city life," write Bart Keunen and Bart Eeckhout, "make clear that the 'urban referent' has become ever more complex in the postwar period. . . . The contemporary American metropolis is no longer a relatively clear spatial entity with a nucleus characterized by density and congestion."[104] Those old dartboard maps of concentric rings that Chicago School sociologists once used to give shape to the industrial city are out of date. Not only does the city of today sprawl laterally into the hinterlands, forming nodes, edge cities, and exurbs, it is crisscrossed as never before by global flows of capital and labor. In this context the urban neighborhood, rather than the city as a whole, is a more manageable space, an easier place for the novelist to concentrate, in both senses of the word. For recent crime writers, the urban neighborhood serves as a framework for interrogating large and harder-to-figure transformations, changes that are challenging to map at scale but are acutely observable in the new buildings, new people, and new tensions on a neighborhood's streets. For novelists, the neighborhood serves an access point for understanding regional, national, even global developments; at the same time, it is a fast-fading preserve of older ways of life that are slipping from history and memory.

The neighborhood turn in crime fiction, moreover, should be understood as a sign of a transformation in the economy, should be seen, in fact, as a sign of the postindustrialization it thematizes. As globalization and gentrification homogenize urban space, they give rise dialectically to the demand for urban particularities and differences, the desire for niche experiences, unusual stories, and unique products that more often than not are centered in, or signify upon, ethnic and working-class life and neighborhoods. The twenty-first-century postindustrial economy values artisanal and locally made commodities over the standardized, mass-produced goods stuffed into suburban homes and horded in attics and garages at midcentury, a shift also evident in the changing tastes for culture, novels included. "In the postindustrial urban economy," observes the sociologist Jan Lin, "the neighborhood is a growing force as a unit of cultural production."[105] Local museums and galleries, ethnic markets and restaurants, cultural centers, and gimcrack trinket shops have filled in some of the holes left behind by the loss of Fordist-era manufacturing. Lara Belkind similarly argues that "with the declining importance of large-scale industrial production, cultural intermediaries, often members of urban subcultures, became essential to the search for new niche markets and marketable differences." This has "meant that cultures once thought to be peripheral—including that of the ghetto and the urban disenfranchised—could be appropriated within the culture industry as sources of content."[106] As a means of empowerment, this is suspect at best. Certainly the rise of the working-class and ethnic neighborhood as an engine in urban economic development signals a turn away from the state and a turn toward neoliberal free-market solutions for neighborhood revitalization. Arlene Dávila's research on the Upper Manhattan Empowerment Zone and its Cultural Investment Fund, which I consider in further detail in chapter 4, demonstrates as much. In order for racial and ethnic neighborhoods, such as Harlem, to receive grant funding, they are required to market their culture in ways that are recognizable and unoffensively palatable to outsiders and day-trippers visiting the area. Dávila argues that ethnic and racial differences have been mobilized and monetized for the purposes of urban development at the same time that their more resistant and more politically or culturally radical differences and demands have been discounted or downplayed. With hypergentrification homogenizing the central districts of major cities in terms of class and culture, neighborhoods on the social and geographic margins have been commodified, marketed, and branded as places of subcultural vitality and ethnic history, the heart and soul of the city, so to speak. Their storied pasts and cultures serve as selling points for short-term tourism and long-term real-estate investment. In sum, in the postindustrial urban economy, ethnicity is reasserted as a method of enterprise just as it is increasingly denied as a political category.[107]

Crime stories, as a variant of local-color fiction, can be seen as part of the culture industry that caters to a desire by today's readers for urban stories originating in parts of the city that might be off the radar for most. The novels in *The Gentrification Plot* zero in on a single neighborhood—an ethnic enclave, a gritty working-class redoubt, a historically Black area—as opposed to the city at large. In doing so, they produce textual spaces for those seeking stories about something different and something authentic while it can still be found, a locale and cast of characters they would not encounter in the corporatized nonspaces of any no-name midtown anywhere. Crime writers today hunt down their material on the gritty edges of the city, neighborhoods in which battles over crime, policing, gentrification, and urban preservation are still ongoing. Even as crime rates have precipitously fallen across New York, in the transitional neighborhood lurks danger and a story to tell about a besieged Latinx community or a polluted blue-collar district being rezoned for condos. "In Brooklyn, life is pretty much out on the street, out on the stoop, out on the waterfront," Gabriel Cohen remarks when explaining why he chose the outer borough for his

Jack Leightner series, rather than Manhattan with its glass and steel sky-scrapers.[108] Though Richard Price sets *Lush Life* in Manhattan, he keeps his story to the geographic and social fringe: the historically Jewish and later Puerto Rican Lower East Side. "It's not like this new Disney Times Square, by any stretch of the imagination," he has asserted in interviews, referenc-ing the family-friendly zone in Manhattan's midtown that was scrubbed of its associations with vice and working-class life by Giuliani in the mid-1990s.[109] For her part, Nadelson depicts the titular waterfront in *Red Hook* with a thick impasto of grease and oil, signifiers of a superannuated indus-trialism of an older New York that contrasts with the gleaming world of Manhattan's financial district on the other side of the harbor.

The writers in *The Gentrification Plot* tell the story of the postindustrial city's neighborhoods in crisis, at one and the same time overpoliced and underprotected. In this literature, postindustrial New York is economically revived by the decline in crime and the spike in development, and as a result its neighborhoods are safer yet more expensive, crackling with new energy yet losing touch with their historic roots. "The streets are cleaner," Cohen has remarked in an interview, "but in terms of its fading independent cul-ture and non-support of local businesses, the city has definitely paid a price."[110] The mystery the writers in this book confront is the postindus-trial city's great inequalities and its canyon-like social divides. The work of the detectives in many of these novels hastens gentrification, which in turn leads to stories of what the neighborhood used to be like and of everyday struggles to hold onto one's apartment or one's turf in New York. These nov-els tell stories of working-class cops who can barely afford to live in the neighborhoods they police and of working-class, Black, and brown residents whose lives are policed as they struggle to maintain a foothold as the neigh-borhood changes. Some fight for a feeling of cultural rootedness wedded to space. "I own an apartment," asserts Quiñonez's Puerto Rican protago-nist, "A real space with walls, doors and locks. It is mine."[111] Others, as in Price's and Chang's texts, just want to leave, put the neighborhood and the past behind them, and start over, if possible. Others still, as in Platzer's novel of gentrification, lash out in rage by hurling bricks through the stained-glass windows of a rehabbed 1890s brownstone, literally breaking windows in defiance of broken-windows policing.

"We must be insistently aware," Edward Soja urges, "of how space can be made to hide consequences from us, how relations of power and discipline are inscribed into the apparently innocent spatiality of social life, how human geographies become filled with politics and ideology."[112] Space is guilty as charged, an accusation leveled by recent crime fiction that depicts urban space as shot through with power and politics. By bringing a historical and spatial analysis to the discourse of crime literature we obtain a fuller understanding of its complex, if sensationalistic, representations of urban crisis, ethnicity, race, poverty, and violence. Much of this literature turns out to be a literature of the double binds ethnic and racialized subjects face over competing loyalties to family and community, on the one hand, and to self-independence and self-advancement, on the other, narratives that are also stories of spaces, of leaving the neighborhood or sticking it out to put down roots. They are narratives of how communities survive and thrive, how culture is emplotted and uprooted, and how the transformation of urban orders through decline, suburbanization, and renewal gives rise to backward-glancing nostalgia and new structures of feeling that imagine a different future for the urban neighborhood. In sum, these writers are part of a contentious conversation about the American city and the activities of making and unmaking places. Some of them write from the outside looking in and others from the inside looking to get out. Regardless of the perspective, they engage with the formal challenge of signifying urban spaces that are difficult to apprehend both because of their internal social complexity and their ever-evolving transformation by external forces, from local practices of policing and urban redevelopment to global patterns of capital and labor migration affecting city life. As a work of literary spatial studies *The Gentrification Plot* brings a spatial and historical imagination to contemporary crime fiction so as to understand how a death in a place—in the gentrifying working-class, ethnic, and African American neighborhoods of New York—launches an investigation into the death of a place and the death of a way of life in the postindustrial city.

The Gentrification Plot's examination of crime fiction and gentrification starts in chapter 1 in the neobohemian neighborhood of the Lower East Side during the early days of the real estate boom, the setting of Richard Price's eighth novel, *Lush Life* (2008). The area's transformation from a neighborhood synonymous with poverty, drugs, and crime in the 1970s and early 1980s to one known for trendy nightlife and upscale boutiques in the 1990s and early 2000s was a test case for subsequent redevelopment of marginalized neighborhoods throughout New York City. But to the extent that the Lower East Side's gentrification was prototypical, it was also singular, given its status as *the* immigrant site of first landing, which has made it, in Price's estimation, "the most important neighborhood in American history."[113] Its metamorphosis from a mythic launching pad for the poor to the postindustrial city's "MFA playground" for the privileged signals the end of one culturally central storyline Americans have told themselves about the American dream of upward mobility, a dream that has always been spatial—a flight to a better location, a better neighborhood.[114] Set in 2002, *Lush Life* unfolds in the area's new cocktail lounges and expensive restaurants and also in the decaying liberal state's midcentury public housing projects on the Lower East Side's perimeter. Price tells a tale of two neighborhoods in one, split by racial and class divisions that are inflamed by broken-windows policing and the murder of a hipster that the lead cop on the case knows will jeopardize the Lower East Side's new reputation. *Lush Life*'s concerns with place, identity, history, and capital are also found in nonliterary discourse on the neighborhood analyzed in this chapter, in particular the activist-oriented report "'A Divided Community': A Study of the Gentrification of the Lower East Side Community, New York" (2004). While *Lush Life* dramatizes the violent underpinnings of gentrification and its backlash, it also ironizes real estate marketing strategies that sell gritty subcultural and ethnic differences as subversive style to newcomers. Moreover, Price's novel underscores that in the midst of disorienting change, long-term urban residents are haunted by history and respond by constructing geographies that reinforce personal and social boundaries and by gravitating to residual signifiers of history and ethnic identification. However, efforts to establish a stabilizing geographical rootedness as long-standing cultural meanings of place are being uprooted fail in Price's novel, further underscoring the painful challenges gentrification poses.

As chapter 2 shifts the focus to the ethnic enclave of Manhattan's Chinatown, a new set of urban issues rises to the fore, including neighborhood memorialization, the double binds of ethnic identity, and Sinophobic representations of Chinatown in U.S. culture and in the crime genre. Representations of Chinatown as culturally inscrutable and physically dirty have both underwritten Chinatown's historical quarantining from the rest of the city and, more recently, have legitimized its intrusive policing and cleanup. Discourses of urban blight, as Marisa Solomon argues, "naturalize the 'need' for betterment" of disorderly neighborhoods and thus are harbingers of gentrification. Until the early 2000s, Chinatown could claim to be the last ungentrified neighborhood in Manhattan south of Ninety-Sixth Street, but by 2010 sociologists and cultural observers were noting that Chinatown was on the verge of disappearing "like many other old immigrant communities in the past."[115] This chapter reads the first three books of Henry Chang's Jack Yu series—*Chinatown Beat* (2006), *Year of the Dog* (2008), and *Red Jade* (2010)—as pregentrification narratives that wind back the clock to 1994, when broken-windows policing was first enforced and when the recent socioeconomic transformations that would alter Chinatown were still in embryonic form. With their start in the year Giuliani is inaugurated, the series functions as a narrative and literary memorialization of life in a neighborhood that is shadowed by a future we know is coming, the reality of realty. To help frame the narratives of economic and cultural struggle in these novels, I draw upon archival material from the Museum of Chinese in America's oral-history project, "Archaeology of Change: Mapping Tales of Gentrification in New York City's Chinatown." This chapter also reads for representations of cultural inscrutability and insularity and physical squalor and grime in Chang's series as figures for urban blight and the temporality of gentrification. Chang's exceptionally ambivalent series textually preserves the old neighborhood and mourns its erasure, which is hastened by the cleanup work of Chang's Giuliani-era detective. His protagonist understands the old neighborhood as freighted with burdensome ethnic obligations that he wishes to shake off, even as he is troubled by their loss. The series offers thick descriptions of Chinatown that immerse non-Chinese readers in the extraordinarily complex neighborhood; at the same time, these texts deploy and resignify the stereotypes of Chinatown's insularity and inscrutability as a way of safeguarding the enclave from outsiders.

The story of gentrification and crime moves in chapter 3 to the working-class port of Red Hook, Brooklyn, which Bloomberg singled out for revitalization and that since the 1990s has been the subject of no fewer than four major urban revitalization initiatives, evidence of the neighborhood's unsettled status in the urban imaginary. The chapter argues that Cohen, Nadelson, and Pochoda use Red Hook as a microcosm to anchor a metanarrative of the erosion of Fordist industrialism and the rise of neoliberal postindustrialism driven by real estate, tourism, and the culture and service sectors. Animating this metanarrative in their work are simmering class tensions that boil over when the neighborhood is retrofitted for a new economy. By bringing class issues to the fore, a number of concerns not encountered in earlier chapters surface, including white working-class grievances over the loss of economic and racial privilege, contemporary gentrification's reawakening of the personal traumas of midcentury urban renewal that led to working-class displacement, and competing views of how we remember and literally write the history of the industrial waterfront. In Cohen's *Red Hook* (2001), Detective Jack Leightner cracks a murder case in which a developer kills to keep secret a plan to build a waste-transfer station in the neighborhood just as the area is showing new signs of life. As Jack pursues his investigation in the present, he relives two defining traumas: the bulldozing of his family home by master planner Robert Moses and the death of his brother in a racist confrontation in 1965 with two Black teenagers. In Cohen's detective, we find a protagonist whose nostalgia for the industrial neighborhood's social order evinces a desire to turn back the clock to a putatively simpler era governed by white, working-class masculinity. Nadelson's Bloomberg-era novel, also titled *Red Hook* (2005), mobilizes crime to narrate a transition from the "old industrial city" with its rotting piers and empty factories to a "brand new city" of marinas and glass condos. While *Red Hook* is part of Nadelson's long-running Artie Cohen series, the heart of the novel belongs to Sid McKay, a member of the Black bourgeoisie who is obsessively working on a memoir of Red Hook. At its core, Nadelson's novel is about how one writes a history of the white, working-class neighborhood when one has been excluded from it, desperately needs "information" about it, and is willing to kill for it. "Information," I show, is a key term in the novel that signifies the information-driven postindustrial economy that is altering the waterfront neighborhood. The chapter closes with Pochoda's *Visitation Street* (2013). While Cohen's and Nadelson's narratives are organized around the point of view of the police detective, Pochoda's dialogic literary thriller interrogates the neighborhood from multiple viewpoints of everyday residents trying to solve the mystery of a working-class Italian American girl's vanishing. Her disappearance signifies the waning of Red Hook's blue-collar community. The fact that the novel's innocent African American character is a suspect in her disappearance underscores the way racialized subjects are targeted at the first sign that gentrification's "forward progress" may be stalling. Since Red Hook is a shipping port, its stories are littered with the detritus of waterfront industrialism, as well as shiny new images of the mode of production replacing it. In this chapter I argue these synecdoches—rotting piers, dilapidated docks, polluted canals, rusted shipping cranes, as well as recreational watercraft and gleaming cruise ships—are stand-ins for abstract flows of social and economic forces that engulf and drown characters in these novels. They are also signifiers of what gets left behind in the neighborhood, what of industrial urbanism's remnants get salvaged and repurposed by gentrifiers, and what gets newly privileged in a neighborhood in flux.

Chapter 4 turns to Harlem's central and eastern sections, New York's most storied Black and Latinx neighborhood, and to novels by two writers, Grace Edwards and Ernesto Quiñonez. This chapter reads their representations of Harlem in the context of the historical racialization, disinvestment, and decline of the neighborhood and in the context of its recent gentrification following its designation as an Empowerment Zone in 1994. The Upper Manhattan Empowerment Zone legislation not only poured tens of millions of dollars into Harlem to spur corporate development; it also incentivized Harlem to market and sell its cultural heritage to tourists as another means of revitalizing the neighborhood. In the chapter, I examine Edwards's *If I Should Die* (1997) for how it seeks to safeguard the local culture and everyday way of life of Harlem residents and for how it exposes the racist violence of the NYPD in the community. Edwards's text sees Harlem through the eyes of Mali Anderson, an ex-NYPD officer, who was fired for protesting racism in the police department and who now is completing graduate work in sociology. Edwards thus provides a uniquely trenchant perspective on the racial underpinning of policing and urban planning. As her protagonist works to expose a drug, child prostitution, and murder conspiracy, we hear the buzz of redevelopment in the background of the text. While Mali's sleuthing successfully shuts down the criminal plot, the text itself seems to have no answer for how to stop the incipient gentrification that is already displacing Black culture in the neighborhood. To better understand Harlem as a whole, the chapter turns to its eastern section and to Quiñonez's *Bodega Dreams* (2000) and *Chango's Fire* (2004). The chapter shows how both texts mobilize East Harlem's history of urban crisis and decline as a way of thinking through its recent gentrification. In particular, the chapter reads for the legacy of the fires that swept the area in the 1970s and 1980s as a result of disinvestment and reads for the signs of the FIRE industries (finance, insurance, and real estate) that swept it in the 1990s and early 2000s. What Quiñonez's writing underscores is that the metaphorical burning of Harlem by the FIRE industries reenacts the same logic and results in many of the same outcomes (displacement and inequality) as the literal burning of the barrio in decades past. At the center of both novels are Latino protagonists who are the ethnic embodiments of the neoliberal values of self-improvement, personal responsibility, hard work, and homeownership. Their entrepreneurial mindset enmeshes them in criminal enterprises as a way of supplementing their income to help make their dreams of upward mobility a reality in the gentrifying neighborhood, only to be badly burned for their aspirations. To compensate his protagonists for their losses, Quiñonez promises them an immersion in their neighborhood's culture and stories, the very fulcrum by which Harlem was remarketed by the Empowerment Zone's Cultural Industry Investment Fund in the 1990s and early 2000s. Reading for crime in these literary, but crime-filled, novels reveals the affective dimension of Latinx precarity and desperation engendered by neoliberal urbanism but also the feelings of opportunity and possibility that it produces in people.

Chapter 5 tracks the stories of New York's gentrification to Bedford-Stuyvesant, Brooklyn's largest African American neighborhood, and Wil Medearis's *Restoration Heights* (2019), Brian Platzer's *Bed-Stuy Is Burning* (2017), and, briefly, Brandon Harris's memoir *Making Rent in Bed-Stuy* (2017). To contextualize the literature, the chapter reflects on the economic processes that transformed Bed-Stuy into a nearly 100 percent racially homogenous Black neighborhood in the 1970s and 1980s and the more recent processes of gentrification, which are also highly racialized, that cut Bed-Stuy's Black population in half. As Black residents have left behind the neighborhood's highly coveted brownstones, gentrifiers have moved in, resulting in a 600 percent increase in its white population. Together these transformations have created the conditions for a flurry of new narratives of the neighborhood. The chapter's main argument is that Medearis's and Platzer's texts underscore how the processual nature of gentrification provides scripts for how whiteness is constructed and reinforced, how whiteness is built (and also how it falls apart) around homeownership and the right to the Black neighborhood. Set against Medearis and Platzer is my short reflection on Harris's memoir of Black precarity in the gentrifying neighborhood still troubled by crime. In Medearis's noirish thriller, the efforts of Reddick, the well-meaning white protagonist, to save Bed-Stuy from villainous white property developers leads to the dissolution of his benevolent white fantasies about the Black neighborhood and leads ultimately to his awareness of his complicity in the "crime" of Bed-Stuy's gentrification. Medearis's text narrates gentrification's redescription of Bed-Stuy as a "community" to a "territory," which is to say, it enacts its redefinition as a place of racial affinity and cohesiveness to a place of pure mercenary self-interest ripe for exploitation. If Medearis's white protagonist tries to save the neighborhood for Black residents, the wealthy white family at the center of Platzer's novel tries to save themselves from a violent uprising against broken-windows policing. Ultimately Platzer leverages the narrative of a neighborhood's social and physical transformation for the enrichment of white gentrifiers at great cost to the Black residents of Bed-Stuy. As the chapter closes, I posit that literary fiction is the byproduct, and maybe even the culmination of, the completely gentrified neighborhood in which violent crime, poverty, and delinquency have been mostly eradicated (or shunted from view). Platzer's novel in the end turns away from the strife of crime fiction and toward the traditional subjects of a certain kind of upper-middle-class literary fiction—meditations on matters of family life, romantic love, wealth accumulation, and self-discovery. In doing so, it expresses a longing for the end of the racial and class struggles of gentrification, a longing, in effect, for a pacified neighborhood where one might instead blissfully focus on the pleasures and challenges of domesticity and the stories that can emerge from it.

Finally, in a short epilogue, I consider the impact of COVID-19 on the uber-wealthy new neighborhood of Hudson Yards and reflect, more broadly, on the pandemic's early effects on gentrification and crime in New York City.

Chapter One

THE LOWER EAST SIDE

Cops, Culture, and the Creative Class

The Lower East Side, the downtown Manhattan neighborhood south of East Houston Street and east of Bowery, dramatically showcases the nadir and apogee of *The Gentrification Plot*'s story of urban change. It makes sense for many reasons to start here. For hundreds of thousands of immigrants processed through Ellis Island in the nineteenth and early twentieth centuries, the Lower East Side was the site of first landing and the gateway to the city and the nation. As a result, more stories of America begin in the Lower East Side than anywhere else. Historically, this working-class, immigrant neighborhood crammed cheek by jowl with garment workers, fruit sellers, printers, dry-goods shopkeepers, and pushcart vendors was the place where you established your foothold in New York. The Lower East Side was also the neighborhood you fled as soon as you had enough money to relocate to Bay Ridge or Westchester or almost anywhere else. The neighborhood by the 1970s was "the poorest in Manhattan outside Harlem" and regarded as "one of the most undesirable places to live in the city," a "free-fire zone" blighted by high rates of violent crime, open-air drug dealing, stubborn poverty, and dilapidated housing after years of disinvestment, demolition, and white flight.[1] Yet by the late 1990s, when this neighborhood once left for dead was buzzing with upscale restaurants, candlelit lounges, and glass condos in ways previously unimaginable, it might just be the place you wanted to live the most. Certainly other neighborhoods in New York gentrified before the Lower East Side; one thinks of SoHo in the early 1980s, but its gentrification was relatively contained. When one looks back at how gentrification spread across the city in the early 2000s, one sees the Lower East Side was where the fires of gentrification were first lit. For this reason, too, it makes sense to start the story of *The Gentrification Plot* in this neighborhood.

There are many ways of telling the story of the Lower East Side's post-2000 demographic overhaul. The crime novelist Richard Price in his eighth novel, *Lush Life*, chiefly tells it as a story of real estate and gentrification in the neighborhood where long-term residents are "hanging on by [the] fingernails" and where wealthier newcomers are elbowing their way in to make a place for themselves and pricing out others in the process.[2] By 2008, the year *Lush Life* was published, the ethnic and class succession of the Lower East Side had largely been accomplished. When walking the neighborhood in search of a story to tell, Price remarked how he had said to himself, "I want to write about this now," but then noted that "*now* is over. . . . The *new* Lower East Side is pretty old. But pump it back a decade, when it was first catching fire."[3] Accordingly, he set his novel a few years earlier, not quite a decade before 2008, but in 2002 to be exact, when the ownership of the neighborhood was still up in the air, when the neighborhood was changing but still undefined—was it an ethnic enclave, a neobohemian playground, an emerging upper-class residential district?—and when its status and future were still being actively fought over. Only a six-year difference, you might protest. Yes, but in gentrifying New York that's practically a lifetime. *Lush Life* narrativizes an old neighborhood order breaking apart, a neighborhood fiercely divided over housing and public space, creative-class whites in one area, Blacks and Latinos in another, trespassing occasionally into each other's territory with deadly consequences. The fatal encounter that launches the novel unfolds between a twenty-something hipster writer and bartender named Ike Marcus and a seventeen-year-old Puerto Rican drug dealer named Tristan Acevedo. Nervously attempting his first mugging with his partner in crime Little Dap Williams, Tristan panics and shoots Ike, killing him with a single .22 caliber bullet to the chest. The duo flee in the four-AM darkness down Delancey Street back to their turf, the public housing projects along the perimeter of the neighborhood, leaving Ike to bleed to death in the street and his two heavily inebriated companions, Eric and Steven, to piece together what just happened.

In interviews Price has made clear that he sees the machinations of the real estate industry, one of the main pistons of today's postindustrial FIRE (finance, insurance, and real estate) economy, as instrumental to understanding his novel. "Real estate is violence. It's physical violence, but it's also uprooting, it's clashing, it's tectonic plates," he has remarked.[4] The observation underscores an infrequently recognized but essential point: real estate is not merely a collection of buildings in space but a social and spatial process through which spaces, places, and ways of life are made and unmade via struggle. It is an arena of political, economic, and cultural conflict that can be so violent that it feels "tectonic" to the characters of *Lush Life*, as though the mantle of the earth has moved. Yet Price has also called the real estate industry the "greatest crime fighter in the word," better than the cops at taming the neighborhood. But, as we will see in Price's novel, the real estate industry needs the cops too in order to survive. "Really aggressive policing and real estate needing a place to go," Price contends, was the one-two punch that flipped the Lower East Side. Soon enough "the place that used to be a heroin apartment is now going for a million dollars."[5] In *Lush Life*, real estate gentrification deracinates the neighborhood's residents, making them lose touch with their roots, and then it displaces them, putatively making the new whitewashed neighborhood calmer and more crime-free for those residents who can afford to remain.

What is helpful to keep in mind when reading *Lush Life*, as well as the other novels in this study, is that real estate is never just about real estate, just as crime is never just about crime. In Price's work, real estate and its cognates, such as tenement apartments, high-rise public housing, and upmarket restaurants and lounges, are stand-ins that condense and concretize abstract social, economic, and spatial transformations that are difficult to see or simply too messy to make sense of in other ways. In telling the story of the social convulsions unfolding in one small but important neighborhood, Price tells a much bigger story of the tumultuous transition from the welfare state to the new neoliberal order, a national story about the dismantling of midcentury liberalism, embodied in the novel's housing projects where Tristan lives, and the new strategies of quality-of-life policing, embodied in the novel's roving patrols that eventually solve the murder. The police keep people of color and the poor in line while securing the flow of private capital that is remaking Price's Lower East Side into a neighborhood for the professional classes. Such is the function of the cops in this novel. Ultimately, *Lush Life* is an urban crisis narrative in a neighborhood known for being in perpetual crisis; it is just not the kind of crisis readers might expect. Rather than telling the story of a neighborhood in the last gasps of its decline, Price tells the story of the Lower East Side's violent rebirth in postindustrial New York.

The subjects of cops, crime, and gentrification are central to all of the neighborhoods examined in *The Gentrification Plot*. What makes the Lower East Side different, apart from it being, as Price has called it, "probably the most important neighborhood in American history," is the manner in which culture has been expropriated for redevelopment of the area.[6] As Suleiman Osman has argued, historical preservation has been a tool for gentrifying New York neighborhoods, especially in brownstone Brooklyn, neighborhoods that began as upper-middle and upper class, suffered a period of decline, and then rebounded largely on the strength of their architectural beauty.[7] These wealthy neighborhoods—such as Park Slope, Brooklyn Heights, and Cobble Hill—have used historical preservation districting to boost property values, tightly regulate the physical alteration of the streets and brownstones, and limit the intrusion of big-box retailers. This deliberate strategy—shot through with all kinds of racial and class implications—has had the added value of conveying a sense of an authentic neighborhood preserved from the erosions of time and the tawdry corruptions of the marketplace. The Lower East Side, which was poor and marginal from its earliest days, has had a different relationship to its storied past. Since the late 1990s and early 2000s, its relationship to its past has not been so much the preservation of its history but the postmodern salvaging of it, an ironic recycling and thematization of it, in other words, not so much a nostalgic restoring of its past to its original state but a contemporary repurposing of it for new uses. The urban planner Lara Belkind argues that this has come in the form of upcycling old storefronts, "defunct façades, signage," and the remaking of the spaces of synagogues, beauty salons, tenement sweatshops, massage parlors, "and other physical traces of the neighborhood's working-class and immigrant past." The selling of gritty subcultural and ethnic differences as subversive style and cultural capital to creative-class newcomers in the Lower East Side "has been translated by the market into real estate value," and "this new value has sharpened the struggle for space between new and existing resident groups and land uses."[8]

As we will see in Price's work, gentrification's processes create and compel new scripts of identities—new habits of consumption, new practices of socializing, new ways of being in the city, and new codes by which groups recognize, affirm, or resist one another. Thus how space and history is repurposed, represented, and made meaningful in the gentrifying neighborhood turns out to be central for understanding the geographical construction of subjectivity and the narratives of geographical struggle in *Lush Life*. What does the neighborhood mean to me? What is my place in it? How does my being here or not being here change this place? Questions like these suffuse Price's novel, even when they are not asked directly. Further to this point, *Lush Life* shows that in the midst of disorienting change, long-term urban residents are haunted by the history that urban redevelopment excavates and repurposes, and they respond by constructing geographies that reinforce personal and social boundaries and by gravitating to signifiers of history and ethnic identification. However, the work of establishing a feeling of geographical rootedness as the cultural meanings of place are being uprooted and resignified fail in Price's novel, underscoring the painful challenges of gentrification. This chapter will also show that in Price's hands the upscaling of the Lower East Side—its metamorphosis from a mythic launching pad for the poor to the postindustrial city's "MFA playground" for the privileged—signals the end of one culturally central storyline Americans have told themselves about the American dream of upward mobility, a dream that has always been spatial: a flight to a better location, a better neighborhood.

MAPPING THE NEIGHBORHOOD

Before diving into Price's Lower East Side, it helps to get a lay of the land, something we will do for each of the neighborhood-novels in *The Gentrification Plot*. Today's Lower East Side, as noted, stretches from East Houston Street down to FDR Drive and from Bowery to the East River, where the Williamsburg Bridge's latticed trusses, inspired by the Eiffel Tower, span over into Brooklyn. A small cutout along East Broadway near Seward Park in the southern part of the Lower East Side is often designated as Chinatown, the sprawling neighborhood that borders the Lower East Side to the west. Cross East Houston heading north, and you enter the East Village, which stretches to Fourteenth Street.

These weren't always the Lower East Side's boundaries. The neighborhood's borders historically have been fungible, shifting with the influx of new immigrant groups and with the whims of the New York real estate market. Neil Smith explains that for much of New York's modern history, the entire eastern section of Manhattan south of Fourteenth Street was designated as the Lower East Side until "real estate agents and art world gentrifiers . . . anxious to distance themselves from the historical association with poor immigrants" rechristened part of the neighborhood as the East Village.[9] The effort was to rebrand and remarket the East Village as a desirable place to live by aligning it with the more upscale district of Greenwich Village and disassociating it with the poverty, crime, and cholera outbreaks south of East Houston.

In everyday life urban boundaries are never as fixed as they are on official maps. The streets near the edges of the Lower East Side are liminal spaces, less hard divisions than transitions and places of contact and friction between different groups. For instance, Eldridge Street is a mix of Asians and Latinos and is where one finds a corner bodega with the awkward yet oddly fitting name Chinese Hispanic Grocery. Also fittingly, this stretch, which was ungentrified in 2002 (and remains somewhat so today), is where the murder occurs in *Lush Life* when Ike and his white friends wander away from the safety of the neighborhood's central streets and run into trouble. Both separating and joining the neighborhoods of the Lower East Side and Chinatown is Sara Delano Park, a scrubby belt with several handball courts and basketball hoops encircled by a jogging track, each catering more or less to the three dominant groups in the area: Chinese, African American, and white. Within the borders of the Lower East Side, different communities lay claim to their own areas—corners and blocks are distinguished by Yiddish, Mandarin, Cantonese, Spanish, or English used in commercial signage and in daily life on the street and are distinguished by the types of establishments—chic wine bars, dumpling houses with untranslated menus, fish and fruit stands, karaoke bars, boutiques with three racks of monochromatic clothing, cluttered trinket shops—and by the presence of different houses of worship—synagogues, Buddhist temples, mosques, and Catholic churches. Lining the neighborhood's central blocks—Ludlow, Orchard, Rivington, Thompson, and Allen—you find luxury hotels and residential towers, such as the Hotel on Rivington (THOR), Thompson LES, and a bit further south, the cumbersome Blue

Condominium, whose blue-and-black pixelated glass exterior bulges out over the tenements below. Out of scale with the neighborhood, the building appears at once totally insular and aggressively elbowing for space. Along the southern and eastern scrim, one finds many of the monolithic towers of midcentury NYCHA housing (New York City Housing Authority): the Jacob Riis Houses, Lillian Wald Houses, Baruch Houses, Vladeck Houses, and Alfred E. Smith Houses. For years, including the time when *Lush Life* is set, these public housing towers were immovable obstacles to gentrification, an outer limit to how far it could push. That no longer appears to be the case. Following a 2013 decision by NYCHA and the subsequent drafting of an infill plan, open spaces on public housing sites can be leased to private developers to build market-rate housing that is all but certain to block the light and air of residents in the towers.

The Lower East Side of the late nineteenth and early twentieth centuries—residues of which are found in the pages of Price's novel and off them—was an almost unfathomably congested immigrant enclave. In the 1890s, the population density in some wards reached 1,500 people per acre, which if reproduced across Manhattan would equate to approximately twenty million residents, or roughly ten times the borough's population a hundred years later.[10] Then, as now, it was a heterogeneous neighborhood, though it was known mostly for its communities of Eastern European Jews and southern Italians. It was this culturally rich and economically poor enclave that

FIGURE 1.1. High-rise development on the Lower East Side. *Source:* David Shankbone, CC BY 2.5 (https://creativecommons.org/licenses/by/2.5), via Wikimedia Commons.

FIGURE 1.2. Alfred E. Smith Houses, from Brooklyn Bridge, Manhattan, New York. *Source:* Ken Lund from Reno, Nevada, USA, CC BY-SA 2.0 (https://creativecommons.org/licenses/by-sa/2.0), via Wikimedia Commons.

gave us Abraham Cahan's novella of acculturation *Yekel* (1896), Hutchins Hapgood's warm account of Jewish life in *The Spirit of the Ghetto* (1902), Anzia Yerierska's three-volume bildungsroman *Bread Givers* (1923), and Theodore Dreiser's vignettes in *The Color of a Great City* (1923). The severely restrictive Immigration Act of 1924, however, altered the neighborhood by reducing the influx of new Jewish and Italian immigrants at the same time that many of the older arrivals were migrating to the outer boroughs and the manicured lawns of Long Island and New Jersey. Over the subsequent decades the neighborhood's demographic composition kept changing, especially in the years following the passage of the Immigration and Naturalization Act of 1965, which liberalized immigration policy. With the lifting of immigration caps, Chinese, Filipinos, and Dominicans arrived, filling the vacancies left by the original ethnic-American exodus. So too did Puerto Ricans, fleeing the crumbling economy on the island in the 1950s and 1960s. They settled en masse in the Lower East Side and Spanish Harlem (chapter 4) "to work in New York's garment industry," an inopportune moment because much of that industry was actively being outsourced overseas.[11] The 1970s saw the neighborhood spiral into a crisis of poverty and, as often follows on its heels, violence that transpired in the context of ongoing suburbanization, bank redlining, lost tax revenues, the near bankruptcy of the city, and the steady decline of manufacturing jobs in New York. For much of the 1970s, the Lower East Side was a "rubble of disinvestment," a bombed-out landscape of weedy lots, charred tenements, squats, and cheap housing that appealed to young artists, musicians, actors, and writers who moved into the neighborhood, bought apartments *in rem* from the city, set up artist collectives, planted community gardens, and the like. Decades of abandonment and neglect, combined with the green shoots of artist-led revitalization, created the "conditions and opportunity for a whole new round of capital reinvestment" when the Lower East Side's high rent gaps and prime downtown location made the neighborhood fallow land for "entrepreneurial exploitation" and real estate development in the 1990s.[12] These latest developments have given us the racially and economically polarized neighborhood we find in Price's novel and that we also find in the 2004 report " 'A Divided Community': A Study of the Gentrification of the Lower East Side Community, New York" (2004) by the activist-oriented Two Bridges Neighborhood Council.

The Two Bridges report depicts the Lower East Side as living on borrowed time. Drawing on data from the 2000 U.S. Census, it underscores how the Lower East Side exhibits many of the hallmarks of white-collar colonization: systemic evictions, a declining Latinx population, high-levels of rent distress among low-income residents, a falling number of renter-occupied units, a rising number of owner-occupied apartments, and an "ever-growing gap between rich and poor."[13] While these trends are the latest evidence of the large-scale and long-wave postindustrial restructuring of New York to serve the needs of its professional managerial class, the report pointedly singled out one entity in particular—the Lower Manhattan Development Corporation (LMDC)—and faulted it for exacerbating the displacement of poorer residents of the neighborhood. The LMDC was created by Mayor Giuliani and Governor Pataki in November 2001 to help Lower Manhattan neighborhoods recover from the September 11 terrorist attacks by allocating nearly three billion dollars in federal grants for affordable housing and economic development. The Two Bridges report, however, in so many words, charged it with disaster capitalism par excellence by opportunistically seizing upon the 9/11 tragedy to hasten the class remake of the neighborhood. The "LMDC grant policies," the council's president Victor Papa contended, "did more to assist landlords and wealthier residents than the lower income residents," who have been displaced.[14] "This trend was, without question, accelerated by the increased real estate speculation activity that occurred after 9/11," speculation that the report labeled "destructive" and "feverish."[15] The "traditional immigrant" neighborhood that was "once a reliable haven for working families," Papa lamented, was now on the verge of "succumb[ing] to the tidal wave of the ever-accelerating gentrification process" that will render it "a tourist curiosity" and "a historical footnote."[16] For the Two Bridges Neighborhood Council, the Lower East Side community was divided against itself for many reasons, but the main one was housing. As we will see, it was too for Price in *Lush Life*.

DEAD ENDS IN RICHARD PRICE'S LOWER EAST SIDE

To understand Price's novel, we have to acknowledge something uncomfortable at the outset. Price does not care much about Ike Marcus. He shows less interest in Ike's life than the place where he dies. Evidence for this claim is found in the formal and narrative peculiarities of *Lush Life* and in the generic expectations and pleasures that Price withholds from readers of crime fiction. Ike dies in the opening pages, before the reader has the opportunity to know or, frankly, care much about him. When one learns his backstory, which comes much later, it feels like filler, a novelistic obligation to provide depth and emotional resonance that falls flat. It is true that homicides almost always occur early in detective novels, serving as the event that triggers the narrative of investigation that rounds up multiple suspects, progressively winnows down the possibilities, and finally zeroes in on a culprit and a motivation. But Price's novel refuses the game of whodunit or even whydunit. The reader is never in doubt about the name and whereabouts of the murderer. As far as Tristan's motivation is concerned, strictly speaking none exists. When NYPD Detective Yolonda Bello in the waning pages of the novel asks, "What did [Ike] do to you?" Tristan replies, "Nothing. . . . He started to like, step to me, and I flexed. Bap" (438). When she tries to fish out of him a childhood-abuse narrative as a mitigating circumstance, she again comes up empty. Price steadfastly redirects readers from the subject of the personal and psychological motivations for crime to its social causations. With Tristan, they are the many, if standard, urban ills of poverty, drugs, and a dysfunctional home life. No suspense propels *Lush Life* forward, and no surprising revelation awaits readers at the end. The climax comes early when Tristan shoots Ike in the heart, and the rest is anticlimax. This is not meant as a criticism of *Lush Life* but as a recognition that Price's own heart is elsewhere.

So what exactly is Price up to in *Lush Life*? To answer this question, let us pause a moment over the difference between genre and genre fiction. As I discussed in the introduction, the scholar Jeremy Rosen reminds us that "genre" designates an "existing literary framework" that is marked by its "generative capacity and plasticity."[17] In other words, it is adaptable, flexible, stretchable as silly putty; writers of serious literary intent can incorporate into its fungible frameworks varied prose styles—postmodernism or magical realism, for instance—and can put them into the service of exploring complex areas of identity, politics, philosophy, or cultural critique, the stuff we normally associate with literary fiction. For its part, "genre fiction," such as romance, westerns, or detective fiction, often uses the frameworks of genre in predictable ways to produce a relatively standardized product, fiction that is "fun, plot-driven, and accessible" and generally considered "subliterary."[18] A writer with a literary sensibility, Price has planted himself firmly within a commercial genre while also refusing to be hemmed in by the expectations and limitations that come with it. He has not been shy, either, about hiding his apparent boredom with detective fiction's hardwired formulas. "I don't even care who did it [the murder]," Price remarked in 2008 when discussing *Lush Life*, adding, "It's an excuse to get into the world. I would rather say who did it in the first sentence and get it out of the way. There are so many dead ends in this book, so many things that go nowhere."[19] Price's comments seem designed to preempt frustrations by warning readers about what and what not to expect. In regard to plot, there's not much of it. Indeed, much of the book "go[es] nowhere." Price has the homicide unit, led by Detective Matty Clark, bungle the investigation with a series of knee-jerk assumptions, which compounded with the NYPD's red tape, create one delay after another. The most costly misstep is the long, humiliating interrogation and arrest of Eric Cash, who was with Ike on the fateful night. His account of the shooting initially raises suspicions, but these are ultimately unfounded. The experience sends Eric in the second half of the novel into a tailspin of depression and drug use and eventually leads him to move out of the neighborhood he has called home for eight years. Stretching well over a hundred pages, the fruitless police interrogation of Eric leaves readers (or this reader at least) feeling increasingly impatient. A fair question to ask is why Price plays it out for so long. He has his reasons.

"The geographic location drove the story and the characters came after it," Price has divulged.[20] One might even argue that the location is the main character. By stalling the forward thrust of the investigation, Price causes the story to circumambulate through a series of detours, which, far from being needlessly distracting, are fundamental and consequential to the novel's larger aim "to get into the world." In *Lush Life*, the delays that "go nowhere" allow Price the time and space to world-build, to create a thick description of the urban environment, a verbal impasto of the ever-changing and increasingly divided Lower East Side. Around the skeleton of a relatively thin murder plot, *Lush Life*'s 450+ pages flesh out a neighborhood undergoing dizzying physical transformation and symbolic resignification under the pressure of a speculative, ruthless, and amoral real estate market.

To tell his story of crime, policing, and gentrification in the neighborhood, Price recreates the geography of the Lower East Side through granular attention to its social and physical landscape, so that in the end the novel's sense of place feels real. He makes repeated direct references to in-the-know places in the Lower East Side that also exist off the page and oblique references to others whose names are changed but whose identities and locations are obvious. For instance, he renames the Alfred E. Smith Houses, a "grubby sprawl of fifty-year-old high-rises," as the Clara E. Lemlich Houses (219). This is where Tristan and Little Dap live. Keith McNally's locally well-known Schiller's Liquor Bar, with its distinctive exterior white tiles and casement windows, graces the novel's cover and is reborn inside the pages as Café Berkmann, where it lives forever. An early outpost of Lower East Side gentrification when it opened at 131 Rivington Street, Schiller's folded in 2017, a victim of rising rents. The 150-year-old First Romanian-American Congregation Synagogue, also on Rivington, that imploded in 2006 is anachronistically a pile of rubble in Price's 2002 setting. The "laboratorio del gelati" that Eric walks past on his way to Berkmann's is Il Laboratorio del Gelato, a retail anchor of a luxury condominium building on Ludlow and East Houston. Moreover, the "Asian massage parlor turned kiddie-club hot spot" that he strolls by is the aptly named lounge

Happy Ending that repurposed the space of Xie He Health Club at 302 Broome Street, retrofitting its basement-level shower stalls into tiled banquettes for drinking while leaving intact the massage parlor's original awning. The latter stylistic choice was known to create confusion for overseas tourists searching for something other than a stiff drink. Happy Ending unhappily shuttered, too, in real life in 2017, also a victim of skyrocketing rents. Moreover, Price uses numerous exact street addresses (27 Eldridge, 32 St. James, One Police Plaza) and landmarks (the Williamsburg and Brooklyn Bridges, the World Trade Center site) to orient readers and create the impression of geographical and social authenticity. Despite all of this geographical authenticity and familiarity, Price's personal relation to the Lower East Side is one of sudden discovery or that of a man who has come late to the party. "I had no idea what to expect when I went down there. I was still thinking 'historical.' And then I just saw all the chaos," he has remarked. The phrasing—"down there"—reveals his physical and imaginative distance from the Lower East Side, a neighborhood a world away from the genteel reserve of Gramercy Park, where Price lived while researching and writing *Lush Life*.[21] By "still thinking 'historical,'" Price betrays that his sense of the neighborhood was out of date and discloses that what has happened to history in the Lower East Side was on his mind from the start.

One of the through lines of *The Gentrification Plot* is how racial, ethnic, gender, and class identities are constituted and inscribed geographically and how these identities reshape the geographies in which they are enacted. This sociospatial dialectic is always already operative in a network of relations between humans, space, and politics that form the habits of our social and physical being: the way, for instance, we consciously or unconsciously divide up a neighborhood into the good and the bad parts, the center and the margins, up here or down there. Gentrification makes observable the processes by which subjectivities are spatially produced. On this point, the geographer Liz Bondi contends that gentrification makes plain "the creation and constitution of distinctive social groups," whose relation to one another is primarily through conflict.[22] Price knows this and makes of this his novel. Price's Lower East Side is a community as divided as the one cleaved in two in the Two Bridges report. It is two neighborhoods in one, segregated by geography, class, and ethnicity. One part of the neighborhood—the wealthier, whiter part, a creative-class haven and an "MFA playground"— constitutes Ike's stomping grounds.[23] There one finds trendy bars, galleries, boutiques, and restaurants clustered along the northern portions of Orchard, Ludlow, and Essex. Tristan lives in the other part, the perimeter blocks of public housing watched over by "the Eighth Precinct station house, an octagonal Lindsay-era, siege-mentality fortress" (47). Bringing his tale of two geographies to life, Price at first conceives a Janus-faced tale, with a white face and a brown one staring away from each other.

The first face is Ike's. He functions as a demographic and psychographic composite of the transformative forces in the Lower East Side. With "a shaved head and a menagerie of retro tattoos" and a smile "as clean as a cornfield," he is a "poster boy for the neighborhood," the face of the area's newest faces—the edgy but not-too-edgy white creative class theorized by Richard Florida who have flooded the Lower East Side in Price's novel (20). While the levers of power in the neoliberal economy are undoubtedly in the hands of more MBAs than MFAs, the latter hold an outsized symbolic role as the embodiment of the creativity, innovation, flexibility, and ability to "think different" required for success now that the industrial-era values of standardization, regulation, and routinization are increasingly out-moded. This is what Ike stands for. Ironically, he also stands for the idea that the Lower East Side is now a safe place to work, live, play, or invest. Ironic—because Tristan shoots him dead ten minutes into the novel. NYPD Detective Matty Clark, the overworked, divorced father of two who assumes the lead on the case, knows full well the stakes if the neighborhood goes south, which is why he remarks after the killing that "a media shitstorm" is about to break (41). Furthermore, Ike's retro tattoos of hula girls, mermaids, and devils stand for the resignification of the Lower East Side's golden age of punk made famous by the Ramones, Television, and Blondie playing in the fetid atmosphere of CBGBs, a world that for Berkmann's patrons has passed from life into legend. Two years before *Lush Life* was published, the fabled bar closed, and the high-end designer John Varvatos opened a store in its place. It is a legend that once declawed can be marketed to new resi-dents and visitors as a sign of an exciting urban lifestyle, a gritty glamour for young professionals. In this sense, "clean as a cornfield" Ike is a walking billboard to Midwestern transplants that the Lower East Side is safe. Or looks safe enough, until Ike dies.

Tristan functions as an urban type as well, the embodiment of the pathol-ogies found in the culture-of-poverty discourse formalized by Oscar Lewis in the 1960s and reprised in the 1980s and well beyond in the conservative writings of Charles Murray and Edward Banfield. Tristan, too, is a poster boy for that part of the neighborhood—a face on a wanted poster and a sign that in the still-gentrifying neighborhood danger lurks. A police sketch renders him a "generic lynx-eyed urban predator," the metaphor foregrounding animalistic lethality in the age of mass incarceration (343). As we will see, between these two faces, Price eventually inserts a third, the ghostly visage of the neighborhood's late nineteenth-century Jewish residents, whose history of tenement life surfaces in the narrative. They serve as an imagined community that indexes a time before one part of Price's Lower East Side came to be defined by its ceaseless commodification of history and geography for profit and before the other part of the neighborhood became caught in a cycle of neglect, violence, drug trafficking, and personal despair.

The novel opens with three verbal maps of the Lower East Side that orient readers in the neighborhood and eventually lay bare its divisions. The first mapping is carried out by the Quality of Life Task Force, a group of boorish cops on an all-hours patrol. They play a small but critical role in the story as Price's enforcers of the broken-windows policing theorized by James Wilson and George Kelling. For Wilson and Kelling, the key to cleaning up cities and making them livable again was not to clean up their dirty spaces through massive, urban renewal efforts that we associate with the midcentury liberal state, in general, and Robert Moses, in particular. Rather it was to clean out their dirty people through police harassment and incarceration. In *Lush Life*, the Quality of Life Task Force sleeplessly circles the Lower East Side beginning on the opening page, framing the reader's entry into the story of the neighborhood under tense surveillance. They hunt for any sign that the newly trendy neighborhood might backslide into its bad old days. The squad reappears every few chapters as they scour for the tiniest real or imagined infraction, a busted taillight, someone walking oddly, someone spray painting graffiti, a driver driving too carefully, any minor quality-of-life violation that they might use to shake out a gun or at least a bag of weed that will lead them to bigger crimes.

Price's description of their patrol of the Lower East Side is worth quoting at length because its reductive parataxis paradoxically signifies the urban excess the police need to control: "Restless, they [the Quality of Life Task Force] finally pull out to honeycomb the narrow streets for an hour of endless tight right turns: falafel joint, jazz joint, gyro joint, corner. Schoolyard, crêperie, realtor, corner. Tenement, tenement, tenement museum, corner. Pink Pony, Blind Tiger, muffin boutique, corner. Sex shop, tea shop, synagogue, corner. Boulangerie, bar, hat boutique, corner. Iglesia, gelateria, matzo shop, corner" (3–4). This list, which goes on for several more sentences, indexes a neighborhood still in transition, a still potentially unruly hodgepodge before the advent of the next phase of gentrification marked by corporate bank branches and generic chain stores. David Schmid rightly remarks that in crime fiction, the city is the site of "semantic overload," but when we look a little closer at Price's language we can see a logic to its semiotic excess.[24] What we have here are diverse "signs" rather than "diverse" people. Or put another way, Price depicts postindustrial urban diversity as a series of diverse consumer goods (Middle Eastern, Jewish, French) in the form of upscale retail or cheap ethnic food after a night of boozing. Sex shops share the block with synagogues, bougie crêmperies with real estate offices, hipster bars with artisan boutiques, Spanish-language churches with new shops peddling gourmet ice cream and older ones hawking matzo, and whole blocks composed of tenements or the memorialization of them as museums. What is noteworthy, too, is how an otherwise unmanageable jumble—a heterogeneous mixing of people who might stand, literally, under these "signs"—is formally arranged in neat rows that are monitored and kept in line. Price's Quality of Life Task Force performs not so much the traditional police work of solving crimes but what Wilson and Kelling term an order-maintenance function to prevent crimes from happening in the first place. The job of the police is to maintain the new status quo, to keep everyone and everything in order in the capitalist city, an idea that Price mimics at the level of his syntax.

The NYPD's quality-of-life policing was a tactic to foster an environment conducive to investment in economically moribund neighborhoods. *Lush Life*'s police circulate through a Lower East Side whose blocks are now jammed with commerce, no sign of an empty lot, vacant storefront, or "rubble of disinvestment" of the 1970s anywhere between Price's compressed commas, signifying a postindustrial economy running at full throttle.[25] A further close reading of his block-by-block delineation reveals the hallmarks of the new economy: expensive niche markets specializing in the small-batch production of commodities ("hat boutique"), the presence of the real estate industry ("realtor"), and the prominence of the service ("crêperie" and "tea shop"), culture ("tenement museum"), and entertainment sectors (the clubs "Pink Pony" and "Blind Tiger"), which have steadily replaced the old industrial urban order in much of the United States. Price brings the list to a stop when the police spot "finally, on a sooty stretch of Eldridge, something with potential: a weary-face Fujianese . . . trudging up the dark, narrow streets followed by a limping black kid half a block behind" (4). Signs of ethnic and racial difference ("gyro joint" and "jazz joint") may exist side by side peacefully as *commodities*, but as *people* . . . the police seem to think "not so much." In Price's text, a "black kid" possibly faking a limp and stalking a Chinese restaurant worker carrying his week's wages through the streets of the Lower East Side is cause for investigation.

Price provides two other maps through the eyes of two Lower East Side residents: Eric Cash and Tristan Acevedo. Their walks through the neighborhood epitomize how the act of navigating urban space is an exercise of one's power or lack thereof. How we orient ourselves in city space, Price implies, reveals as much about us as it does the city. Eric's and Tristan's walks are from two different angles and places. Eric's is from the central streets near Ludlow and Orchard, where many of the neighborhood's iconic nineteenth-century brick tenements that once housed Jewish and Italian immigrants are clustered. Tristan's is from the southern and eastern fringes, where the Latinx and African American public housing projects are located, a legacy of midcentury racial liberalism that warehoused residents displaced by urban renewal. These two vectors represent not just two different people but two different historical forces. Eric and his companions, Ike and Steven, as wannabe writers and actors, are the low-tier creatives that Florida celebrates as the vanguard of late 1990s gentrification.[26] Tristan and his companion Little Dap, for their part, are the products of the increasingly superannuated liberal state's inability to provide meaningful life choices for poor people of color in American cities. As "a dark kid with a gun," Tristan functions in the text as an unconscious expression of pent-up resistant energies waiting to lash out at any visible manifestation of gentrification, even if as a character he'd never quite frame it in these terms (194). After these two vectors are launched, they fatally collide.

The first of these walks is Eric's. Making his "daily four-block commute" to work at Café Berkmann, the thirty-five-year-old manager and writer, "an upstate Jew five generations removed from here," observes the architecture of the street. What catches his attention are "traces of the nineteenth-century Yiddish boomtown everywhere: in the claustrophobic gauge of the canyonlike streets with their hanging gardens of ancient fire escapes, in the eroded stone satyr heads leering down between pitted window frames above the Erotic Boutique, in the faded Hebrew lettering above the old socialist cafeteria turned Asian massage parlor turned kiddie-club hot spot" (15). What draws Eric to the neighborhood is not nostalgia for its nineteenth-century history of Jewish life and political radicalism. Rather, what excites him is actually "its right here and nowness" (16), the juxtaposed and palimp-sestically layered signs that comprise a postmodern "ethnohistorical mix 'n' match" that defies historical sequencing by showcasing history and culture synchronically, making it available all at once as a pleasurable aesthetic object (15). Filling out the opening paragraphs, Price points out within a block or two, one finds "laboratorio del gelati, the Tibetan hat boutiques, [and] 88 Forsyth House with its historically restored cold-water flats not all that much different from the unrestored tenements that surrounded it" (15). What do we find here in this additional catalog? Italian ice cream scooped out in a hypermodern, white-box lab, next to Eastern mysticism purchased off the shelf as style, next to the frozen-in-time social memory of immigrant poverty, next to the unfolding-in-time experience of bourgeois tenement living today. In the new globalized economy all of history and all of the world's cultures are available for purchase, if one has the cash. Yet one cannot help but feel an element of insidious control lurks under this consum-erist surveillance. We sense this when we recognize how the language describing Eric's walk closely repeats in form and content the descriptions from the patrol a few pages earlier, the policing that makes such consum-erism possible. Furthermore, in Price's repetitive sentence structure we can discern something else. For sale in the Lower East Side is not authenticity, history, or real cultural differences but a series of reproducible commodi-ties that appear as exchangeable textual signs that the novel repeats in the first chapters. This point, subtly made in the opening, emerges in time as one of its major themes.

Eric's walk establishes the neighborhood from his point of view. It also foregrounds how he orients himself in space by using the language of real estate and gentrification to formulate his class, race, and gender identity. Consider his scolding response to the ethnic difference in the Lower East Side that annoyingly slows him down. The scene is a line of people filing into a bodega to see, for a buck, the apparition of the Virgin's face on a refrigerator's wet glass door. Eric's flinty egoism dismisses the spectacle. "Whatever this was, it had nothing to do with him; the people were overwhelmingly Latino, most likely from the unrehabbed walk-ups below Delancey," writes Price, referencing the busy four-lane thoroughfare bisecting the Lower East Side from west to east, which in the 1990s and early 2000s served as something of a firewall that gentrification has since jumped (16). The people from the "unrehabbed," ungentrified south side of Delancey, Eric thinks, are denizens of "the half-dozen immortal housing projects that cradled this, the creamy golden center of the Lower East Side" (16). Not surprisingly, he geographically orients himself in the neighborhood so as to place himself at the comfortable center and those who are marginal literally at the margins. Assigning a type of face to a type of place, he linguistically undoes the area's "mix 'n' match," which was a visual pleasure when merely a hodgepodge of consumer signs but is a nuisance when manifested as live bodies. The scene exemplifies gentrification's uneven process, how it shuffles the urban tiles, piles people on top of one another who would rather not be so close. "I wanted to write about how these different groups of people occupy the same physical space, but seem not to even see each other," Price told Nicholas Wroe in the *Guardian*.[27]

On the heels of Eric's walk is Tristan's. One of the first thing Price reveals about him is that he has been "ROR'ed" a few times, circulating in and out of police custody for minor violations (26). "The usual shit," writes Price, "possession, trespassing—aka hanging out in the park after curfew—for fighting that one time, pissing out the bedroom window" (26). Tristan lives in one of those "immortal housing projects" with his physically abusive, alcoholic ex-stepfather, who terrorizes the house from his recliner where he is perpetually glued in a half-daze to the TV (16). He, too, constructs his own geography, though one that has far less purchase than Eric Cash's. As Tristan walks with Little Dap through the Lower East Side, Price provides a window into how he orients himself as an alienated racial subject in relation to the city, whole regions of which feel off-limits and foreign. "They were only five or six blocks from the Lemlichs," writes Price, "but Tristan could almost count the times he'd been this deep away from home when he wasn't making a delivery. He didn't like going north of Houston or west of Essex, and he hated delivering dope to the doctors and nurses up at Bellevue or NYU Special Joints, both so far uptown they might as well be in another country" (27). At this early moment in the novel, before the shooting, Tristan is unsure of himself, constantly deferring to his friend, his teenage masculinity in the tenuous period of forming and hardening in an urban environment that is also changing.

As the novel unfolds Tristan grows more assertive and seeks to own the spaces immediately around him, as well as those in Eric's "golden center" of the neighborhood (16). In the end, he wants to reclaim the entire Lower East Side as his turf. The hip-hop lyrics he writes are filled with fantasized images of unfettered access to the city: "King of Hell / Know him well / I walk right in / Don't ring the bell" (374). While such lyrics are Price's way of underscoring Tristan's symbolic empowerment and trespassing of the polarized geographies of the gentrifying city, the all-too-real gun he tucks in his waistband—a remasculinizing phallic signifier—is what reopens urban space to him. Late in the novel, Price replays the earlier scene of Tristan's walk, only now all the streets of the neighborhood belong to him: "He just left the building and went off to walk the streets. He had no destination, no itinerary, except to hit every one from Pitt to the Bowery, from Houston to Pike, walk down every street, pass every building, go into every store that he'd ever felt bad or afraid or stupid in front of and, with the .22 snug up against his belly, reclaim them all" (300). The streets Tristan walks, Houston, Pike, and the Bowery, form borders of the Lower East Side, with Pitt Street running through the middle, suggesting his effort to "reclaim them all" is to own the neighborhood in its entirety, from the gentrified middle to the racialized margins, "every street," "every building" secured by the potential for violence already acted upon once by his murder of Ike. When NYPD Commissioner Bratton laid out his plan to effectuate broken-windows strategies, he did so in the treatise "Reclaiming the Public Spaces of New York" (1994). Its title implied a theft, as though the city had been stolen from its hardworking, law-abiding residents and now the cops were going to get it back. It is fair to say that this urban reclamation project has meant the removal of people of color through incarceration and gentrification. Tristan's act of reclamation is exactly the opposite. He seeks to expropriate what the racialized logic of gentrification as stolen from him.

Price's eye operates primarily at street level, more fascinated by the experiences of cops in squad cars, grifters in the street, and small-time drug dealers on the corners and in the projects than with the larger designs and machinations of police commissioners, urban planners, and politicians. So it is significant when Price's novel assumes the proverbial thirty-thousand-foot view with an aerial perspective that offers yet another type of map for the reader. These moments, which occur twice in the text, situate the dismantling and replacement of the Lower East Side's older economic and demographic order within a larger frame.

In the first scene, two housing cops stand on the roof of Tristan's building, surveying the area and its surroundings: "Wall Street, the bridges, the Brooklyn Promenade, the Heights. 'A kick-ass Trump view,' one cop [says], then speculating how much it would go for on the open market. 'All you got to do is lose the fifteen stories' worth of shit skins living under it'" (153). In the second, Matty, standing on the balcony of his modest Lower East Side apartment, "look[s] down on the neighboring streets to the west, an aerial checkerboard of demolition and rehabilitation, seemingly no lot, no tenement untouched; then look[s] south to the financial district, to the absence of the Towers" (159). At this height one sees the material manifestation of the flow of capital across the city, impeded only by the stubborn persistence of public housing that prevents valuable real estate from being privatized and sold off. The elevated views of "demolition and rehabilitation" and free-market Trumpian real estate speculation contextualize the Lower East Side vis-à-vis Wall Street (the source of finance capital) a few blocks to the south and west, Brooklyn Heights across the East River (the first suburb for New Yorkers fleeing downtown poverty and crime in the nineteenth century), and the destroyed World Trade Center, which led to the creation of the LMDC that the "'Divided Community'" report excoriates for eliminating units of low-income housing in the area. Price does not explicitly connect the dots on this map. That's for readers to do. The novel's street-level views paired with the higher-order perspectives invite us to understand the upheavals of the contemporary Lower East Side within the local and global contexts of housing bubbles, histories of suburbanization and white flight, terrorism, and most recently, gentrification.

EVERYTHING HAS A PRICE

In a key moment in *Lush Life*, Price shows Harry Steele, the owner of Café Berkmann and a neighborhood landlord, purchasing several of Jacob Riis's famous glass negatives of nineteenth-century Lower East Side poverty, crime, and ethnic difference for his growing collection of historical ephemera. Harry is lounging at the restaurant when a man sits down and slides across the table an aluminum attaché case, a scene with the trappings of a drug transaction one might have witnessed in a grittier era before Café Berkmann ever existed. Eric, the restaurant's manager, makes the association explicit: the shady dealer reminds him of "too many shadow players from back in the shame days" (20). The perennially packed Café Berkmann has only been in the neighborhood for ten years, but with its "partially desilvered mirrors," "industrial-grade chicken-wired glass," and "faux-aged wooden dowels" (19), it is designed to look like it has "been there forever" (433), perhaps a place frequented by Riis. Café Berkmann is a "restaurant dressed as theater dressed as nostalgia," Price pithily comments (19). As noted, he has modeled it on Schiller's Liquor Bar, by the restaurateur Keith McNally, who, one also duly notes, started off as a theater set designer.

More than any other book, Riis's *How the Other Half Lives* (1890) put the Lower East Side on the map. Riis's exposé is fundamentally a muckraking depiction of spatial disorder—disorderly people in disorderly houses in disorderly parts of the city. Too many different kinds of people piled on top of one another was cause for alarm. Hence, Riis begins by warning of the fearful possibility of "crimes against property" by those without property and ends by citing "the sea of a mighty population, held in galling fetters, [that] heaves uneasily in the tenements."[28] However, the real criminals in *How the Other Half Lives* were not the restless tenants but the landlords, a point not often remembered. They were the ones that Riis lambasted for their "greed and reckless selfishness" and their immorality for charging "exorbitant rents."[29] The best way to tackle the city's lack of decent affordable housing for its immigrant poor, thought Riis, was to rein in the market so it was compelled to better serve the poor and in the process improve them morally and physically. The spatial reforms inspired by *How the Other Half Lives*, such as the landmark 1901 Tenement Housing Act, resulted in improved housing, relatively speaking: better ventilation, courtyards, and at least one toilet for every two families. But before those reforms could ever be considered, Riis had to help people imagine what life was like in the city's lower wards. Riis, who cut his teeth as a police reporter for the *New York Tribune* and was a confidante of the then–police commissioner Theodore Roosevelt, was known to push open tenement doors unannounced. Armed with a flash-cube camera, he'd capture what he saw with a sudden blast of light: the startled and dazed faces of Jews, Italians, Chinese, and African

Americans sitting in the near-dark of their often windowless living rooms minding their own business. On at least one occasion, the spark from Riis's camera briefly set an apartment on fire.

These are the kinds of images Harry eyeballs as he picks through the negatives, deciding which ones he would be delighted to own. The briefcase holds some of Riis's most iconic shots—"Ludlow Street Sweatshop," "Blind Beggar, 1888," "Passing the Growler," and "Bandits Roost" (20). The irony is that what makes the slides valuable as *aesthetic* objects is how far removed they are from being *sociological* ones documenting nineteenth-century poverty, crime, and alcoholism. Owning the negatives now means owning a piece of art and a piece of urban history.

This scene with Harry allegorizes the buying and selling of signs of cultural difference and urban decay, something Harry knows well. He lives in "a desanctified synagogue on Suffolk Street," where beneath a huge Star of David he has a "built-in Torah ark" holding his "collection of eighteenth- and nineteenth-century cookbooks" (247). He has decorated the rest of the apartment with artifacts of historical and contemporary vice, some of it recently shoveled out of the ground: "a handwritten Eighth Precinct incident book from 1898, a leather medical case holding instruments used to examine immigrants for trachoma and other rejectable eye diseases at Ellis Island, an eighteenth-century Dutch clay pipe unearthed in Steele's backyard privy mounted alongside the twentieth-century glass crackpipe found lying in the grass next to it" (249–50). As Elizabeth Gumport explains, fictions of gentrification "subsume . . . questions of class and race in discussions of interior design."[30] Harry's arrangement of these objects into an aesthetically appealing horizontality, as if they were all equal, masks the racial and class hierarchies of gentrification that have permitted him to buy them in the first place. Moreover, as a landlord, his resignification of images of cultural marginality into signs of sophisticated urban edginess fosters, in its small way, real estate demand for what might otherwise be thought of as low-quality housing in a low-status neighborhood. The old rigid modernist dichotomies between normative and deviant and suburb and slum that in the past have been marshaled for urban renewal predicated on the erasure of the devalued Other—the removal from sight of marginal cultures, peoples, and histories—are no longer in place. In Price's Lower East Side, they have been replaced by a shallow form of inclusion. What we see not just in Harry's apartment but throughout the novel are postmodern coagulations of cultural heritage and subcultural differences that allow residents and visitors to construct, test out, and inhabit varied lifestyles through the purchase and display of specialized consumer goods. In Price's pages residents are "sporting Shriner hats, top hats,. . . frogged and beribboned tunics, aviator goggles, and Salome veils," as if they have just raided a nineteenth-century wardrobe. The Lower East Side that we find in the novel is not so much a neighborhood but a stage (309).

In *Selling the Lower East Side: Culture, Real Estate, and Resistance in New York City* (2000), the historian Christopher Mele chronicles how in the 1980s and 1990s the area's history of immigrant cultures, subversive politics, and deviance were repackaged by developers and the real estate industry to attract consumers and new residents seeking a putatively "real" urban environment, someplace different, edgy, and more avant-garde.[31] This marketing tactic continues today. To cite one recent example, the marketing team for the Ludlow, a twenty-three-story luxury apartment building on the neighborhood's northern border, entices potential renters with a thumbnail history of what they call "the narrative behind the Lower East Side."[32] Its boosterish "narrative" quickly notes the neighborhood was "once home to two great estates and a smattering of working-class artisans," later became a "famous refuge for immigrants from faraway lands," and then in "the late 19th and 20th centuries" was a "sanctuary" for "radical politicians, performers such as Al Jolson and the Gershwin Brothers, as well as poets and writers from the Beat era." The foreshortened history concludes this way: "By the 1970s, punk rockers and artists settled in this area until gentrification caught up with the market by the early 2000s. Now, the Lower East Side is considered to be one of the hippest, trendiest places to live in the entire city. Now that's authenticity!" That's also teleological. This conflict-free real estate story, in which gentrification is a passively enacted phenomenon that happens on its own, endeavors to capture in words what no longer exists, what is no longer there because it has been displaced by the very kind of development the Ludlow represents and sells back to newcomers in search of luxury apartments. "Authenticity, it seems, always comes after, and then primarily as loss," the urban theorist Andreas Huyssen contends, though the Ludlow's developers understand it primarily not as a loss but as an economic gain.[33]

What is important to stress here is how much the approach to cleaning up the neighborhood has changed from the days of Riis and later Robert

Moses. Progressive housing reform and midcentury urban renewal were predicated on the wide-scale elimination of physical signs of cultural alterity. Urban development today, however, makes a safe space for it as a consumer spectacle and commodity, if not for the actual residents who produce it. Street art, ethnic food, histories of protest, revolutionary politics, and countercultural literature are enticing signifiers of authenticity, local color, and raw energy that sell upscale property. One thinks here of the eighteen-foot-tall copper statue of Lenin with one hand raised in mid-oration atop Red Square in 1994, the sardonically named luxury apartment building on the northern border of Price's Lower East Side. Yet even as developers redeploy "*symbolic* representations of cultural differences," Mele argues that "municipal leaders . . . under the guise of 'quality-of-life' initiatives . . . have employed strategies that restrict *public expressions* of social and cultural diversity."[34] Price's novel enacts this logic. In one scene, the cops in the Quality of Life Task Force pull up as Little Dap, whom the police have not yet connected to the murder, is standing in front of the housing project where he lives. He is busily "putting the finishing touches on a laundry-marker dick in the ear of the solider on the bus-shelter recruiting poster" (290). "Vandalize government property?" the cop asks while frisking him (290). Graffiti is one thing in an art gallery, but Price suggests that on the streets it is something else entirely.

As *Lush Life* unfolds, real estate moves to the center of the text, eclipsing the crime that began the book. Circulating through the novel like extras in a film are the numerous, unnamed would-be writers, artists, and hipsters who are playacting with their identities, twentysomethings "too young for their beards and handlebar mustaches," writes Price (309). They may find delight in the Lower East Side's "ethnohistorical mix 'n' match," but the neighborhood's real estate, increasingly in the grasp of the well-heeled, is beyond their reach (15). In *Lush Life*, the neighborhood is not unlivable because it is uninhabitable, as the old story of urban decline proposed, but because it is now unaffordable. With a name synonymous with capital, Eric Cash unwittingly primes the area for the next wave of gentrifiers— people working in finance, advertising, information technology, and the like. "This whole neighborhood, I mean, it's all what the realtors want it to be anyhow," Eric says (433). His boss, Harry, has seen the so-called home-steaders in search of cheap rent replaced by investors with deeper pockets. Surveying the past decade, he expounds:

The whites. The, the "pioneers" . . . The Latinos? The Chinese? The ones been living here since the Flood? Couldn't be nicer. Happy for the jobs. The thing is, the complainers? *They're* the ones that started all this. We just follow them. Always have, always will. Come down here, buy some smack squat from the city, do a little fix-up, have a nice big studio, rent out the extra space, mix it up with the ethnics, feel all good and politically righteous about yourself. But those lofts now? Those buildings? Twenty-five hundred square feet, fourth floor, no elevator, Orchard and Broome. Two point four mil just last week.

(124)

"It's called revitalization," Harry remarks (124). Before Café Berkmann opened, the neighborhood was a "hellhole," he says (124). His "frontier language" of heroic urban pioneers "camouflages a raw economic reality" and "rationalizes the violence of gentrification and displacement."[35] He has been in the neighborhood long enough to pay witness to the changes he profits from, while downplaying culpability in gentrifying the area with his restaurant and portfolio of apartments that he wants to convert to market rate.

One of Harry's tenants is Avner Polaner, who is interviewed by the police under the assumption that his earlier mugging may be linked to Ike's murder. After he remarks that "the price of living here" is that occasionally on a dark street one runs into "a dark kid with a gun" (194), he sounds off about the real price of living in the Lower East Side: "I pay top dollar, sixteen hundred for an apartment so small I have to leave the room to change my mind" (195). Price, price, Cash, cash: the prices of everything—market values and their social costs—in the Lower East Side are always on Price's mind. Avner derails the interview by continuing to rant about real estate and gentrification, in effect suggesting the NYPD is hunting for the wrong kind of criminal: "[Harry] says he'll pay me ten thousand if I move . . . says I'm paying close to market value already, so what's the big deal. The big deal, Mister Hot Shit Harry Steele, is I was here *before* you opened the restaurant, I was here *first. You* move" (196). Ontological privilege and historical priority are two of the ways we lay claim to a neighborhood and deny others their claims in the process: Aver, who like Harry is Jewish, opts for the latter. Tristan is guilty of a murder in the neighborhood, but Harry and his ilk are the ones who are really making a killing by killing it, Price implies through Avner.

Scenes like the one just described perhaps suggest that Price merely writes the latest chapter of demographic succession in a neighborhood defined by it. But I would caution that this misses the point about what makes the story he tells new and important. When Price remarked that "the Lower East Side is probably the most important neighborhood in American history," he qualified his comments by conceding that while hundreds of thousands of immigrants landed there, few actually wanted to live in the area for long. Its importance, he said, was "in terms of people coming off the boat, settling there, taking a look around and saying 'we gotta get out of here.' "[36] Historically, the Lower East Side has been shorthand for the archetypal immigrant American success story of first settlement, acculturation, hard work, and savings, followed by an exodus to a better urban neighborhood or the suburbs, which conveniently freed up space for the next arrivals, those who—and this is the key difference—were economically less secure, not more. The tidiness of this cultural narrative, a literary and national plotline periodically refreshed with a different set of ethnic characters, is fraying, as *Lush Life* underscores, because of the realities of poverty that many do not rise up out of and the fact that once settled many cannot or do not wish to leave. Yet gentrification has further complicated the narrative of the Lower East Side in a profoundly different way, too. As dramatized in Price's novel the latest white, college-educated entrants—the young professionals in the novel's dim lounges staffed by suspended mixologists using eyedroppers to serve cocktails made with top-shelf "single-batch Curzan rum"—have broken the historical and demographic pattern (36). Changes to the neighborhood in the last two decades, Price implies, have upended the meaning of nearly two hundred years of social history, fundamentally rewriting the narrative of in-migration, displacement, and out-migration that has not only been central to the Lower East Side and New York City but to the entire American story that correlates upward economic mobility with geographic mobility. This quintessential American narrative (whether or not true in practice) has relied upon the social and cultural geographies of the Lower East Side to function as a worldwide rhetorical selling point for American life—a story many immigrants heard and hoped for before their arrival in the United States. Unlike their historical predecessors whom they are rapidly displacing, the latest arrivals come equipped with the tools for their own success (English literacy, a college education, financial support from home, racial privilege, a full complement of citizen-ship rights). These are already bestowed or achieved in advance rather than obtained through the mysterious processes of assimilation and accul-turation, pithily known as the making of Americans. That older narrative, which made the Lower East Side "the most important neighborhood in American history," is in Price's estimation effectively done and over.

HAUNTED HISTORIES AND GEOGRAPHIES

It should go without saying that Price's novel endeavors to do more than mirror the socioeconomic and historical conditions and materials out of which it is fashioned. While establishing historical and geographical con-texts around *Lush Life* is critical for a richer understanding of the text, it is more important still to unpack how the text attempts to give shape to and reimagine these contexts within its own narrative space. As an interven-tion into the neighborhood at the moment of its recent restructuring, *Lush Life* provides an entry point for understanding how individual subjects respond when the personal, cultural, geographical, and historical narra-tives that have shaped their relation to the past, present, and future cease to have explanatory power. Price attempts to answer this question but, as we will see, the answers—which range from spectral relations to history to a cynical embrace of the forces of commodification—are unlikely to be satisfying.

Lush Life underscores that the act of imbuing time and space with mean-ing is an inherently material process. The stories Price's characters tell themselves about the old neighborhood are crafted out of the material objects (and the histories sedimented in them) that redevelopment literally unearths. In *Lush Life*, capital's churning of the urban landscape—the dig-ging up of the streets, the razing of old buildings, and the raising of new ones—causes buried histories to surface.

Price lays the groundwork for this logic early. While Eric strolls to work before the night of the murder, he bumps into Ike, and together they take a detour to inspect a recently collapsed synagogue. Its neglected condition led it to cave in on itself. In the midst of the rubble are a cantor's table, meno-rah, and candleholders that Price describes as "props" in "an open-air the-ater" (22).

As we have seen, "props" like these wend their way into Harry's growing collection of historical ephemera that he arranges in his recycled synagogue of a home. In a lengthy description, Price has Matty walk through the apartment, reading it for clues, not for who killed Ike (Harry is never a suspect), but for what has happened to the neighborhood he polices. In *Lush Life* the disruptions of the present reanimate histories that cling with a ghostly residue to Harry's aestheticized objects. "He could still feel the holy-of-holies aura that lingered here," Price writes of Matty, "no matter that the long-dead immigrant worshippers had today been replaced by a group of Berkmann managers, hosts, and bartenders" (248). As Matty continues to survey the apartment, he sees the material objects but senses their spirits, "the double layer of evicted ghosts—pauperish tenants, greenhorn parishioners," the stress falling heavily on "evicted," "the double layer" signifying a double temporality, past and present (250). "This fucking place [is] haunted, he'd swear it," Price writes (250). What haunts Harry's apartment is not an immigrant history that in refusing to be repressed demands acknowledgment. It is nothing as metaphysical as that. What haunts it is a truth that cannot be acknowledged, the truth that his class power is dependent upon but disavows the exploitation and displacement of others in the Lower East Side. This class power is aesthetically reduplicated in his collection of displaced, appropriated, and fetishized tchotchkes, which Harry has purchased from the profits from Café Berkmann and his exploitative real estate holdings.

For Eric the feeling of being haunted by history assumes a different significance, attributable in no small part to his economic precarity relative to someone like his boss. For him, the "ghosts," or the reanimated history of the Jewish Lower East Side, act as props he uses to reconstruct his sense of self, which has largely collapsed in the weeks since Ike's shooting but which also simply has been worn down in the accumulated grind of barely getting by in the neighborhood. While working at Café Berkmann, Eric has been plugging away without much progress on a screenplay about "the Lower East Side in its heyday, Aka Jewday" (22). "A former Alphabet City squatter turned real estate gorilla" commissions the piece, a screenplay one can imagine could be used to drum up investors' interest in the area (22). But Eric's writing is going nowhere, and after the shooting he realizes the hopeful idealism of his hyphenated class identity (writer–bar manager) has been broken in half by the reality of a life of unfulfilling labor. His writerly identity is a ghost of his former self, who has been killed off by just trying to stay alive to pay the rent. By evidence of his last name, professional ambitions, and ethnicity, Eric Cash is clearly a counterfactual stand-in for a younger Price had the novelist's writing career never panned out.

Pushed over the edge by Ike's murder, Eric engages in increasingly destructive behavior, which takes up much of the novel's thick middle while the police investigation spins in circles in the background. He snorts more and more cocaine, steals a greater share of tips from his workmates than he usually does, and heads to the projects to buy drugs. Eric is subsequently robbed and assaulted in the stairwell of his building by dealers who tail him back to his part of the neighborhood, the center of the neighborhood that he calls "inland" and the Lemlich residents tellingly label "*white* land" (383). The social relations of racism are configured in starkly different spatial languages in the novel. The beating lands Eric in the hospital, where his dreams are populated with the Jewish Lower East Side of the nineteenth century: "His building had come back to life with the tenants of a hundred years ago, everybody walking, running, trudging up and down the stairs carrying all sorts of shit—suit patterns, buckets of water, chamber pots— the entire building reeking of sweat and heavy cooking and excrement" (392). These "reanimated tenants," ghosts from Riis's era, are dressed in "battered derbies and tattered waistcoats and multi-layered dresses" that signify as layered signs of squalor, food, and bodily excess. At first glance, they appear to be a forgotten past newly exhumed by the violence of the present. However, these "reanimated tenants," as Eric remembers later, have "something funny" about them (392). They are not just the positive image of Riis's negatives. "They had long, curved nails on their left pinkies," Eric recalls, "like all the pimps and hustlers and every kind of mack pappy player back in the seventies, the sole purpose of which was to more easily scoop coke from a baggie" (392). Eric's battered dream of the past turns out to be a mash-up of nineteenth-century immigrant poverty and fantasies lifted from 1970s Blaxploitation flicks of hustlers and hoodlums. The mash-up discloses that Eric sees the world around him and the past behind him filtered through the ideological colorings of literature, movies, and other urban discourses that give shape to the city and neighborhood. But more than this, it discloses "something funny" about white identity, reveals it as a haunting at the center of the neighborhood that displaces its own vices onto the Black body at the neighborhood's margins. After all, the only one scooping cocaine in the novel is Eric.

The spirits of the Jewish ghetto are not ghosts, of course. They are textual inscriptions, tropes, or metaphors that Eric increasingly thinks about as he loses his grip on the neighborhood. He dreams, in part, about the haunted faces in Riis's photographs because he himself writes about them. Returning to his characterization of his screenplay makes this clear. It is "historical, about the neighborhood. . . . It's kind of like a ghost story. But not about *ghosts* ghosts? It's more like, metaphorical ghosts," he tells Matty (92). The Lower East Side is haunted in his dreams because Price predisposes him to imagine it that way through his own writing. The present-day conflicts over gentrification awaken in him a romantic longing for his own Jewish history that, five generations removed, is in the distant past, leave him searching for a way to center himself, a way to reattach.

One way forward for Eric is actually backward and downward. Actively reconnecting with his roots sedimented in the urban locale serves as an ameliorative strategy, a way for Eric to ground himself in ground that is being torn up. Price plays out this idea in the most literal of ways. We see this in the several scenes in which Eric descends into Berkmann's "fungal coal cellar" when the buzzy restaurant and the Lower East Side more generally become too much (172). He hides out in the cellar to get away from it all and do a little blow, but Price clearly means it to signify something else, too. His descent is into a historical past, one putatively purer than the commodified symbols—Berkmann's faux-aged interior—on the surface. He discovers beneath the café "four crude hearths that still stood like neolithic kilns" (172) and two Yiddish words scratched into a beam, "*Gedenken mir.* 'Remember me,'" which in desperation he runs his fingers over and says aloud (328). These signs strike a chord with Eric, who believes they are ethnic history speaking to him and for him. In his mind, the haunting plea "*Gedenken mir*" is in some manner his own. With his sense of self unraveling, Eric wishes to write himself into historical memory and into a narrative of the Lower East Side that also has unraveled both as a story and place. Hunkered down beneath Café Berkmann, he imaginatively rewrites nineteenth-century Jewish history so that he becomes its subject and its fulfillment, as if he is its telos: "And now I know," he says on the verge of tears, "what that squiggle, that hand, was trying to tell us. It's like, from the whole, millions coming over, here's this one infinitesimal voice that says, 'I am, I was' " (328).

This is Eric's attempt to bond himself to history, to carve a grammatical space for himself as an "I" in the gentrifying neighborhood's narrative, to say, in effect, like the Jewish immigrants who came before me, I too am and was here and will be remembered. It does not work. The Lower East Side's Jewish history in the era of gentrification is not fully recoverable as a complete or uncorrupted artifact but is only available as traces that signify an absence exacerbated by the pressures of the current historical moment. They cannot be integrated, Price suggests, into a new narrative of identity with an anchor securely in the past, especially not in the context of the relentless commodification and simulation of history in the early twenty-first century. Carrying the logic of cultural and historical simulation to its absurd end, Price in the final pages has Eric leave the neighborhood and relocate, of all places, to Atlantic City, to work in a hotel and casino in a newly built "New York theme park" (451). It is replete with a "Times Square Land" with "neon girlie-show signs," a graffitied 1970s "Punktown," and a "Yidville" anchored by a replica of Café Berkmann that is a simulacrum of an already simulated history (451). It is not so much a simulation of a rougher, dirtier New York as a simulation of the mopped-up Disneyfied New York of the early 2000s. Except it is worse, because it is in New Jersey. Evoking the Lower East Side's long historical association as a place for by-the-bootstraps self-reinvention, Eric's boss urges him to relocate to the even faker version of Berkmann's in the New Jersey theme park of old New York. "It'll be a new start for you," he says (434). He means it earnestly, but one cannot help but hear the cynicism bleeding through. Eric's departure signals the completion of the Lower East Side's gentrification, the artist's cultural capital no longer needed.

While ghostly traces of nineteenth-century Jewish culture haunt Price's Lower East Side as symbols, the real presence of people of color—in particular the Puerto Ricans and Dominicans occupying its edges—haunts it in another way. Their daily life stories are more difficult to incorporate into the narrative of gentrification as progress. The Lemlich Houses, where Tristan and Little Dap live, are shadowed by One Police Plaza and the "massive futuristic" building of Verizon's headquarters (219, 220). The former functions as an alternative form of "housing" in the age of the mass incarceration of people of color, the latter an edifice of the new postindustrial economy's information technology, whose rewards have been unequally distributed by race, to put it mildly. Price calls the Lemlich Houses "immortal," insinuating that they represent the intractable social problems of poverty and racial isolation, which the liberal state cannot solve and whose housing policies have exacerbated (16). Yet the Lemlichs too are changing. "You din't live round here back in the heyday, so no way you'd know, but about ten, twelve years ago. . . . Man, it was, there was some bad dudes up in here," Little Dap says to his fellow residents (24). These stories of "the heyday" are "immortal" in another sense: they have passed into legends. "Now it's like just the Old Heads out there sippin' forties and telling stories about yesteryear," Little Dap adds (24). The "loss of the historical quality of things" constitutes myth, Roland Barthes once proposed. But so too, as Neil Smith argues, does "the loss of the *geographical* quality of things."[37]

In the end, Matty's legwork does not lead to Tristan's arrest. The Quality of Life Task Force solves the case when it snags Little Dap on a minor offense, marijuana possession, an apparent validation of broken-windows policing by the novel. The cops on the task force use the possession charge as leverage to see what Little Dap knows about Ike's murder. He quickly coughs up his accomplice's name to reduce his charges. Tristan exits the novel in police custody, "exhal[ing] like something punctured, his body slowly sinking in on itself," as if shot, like Ike, through the chest (438). *Lush Life* ends with another person of color leaving the neighborhood for jail, likely to the Manhattan Detention Complex, also known as the Tombs.

Urban literature is one of the main discourses that provides us with scripts for living or at least imagining living in a city; it also provides us with scripts for the city itself, scripts of decline, scripts of nostalgia, scripts of rebirth. *Lush Life* tells the story of crime, culture, and gentrification in one of New York's changing neighborhoods, a neighborhood that also has been a critical site, arguably *the* critical site, for American mythmaking. Price's novel dramatizes how culture is enlisted in the service of real estate speculation. The novel itself is, as a material object circulating in the economy of ideas about the Lower East Side, also directly implicated in the neighborhood's transformation. On this note I wish to conclude.

In 2010 two curators, Franklin Evans and Omar Lopez-Chahoud, organized an exhibition titled "Lush Life" at nine galleries, eight of them in the Lower East Side, each in dialogue with the novel's nine chapters. In a press release for the shows, they stated they were drawn to Price's novel as a

FIGURE 1.3. The north building of the Manhattan Detention Complex ("The Tombs") at 100 Baxter Street. *Source:* Beyond My Ken, CC BY-SA 4.0 (https://creativecommons.org/licenses/by-sa/4.0), via Wikimedia Commons.

vehicle for "the consideration of community as voices compete for, ignore and occasionally share the same physical and conceptual space." "Our intention," Lopez-Chahoud revealed in an interview with Jane Harris for *Art in America*, "was to present work that talked about these forgotten communities in one way or another."[38]

Harris seemed skeptical about whether the exhibits had accomplished that mission. "How do you think your show includes or engages these communities, if at all?" she asked. In spite of the curators' claims, the forgotten communities themselves appear to have been overlooked in the often abstract and conceptual exhibition. The art historian Media Farzin noted in *Art Agenda* that "there was little to be found of the neighborhood's layered history, few works that attempted to dispel the spectacular opportunism of its recent immigrants, or even consider their real dilemmas—no attempt, in short, to really reflect on its being embedded in the neighborhood."[39] I do not wish to argue that realism as an aesthetic has a purchase on life that other modes and styles do not. Rather, what I want to underscore is the easy slippage between "physical and conceptual space" in which people and places become ideas or abstractions.[40] Their dematerialization is a step toward their eventual removal. The curator Franklin Evans ended up admitting that the exhibition is in the final analysis about "the idea of forgotten communities rather than communities specific to the LES and/or its past."

To bring attention to the neighborhood's new art boom on the occasion of looking at signs of communities erased not once (in physical space) but twice (in conceptual space), the galleries issued a map, nearly three feet by two. The map pinpoints the galleries' locations through impossible-to-miss star icons. However, the rest of the neighborhood—historical sites, cultural centers, restaurants, and shops—is barely represented, with the exception of a few playgrounds, parks, and most notably "THE TOMBS," New York's infamous jail, in a huge all-caps font with an arrow pointing southwest where visitors on the art stroll could, should they wish, visit. This notorious incarceration facility has in a real way helped clean up the area to make the galleries possible. As Rosalyn Deutsche and Cara Gendel Ryan contend, art galleries alter and produce the spaces they represent. Price had remarked in 2008 that "the *new* Lower East Side is pretty old," but he hedged and added its gentrification was not "a done deal."[41] But the truth be told, it was. A novel about the human costs of redevelopment, *Lush Life* was translated into the conceptual spaces of the Lower East Side's galleries, whose mere presence was a sign that its gentrification in 2010 was fait accompli.

If the fate of the Lower East Side was sealed by cops and developers, the future of the neighborhood next door, Chinatown, was still up for grabs. It is to that complex neighborhood and the crime novels of Henry Chang that *The Gentrification Plot* now turns.

Chapter Two

CHINATOWN

Policing the Ethnic Enclave

While gentrification has telltale signs, such as upmarket commerce, rising rents, and class displacement, which we can see in any neighborhood that is being upscaled, it is also expressed and experienced differently in each neighborhood in *The Gentrification Plot*. Each neighborhood's distinctive built environment, immigration history, and current demographics mean that its experience of gentrification will be unique. As this chapter turns from Richard Price's *Lush Life*, set in the neobohemia of the Lower East Side, to Henry Chang's crime novels, set in the ethnic enclave of Manhattan's Chinatown, a new set of urban issues rises to the fore, including neighborhood memorialization and the double binds of ethnic identity (dramatized by Chang's Chinese-American police detective). What also rises to the fore in this chapter are the Sinophobic representations of Chinatown that have underwritten its historical quarantining from the rest of the city as a physical and cultural miasma and, more recently, have legitimized its intrusive policing and cleanup. Give these Sinophobic representations, this chapter reads for the political meanings of dirt, grime, and squalor, the tropes of urban blight that "naturalize the 'need' for betterment" of disorderly neighborhoods and thus are harbingers of gentrification.[1] Nearly every urban ethnic enclave has been labeled as dirty and congested at some point in its history, but added to these common charges for Chinatown are accusations that the neighborhood's putative squalor is part and parcel of it being culturally inscrutable, unfathomable, and peculiarly un-American. These stereotypes assume newly urgent meanings in the context of gentrification that seeks to infiltrate, colonize, and whiten the enclave. To clean up and gentrify Chinatown is to compel it to be socially, culturally, and physically legible through the erasure of the ways of life and the residues of history and memory that have built up there for decades. As we will see, even as Manhattan's Chinatown has been subjected to many of the same socioeconomic forces that made the adjacent Lower East Side a testing ground for the postindustrial city, gentrification in Chinatown has produced its own problems and its own distinctive set of stories.

Until the early 2010s, Chinatown was the last ungentrified neighborhood in Manhattan south of Ninety-Sixth Street. As the Lower East Side was experiencing a dizzying transformation into what Price termed a "yuppy-buppy-schmuppy playground," the sprawling neighborhood of Chinatown on its borders still appeared to many as a low-income immigrant ghetto of aging tenements, sweatshops, and small businesses.[2] However, in the eyes of scholars who studied it, Chinatown was showing signs that its historic status was beginning to fade away. Chinatown "will most likely disappear," the sociologist Peter Kwong remarked in 2009 to the *New York Times*.[3] His comment was not part of a declension narrative: the neighborhood was not in decline, at least not economically. It was disappearing because it was on the ascent, because those who were better off, at least economically, were moving in. Four years after his prediction, the Asian American Legal Defense and Education Fund (AALDEF) issued the report "Chinatown Then and Now" (2013), whose "block by block and lot by lot" year-long mapping revealed that the neighborhood's tenements, garment factories, mom-and-pop noodle shops, nail salons, produce stands, and fish markets were being replaced by "luxury condominiums, high-end businesses, hotels, and other upscale services." The gentrification that had swept over the Lower East Side nearly a decade before had arrived at last. Median rents were spiking, housing values were up, and the white population was growing much faster in Chinatown than the rest of Manhattan, the report noted. "At what point does Chinatown cease to be Chinatown" and become "little more than a caricature of [its] cultural heritage?" the authors asked, before declaring: "Chinatown must be preserved for future generations."[4]

At issue in the report was what preservation actually meant and what was to be preserved. Neighborhood preservation as a strategy and philosophy can assume different forms, such as landmarking buildings, streets, and entire districts as a recognition of their historical or architectural merit. As overseen in New York City by the Landmarks Preservation Commission, the designation freezes buildings and neighborhoods in time, encasing them in a kind of legal carbonite. It does so to prevent their erosion through benign neglect or their alteration or destruction through active development, and it does so with the good intention of promoting tourism and civic pride, improving property values, and safeguarding culture. Yet as preservation makes a neighborhood more attractive, it hastens gentrification, rather than slowing its pace. As a result, neighborhoods that are preserved often end up reduced to a pretty but haunted shell of their former selves, their original residents priced out. "Urban planners and preservationists often tout the need for neighborhoods with distinctive cultures," the report commented, adding, "The residents who create that culture are often forgotten. An historical plaque in Chinatown is no substitute for a real life working community full of residents and vitality that such immigrants produce."[5] The outward markers of Chinatown might be preserved, but at a cost to Chinese Americans themselves.

Preservation can take less obviously material forms too, such as through the writing and recording of personal, cultural, and historical memories, narratives, and stories. In this chapter, I take up the first three installments of Henry Chang's hardboiled Jack Yu series—*Chinatown Beat* (2006), *Year of the Dog* (2008), and *Red Jade* (2010)—to argue that its narratives function in complex and contradictory ways as a textual preservation of Chinatown and its communities in the face of what Chang, referring to gentrification, calls "the reality of realty."[6] Yet what is paramount to remember at the outset is the obvious but often forgotten point that these stories are not "merely a window on material reality" or urban sociological data in narrative form and should not be read as such.[7] The neighborhood they represent to readers is indelibly shaped by a genre prepackaged with expectations: noirish locales, the prevalence of certain urban types (femme fatales, solitary detectives, corrupt cops), the duplicity of human relationships, and so on. Having acknowledged this, we should also recognize that Chang himself sees his novels as "less conventional mysteries than studies in Chinese-American culture." "I can't get enough history and sociology into these books," he has remarked.[8] They are crime novels, but Chang views them as something more. What that something more is is what this chapter is about.

While the first three books of the Jack Yu series textually preserve Chinatown, they do not freeze it in time at the date stamp of each book's publication. Instead, these books from 2006, 2008, and 2010 dial back the clock to 1994, when the recent socioeconomic transformations that would gentrify Chinatown were in embryonic form.[9] Chang teleports readers to Chinatown to write what I contend is a pregentrification narrative shadowed by the future, when the neighborhood as we know it "will eventually disappear." One cannot read these novels without thinking just how much Chinatown has changed in the interim. We will not find in Chang's novels creative-class hipsters overrunning an enclave of artisanal bakeries and candlelit lounges. They were not clamoring at the gates in 1994. However, what we do find are early instances of quality-of-life policing in Chinatown and evidence of real-estate rehabilitation on the horizon that together would upend the neighborhood. In these books we find as well Chang's surprisingly virulent critique of the liberal welfare state that many held responsible for the urban crisis of the 1970s and 1980s, which brokenwindows policing and gentrification were later said to solve. The timing of the series is especially critical, coming as it does months into the Giuliani administration and its crackdown on quality-of-life violations helmed by NYPD Commissioner Bratton, the boss of Chang's protagonist. Chang's decision to launch his novels in 1994 allows him, on the one hand, to navigate a grimier and grimmer city familiar to hardboiled fiction readers and, on the other, allows him to implicate the twenty-seven-year-old Detective Jack Yu in Chinatown's clean-up, which catalyzed the gentrification of the neighborhood that these novels lament. What we find in the figure of Jack that we did not find in Price's *Lush Life* are the double binds of ethnicity that ensnare the Chinese-American detective, who is compelled to navigate competing demands and tensions between cultural and professional loyalties, demands and tensions that gentrification worsens. Chang's protagonist understands the old neighborhood as laden with burdensome ethnic obligations that he wishes to shake off, even as their loss troubles him.

As we will see, Chang's novels are contested terrains in many different ways. They dramatize the bloody contests between rival tongs for control of Chinatown's streets. This violent intraethnic factionalism between organized criminal syndicates drives Chang's storylines. Furthermore, the novels themselves are contested ideological terrains that, on the one hand, seem to advocate for the cleanup of Chinatown and, on the other hand, exhibit highly ambivalent and skeptical attitudes toward outside forces policing the neighborhood's perceived disorder. Finally, the series exemplifies how the genre of crime fiction is a contested terrain for the ethnic detective writer. Crime fiction has often trafficked in xenophobic depictions of yellow peril and Orientalist caricatures, which as a Chinese-American crime writer Chang is compelled to wrestle with but which white crime writers are simply spared. His work, as this chapter will also show, articulates a multifaceted representation of Chinese-American identity that resists the genre's stereotypes. Yet even as his work rebuts these stereotypes, it mobilizes cultural caricatures of Chinatown as an inscrutable mystery, unfathomable puzzle, a world unto itself. As we will see, Chang's books simultaneously offer two seemingly contradictory and irreconcilable positions: they provide thick descriptions of Chinatown through the street-level eyes of the detective, which introduce to and immerse non-Chinese readers in the extraordinarily complex neighborhood and its culture; at the same time, these texts deploy and resignify the tropes of Chinatown's insularity and inscrutability in subtle ways to preserve Chinatown, to keep it a secret, if you will, from non-Chinese outsiders who might disrupt its way of life. In a period of accelerating gentrification, we can understand Chang's resignification of the cliché of inscrutability in this manner as functioning as a kind of protection from exterior forces as the terrain of Chinatown is fought over.

However, for all of the complexity that Chang's novels afford Chinese identity, his work evinces less generosity in its depictions of African Americans residing on the borders of Chinatown, a subject that this chapter will also address. I refer here to the series' sensationalistic depictions of random *"Black-on-Yellow crime"* and instances of racial resentment directed at African Americans collecting welfare while dealing drugs in government-subsidized projects (*Chinatown*, 86). To understand, but not excuse, representations like these, we have to see how Chang triangulates Blackness, whiteness, and Chineseness, negatively contrasting African American life with life in Chinatown in an inherently fraught effort to do positive cultural work for a neighborhood that has suffered its own stigmatization. Gentrification here too serves as an illustrative framework. The Chinatown of the Jack Yu series is a community with its own strict value and honor codes, a community distrustful of the state in all of its manifestations—from the police to public housing. It is a "community [with] its own system," its own way of doing things, Chang has commented. It is also a community of everyday residents and shop owners trying to lift themselves up one more greased rung on the American class ladder. "I wanted to tell these stories about regular people as well," Chang has remarked, not just gangsters but "regular, hardworking people, immigrants who are struggling to find their little place in America."[10] This Chinese-American community, which Chang's novels wish to preserve into the future in spite of gentrification, ironically evinces a do-it-yourself work ethic fitting for a gentrifying neoliberal city that is wearing away at the edges of Chinatown. As we will see, this industrious persevering community stands in stark contrast to an image of an urban African American community that these novels align with the moral corruption and lassitude of the old midcentury welfare state, which it would prefer not to preserve into the future but confine to the past.

THE ARCHITECTURE OF MEMORY

Manhattan's Chinatown stretches laterally across much of the eastern and central section of the island, where it runs up against and in some cases overlaps with several neighborhoods, including the Lower East Side, the ever-shrinking district of Little Italy, and the affluent avenues of TriBeCa. It is the largest concentration of Chinese in the Western Hemisphere, and it is coveted real estate, a short walk to work for a newcomer with a job on Wall Street or a government lifer hoofing it to City Hall. The neighborhood's borders are roughly Canal Street to the north; Leonard, Baxter, and Henry Streets to the south; and parts of Broadway and Essex on the west and east. But with numerous cutouts and odd angles, the neighborhood's frame is more complicated. About 150,000 people live here. When you see more signage in Chinese characters than in English, you know you are probably in

Chinatown, though this is no longer a surefire sign. The white population has increased over 40 percent since 2000.[11]

One prominent example of the new discourse to preserve the stories inside this fluid urban frame is the archival project "Archaeology of Change: Mapping Tales of Gentrification in New York City's Chinatown," by the Museum of Chinese in America (MOCA). As we will see, this project provides a point of comparison and contrast with Chang's work and helps situate the latter as participating in a larger effort to narrate stories of the neighborhood at a time when such stories are in danger of being lost. The leaders of the project, Lena Sze and Tomie Arai, interviewed Chinese and non-Chinese former and current residents, including businessowners, artists, community activists, and at least one Chinese police informant and mob enforcer, who with the vividness of a hatchet man in Chang's crime novels, spoke off the record about his firsthand knowledge of gangland violence, including homicides, in Chinatown. The interviewees were asked about their memories of the neighborhood, where they would draw the geographical boundaries of Chinatown, their impressions of its gentrification, and their thoughts on one or more of six buildings that embody both its immigrant history and its recent upscaling. The buildings were the Grand Machinery Exchange building at 215 Centre Street, which now houses MOCA; the Jewish Daily Forward building at 175 East Broadway, once home to a socialist paper of the same name for Yiddish-speaking immigrants, subsequently replaced by a Chinese church and now a high-end condominium building; the Music Palace at 91–93 Bowery, an old Chinese movie house, now a Wyndham Hotel; the Oltarsh building at 277 Canal Street, originally a theater before it housed the locally famous Chinese importer Pearl River Mart, which has since relocated to Chelsea Market, a tourist food mecca and overpriced mall; the Machinery Exchange building at 136 Baxter Street, also now a luxury condominium; and the Phoenix Poultry Market at 159 Grand Street, once the site of a thriving slaughterhouse, now the boutique Solita SoHo Hotel, from whose name any sign of its Chinatown location has been plucked and severed.

The "tales of gentrification" Sze and Arai collected run the gamut from laments over the passing of the old enclave, to acceptance (sometimes grudgingly) that the area has improved with lower crime and more

FIGURE 2.1. The Forward Building, New York. *Source:* Jim Henderson, public domain.

renovated buildings, to a laissez-faire response that decay and renewal are part of the natural urban ecosystem. "That's just the way it is, you have to change. If you don't change, you'll be wiped out," asserts Ching Yeh Chen, owner of the Pearl River Mart.[12] Chen's Darwinian tooth-and-claw narrative of living in New York City was echoed by the photographer Dirk Westphal, a self-described "yuppie gentrifier" with a commercial studio on Centre Street, who has come out on the winning side of the survival of the fittest. "I always feel sorry for people that are displaced but I also kind of feel like that's what makes a city," he says, adding, "gentrification isn't a bad word, and it's just this thing that kind of happens."[13] The reductive idea that cities change and that change just kind of happens obscures the questions of who or what causes them to change and who benefits from the changes. These are profoundly political questions that go to the heart of issues over power and representation that lay bare the truth that nothing about the redevelopment and gentrification of neighborhoods is natural. The urban ecosystem is itself, of course, not a naturally occurring phenomenon but a highly gendered and racialized capitalistic structure maintained in place by political and legal choices that have been made by humans and can be remade by them.

One of those choices is the kind of policing that is implemented, another the kind of development that is permitted. Jan Lee, a forty-two-year-old life-long resident of Chinatown, remarks to MOCA's interviewers that the neighborhood was a place where he had to constantly look over his shoulder. "My mother would tell me, 'Never walk on Pell Street.' It was just too dangerous," he recalls, remembering the "bullet holes in the telephone booth" from the "guys [who] used to shoot down that street." "I have a lot of problems with Giuliani, particularly about how he treated Chinatown," Lee says, but he praises him too: "He arrested all of the kingpins of my childhood all in one fell swoop." Among the stories Lee and others tell is of widespread extortion, small businessowners forced to fork over protection money for their nice little shops lest something unfortunate happen to them. Much of this is now in the past; in Lee's eyes, the gentrification of the neighborhood has been swift. "Much more accelerated," he says, noting that "in my short lifetime we've gone from being a ghetto" to being a place where non-Chinese newcomers to New York "*want* to live." The most visible signs of change have been the new development—"throwing up condos"—but it has been built on the backs of Chinese residents who for years have sweated and fought to better their own neighborhood. Lee notes "all the sacrifices to make Chinatown *that* desirable," an invisible labor done by "families [who] made tremendous sacrifice to build up the equity," families who are "very blue-collar," managing "funeral parlors" and "laundries" but getting "no credit."[14] Some of the rapid gentrification of the neighborhood has come from *within* the community, such as by Spring Wang, a former "radical Marxist" and now "developer" who "pick[s] up dilapidated buildings"— "lofts and brownstones"—"do[es] renovations, and manage[s] them or sell[s] them." Development, however, is not just putting up new buildings;

it is tearing down old ones. When the interviewers ask the artist Kam Mak about what places in Chinatown are personal landmarks, he responds, "Oh my god. They're all gone."[15]

If one pulls back from the individual memories located in the "Archaeology of Change" archives and focuses instead on the transformation of the six buildings singled out in Chinatown, one glimpses a larger story of postindustrial urbanization. From one angle this is the story told via the Jewish Daily Forward building, once home to America's most famous socialist newspaper, the story of ethnic and class succession from Jewish to Chinese to those, regardless of race or ethnicity, who are wealthy enough to rent a one-bedroom apartment at the building's current market rate of $6,500 a month.[16] The bas reliefs on the frieze above the entrance feature the visages of Karl Marx and Friedrich Engels, their stoic faces preserved in stone while their bodies surely roll in their graves. From another angle, this is the parallel story of the dismantling of New York's older urban industrial order, which depended for decades on blue-collar ethnic labor. The Grand Machinery Exchange building, the Phoenix Poultry Market, and other buildings that once housed the metalworking machines, bronze forgers, food canners, garment factories, warehouses, and meat-processing plants of New York's industrial urbanism have either been repurposed and transformed into luxury apartments and museums or demolished and replaced by hotels. In the succession of Chinatown's spaces one can track the succession of an economy driven by the heavy machinery of mass production, storage, and distribution of textiles, food, tools, and machines to make other machines to an economy driven by cultural heritage, the real estate industry, tourism, information production, and the rise of freelancing and flexible specialization (connoted by lofts and live-work spaces). In a nutshell, we witness here the transformation variously described as from Fordism to post-Fordism, from Keynesianism to neoliberalism, from industrialism to a postindustrial services economy, a whole reorganization of how and where we work and live. At the local level this is change we often call "gentrification."

Henry Chang's richly textured crime novels set in Manhattan's Chinatown can be seen as an extension in literary discourse of the oral histories and neighborhood mapping of MOCA's "Archaeology of Change" project. It is no coincidence that *Chinatown Beat* is almost exactly contemporaneous with MOCA's gentrification archive initiated in 2007. Chang himself was interviewed at length in 2013 by Tomie Arai for MOCA's related project "Portraits of Chinatown," during which he reflected on the changes to the neighborhood in recent decades. Both Chang's novels and MOCA's archival efforts respond to the timely need to memorialize the everyday, street-level histories and legends that the data in the report "Chinatown Then and Now" suggested were in danger of erasure. For Chang, whose working-class family moved to Chinatown when he was five—living first in a railroad apartment at 8 Pell Street and then nearby in a slightly larger two-bedroom flat on Mott—the prospect of this loss is personal. His connection to the neighborhood is long-standing, intimate, and familial. His immigrant father was a waiter, his mother a sweatshop laborer, both toiling in Chinatown. "I have a special connection to the people down here who have a special connection to the stories," he stressed on a walking tour of the neighborhood for Asia Pacific Forum, "because it is their story as well. They remember the places and the other people, many whom and which are no longer around."[17] "I've learned to bring a pad and pen with me and I'm always noticing stuff—what things sound like, what they smell like," he remarked, describing how he gathers material for his novels.[18] His notes for his gritty debut came not only from walking the streets but from his time hanging out in Chinatown's poolrooms, bars, and underground gambling dens. Chang has said that emerging out onto the street at 3 AM, "I'd tried to get all these stories down," "scribbling on a napkin or whatever piece of paper I could find." When asked by Arai what he thought the future of Chinatown would be, he mourned, "I think it may be greatly reduced . . . just a shell of a community," a place "just for tourists," not a real neighborhood but something more "like a movie set."[19] If the activists and academics of the AALDEF sought to prevent the neighborhood's physical and social profile from vanishing through, as they recommended, more affordable housing and subsidies for local businesses, then Chang sought to record, like MOCA's oral archives, what we might call the neighborhood's softer architecture of stories, memories, and legends through his pad and pen before they too vanished.

One rightly asks, then, just what kind of stories does Chang tell? What kinds of stories does he want to preserve as Chinatown gentrifies? In the unexpected answer to these questions lies the complexity of his work.

Readers looking for a tender portrait of an urban ethnic neighborhood collectively coping with the travails and tribulations of gentrification and policing have to look hard to find it. What he offers upfront is a portrait of an enclave ripping itself to shreds by intraethnic factionalism, co-ethnic labor exploitation, and rampant Chinese-on-Chinese tong violence for ownership of the neighborhood. However, what he presents in the background is what I see as the secret story of these books, the under-the-radar working-class ethnic community of ordinary people toiling away in the midst of all of the in-fighting over property and power. They are the residents who Jan Lee told MOCA's interviewers work hard but receive "no credit" but who in Chang's work are given dignity and representation as they struggle to stay alive and maybe even live a little bit better in a changing neighborhood.[20]

The Chinatown in Chang's narratives at first glance resembles the one described by the police informant and hitman Kayo Ong in the "Archaeology of Change" archives. It is one where Ong flatly stated "everybody was territory" (a spatial ontology, if there ever was one), a neighborhood where Fukienese, Cantonese, and Toishnese gangs battled one another on Pell, Doyers, and Grand Street with guns, "pipes," and "cleavers." In what could be a scene lifted from the pages of Chang's noir thrillers, Ong remarked how Chinese gang members ambushed each other: "They would . . . go up to the guy and just hack him." "That was Chinatown," he recalled, "so there was a lot of recorded killings," and apparently a lot he was recording for the first time—at the risk of legal liability—into the microphone of MOCA's curators. "I'm an unusual man, with a lot of unusual connections," Ong boasted. "I had to put a contract on my own cousin's son," "the right-hand man" of a Flying Dragon leader, he said. He started to explain, "So I had to . . ." only to trail off in silence when the interviewer nervously tried to change the subject.[21] To fully understand Chang's depiction of Chinatown as riven by just this kind of widespread internecine warfare, a portrayal that might appear to confirm stereotypes of the neighborhood as a violently clannish society, requires situating his work within the larger scope of the discursive portrayals of Chinatown by municipal leaders, writers, and filmmakers. In doing so, we will see that Chang's books about crime are indeed tales of gentrification and preservation for an ethnic enclave whose cultural status and physical territory is highly contested in the early twenty-first century.

FORGETTING CHINATOWN IN HENRY CHANG'S
JACK YU SERIES

The dramatic storyline Chang loosely weaves across his first three books follows Detective Jack Yu on his investigation of Mona, a former karaoke hostess–turned-mistress to the abusive criminal godfather Uncle Four, whom she murders in *Chinatown Beat*. After stealing his stash of gold coins and diamonds, she flees to Seattle by the third book, *Red Jade*. Uncle Four's death leaves others scrambling in all three novels to fill the power vacuum, sparking a war between tongs vying for turf once under his thumb. Several side plots are grafted into the dominant storyline, including the crimes of a Chinese pedophile, the gruesome murder of a Chinese teenager by "black devils" in the housing projects, two murder-suicide stories by Chinese men who have lost face over financial instability and probable marital infidelity, and the brazen shootout between two factions of a Chinese gang that leaves multiple people dead.[22] What launches the series are the fairly standard investigatory questions of crime fiction, but one cannot help but note that Chang's books often fail to pursue these questions for several chapters as the narrative spins off into side plots, subplots, and digressions. This structure, as discussed in the introduction, exemplifies the way crime fiction centrifugally incorporates non-crime-related matters. Put another way, it is how Chang's crime books, which wander into every nook and cranny in Chinatown, morph into "studies in Chinese-American culture."[23] Given the recurring characters, common setting, and interlinked plots of these novels, I will consider them as a body of work rather than take up each individual text for analysis. Considering them together allows a set of concerns—both within the world of the texts and the world in which these texts circulate—to come into focus.

What becomes immediately clear is that these books are about Jack's troubled relationship with Chinatown's old ways, which are fading with the death of his father in 1994. What becomes clear, too, is that Jack thinks of his father's Chinatown as dirty, even blighted, and that this blight signifies how tightly his immigrant father clung to tradition and how far he was from ever assimilating. In the first pages of the debut, Jack wants nothing more than to flee the neighborhood where he was born, wants nothing more than to free himself from his father's "fierce Chineseness" and "the burden his past here placed on him" (*Chinatown*, 10). Ironically, in trying to forget what his father represented, he ends up memorializing it for posterity. Chang continually sets off this old Chinatown in italics as though to separate and preserve it within the text. *"Remember where you came from. Know who you are. Know where you are going"* are the words Jack's dying father penned in a letter that haunts him (*Chinatown*, 83). He cannot stop thinking about his father's old Chinatown; even as he seeks to escape it, it ferments in his memory. *"His jook, his Chinese newspapers, his particular baby bok choy. All his excuses to stay rooted,"* Jack muses (*Year*, 67), reflecting on his father and those "old-timers" who took "pride in their disdain for American ways, Jack's ways" (*Chinatown*, 10).

Much to Jack's dismay growing up, his father's fealty to his ethnic identity and the ethnic enclave were more important than any semblances of a better life that might come with leaving both behind. "Time and again Jack had asked Pa to move. Uptown. Crosstown. Queens maybe. A decent apartment they could rent somewhere," Chang writes, but "Pa wouldn't hear of it" (*Chinatown*, 9). For Chang, the conflict over the space (the father's tenement apartment with its rats and drafty windows) allegorizes the first-generation ethnic subject's internal conflict between assimilation and cultural fidelity, as well as the masculine subject's assertion of cultural and spatial autonomy from the father's lingering shadow. In the series, Chineseness and Americanness are constituted by differing responses to cultural objects that connote rootedness, responses that are repeatedly performed ("all his excuses") to make one Chinese or, conversely, American, the two identities contingently related, each antagonistically defining the other. These are novels where one cannot separate one's ethnic identity from one's place and where urban space is an expression of one's ethnicity. Chang metaphorizes unassimilated ethnicity as a sticky, built-up residue, calling it "tenement squalor" and "grime in the hallway" that Jack would like to wash away (*Chinatown*, 9, 10). His father's Chinatown is unmistakably dirty, unabashedly Chinese, and authentic. Dirt and blight here are markers of time, signs of a racialized temporality in which "fierce Chineseness" is confined to a past that has no future (*Chinatown*, 10). His father's Chinatown is Chinatown before it is gentrified, Americanized, and whitened.

The cultural expectations dramatized in Chang's series are difficult for any first-generation subject to negotiate, but for Jack as a police detective, they are well-nigh impossible. He leaves his father's dirty Chinatown behind, only to be called back to clean it up, a job he does and does not want. In the series, trash, dirt, and grime are evidence of years of racialized poverty, but they also are "an index of backwardness" and a tacit "justification for (eventual) redevelopment" after intensive policing. In the context of racialized and devalued urban space, as Marisa Solomon has argued, trash, grime, and squalor are taken as "the obvious material evidence required to enroll neighborhoods and cities into a teleological narrative" from "worse to betterment," from "poverty to upward mobility."[24] If the old Chinatown reminds Jack of the unasked-for burdens of a Chinese identity hopelessly stuck in the past, one can surmise that the clean slate of gentrification, which these novels spy in the distance, will make him aware of what he has lost and forget what he does not want to remember.

For Jack, ethnic identity feels like an albatross, a set of cultural loyalties and attitudes that he does not want to have to carry: "I don't like boxing myself in," he says in response to another character's assertion of their shared ethnicity (*Chinatown*, 87). The series starts with Jack's desire to leave Manhattan's Chinatown for good, and then in book after book Chang ensnares his protagonist more and more within it. The NYPD has stationed him in the neighborhood's precinct because he is one of the few Chinese-American detectives on the force. It epitomizes an effort to put a familiar face on the police, who are viewed with suspicion by residents, but mostly it is a tactic for infiltrating the neighborhood and ferreting out information about ethnic crime. For Jack, being stationed back in Chinatown causes memories, most of them unpleasant, to come flooding back. "The transfer had brought Jack back to the o-Five," Chang writes, "back to the old neighborhood, where he'd grown up, where he'd lost boyhood friends and his innocence, and from which he'd thought he'd finally escaped."[25] At the conclusion of Roman Polanski's neo-noir thriller *Chinatown* (1974), the private investigator Jake Gittes is famously urged, "Forget it, Jake. It's Chinatown," a line Chang eventually quotes and recontextualizes.[26] Through these novels Chang himself wants to remember Chinatown, but his protagonist desperately wants to forget it. Unfortunately for Jack, he cannot. This struggle amounts to the emotional core of the series.

One cannot fault Jack for wanting to forget where he came from. Chinatown's association with human trafficking, tong warfare, ramshackle apartments, and filthy streets have been long-standing. Its status as an unsettled place in the American imagination, one compelled to bear wholly contradictory and incompatible Sinophobic significations, can be traced to the fact that it was at its founding an ideological and material white construct created, regulated, and quarantined by urban planning, zoning, policing, immigration policy, and other levers of state power. From the moment Chinese immigrants arrived in the United States in the mid- and late nineteenth century, they were prohibited from owning property outside of designated areas that were in most cases already slums. Those areas, labeled as Chinatowns, were routinely and incongruously characterized as enervating yet violent, as insular yet contagious, as tightly knit enclaves held together by ancestral traditions yet as zones bubbling over with social and physical squalor and disorder. Such contradictory images, which are a mainstay of sociological studies, newspaper reporting, urban planning documents, and narratives in popular culture, derive from the incommensurate ways Chinese immigrants have been stereotyped as exotic foreigners but also as model minorities, as lazy and easily susceptible to vice but also as more industrious than white ethnic Americans, as cunning but meek. In *How the Other Half Lives*, Jacob Riis remarks that "stealth and secretiveness are as much part of the Chinaman in New York as the cat-like tread of his felt shoes" and adds, "Trust not him who trusts no one" is a "safe rule in Chinatown." "A constant stream of plotting and counter-plotting makes up the round of Chinese social and political existence," Riis claimed, who accused the Chinese of a paradoxical "crafty submissiveness" in all their dealings, as if they are the very embodiment of urban deceit and mystery.[27]

In the discourse on Chinatown, the odoriferous nature of the neighborhood, which is nearly always mentioned, describes not only the pungent reality of the enclave for visitors but also served as a panic-filled metaphor for the geographical uncontainability of Chinese culture, its putative ability to waft, drift, and ultimately contaminate the city and nation. Such sentiments permeate, for instance, the descriptions found in Elodie Hogan's travel report "Hills and Corners of San Francisco" (1893) of Chinatown's "reeking sidewalks, foul with unknown trash," and of its "nauseous odors [that] vomited from black cellars."[28] But just about as often as Chinatown was accused of being a metastasizing yellow peril spilling across borders, it was accused of being an inward-looking community whose residents kept to themselves, clung to traditions, and refused to adapt to American customs. "They are attached to their own country by a superstitious bond," railed San Francisco's Mayor James Phelan in 1901, "and never think of leaving it permanently." Phelan was instrumental in the renewal of the Chinese Exclusion Act in 1902 that sealed off national borders to Chinese immigrants until the Immigration and Nationality Act of 1965 lifted the ban. "They cannot and will not assimilate with the white population; they live in colonies separate and apart," he continued, without acknowledging that U.S. jurisprudence had created those "colonies."[29] "There is no remedy for the evils of Chinatown apart from its utter demolition," he announced in "The Case Against the Chinaman" (1901).[30] Preservation was not on the table for Phelan.

As K. Scott Wong argues, images like the ones surveyed here "tended to cluster around a number of common themes: the physical 'mysteriousness' of Chinatown, unsanitary living conditions, immoral activities, and the general Otherness of the Chinese themselves, all of which contrasted with familiar idealized images of 'American' communities" that quality-of-life policing and gentrification would later seek to preserve or restore.[31] While such rhetoric speaks to the late nineteenth-century zenith of anti-Chinese sentiment, the characterization of Chinatown as a blighted neighborhood beset with intractable social problems continued well into the late twentieth century. Jan Lin maintains in *Reconstructing Chinatown: Ethnic Enclave, Global Change* (1998) that "Chinatown continues to be seen as a backward, somewhat byzantine society, an urban backwater." The point to stress is that narratives of Chinatown's physical and cultural disorder licensed the intensive policing of the neighborhood, led to its current redevelopment, and provided the context for filmic and literary narratives that dramatize police crackdowns that work in concert with gentrification. "The social problems perspective," Lin emphasizes, "feeds popular cultural images of Chinatown as a defiled and degraded place that needs to be cleaned up by investigative cops and aggressive district attorneys."[32] Images like these are not confined to the early twentieth century. In Michael Cimino's thriller *Year of the Dragon* (1985), the rhetoric remains depressingly familiar. Over dinner in a Chinese restaurant in the minutes before its patrons are machine-gunned in an unfolding tong war, the aptly named NYPD Detective Stanley White tries to convince the TV reporter Tracey Tzu to launch an exposé on the neighborhood's deteriorating conditions. The detective's ostensible target throughout the movie is Harry Yung, the head of the Chinese mafia threatening to push past Canal Street and force out the Cosa Nostra, but at the dinner table he redirects his fire from organized crime to what one suspects is his real target, the area's supposed cultural Otherness and physical disorder. Mansplaining to Tzu the evils of Chinatown, the white detective declares, "[Chinatown] stinks. . . . You got thirty people living in a room. You got the highest rate of TB and mental illness in any city neighborhood."[33] Cleaning up Chinatown, White infers, is a way of preventing the neighborhood from spreading.

Historically, Chinatown has been (and remains) a contested terrain fought over by residents, developers, police, and health inspectors. So too is the genre of crime fiction a fought-over discursive terrain, freighted as it is with Sinophobic caricatures and storylines of Chinatown as a cultural riddle to be cracked or a social problem to be eradicated. The two most famous Chinese characters in crime fiction—Sax Rohmer's Dr. Fu Manchu and Earl Biggers's Detective Charlie Chan—embody, respectively, Chinese criminality and malicious hyperintelligence and male effeminacy, and ethnic submissiveness, thus burdening Chinese-American protagonists with fighting off pernicious ethnic stereotypes while attending to the already time-consuming investigatory work they are paid to do. In a scene in *Chinatown Beat* in which Jack argues with Lucky Louie, the leader of the criminal underworld organization Ghost Legion, Louie snidely remarks, "When the fuck did you become Charlie Chan," essentially accusing him of cultural disloyalty for his work as a cop (170). Played in yellowface by the Swedish-American actor Warner Oland in films in the 1930s, Biggers's portly sleuth has been excoriated as an image of racial minstrelsy and humiliation by the novelist Frank Chin. Elaine Kim has decried the character as "a non-threatening, non-competitive, asexual ally of the white man."[34] Jack's efforts to free himself from his father's "fierce Chineseness" by becoming a detective open him to accusations that he is little more than a police stooge (*Chinatown*, 10). Louie's insult echoes the very terms by which Jack is seen as too Chinese within the NYPD. "Jack wasn't one of them. Any of *them*," Chang writes, "He was becoming the loner in his professional life that he was in his personal life. So *they* couldn't figure him out; the inscrutable Oriental, Detective Charlie Chan, they joked behind his back" (*Chinatown*, 98). The man who "live[s] in two worlds at the same time" is either too Chinese or not Chinese enough (*Chinatown*, 8).

Chang's own position as a writer is fraught within the terrain of the hard-boiled tradition, carrying as it does this history of embarrassing discursive

ethnic embodiments that do not impugn white writers and their protagonists, such as Raymond Chandler's solitary Philip Marlowe or Dashiell
Hammett's reticent Sam Spade. In the detective genre, the emotional
remoteness of white masculinity and its bare-bones physical separateness
and simplicity—a twin bed and a nightstand, or a plain desk in a purely
functional office such as one finds in Edward Hopper's paintings—are signs
of strength and ethical purity that counter the corruption, duplicity, and
enervation that this fiction associates with ethnic minorities. In Chandler's
The Big Sleep (1939), the Chinoiserie of Arthur Gwynn Geiger's apartment
cries out that he is a "pervert," a bisexual to be exact. In Chang's novels,
Jack's asociality and masculine reserve are treated not as evidence of his
tough-mindedness but as proof of his Chinese hermeticism. His male subjectivity is inseparable from his ethnicity, both arising from his alienated
relation to the ethnic enclave in which he was raised. Underneath the inscrutability lay no essential or even socially agreed-upon Chineseness but only
painful social contradictions mystified as ethnic unfathomability. Dolores
Hayden notes that "the power of place" emerges from the struggle over the
control and possession of urban space and the meanings and memories that
layer the city landscape over time.[35] In Chang's work this struggle is not
only over the place of Chinatown but over his own place in the genre of
crime fiction.

Through his detective, Chang escorts the reader into Chinatown and signifies on many of these pathologizing tropes of the neighborhood. Jack, in
effect, works double duty as an officer in the Fifth Precinct and as a cultural mediator or tour guide for readers, not unlike Chang himself, who
has worked as a corporate security director and has given walking tours of
Chinatown. As a police officer, Jack is armed with the legal authority to
enter into the depths of the neighborhood to enforce the law. As a mediator and as someone who "had grown up in Chinatown, knew what it felt
like to look and breathe Chinese, to savor *foo yee*, *ga lei*, pungent and spicy
aromas that white precinct cops wrinkled their noses at," he is equipped
with an intimate knowledge of everyday life in the area (*Chinatown*, 8). He
crosses linguistic and spatial borders into domains inaccessible to English
speakers. Deploying, then translating, Chinese phrases on nearly every page
("*gow say gow say*, twice a dead dog," "the *fung sup*, arthritis," "Loo *je*, sis-
ter Loo"), Chang rhetorically constructs authentic linguistic difference,
simultaneously joining and holding apart disjunctive cultural realities

(*Chinatown*, 11, 46, 9). Yet Chang's typographical presentation of Chinese treats the language as visually exotic, a language not fully integrated into the text. The translated phrases furthermore imply that Chang does not imagine a bilingual reader but a monolingual English one whom he can bring over into Chinatown's culture without discomfiting their reading experience with what would be to them incomprehensible foreignness. In short, Chang's protagonist is an armed tour guide and translator through the world of Chinatown.

Yet what is constructed in Chang's novels still turns out—at least at first glance—to be a Chinatown that is incomprehensible and foreign, an illegible urban space that is knowable only in its unknowability. The narrative transmits back to the reader a neighborhood of rival tongs (Hip Ching, Ghost Legion, and Fuk Ching), multiple dialects (Cantonese, Mandarin, Toishanese, Hakka), Confucian concepts of social hierarchies, fortune tellers and mahjong players, exotic foods and counterfeit merchandise, a physically deceptive neighborhood where brothels are hidden behind red curtains in barbershops and where gangsters confront each other in back alleys and concealed passageways. All in all it epitomizes a "secret society," as Chang labels Chinatown (*Year*, 109). Such images would seem to compound the well-established trope of Chinatown's urban unfathomability, where bewildering cultural chaos is bound by a tightly wound cultural riddle of ethnic criminality. At the end of *Chinatown Beat*, Chang sums up the neighborhood, leaving the threads still neatly tied: "Chinatown was a paradox, a Chinese puzzle" (209).

How should we understand such stereotypical depictions from a Chinese American writer? I will return to this question to argue for the ways that Chang's work sees through and demystifies the riddle. But here I would note that one way we may understand Chang's deployment of well-trodden tropes of Chinatown as inscrutable, insular, and violent is as an extension of the hardboiled novel's history of, and formula for, representing the city as a whole as duplicitous and dissembling. The city in crime fiction is a place of arabesque conspiracies where nearly all social exchanges are characterized by misinformation, half-truths, and outright lies concealing darker motivations. The genre's hermeneutics of suspicion accepts nothing at face value, as it pledges to spy an underlying meaning in the disorder and confusion of the city. Thus one way to view Chang's series is to see the texts as crime novels first and foremost, which, had they been set in another

FIGURE 2.2. A street in Chinatown, Manhattan, New York. *Source:* Stig Nygaard https://www.flickr.com/photos/stignygaard/, CC BY 2.0 (https://creativecommons.org/licenses/by/2.0), via Wikimedia Commons.

neighborhood in the city, would have found similar dark streets washed in the same neon glow. Yet ultimately this misses the point. Such a view ignores the difference that both Chinatown and Chang bring to the genre. Ultimately, I argue that one of the projects of Chang's texts—deeply conflicted and contradictory as they are—is to reveal that the pathologizing images of Chinatown emerge from urban political economy, capitalist development, and institutional and discursive racism and not from some immutable Chinese otherness. In this regard, Chang contributes to efforts by Frank Chin, Amy Tan, and Maxine Hong Kingston, whose cultural interventions, Sau-Ling Cynthia Wong argues, entail promoting more complex representations of Chinatown and Chinese culture.[36] But as a hardboiled crime writer, he also recognizes that representing Chinatown as a fearful cipher lends his work irresistible atmosphere and drama, which he deploys to maximum effect.

PLOTTING ETHNICITY, RACE, CLASS, AND CRIME

Early in *Chinatown Beat* Jack maps Manhattan at night, a common gesture in crime fiction, one that takes the shape of the setting on foot, from above, or, here, from a car. As Jack drives, Chang sketches a landscape of ethnic poverty and crime that will be his setting for the next several books. Yet one can already sense the value judgments and blind spots of this map, can already see what it leaves out and what it makes sure to leave in. Starting at "the corner of Mott and Bayard" in Chinatown in his "midnight-blue Dodge Fury," "he rolled through the extended communities of Fukienese, Malaysians, Chiu Chaos, settlements stretching east to Essex and north to Delancey, into areas longtime Hassidic, Puerto Rican," Chang writes (14–15). Jack "continued east" past

> the Greater Chinatown Dream, the Nationalists had called it: an all-yellow district in lower Manhattan running from the Battery to Fourteenth street, river to river, east to west, by the year 2000.
>
> Then he turned the car north and made all the green lights through *loisaida*, the Lower East Side, past the Welfare Projects—the Wagner, Rutgers, Baruch, Gouverneur—federally subsidized highrises, which ran along the East River, blocs of buildings that stood out like racial fortresses. Blacks in

the Smith Houses, Latinos in the Towers . . . a patchwork quilt of different communities of people coexisting, sometimes with great difficulty. (*CHINATOWN*, 15–16)

The tour continues "north through Gramercy Park and Murray Hill" and the Upper East Side, as Jack escorts the reader to "Spanish Harlem, the decay suddenly evident," then "west toward Morningside Heights and the enclave of Dominicans, a drug-dealing hub that connected New York, Connecticut, New Jersey," before he finally pauses to stare at "the city spread out before him" (16). Jack completes the tour's circuit by looping back to Chinatown, driving south along its "sinking potholed streets and garbage-strewn parks" (17). Jack's mid-1990s New York is a "city [that] was dying," an "unforgiving metropolis" far different from being the safest big city in the United States when the books were published (*Chinatown*, 16, 120).

Chang's survey of New York's tessellated geography of crime is extremely precise in places and frustratingly vague in others. For starters, we see that predominantly wealthy, white areas—Gramercy Park, Murray Hill, and the Upper East Side—are merely noted by their place names, silently existing as a kind of blank space in the text until "the decay [is] suddenly evident" once Jack enters Spanish Harlem. These unremarked-upon, low-crime, white neighborhoods serve to throw into greater relief the ethnic and racial tensions, poverty, and criminality of the city's racialized zones. The two main criminal geographies in Chang's imagination are the two already delineated as such on his map—the racialized spaces of the housing projects in and around the Lower East Side and the ethnic enclave of Chinatown itself—but Chang treats them in radically different ways. The former he singles out for particular animus, drawing upon common typologies of Black urban criminality. The latter, too, is a violent and dangerous enclave, but as we will see, Chang's writing eventually works to complicate and subvert its pathologized status.

Let's take a closer look at how Chang represents Lower Manhattan's "racial fortresses." The Alfred E. Smith Houses, "located in the bowels of the Lower East Side," are a "low-income housing development" bordering Chinatown's southern edge (36). Chang's language of "bowels" likens the Houses with excremental uncleanness. If grime connoted both economic hardship and the accumulated years of cultural defiance in Jack's father's

Chinatown, in the projects it connotes sheer cultural deviancy and criminality. "Pa had told Jack not to go down there," writes Chang (36). As a cop,
he is summoned there constantly. Chang's descriptions of the Smith Houses
as rank and despoiled is unmitigated by other kinds of images. Nothing
about the complex is redeemable. The buildings are suffused with "the
stench of junkie vomit," their "graffiti-covered walls" spray-painted with
"NWA, the rap group Niggers With Attitude" (37).[37] Later in *Chinatown
Beat*, Chang labels the residents of the projects "The low-life scum of New
York City, thrown down here with the Chinese because no other community wanted them" (102). Things get worse in *Year of the Dog*. One of its side
plots contains a grisly murder in the Riis Houses of a teenage Chinese-
American delivery boy, the outside of the building tagged with "NIGGAZ"
(159). Jack "felt the *word* was just niggers with a different shine on it. It was
a *black thing*, he'd been told; *you* wouldn't understand," writes Chang (159).
The three perps who kill the delivery boy are DaShawn, Jamal, and Tyrone,
their names racial signifiers of unmistakable Blackness. They exemplify the
superpredatory gangs that Chang labels a "wolf pack" in *Red Jade*, a dog
whistle that described Black teenagers in the aftermath of the brutal assault
on the Central Park jogger in 1989 (57). The three gleefully stab the boy with
a knife and smash his head with a hammer, then laugh that the "Chinee
muthafucka only had fitty-one dollars," not even enough for new "Air Jor-
dons [*sic*]" (*Year*, 170). The assailants' "run-down projects apartment" where
all this happens is a grotesquerie of the worst nightmares of Black urban
life. Roaches crawl the walls; "fuck magazines" like "*Ghetto Bitches*" litter
the floor; the living room is a pigsty of "filthy sleeping bags" and "stained
furniture" (*Year*, 160). Perhaps most damning is when Chang writes that
the "apartment was typical" (*Year*, 160). Swing open any door in public
housing and this is what you'd find, Chang imagines.

Regrettably, Chang's depictions of this "environment of violence and
drugs," a place of "junkie absentee parents and illegitimate drop-out children," is neither new nor nuanced (*Year*, 160). However, when we probe further the social meanings of these representations, we can see them for
what they are: Jack's displaced animus toward the liberal welfare state for
its socioeconomic failures, displaced because it is aimed not at the structures of the state but at its most marginal citizens. It is victim blaming, much
like the culture-of-poverty discourse by Oscar Lewis, Patrick Moynihan,
and others that Chang draws upon, wittingly or not, for his novels' images

of Black familial pathology. In Chang's work, the Smith and Riis Houses are where families "lived off Welfare programs, generations growing up on WIC coupons, and food stamps" (*Chinatown*, 36). All around the projects are drugged-up "loitering zombies" who, Chang states, "trade WIC coupons [and] food stamps" and "then infest Chinatown seeking opportunities to steal, maybe rape" (*Chinatown*, 102). The overall impression the novels leave one with is not just of criminality and violence but of un-American laziness, a culture of dependency on government handouts, a warped value system, and a willingness to steal what others (i.e., Chinese-Americans) have worked mightily to obtain by playing by the rules.

One can understand then, if not sanction, that the second social function of Chang's stigmatizing depiction is to triangulate Blackness, Chineseness, and whiteness in a way that throws into relief the very Americanness of Chinatown's self-driven, goal-oriented community, a social and political status historically denied to it. In Chang's work, Chinatown's national belonging is defined, ironically it would seem, in large part by its separation, self-reliance, and lack of dependency on the nation-state that houses it. His contrasting representation of the family of the murdered Chinese teenager makes this painfully evident. They are the sentimental embodiment of traditional heteronormativity and up-by-the-bootstraps American values, checking all of the boxes of what it means to be an aspiring American in Chang's imagination. They are small businessowners, running a "take-out joint" where the mother and father work "grinding restaurant hours," "a generation of sacrifice for their little piece of the American Dream" (*Year*, 131). On the evening their son is murdered, the mother and father were on the verge of closing up for "a family night" together— Christmas night, to boot (132). Chang writes that he was their only son, "a good boy, responsible," "a high-school scholar," details signaling the family's ascension in years to come into the professional upper middle class (132, 161). No absentee parents or high school dropouts here.

The larger point to take from these representations is that they are Chang's implicit way of figuring a rejection of the socially retributive welfare state that quality-of-life policing would target as a site of crime and disorder and as an obstacle to the redevelopment of Chinatown. In the 1990s in New York, writes Julian Brash, "There was a sense (mostly among whites) that an overly generous and permissive liberal state had led to urban 'disorder' and that retrenchment was required."[38] We can see that retrenchment dramatized in Chang's texts in stories of policing and crime. In the portrayal of the Chinese victims, we can also see an embrace of the independent entrepreneurialism that neoliberal urbanism not only champions but requires. The belief in personal effort as the means by which one obtains a better life, one that is effectuated in the private marketplace, is what underscores the pioneering spirit of gentrification. This is not to suggest that the hardworking Chinese in these texts are themselves gentrifiers, but it is to suggest they embody a mindset that underwrites the tacit antistatist critique that these novels articulate. It is a critique that legitimizes neoliberal urbanism's dismantling of the welfare state, concretized in the towering projects that are a physical impediment to gentrification and a site of nauseating disorder and stomach-turning crime in Chang's texts. In doing so, the novels license the policing of Black spaces and their removal for the city's entrepreneurial citizens.

Chang's sentimental portrait of the Americanness of the Chinese in America is not the culturally dominant one. As noted, Chinatown has been subjected to pathologizing tropes of it as an undifferentiated, incomprehensible, cognitively unmappable, and criminal Chinese mass. That's how the NYPD views it in Chang's series. In Chang's novels, for the white police officers (who live out in the 'burbs) "Chinatown was like a foreign port . . . full of experiences confounding to the average Caucasian mind. . . . They were able to dismiss it as a troublesome nightmare, half-remembered and unfathomable. These Chinese were creatures unlike themselves, existing in a world where the English language and white culture carried little significance" (*Chinatown*, 8). The port metaphor insinuates that the neighborhood is not really a part of the city but a marginal and liminal space associated with the flotsam and jetsam of human cargo (or something less than human, even "creaturely"). This totalizing Sinophobic description is, however, Chang mockingly suggests, a product of the limited imagination of whites who are either blind to or easily confused by urban difference. In Chang's writing Chinatown *is* a criminalized geography. But it is a different kind of urban criminality than one finds in the projects.

The NYPD's totalizing view in Chang's work suggests Chinatown's social diversity and cultural complexity has been invisible or actively denied by outsiders. "The existing literature on New York City's Chinatown," Lin observes, "generally views the district as a unified enclave."[39] Chang's writing puts a lie to these views. Part of the cultural work that Chang's writing performs for readers is to rhetorically construct a neighborhood on the page that is as kaleidoscopic—not "united" but extraordinarily divided—as the "real" Chinatown off of the page. The Jack Yu series does this by depicting the neighborhood with a level of block-by-block granularity that reveals its cultural nuances and heterogeneity. Chang's Chinatown is a neighborhood split by cultural divisions that map onto immigration patterns from various regions of China and Taiwan, by linguistic divisions that render communication between residents difficult, and by contentious political divisions traceable to the Chinese civil war between the nationalists of the Kuomintang and the Communist Party of China. Or in the words of Chang, it is a Chinatown with "more diversity . . . but less unity" (*Red*, 105). In these novels, the gangs divvy up the ethnic neighborhood as an exercise of power, an observation Chang underscores in the very first sentence of his very first book when a Chinese character rolls up in a black Lincoln on a "narrow street, territory of the Hip Chings," a street where he does not belong (1).

Through the process of working Uncle Four's murder case and the homicides and suicides that occur throughout the series, Jack reveals a neighborhood composed of carefully partitioned but constantly disputed zones that are ruled by different gangs with differing class alliances, regional origins, and global flows of labor and capital. For instance, one of the larger criminal underworld operations is the Ghost Legion, whose members are wealthy Hong Kongese. They "sneered at the ship-jumpers, the waiters and dishwashers, the laundrymen, who joined the rival Hip Chings," a gang that hails from "mainland China, Southeast Asia, and Taiwan" and answers locally to Uncle Four (*Chinatown*, 44). Both groups increasingly contend with the Fuk Chings, composed of Fukienese immigrants at the bottom of the intraethnic urban hierarchy. In the series, long-term Chinatown residents view the new Fukienese immigrants as culturally backward and see their cheap labor as a threat to other working-class Chinese. With new labor migrations, "power was shifting," changes Chang maps onto shifts in urban territory (*Year*, 20). Hip Chings operate restaurants on the southern corners of "Essex Street," but they are "shaken down by three rival crews, one of them being Dragons" (*Chinatown*, 27). With Uncle Four's death, Louie's hand as the leader of the Ghost Legion strengthens, but only momentarily. From their stronghold on East Broadway, the Fuk Chings encroach on Pell and Division Streets, the heart of what Louie calls "*his* turf" (*Year*, 20). "The Fukienese were driving the boundaries north and east," reflects Louie, "challenging all corners to the long stretch of East Broadway and the side streets" (*Year*, 71, 72).

Admittedly, these fluid boundaries are a little hard to keep straight. One thing is crystal clear: Chang's Chinatown is not a hermetic world unto itself. Almost nothing is insular about this global neighborhood. The crime writer S. J. Rozan's *China Trade* portrays Chinatown as "a city within a city . . . a world all its own."[40] In contrast, Chang's work undermines the notion of the neighborhood's insularity, though as we will see later, it ends up also redeploying this trope as a way of protecting Chinatown. Chang's Chinatown is tied to and shaped by the world outside of it, a neighborhood locally affected by global transformations in the economy that unleash flows of money, labor, and commodities across borders. "Chinatown doesn't end at Delancey Street, Captain. It stretches to Hong Kong, and Taiwan, and China," says Jack to another police officer (*Chinatown*, 204). The connections woven in Chang's series between the concentric circles of the local, the regional, and the global are fundamental to the logic of his books and to contemporary crime fiction more generally. The genre focuses on a specific crime in a specific urban neighborhood that it examines for its singularity and maps onto the larger urban system's interlocking class, race, and ethnic orders, which are tied to intertwining regional, national, and global trajectories of labor and capital.

The point to note is what actually lies behind Chang's representation of Chinatown as caught between greedy tribes battling in a kind of Hobbesian war. The mysticism of the tongs is "Fu Manchu bullshit" (*Year*, 74), a smokescreen for the global dealing of commodities—stolen "video camcorders, digital cameras, Walkmen and laptop computers" through a "network of merchants" (*Year*, 123) "in Europe, and in Central and South America. More recently . . . North America" (*Year*, 74). "Every time business was transacted, there were the lawyers, the brokers, the city officials, the bank regulators," Chang remarks (*Chinatown*, 30). Once demystified, these enigmatic tongs are corporations by another name. Their structures are homologous to legal businesses with supply chains, distribution systems, and retailers. And the people who make both kinds of organizations work are functionally the same: middlemen, bankers, politicians, and attorneys. The radical critique Chang makes is to imply that the tongs' planned and organized crimes are inseparable from the "crimes" of capitalist exploitation. Yet the conservative critique he also makes is to imply that the tongs' crimes are categorically distinct from the random and senseless Black crime on the neighborhood's fringes. In the final analysis, these novels show that the violence in Chinatown is a product of global labor migration, a desire to lay claim to the neighborhood's spaces, and a pursuit of greater market share or total market dominance. As such, there is nothing mysterious or insular about them.

GENTRIFICATION, GIULIANI, AND EVERYDAY LIFE

The gentrification of Chinatown in the early 2000s, which was when Chang began publishing his Jack Yu series, followed on the heels of the cleanup campaign by Giuliani's NYPD, which was initiated in 1994 when Chang's novels begin. Giuliani's campaign was not only a campaign to clean up the streets through quality-of-life policing but also to clean up the corruption and extortion of the Chinese mafia (the tongs in Chang's books) to make the area more friendly to the lawful commerce that gentrification depends upon. This point is essential for understanding the logic of Chang's texts. As Jan Lee told MOCA's interviewers, Giuliani "arrested all of the kingpins" in the neighborhood. Rooting out the ethnic gangs opens up the neighborhood for its colonization by legitimate capital. As a member of the NYPD, this puts Jack in an increasingly tense and seemingly untenable situation where by merely doing his job, he is guilty of betraying his community. "We own the streets, not them [the police]," Louie says to Jack, adding, "See, to me, to the boys, Chinatown is our life. Not a job, not a paycheck. Every minute, every day, we're here to stay" (*Chinatown*, 169). "That badge ain't shit down here," Jack is told (*Chinatown*, 147). At heart, it is a question of to whom does the neighborhood belong. Increasingly, Jack feels he belongs nowhere.

Louie's assertion of control over Chinatown's streets betrays his fear he is losing them to the police's intrusive presence. He frets the new mayor "was a law-and-order guy, an ex-DA who'd already stated publicly that he was going to crack down on organized crime. In the past that had meant the Mafia . . . but now included . . . the Chinese tongs" (*Year*, 21). What draws the NYPD to the neighborhood is not only organized crime; it is also disorganized streets. In *Chinatown Beat*, Alexandra Lee-Chow, an attorney for the Asian-American Justice Advocacy and a recurring character in the series, complains about the police hassling unlicensed street vendors, everyday people eking out a living by selling dragon fruit or clothing on sidewalk tables along the streets of the neighborhood. These are the same people the report "Chinatown Then and Now" argued were being cleared out for "luxury condominiums" and "upscale services."[41] "Tell me, why is it that you can't walk down the street in Little Italy, there are so many sidewalk cafés, but the Chinese guy with the fruit stand or the grandmother with the tray of socks rates a hundred-dollar summons and gets hauled away in handcuffs," Alexandra says with exasperation (*Chinatown*, 106). The designation of the streets as disorderly, as opposed to differently ordered, legitimizes their policing as a precursor to their gentrification. Chang's Chinatown finds itself on the verge of gentrifying in no small part because of the NYPD's clampdown on misdemeanors that the Giuliani administration prosecuted by zealously implementing James Wilson and George Kelling's order-maintenance policing. Giuliani's policing compromised the cultural integrity of Chinatown and set the stage for development under Bloomberg, a historical and spatial context that is not only a frame around Chang's novels but is immanent within them. Giuliani may be a minor figure in the Jack Yu series, but his glowering, golem-like visage is inescapable. He hangs over these books.

Efforts to curtail public disorder are not the main focus of the novels but rather are quietly and not so quietly operating in the background, displacing unwanted people from valuable urban real estate. Jack is not engaged in this low-level police work, yet when Alexandra challenges him in *Chinatown Beat* about the police's harassment of poor and working-class people, challenges him on "how screwed up the system is," he feels guilty by association (106). Yet when he is called out further and asked, "Can't the precinct find better ways to utilize manpower," he protests that he bears no responsibility (105). "I'm working homicides," he retorts, as if that has nothing to do with cleaning up the neighborhood (105). Still chastened, he softly remarks that the quality-of-life policing must have to do with the "zoning or health code," an allusion to the long history of stereotyping Chinatown as a contaminated space to be sanitized and modernized both physically and culturally (106).

Crackdowns on quality-of-life crimes are indistinguishable from crackdowns on culture when they occur in the context of gentrifying ethnic neighborhoods. Chang suggests as much about the relation between policing and ethnic culture in a scene in *Red Jade* that is fundamental to understanding how policing, ethnic identity, and urban restructuring are interrelated in these texts. Sitting in a Chinatown bar, Jack glances up at a TV where "the new Italian-American mayor . . . was pitching the idea of banning fireworks in Chinatown, especially Chinese New Year celebrations" (89). "The mayor was citing fire safety concerns," Chang writes, though "it hadn't been a concern for a hundred and twenty-five years" (89). As Chang knows, this proposal strikes at the heart of what it means to be Chinese-American. The artist Kam Mak, interviewed for the "Archaeology of Change" archives, remarked that when growing up in Chinatown the fireworks had glowed in his imagination, connecting him to his community, but "Giuliani changed everything . . . 'No more fireworks.'"[42] Chang implicates Jack in the city's clampdown on Chinatown's most important festival of ethnic identity, further tying him in double binds of having to choose loyalty to his ethnicity or to his profession, binds he never fully undoes.

With this in mind, the scene at the end of *Chinatown Beat*, when the mayor hovers over Jack's shoulder, is both poignant and ominous. After being wounded in a shootout in an unsuccessful attempt to arrest Uncle Four's killer, he is awarded and promoted. "Jack stood on the stage in his neatly pressed blue uniform, before the mayor, the commissioner and an array of the department brass," Chang writes, "all applauding as the deputy chief pinned the Combat Cross above the gold badge over Jack's heart" (206). Curiously, however, Chang calls this shield a "Yellow Badge"—not a "gold" one—in the chapter's title, casting it as a signifier of ethnic difference, one standing for both professional pride and ethnic shame (205). "When he looked out over the auditorium, Jack felt exhilarated yet sad. There was no family in the audience waiting for him. He thought of Pa" and mused "how proud he might have been. Maybe" (206). Reverberating in Jack's mind may be the words of his father's letter: "*Remember where you came from. Know who you are. Know where you are going*" (*Chinatown*, 83). The intense conflicts over ethnic space in Chang's novels are matched by the internal conflicts in the spaces of the heart.

We can understand how policing, gentrification, and Chinatown become inseparably linked if we loop back to the discomfiting scene at the Riis Houses where the Chinese delivery boy was murdered. The former African American occupants of the squalid apartment had dumped the teenager's body "*like a sack of garbage by the gutter*," a description that conflates the quality-of-life violation of littering with murder (*Year*, 161). The rest of the scene bears out this logic. One of the killers, we learn, has a "rap sheet that detailed his ascent of the thug ladder: early busts for loitering, drinking from an open container, turnstile-hopping, then from criminal mischief to," the list continuing until reaching its inevitable end, "attempted murder of a New York City police officer" (164). It amounts to a criminogenic progression, an unstoppable telos that is central to Wilson and Kelling's central proposition. "At the community level," they argued, "disorder and crime are usually inextricably linked, in a kind of developmental sequence."[43] Fail to quash littering, loitering, or public drinking and soon enough you get "attempted murder." Quash all of it, and you might reclaim your city for the wealthy. That's the larger frame for understanding this moment. It is what Jack spies across the East River from the projects, in what I believe is the key scene of the first three books of the series. Literally framed by the windows of the declining welfare state's public housing is a new neoliberal economy in the making, one Jack himself helps make possible. He sees Williamsburg, Brooklyn, once a vibrant, if poor, Puerto Rican and Jewish neighborhood, which, having fallen into disrepair, is now being retrofitted by gentrification into the uberhipster neighborhood it would come to be by the late 1990s. "He saw," Chang writes, "dilapidated docks and crumbling warehouses along the piers, camouflaged by the clean cover of snow. Garages and gritty industrial dumpsites along a graffiti-tagged and run-down shoreline. An area slowly being converted to residential lofts and low-rise condos, with pioneering urban homesteaders paving the way for the gentrification that was sure to come, the reality of realty finding its way across the river from Manhattan" (*Year*, 161). The rundown docks and warehouses signify an inexorable ("sure to come") economic and social transformation that these texts posit is the telos of the policing. What is about to happen to Williamsburg, these books know, will ripple back to Chinatown in due time.

The "reality of realty" is both on its way and already present in Chang's work, if one reads for it as the key to unlocking the puzzle and paradox of his representations of the changing neighborhood. While Jack attempts to escape culpability for these changes by claiming to Alexandra that he only works homicides, the "reality" is that in these novels working homicides cannot be disentangled from the policing that is the frontline of gentrification. The reality, too, is that these ambivalent novels buy into this logic and mourn its eventual outcome as the loss of ethnic community.

I began this chapter by noting that if we closely study the six Chinatown buildings singled out by the Archaeology of Change project, we can detect a shift toward a new postindustrial New York. Doing the same in an exercise of literary materialism with Chang's own representations of the built environment similarly yields insights, revealing abstract flows of capital that the text "preserves." Take, for instance, when Mona stands on her balcony in her modern China Plaza apartment, with its rooftop billboard advertising "Luxury Condominiums" for sale, and surveys the "ghetto detritus" of "discarded mattresses and dismembered plastic dolls . . . the carcasses of gutted refrigerators, air conditioners" strewn across the streets below where she had once seen "a black man on top of a woman, doggy style" (*Chinatown*, 19). In this racially charged image, Chang's text contemplates capitalist spatial contradictions and geographical unevenness, surveying not merely a setting but a system that can produce luxury and racialized degradation that exist side by side before the latter is removed. Later, in *Year of the Dog*, the text takes us to "the tallest building in the area," a "sixteen-story mirrored glass office" tower that is anchored to the street by a "Citibank branch and a tourist-trade gift shop" and is home to the "On Yee Merchants Consortium" on the third floor (70). Here in one architectural image we find a schematic of Chinatown's position and role within the global economy, a portrait of coexisting but ever-changing economies. Chang depicts how an older closed economy governed by ethnic traditionalism shares space with the marketing and commodification of Chinese culture as cheap consumer trinkets, which shares space with a global bank through which foreign and local capital passes into and out of the neighborhood. Along East Broadway, Chang notes "Chinatown vendors with outdoor ATM machines, a MoneyGram shop, and a Western Union at either end of the street," portals for transferring remittances earned in Chinatown's restaurants and garment factories back to the mainland (*Year*, 109). A few pages later, he reflects upon Chinatown's intercity "unregulated tour-bus business," a low-cost means of transporting freshly arrived "coolie workers," supplies, and cash "to restaurants and malls from Richmond to Rochester, as far west to Ohio, and north to Montreal" (*Year*, 111), where "cheap Chinese-speaking labor" is in demand (*Year*, 110).

Chang's precise attention to the details of his Chinatown setting creates a reality effect, immersing the reader in the neighborhood, as all good realistic fiction should. Yet the fact that these details circle back time and again specifically to the movement of capital, commodities, and people suggests something more is at stake, too. What these novels attempt to do is deconstruct the discursive myth of Chinatown's insularity by dramatizing how the daily life of ordinary people in the neighborhood—not just tong leaders—are shaped by the global flows of labor and capital that have made gentrification a worldwide phenomenon across urban landscapes. And in doing so, these novels attempt to find a narrative form for expressing the local and global forces that fundamentally reshape how people work and live in the neighborhood.

Nested within these flows are the spaces of Chinatown's everyday residents and their untold stories, not unlike those gathered by Lena Sze and Tomie Arai for the Museum of the Chinese in America. These are the stories of people trying to get by and make do, stories that Chang likely meant when he spoke of having "a special connection to the people" of Chinatown and when he remarked that his story was "their story as well" that he would memorialize and "remember the places and the other people, many whom and which are no longer around."[44] These, I admit, are the unthrilling stories that make these thrillers more poignant. They are the stories of the poor and working-class characters, their lives mere subplots threaded with or without their will into the dominant storylines of gentrification and crime. They are the stories of Sai Go, a small-time bookmaker who at fifty-nine and dying of lung cancer dreams of a vacation to Florida but ends up leaving his life savings to Bo Lan, a hairstylist who struggles to pay off her smuggling debt from China to New York. Her "small storefront" salon is "sandwiched between a noodle shop and a poultry market on a dilapidated block of Henry Street" and has trouble competing with "the new and shiny hair, nail, and massage 'emporiums'" popping up in the gentrifying neighborhood (*Year*, 79). They are the stories of Alexandra Lee-Chow, whose law office is in a former bodega close to Chinatown's "junkie parks" and "autorepair garages" (*Chinatown*, 103). They are the stories of the young Ms. Gong, a manager at a karaoke club, a job that "was like *freedom*" from her postpartum depression, a story fatally cut short by her jealous husband in *Red Jade* (20).

And they are the story of Jack's life, too, in its quieter moments. They are the stories of his off-duty days and nights, his lonely "workingman's life" in his studio apartment with a "convertible sofa bed," "a Mr. Coffee," and "a wok" in Sunset Park, the Brooklyn neighborhood dotted with late-night Chinese takeout restaurants and a transplanted "Chinese garment industry that had followed low rents out of Manhattan" (*Chinatown*, 59–60). As Jack stares out the window of his apartment, watching freighters loaded with what one assumes are Chinese goods moving through the New York Harbor, Chang tellingly describes Jack's life as composed of "mostly portable, transient, *disposable* items, his life in flux," his "thoughts flashed wide and scattered, his mind adrift" (*Chinatown*, 60). His is a "transient" life without strong ties to community or family, a life "adrift," floating like many others in Chang's Chinatown on waves roiling in a world beyond any single person's control. We might understand Chang's repeated efforts to draw his protagonist back into Manhattan's Chinatown—"And here I am, thought Jack. Back in the 'hood"—as attempts to reincorporate a first-generation ethnic American into his original community, to moor an adrift life by binding it to a culture and a place (*Red*, 25). But that culture and place were already becoming unglued when Chang penned his novels in the early 2000s. The "portable, transient, *disposable* items" flowing through the New York Harbor augur what has in truth already arrived: a postindustrial city of tourists, refugees, and workers.

In highlighting lives in the context of flux, Chang's words draw my attention to the concluding pages of his first three books where everything, as it often does in crime fiction, comes together: Chinatown, crime, inscrutability, and the way all of these have been publicly imagined are concentrated into one moment. Jack and his counterpart in the Seattle Police Department, Detective Nicoll, are meeting at dawn on an icy pier where hours before a shootout left two hitmen from an international triad dead, another badly wounded by a letter opener plunged into his eye, and Mona, whom everyone has been searching for, still missing after she escaped by leaping into the riptides of the harbor. The conversation that ensues between the two detectives is a staple of the genre, the familiar scene when the secret links between the mystery's clues are unveiled and the text's larger social world of labyrinthine deceitfulness and opaque conspiracies is finally made legible. After hundreds of pages devoted to what Chang in the first book describes as "a paradox, a Chinese puzzle" (209), Chang at last prepares Jack to make his case, a verbally unambiguous utterance that will lay bare Chinatown's entangling webs of subterfuge and bring them under the clear, rational order of the law.

Then, remarkably, he refuses.

Here is how the short exchange unfolds: among the evidence gathered from the crime scene is what appears to be the novel's most notable symbol of Chinese culture, and the title of the book itself: a red jade bracelet worn by Mona as a protective charm. In truth, it is a cheap "gift-shop trinket" (*Red*, 74), the disposable kind transported in bulk in shipping containers on freighters and sold as cheap souvenirs in "tourist-trade gift shop[s]" all over the Chinatowns of America (*Year*, 70). So what does Chang make of this inscrutable commodity that contains the secret of our global social relations in condensed form? Nicoll points to it and ignorantly asks, "What is that? Some kind of voodoo," to which Jack replies, "It's a Chinese thing," adding, "I'm not sure you'd understand" (*Red*, 226). As they part ways, Nicoll answers back, "Well then, don't worry about it, Jack," and says, "Remember . . ." Before he can finish, Jack responds wearily, "I know, I know . . . it's *Chinatown*" (226). Remember to forget it, Nicoll is about to say. The exchange, as noted earlier, cites the famous conclusion of Polanski's film, when Jake is pulled away in disbelief from a scene that reveals an unholy union of civic corruption and incestuous insularity in Los Angeles. The irony is that Chinatown does not even appear, not even once, in Polanski's film other than as a word, a signifier for urban unfathomability, a part of the city that is so secret and opaque that apparently it cannot even be represented on the big screen. Chang mocks Polanski's use of the Sinophobic trope but also recognizes it as a widely circulated cultural code shared by the two detectives, as well as the reader. He hints at something else, too. The Chinatown that we are to "forget" in Polanski's film is the Chinatown that in Chang's narratives we "remember," even if we will never fully understand it. In the end, Chang's fiction dispels the riddle of Chinatown's inscrutability, only to suggest it might be best if the police did not understand it either, if they looked the other way, if they in effect left it alone. With this in mind, Chang's comment to the *New York Times* resonates with added meaning: If you were to "come down here looking for the old Chinatown . . . you wouldn't see it," he said, adding, "And that's a good thing. It doesn't mean it's totally gone, but it's behind closed doors."[45]

Chinatown's old way of life and its own way of doing things, legal or maybe not, continue on out of sight of prying eyes, he implies. If the idea of Chinatown as an uncrackable riddle was once a Sinophobic trope, in Chang's hands it is a way of rhetorically pushing away white outsiders and preserving what remains of a neighborhood fading away. Chang's work invites the reader in and shuts them out at the same time.

In the first three books of his Jack Yu series, Chang writes a narrative for a neighborhood that he sees as changing, maybe even in Peter Kwong's word, "disappear[ing]" with gentrification. In these books published in the early 2000s but set in the 1990s, we read of Chinatown's future, one we know has already arrived. When Jack looked out at the waterfront of Williamsburg, he saw the industrial decline that Chang takes as a precursor to the city's reinvention. Next, in chapter 3, we turn to narratives of the declining white, working-class Brooklyn waterfront as another crime scene in the ongoing story of New York City's death and rebirth.[46]

Chapter Three

RED HOOK

Blood on the Industrial Waterfront

It is both impossible to ignore and easy to forget that New York is mostly an archipelago of islands and that its waterfront is the most extensive of any city in the United States. In other major cities, from Miami to Hong Kong, the shoreline contains the priciest real estate, historical monuments, glistening skyscrapers, museums, parks and public esplanades, restaurants, and retail. Not in New York. Not until recently. The most coveted addresses in the city, in Manhattan especially, have been farthest from the soiled edges of the island: Central Park West, Fifth Avenue, and Park Avenue. Conversely, as late as the 1990s many of New York's waterfront neighborhoods were, as a result of Robert Moses's midcentury urban renewal projects, peripheral slums associated with dying industries, government housing, and poverty. Yet within two decades—a short time in the life of any city—their status would radically change. This chapter follows the story of crime and gentrification in New York to one of those waterfront neighborhoods, working-class Red Hook, Brooklyn, and to three writers, Gabriel Cohen, Reggie Nadelson, and Ivy Pochoda, whose novels map and narrate the redevelopment of this isolated, forlorn, yet starkly beautiful place. Better than any other neighborhood in *The Gentrification Plot*, Red Hook and its history—at midcentury as a bustling port filled with stevedores and wiseguys, then from the 1970s through the 1990s as a no-go zone of drug-related violence and poverty, to its current status as a frontier of gentrification—encapsulates the city's transformation into the postindustrial citadel of today. The two gentrifying neighborhoods previously considered, the Lower East Side and Chinatown, have historically been the home to light manufacturing and a lively retail scene but primarily have been home to people, hundreds of thousands of people crammed into tenements. In contrast, for much of its history, Red Hook was an industrial space organized around shipping, warehousing, and waste treatment, the site of backbreaking blue-collar labor. Its residential real estate was, and still is, limited: a few streets of rowhouses, many of them recently rehabbed, close to the docks, and a sprawling community in NYCHA apartment towers further inland. In this one, marginal neighborhood we can detect the erosion of Fordist industrialism and the rise of neoliberal postindustrialism driven by real estate and tourism, and we can detect here too simmering class tensions that boil over into violence when the neighborhood is retrofitted for a new economy.

For non–New Yorkers, the South Brooklyn neighborhood of Red Hook may be less familiar than the Lower East Side and Chinatown. Red Hook is

FIGURE 3.1. Aerial view of Red Hook, Brooklyn. *Source:* Fairchild Aerial Surveys, Inc. Museum of the City of New York. X2010.11.13076.

"uncharted territory," Cohen writes, while Pochoda calls it "the loneliest place on earth." For Mayor Bloomberg, however, Red Hook was on his radar for redevelopment from the day he took office. In his first State of the City address in 2002, he announced that his administration would remake New York's "inaccessible and neglected . . . 500 miles of shoreline." He singled out the "old industrial waterfront sites" in the neighborhoods of Gowanus and Red Hook for conversion "into housing, parks and other developments."[1] He also slated for revitalization Governors Island, 172 acres of prime real estate offshore from Red Hook and a short ferry ride to the skyscrapers of Manhattan's financial district. Furthermore, the "entire waterfront" of Manhattan was to be made "accessible to walkers and cyclists" with a "multi-use recreational" ribbon wrapped along its edges like a bow. "Our crime rate continues to fall," Bloomberg noted, adding, "New York is safe, strong, [and] open for business." To keep crime falling further, he announced "Operation Clean Sweep," which would target "quality of life violations by aggressively policing low-level offenders." It was a far-reaching vision of New York as a low-crime, cleaned-up postindustrial city oriented around business and pleasure. The dirty waterways, long considered an afterthought, were suddenly positioned as of strategic importance to the city's future. By the end of his three terms, Bloomberg did "more rezoning of the waterfront and made more efforts to modernize and encourage reuse of industrial property than has ever occurred [in New York]."[2] "We must bring new life to the waterfront," he declared.

The writers Cohen, Nadelson, and Pochoda offer a starkly different vision of the city's creaky waterfront, one much less sanguine about the future. In their eyes, Red Hook in the late 1990s and early 2000s was being resuscitated, but it was also shot through with the racial and class violence of gentrification. In the context of redeveloping the waterfront, the rhetoric of "new life" was clearly a euphemism for the new people that gentrification would bring to an area whose older forms of life were dismissed as superannuated. The stories told by Cohen, Nadelson, and Pochoda, set in Red Hook in the last years of the twentieth century and the early years of the twenty-first, are as much investigations of homicides and missing persons as they are of a place dying, disappearing, and reemerging as something else.

Whereas chapters 1 and 2 examined stories of neobohemian hipsters and Chinese Americans in two gentrifying neighborhoods, chapter 3 brings issues pertaining to the white working class to the fore. As a result, a number of concerns surface in Cohen's, Nadelson's, and Pochoda's novels set in this waterfront neighborhood, concerns we have not encountered in earlier chapters, including white grievance over the perceived loss of economic and racial privilege, gentrification's reawakening of the personal traumas of midcentury urban renewal, and competing nostalgias between white and Black residents for the old, hardscrabble neighborhood. Since Red Hook is a port, its stories are littered with the oily detritus of waterfront industrialism, as well as shiny new images of the mode of production that is replacing it. In this chapter I read for these synecdoches—rotting piers, dilapidated docks, polluted canals, rusted shipping cranes, as well as recreational watercraft and gleaming cruise ships. As this chapter will argue, they are signifiers of the flow of social and economic forces, signifiers of what gets left behind, what of industrial urbanism's remnants gets salvaged and repurposed by pioneering gentrifiers, and what gets newly privileged in a neighborhood in flux.

In researching *Red Hook* (2001), his debut novel for his Jack Leightner series, Cohen walked around the streets of the neighborhood and wondered what the hell had happened. "To me, it was a profound mystery," he told North Country Public Radio.[3] Cohen's novel was written to explicitly answer the mystery of Red Hook's decline from its halcyon industrial days and its transformation into a different kind of neighborhood by century's end. In the series, the NYPD detective Jack Leightner is a longshoreman's son who waxes poetic for when Red Hook was pulsing with life, yet he is also haunted by its subsequent decades of decay. In *Red Hook*, he works a murder case leading to a developer planning to erect a waste-transfer station in the neighborhood, which just might be the death knell to the area, which is showing early signs of coming back to life. Already displaced once by redevelopment (Robert Moses bulldozed Jack's family's home), Jack evinces nostalgia for the old neighborhood. As we will see, he desires to turn back the clock to a putatively simpler era before both late-century gentrification and midcentury urban renewal, to a time more strongly governed by white privilege and working-class masculinity.

In Reggie Nadelson's novel, also titled *Red Hook* (2005), the crime genre is deployed to narrate a murderous transition from what she calls the "old industrial city" on the waterfront to the "brand new city" for developers who "prowl Red Hook's streets."[4] In her work, the waterfront is saturated with memories of its industrial past, which some will kill to hold on to and others will kill to keep secret. A retired African American newspaper editor, Sid, who was obsessed with Red Hook's white working-class immigrant vitality as a teenager but shut out of its community because of his race, is murdered while trying to gather information on the neighborhood's history for a book he is writing. An undocumented Russian sailor, Meler, whom Sid was searching for to obtain details about the old neighborhood, beats him to death out of fear his immigration status will be exposed by Sid's book. In Nadelson's hands, these crimes signify a violent desire to salvage and repurpose Red Hook's past or to forget it entirely. As we will also see, repurposing or recycling the bones of industrial urbanism is part of the aesthetics and economics of gentrification in Nadelson's book. But since this industrial history is also a kind of "information" (a word that Nadelson uses repeatedly), owning it is a way of figuring the new postindustrial information-based economy that is changing Red Hook.

The chapter closes with Ivy Pochoda's literary thriller *Visitation Street* (2013), in which the case of a missing person constitutes the web of intrigue that holds together this formally polyphonic novel of Red Hook's diverse residents. One night, a fifteen-year-old Italian-American girl, June, paddles into the harbor on an inflatable raft and does not return. The search to discover what happened to her morphs into an investigation by Pochoda into the class and racial politics of urban development. The fact that the novel's main African American character is a suspect in June's disappearance underscores the way racialized subjects are blamed for any sign that gentrification is under threat. As I will show, the real culprit for Red Hook's tumultuous past and present in *Visitation Street* are roiling waves of urban history and capitalist production captured in the novel's ships, rafts, speedboats, shipping containers, sailboats, and new cruise liners, which, deflated, wrecked, stripped apart, sinking, or gleaming, become freighted with lost dreams and hopes for a better life.

RED HOOK IN THE URBAN IMAGINATION

Red Hook's luridly colorful name seems almost too good to be true from the crime novelist's perspective. But it is derived not from the area's reputation for blood and gore but from the color of the soil and the Dutch word *hoek*, meaning "point" or "corner." The neighborhood—a "weird fat lip of land"—juts out into the harbor with unrivaled views of the Statue of Liberty (Nadelson, *Red Hook*, 6). Its northeastern border is the elevated six-lane Gowanus Expressway, completed by Robert Moses in 1941, that connects the often-clogged Brooklyn-Battery Tunnel to the usually jammed Verrazzano-Narrows Bridge, linking (at least in theory) the neighborhood to Manhattan and Staten Island. The diagonal cut of the expressway and eight-laned Hamilton Avenue running beneath it sever Red Hook from the wealthier neighborhood of Carroll Gardens and leave residents trapped behind lanes of traffic that have to be crossed over via a dicey pedestrian bridge or passed carefully under to reach the closest subway station at Smith and Ninth Streets, a mile away. In Cohen's novel, the expressway is a "deep gash," an open wound that years later haunts even those who have left the neighborhood, especially Jack (28).

As a place, Red Hook bears contradictory significations that are unique to its geographical and economic position. One of the first impressions conveyed by urban planners, politicians, and writers who study the neighborhood is its paradoxical interconnectedness to the rest of New York and remoteness from it. "Red Hook is defined by its proximity to water and roadways," write the authors of the redevelopment blueprint *Red Hook: A Plan for Community Regeneration* (1996), a Giuliani-era proposal to transform the area. They go on to note that "while critical to the movement of goods and vehicles, these waterways and transportation structures separate Red Hook from the rest of Brooklyn." The remoteness of the area is actual but also imagined: "To the outside world Red Hook often evokes images of danger and isolation," the authors of the plan remark.[5] Red Hook seems simultaneously inside the city and outside of it. Nadelson's novel figures Red Hook as "the edge of the world" yet only "a couple of miles from Manhattan" (25), literally on the fringe but central (at least at one time) to the city's economy as "the biggest shipyards on earth" and as the city's main port (7). The social and economic changes in Red Hook are "a microcosm" of the transformations to the wider city (281).

The word "transformations" may lend a false impression that changes in the neighborhood have been smooth. In truth, they have been anything but. Red Hook has been beaten and bloodied by decades of passive neglect and active harm. The Gowanus Expressway destroyed the neighborhood's retail corridor by casting it in perpetual shadow and raining down on it exhaust fumes and nonstop noise. Red Hook's status as a busy port for unionized white ethnic laborers rapidly declined in the 1960s. The advent of containerization in international shipping eliminated the need for so many hands to unload cargo. The opening of a larger and better-connected port in Newark, New Jersey, was the coup de grâce to the industry in New York. The publicly subsidized Red Hook Houses, originally built in the late 1930s for dockworkers, had by the 1970s gained a reputation as a notoriously violent African American and Latinx housing project. Its cluster of over thirty buildings, with nearly ten thousand residents, is the largest concentration of public housing in the borough. When the city embarked in 1975 on a $378 million sewage treatment project in Red Hook, it seemed to many residents like adding insult to injury.[6] The city seized houses and businesses along Columbia Street, tore them down to dig a sewage interceptor canal, then paused work when buildings started to collapse because their foundations had been weakened by the dredging years earlier of the Brooklyn-Battery Tunnel. Then the murder of the beloved elementary school principal Patrick Daly in 1992 traumatized the neighborhood all over again. Daly was caught in crossfire at the Red Hook Houses, where he'd gone to search for a nine-year-old who'd left school after a fight. When Superstorm Sandy hit in 2012, it drowned Red Hook in several feet of water and muck. Even despite the influx of wealthier residents in recent years, Red Hook remains poor: in 2014, 49 percent of its households earned less than $25,000 a year, classifying them as "extremely low income."[7]

For a small neighborhood, Red Hook has generated a surprisingly substantial body of literary and filmic discourse. This has included H. P. Lovecraft's "The Horror at Red Hook" (1925), Elia Kazan's *On the Waterfront* (1954), Arthur Miller's *A View from the Bridge* (1955), Hugh Selby's *Last Exit to Brooklyn* (1964), and Matty Rich's *Straight Out of Brooklyn* (1991). The horror at the heart of Lovecraft's anti-immigrant screed, published at the height of 1920s xenophobic nativism, is racial and ethnic mixing. Its protagonist, the New York police detective Thomas F. Malone, tracks down a human smuggler in the neighborhood, which is histrionically characterized as a "polyglot abyss," a "nest . . . of disorder and violence," and where "Syrian, Spanish, Italian, and negro elements," plus "unclassified Asian dregs," live cheek by jowl.[8] In Lovecraft's imagination, Red Hook is less terra firma than a kind of fluid area associated with rootlessness, nomadism, and the noxious mixing of people from different cultures and nations, something liminal, uncategorizable, and polluted.

Arthur Miller's opening image of Red Hook in *A View from the Bridge* is of a "slum that faces the bay on the seaward side of Brooklyn Bridge." But what soon emerges into view is a tight-knit, if fractious, community of immigrant and first-generation longshoremen who are heroic and tragic, driven by loyalty and led astray by jealousies. In Miller's depiction, Red Hook leaves a firm imprint upon its inhabitants. Explaining the frustration and rage of his protagonist Eddie Carbone, Miller declares that he "is not comprehensible apart from [his] relation to his neighborhood."[9] Miller's Red Hook is both a vibrant ethnic community and a toxic stew of incestual desire and class resentment. Carbone leers at his wife's eighteen-year-old niece, who is pursued by an undocumented Italian who Carbone suspects is gay. When Carbone reports him to immigration services, he violates the insular neighborhood's code to enact its own brand of justice, setting up what will be his downfall: a knife in the gut. Published during Red Hook's white, working-class heyday, Miller's play prefigures its decline in Carbone's death.

The part of "the slum that faces the bay" in Miller's work alludes to what is locally known as the neighborhood's "back," its more desirable real estate and the part increasingly gentrified by century's end. "The front," in contrast, refers to the impoverished terrain of the high-rise Red Hook Houses and a wasteland of repair shops and gas stations abutting the expressway. Whereas "the back" is the territory of Lovecraft, Kazan, and Miller, "the front" belongs to the Black film director Matty Rich. Released in 1991, just after New York City's homicides peaked at 2,245 in a single year, Rich's gritty *Straight Out of Brooklyn* reflects public panic over urban crime in Red Hook's subsidized housing. When the authors of *Red Hook: A Plan for Community Regeneration* remarked that the neighborhood "evokes images of danger and isolation," they cited Rich's film as evidence. Taking place in the Houses, *Straight Out of Brooklyn* centers on the teenager Dennis Brown, who wants to flee with money he plans on obtaining by robbing a drug dealer with a borrowed shotgun, a plan that ends tragically. The film leaves viewers with the impression that no one gets out alive.

Collectively this body of literary and filmic discourse represents Red Hook, at its best, as an isolated, closely knit community that polices itself and, at its worst, as a variegated anticommunity, a hybrid mélange overrun with lawlessness. Taken together, it attests to the cultural anxiety Red Hook has consistently provoked in the urban imagination. This anxiety is also implicit in the recent proliferation of urban planning literature on the neighborhood that testifies to Red Hook's unsettled status. Since the crime decline of the mid-1990s, the area has been at the center of no less than four major revitalization and renewal initiatives to gentrify the neighborhood, including the aforementioned *Red Hook: A Plan for Community Regeneration*, *The New Waterfront Revitalization Program* (2002), *Vision 2020: New York Comprehensive Waterfront Plan* (2011), and *Red Hook: NY Rising Community Reconstruction Plan* (2014).[10] In this urban planning literature, Red Hook is always already a work in progress, a neighborhood as fluid as the water around it.

James Throgmorton argues that urban planners are storytellers who write narratives about the urban future. The "stories" they tell through their otherwise technocratic and data-driven reports "guide readers' sense of what is possible and desirable."[11] The latest of the reports on Red Hook, *NY Rising*, crafts a narrative of the neighborhood's transformation as inevitable. "Red Hook is a changing Community," the authors note, before reaffirming a few pages later that "Red Hook is a rapidly evolving neighborhood," and then once more for good measure, "Red Hook is in a time of transition."[12] Left unsaid in this passive phrasing are the underlying socioeconomic and ecological forces that bring about the change that urban planners, we are led to believe, merely struggle to keep up with, rather than actively hasten. Left uncritiqued, too, is "the teleology of waterfront 'development' as 'progress,' the belief that proposed redevelopments are technologically, socially, environmentally, and economically better than what came before." The language and narrative deployed in the four initiatives evoke a vision of a new waterfront that "distances itself from and places itself in opposition to an obsolete and contaminated industrial landscape." In these reports, Red Hook's historical status as a blue-collar shipping port is not denied but rather is relegated to the background, nearly invisible apart from a few photographs of outmoded cranes mixed in with images of sparkling cruise ships and new cafés.[13] The dirty word "gentrification" is also missing from the latest plan's 194 pages but haunts it like a specter. Or maybe it is so obvious that all the references to "change," a community "rising," and a neighborhood being "reconstructed" are euphemisms for "gentrification" that the word need not be uttered. One of the common narratives of urban planning, Throgmorton asserts, is the one that "constructs *the city as a site of opportunity and excitement*, a center for artists and other creative people," a claim borne out by the redevelopment documents. What the plans imagine—and help bring into being—is a future postindustrial Red Hook as a vibrant community of artists, a place of "park and outdoor recreational amenities," a place with water tours for visitors, and a place that memorializes New York's sinking maritime industry in a small museum housed on a wooden boat.[14]

Red Hook's transformation into a place for recreation, artisanal manufacturing, and upscale housing is part of the restructuring of work and life in the city away from heavy industry and toward services and white-collar work. Much of the credit for this change in Red Hook would seem to go to one person: not Bloomberg, but Greg O'Connell, an ex–drug cop turned developer who bought his first building in Red Hook in 1982 and now owns twenty five of them. Over the years, he assembled the largest real estate portfolio in the neighborhood, estimated at $400 million, much of it bought for pennies on the dollar as *in rem* buildings from the state.[15] Red Hook's Fairway grocery store, housed in a block-long nineteenth-century red brick warehouse for storing cotton, is there because of O'Connell. Many of Red Hook's small businesses, including "a hat manufacturer, medical supplies distributor, glass blowers, carpentry shops, [and] an apple processor," are his tenants. Etsy, the online company through which indie craftspeople sell art and jewelry, leases nine thousand square feet of space from him. O'Connell's Red Hook is a veritable postindustrial hodgepodge of boutique and just-in-time manufacturing. As O'Connell has said in interviews, being a detective in SoHo when it started to gentrify gave him a street-level view of what to look for twenty or thirty years down the road, a postindustrial future in the making: "I saw [Red Hook] as an opportunity, a challenge."[16]

Even for all of his outsize presence in Red Hook, O'Connell is, like Bloomberg, a conduit for the impersonal forces of postindustrial restructuring that in the early 2000s created a neighborhood in a state of "transition" with jarring juxtapositions. A neighborhood where rotting piers have been rehabilitated to accommodate luxury cruise liners. Where converted warehouses are home to tech startups. Where a massive housing project looks out onto the blue whale of a 346,000-square-foot IKEA with acres of parking on what was a Civil War–era graving dock (a type of dry dock). As we will see, Cohen, Nadelson, and Pochoda offer a violently contested story of the neighborhood in which its industrial past is not easily forgotten and its postindustrial future is not entirely assured.

THE DEATH OF BLUE-COLLAR LABOR IN GABRIEL COHEN

In the opening of Gabriel Cohen's *Red Hook*, Jack Leightner, a detective on Brooklyn's South Homicide Task Force, kneels in the grass inspecting the blood-soaked body of a mid-twenties Latino. Tied up with rusted wire and rope and cinderblocked around the ankles with a chain, the body has been dumped in a hurry "in a scrub of sun-dry marsh grass" on the banks of the Gowanus Canal, the polluted artery and Superfund site that originates at the waterfront and snakes a mile and a half inland to the neighborhoods of Gowanus and Carroll Gardens (6). Close by in the background, just behind "a fence which marked the rear boundary," Jack catches sight of "abandoned delivery trucks and a rusted black crane" curling downward on the verge of collapse, his eyes lingering, as if he is making a mental note (7). These seemingly minor details—the murky canal, the crane, and the empty delivery trucks—will turn out to be consequential as the industrial backdrop moves front and center in the novel, supplanting in importance even the dead body that has drawn Jack to the neighborhood. Once home to the busiest commercial waterway in the United States, this patch of Brooklyn in Cohen's novel is cut off, fenced in, and abandoned. The flow of raw materials, commodities, capital, and labor between sea and land along the canal is all but stagnant, and the thriving maritime industrial economy that used to define the area is nothing more than a rusted shell of its former self.

Red Hook launches the Jack Leightner series and Cohen's larger project to map across several books the history of Red Hook's industrial decline and its current postindustrial revival. It is also where he crafts the backstory for his recurring character, a fifty-year-old Jewish detective and divorced father with a drinking problem. The son of a stevedore, Jack hails from Red Hook and came of age when the port was already on the wane but when the stories of it as a home to a thriving working-class, white-ethnic community were still vivid. As soon as he was old enough, Jack fled the neighborhood, first joining the navy, then the NYPD, eventually settling into the staid middle-class Brooklyn area of Midwood. As it quickly becomes apparent, however, he cannot stop thinking about the old neighborhood no matter how much he tries and no matter how much he avoids crossing through the shadows of the Gowanus Expressway to the place he grew up. *Red Hook* is a narrative about a neighborhood one never fully shakes off even after fleeing, a place where fresh crimes exhume old memories.

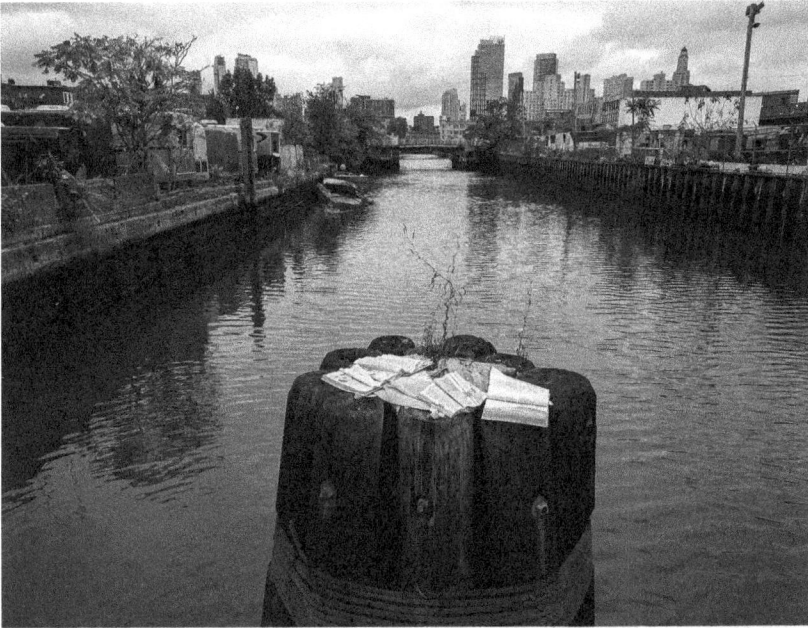

FIGURE 3.2. The Gowanus Canal, Brooklyn, New York. *Source:* Anahita Rouzbeh, CC BY-SA 4.0 (https://creativecommons.org/licenses/by-sa/4.0), via Wikimedia Commons.

In Cohen's novel, the violence of gentrification reawakens old wounds. A seasoned detective, Jack is no stranger to scenes of violence, but Cohen hints that something about this particular murder along the canal haunts him deeply. Turning over the body, he discovers an "ugly slit of a stab wound" in the abdomen and immediately "stagger[s] a few feet away" to "heave up his guts" (11, 12). What we see here is the corpse reanimating an earlier trauma, sending Jack into near fainting spells of nausea. His strong visceral reaction is not to the sight of viscera per se. What turns him inside out is the resurfacing of a familial and social history best left for dead. The NYPD soon identify the victim as Tomas Berrios, who lived nearby on a street tellingly characterized as "halfway between working class and gentrified" and who worked as a porter in the Bentley, a luxurious Manhattan apartment building (37). Eventually, Cohen reveals that Tomas's path crossed—in what will prove to have been a fatal class and ethnic collision— with Randall Heiser, the head of a sprawling real estate holding company.

"It's no accident that the villain . . . is a real estate developer," Cohen has said, who has spoken about how developers "have often ended up homogenizing and blighting already-thriving working- or middle-class neighborhoods."[17] He explicitly likens Heiser to Robert Moses, New York's legendary midcentury master builder whose massive urban renewal and highway construction projects displaced a quarter of a million New Yorkers from their homes.[18] Given Moses's long-standing association with razing poor and working-class neighborhoods to construct highways, naming Heiser's residence after an automobile for the global elite also seems more than coincidental. In fact, the comparison of Heiser with Moses, made near the end of the novel, is not only a key to apprehending the mysteries within Cohen's text but is also more broadly indicative of the reorientation of the genre of crime fiction around contemporary crises of urban real estate development and cultural upheaval.

All roads lead back to Red Hook and all roads dead end in the past in Cohen's book. "I used to live there" (96), Jack reveals to his new NYPD partner Gary Daskivitch as they roll into Red Hook, where "the streets flurried with ghosts" (95). Daskivitch's response, "You're shitting me, right," speaks to his astonishment that anyone was able to get out (96). In this 2001 book, the area is at an inflexion point: it is beginning to gentrify, but its reputation for poverty, drugs, and gang violence lingers. "It used to be different," Jack says, which comes to mean it used to be better (96). "Fifty years ago, the Houses were filled with dockworkers," Jack explains. "We had Italians, Irish, Poles. And Russians, like my old man" (96).

A prominent strain of American city literature is cast in nostalgic hues, narratives bathed in sentimental colors for the days of an imagined past. Cohen's novel is occasionally saturated with these sepia tones, such as when it romanticizes the Red Hook of the 1950s and early 1960s as a harmonious place, an organic community where residents knew one another by name and where boys—like Jack's beloved late brother Pete—were local legends for their baseball skills. While Gary and Jack drive through the neighborhood looking around with "sorrow and disgust" (97) at the "no-man's land" (98), a jumble of flashbacks light up Jack's mind: doo-wop songs from the Crystals, swimming in his underwear with a teenage crush, a neighborhood kid who could "hit a Spaldeen fourteen stories up" (96). "Jesus, life had been simple," he thinks (97). "Back then . . . there was none of this garbage along the streets. The grass in those courtyards was *green*—you could get a five-dollar ticket just for walking on it," he says (96). This language of low-level urban disorder and citations is the language of quality-of-life policing. Jack insinuates that more of it is needed to bring the neighborhood back in line and return it to its former status as his white, working-class Eden. The grass is always greener on the other side of time's fence.

Most nostalgic fictions are fictions not of remembrance but of denial and displacement, principally the denial of the historical and social complexity of the past, which is obscured and displaced by contemporary racial resentment. That's the lesson here. The Red Hook of Jack's childhood is diverse, but its diversity exists within the bounds of white ethnicity ("Italians, Irish, Poles. And Russians"), whose geographical and racial borders were tightly patrolled in his youth (96). The white, working-class world of his Red Hook is indeed very much a shadow of its past. But rather than understanding its disappearance as a consequence of large-scale socioeconomic transformations that have chewed up the community, it is blamed in Jack's mind on African Americans who, like everyone else in Red Hook, are caught up in the same set of forces. For Jack, their presence in the area represents a temporal rupture that retroactively unifies the former neighborhood ("life had been simpler") by paving over its internal differences while simultaneously explaining its decline.

Ask someone to pinpoint the date when the decline started, and what they say will tell you almost everything. Jack pinpoints the beginning of the end of this idyllic period of white working-class sovereignty and clearly delineated racial hierarchies to a day in 1965 when his brother was stabbed in a racially charged altercation. As he reveals near the conclusion in a drawn-out confession at an Alcoholics Anonymous meeting, he and his brother had discovered a case of liquor stolen from the shipyard and when two African American teenagers approached to reclaim it, he let fly a series of racist taunts—"Fuck you, nigger," and again, "Fuck you and your nigger friend"— escalating the fight that ends with Pete's murder (266). Jack confesses he felt emboldened because he spotted a patrol car a block away, assuming the police would protect him simply based on his skin color. The cops, unaware of the fracas, pull into a local diner. In recalling this memory, Jack insists he was not being racist, just being a hotheaded fifteen-year-old: "It wasn't like I had anything against black people. I mean, I used to run with black guys from the projects. . . . I just wanted to piss them off" (266). Yet one cannot help sense that the original sin that spelled the end of Jack's working-class paradise actually has everything to do with racism, his denials notwithstanding. In Jack's rationalization, it was the initial appearance of the wrong bodies in the wrong place—Black kids in a white space—that somehow justified his slurs. "We could have handed [the liquor] over and probably that would have ended it. But I knew they weren't from the neighborhood," he says (265). All of this unfolds at the height of the Civil Rights movement and the changing racial composition of Red Hook once the port largely shut down, a historical context that Cohen's protagonist does not want to fully own. The novel gestures to this context through the historical date of 1965 and then leaves it uninterrogated.

In *The Ninth Step* (2010), Cohen returns to this murder scene, fleshing it out with additional detail and a wider angle that appears to be an effort by Jack to further downplay, even deny, the racial struggle that clearly animates it, while again leaving unaddressed the structural issues undergirding the confrontation. The reader learns in *The Ninth Step* that the local mob had paid the two teenagers to threaten, but not harm, Jack and his brother. By doing so, the mob intended to strongarm Jack's Russian-speaking father into continuing to work for them as a translator so they could partner with Russian mobsters in Philadelphia. But the revelation does nothing to exonerate Jack for his actions, because the circumstances behind the two Black teenagers' appearance in Red Hook were unknown to him at the time. Once again, he rationalizes his brother's death was because he "had said something stupid in an offhand moment."[19] The emotional heart of Cohen's work through four books of the series continues to be this scene of admission and denial during the supercharged racial tensions of the mid-1960s, which were exacerbated by the neighborhood's industrial decline and, importantly, resuscitated by its gentrification in the late 1990s and early 2000s.

The revelation of Jack's feelings of culpability for his brother's stabbing in a confrontation over race, stolen goods, and public space is yanked out of him over hundreds of pages as he works to solve Tomas's murder and as Cohen works to narrativize Red Hook's death and rebirth. The clues to these deaths are seen in Jack's visceral reaction to the "stab wound" at the book's beginning (11). The historical traumas of the urban neighborhood have a double temporality in Cohen's novel. Violence in the present reawakens an original and still unhealed wound: the stabbing of Tomas recalling the stabbing of Pete, whose death symbolizes the beginning of the end of Jack's working-class waterfront. Jack feels this before he knows it, the loss of Red

Hook decades later resurfacing from the "opaque depths" as bodily affect, resurfacing from the detective's own depths as vomit (6). Cohen's narrative thus links personal memory to the history of urban transformation in a way that makes it not an abstraction but a painfully real experience. Yet one suspects that more than the stab wound sends Jack staggering. He sees something else but wishes he did not. Towering in the background over the exposed corpse, dumped like a bag of trash, is the clue in plain sight: the rusted crane on the verge of collapse, a haunting reminder of a form of urban modernity that has now passed, a trace of a past now gone. At its heart, Cohen's narrative mobilizes an investigation into the relationship between social geography and crime, or as Dennis Porter has stated about the genre more broadly, an investigation into the "relationship . . . between site and event."[20] By the novel's conclusion, Jack's investigation will tie Tomas's murder to a secret plan by Heiser to make the rebounding neighborhood into a dumping ground, a place synonymous with urban blight once more.

The narrative structure of *Red Hook* exemplifies what the crime scholar John Scaggs categorizes as a "split narrative." In such narratives, he posits, "events that have led to the current crisis are embedded within" another "narrative of investigation and deduction" that often leads back in time.[21] Porter, for his part, observes that crime fiction is "committed to an act of recovery, moving forward in order to move back," returning to the past to locate an originary point that will explain, and perhaps heal, the traumas of the present. This structure accounts for the genre's "ideological motivation to recover, or return to, a previous period characterised by stability and order."[22] In a moment of metacommentary, Cohen in his later novel *The Graving Dock* (2007) writes that the detective narrative is a reconstructive one: "The essence of the job was to go back in time, to project yourself through the still eye of the storm, and to come out into another whirl of activity, the one that had put the body there in the first place."[23] In its forward and backward movements, *Red Hook* dramatizes this process of investigation. The narrative of the murder is embedded within a narrative of Red Hook's decades-long transition from one mode of production to another. As we have seen, Jack's own narrative of the latter is false, pinning as it does Red Hook's decline to his tragically hotheaded reaction and to the presence of Black teenagers in a white working-class enclave. The deconstruction of this false narrative can be performed by the reader who refuses to take Jack's account of the past at face value and reads past it for clues to another explanation of decline—the polluted industrial canal, the delivery trucks, the crane—lurking in the background.

However, the undoing of Jack's false reading of urban history is also performed in the text itself by way of the Italian-American character Larry Cosenza, a "local historian, philosopher, and community activist," and perhaps most tellingly, funeral director who mourns for a dying neighborhood (224). Larry stands for the white ethnic who held on and fought for his neighborhood through its long downturn, the one who struggled for an alternative future for Red Hook while acknowledging its difficult past. "In the 1960s, when hundreds of middle-class families were fleeing South Brooklyn for the suburbs," Larry "organized to keep his neighborhood intact" (224). He contrasts with Jack, the white ethnic who left the neighborhood and became a cop who wants to give the neighborhood a clean sweep. Jack goes to Larry for insight into the murder investigation but ends up learning another way of historicizing Red Hook's current crisis. One of the roles Cohen assigns him is educator. He teaches Jack about the roots of contemporary urban problems such as poverty, drug addiction, and gun violence in this patch of Brooklyn.

Red Hook was built on the exploitation of working-class immigrant labor, and its decline began when that labor, no longer as useful or as efficient as it once was, was summarily discarded—that's the hard lesson his friend impresses upon Jack, but Jack does not fully absorb it at first. As the two men motor through Red Hook in a second driving scene, the novel stages a debate over urban history. Jack comments that this "place is a mess" (225), noting the visible signs of disorder but not the structural causes under them. Larry argues for a longer view. "Maybe—but you can understand how it happened" (225). Jack does not, or at least not really. He responds, "Yeah, a lot of people discovered that it's easier to sell drugs than to do a real day's work. . . . If people want work, they can find work. Look at my old man" (225). Larry replies in frustration, "Work? What work? There are no jobs. . . . Your father and my father came to this country because the government let a certain number of foreigners in to do the shit work—dig the ditches, build the railroads, unload the ships. Now most of those jobs are gone" (225). The white, working-class stevedores lionized by Elia Kazan and Arthur Miller who unloaded breakbulk cargo on the docks "are gone" with the shift to containerization and automation in Cohen's novel. "How could he fight something as abstract as technology," Jack muses about his father later in *The Graving Dock*.[24] In *Red Hook*, however, he is slower to accept such explanations, even though such explanations themselves betray a kind of technological fetishism that fails to interrogate the class power behind the design and implementation of a technology that destroyed Red Hook's working class. Larry challenges him, "It's not a mystery how the neighborhood ended up this way" (226). "Everyone acts as if the poor were just dropped here by God. . . . As if it's just a fact of life. We don't look at the history," he argues (225). This is the essential sentence in the novel, the one that in denaturalizing poverty unlocks a door that opens onto a wider set of concerns. One death, who killed Tomas, has been replaced by another, who killed Red Hook. The answer to "mystery" is "history" in Cohen's book.

The radical potential of Larry's class critique is quickly redirected by the text and absorbed within a neoliberal ethos. The private market—backed by institutions of law, the police most pointedly—is what will save the neighborhood, suggests the activist Larry, revealing himself to be all too bourgeois. We see as much during the drive when the conversation shifts from Red Hook's decades-long decline to the incipient signs of its revival. Jack asks, "What's been going on around here, real-estatewise?" (227). Larry excitedly responds that "the neighborhood's been on the upswing. . . . We get more patrol cars on the streets these days. Some artists and yuppies have been moving in, buying up old houses" (227). He approvingly points out that the "old piers" are being converted into "artists' studios [and] homes for small businesses" (227). In short, the neighborhood exhibits the typical signifiers of a waterfront renaissance: urban pioneers, repurposed industrial spaces, artist- and artisan-led production, and a stepped-up police presence to protect new, wealthier arrivals. For both men that's a good sign. Commenting on Red Hook as envisioned by Heiser's development plan, Larry ponders, "How many people are gonna want to buy a house here if you've got hundreds of stinky garbage trucks barreling through the streets" (228). "This could be the last nail in the coffin," Larry, a funeral director, adds (228).

In academic discourse, gentrification is frequently portrayed as a mixed bag at best, if not as an entirely deleterious force acting on racial, ethnic, and working-class areas, one that drives up housing prices, displaces long-time residents, and homogenizes the culture of neighborhoods. But in Cohen's text it is the forces working against gentrification that are villainized, a point that cannot be overstated. These forces are embodied in the figure of Heiser, who is trying to impose his will on Red Hook. Heiser does not plan to build more yuppie condos and cafés. He plans to erect a grimy station for hauling garbage into and out of the neighborhood. In the dramatic final pages of the novel, the answer to who killed Tomas and who might kill Red Hook just as it is coming back to life in its post-working-class iteration ends up being one and the same. Having lured Jack alone to a warehouse in the neighborhood, Heiser and his henchmen are about to kill the detective—but not before confessing the whole backstory, a moment of expositional excess that is a trademark of the genre. The reader quickly learns that the developer had Tomas murdered after the porter stole from his apartment the blueprints for the waste station. With the stolen plans, he had attempted to extort Heiser for fifty thousand dollars, a pittance to the real estate tycoon but enough money for the porter to buy a bigger apartment for his family. "Things were going to get better for us," Tomas's late wife reveals (94). It thus turns out that Tomas is not a working-class immigrant who is out for social justice by thwarting Heiser. Far from it. He wants to leverage his insider knowledge of Heiser's scheme for a chance at the alluring bourgeois fantasy of a better life—the fantasy that everyone in the novel wants—as it is materialized in homeownership. Houses and their meanings are never far from the novel's concerns.

Red Hook's narrative drifts back in time as a way of moving forward. But it also moves in circles in a manner that suggests that certain urban issues are less resolvable than they are merely repeatable, returning again and again. By the end, we see that Cohen has created a symbolic circuit that ties the novel's past and present storylines in a loop. In doing so, the text creates uncomfortable resonances between its hero and villain, Leightner and Heiser, that it never addresses but that I think are worth interrogating. The two men, literally opposed to each other, have more in common than one would think. We see this is the case when we recognize that the poor disposal of Tomas's body, whom Heiser calls a "greasy little wetback," leads to a story about waste disposal and environmental racism and then leads back to Jack's racial slur, "Fuck you, nigger" (287). I hear these two slurs echoing each other across the pages. What also echo are two scenes of racial trespass. Cohen implies that what sparks Heiser's plot to murder Tomas is not only extortion but—like the original Red Hook "crime" for Jack—the violation of white space. As Heiser reveals in the climatic warehouse scene, one day he arrived home unexpectedly to find the lowly porter in his apartment watching television with the maid he was flirting with. "He had no right to enter my home. To go into my *den*," Heiser seethes (287). The wrong body in the wrong place again. In Cohen's text, Red Hook is not so much experiencing a revival, as it seems to be at first glance, but is cyclically and compulsively reliving its history of racial and class violence all over again.

In the final seconds before Jack himself is almost killed, one of Heiser's bodyguards, who is, unbeknownst to Jack, an undercover FBI agent, rescues him. After Heiser is arrested, Cohen reveals that the FBI had been conducting "a much broader investigation into racketeering in the national real estate and development markets," suggesting that Red Hook's crisis, notwithstanding its geographical and historical specificities, is part of a larger pattern of real estate speculation (292). What becomes apparent in Cohen's novel is that the state, as represented by local and federal law enforcement, plays a vital role as an enabler of capitalist development. It does so by making undervalued neighborhoods safe for initial investment through crime reduction ("more patrol cars on the streets") but also by protecting those areas from future predatory capitalists, like Heiser, in the marketplace. It polices capitalism from its worst excesses, helping secure a way of life that is important for well-functioning neighborhoods, home ownership, ethnic assimilation, and citizenship: "You weren't really an American until you had money—you were still just a Dominican or a Puerto Rican or a Pole," says Tomas in the novel's prologue, some of the few words he utters before he turns up dead (5). Cohen's blue-collar detective and capitalist villain are opposed to each other as individuals, but as figures representing their respective social positions, it turns out they really are not. This is the novel's profound structural irony. Jack does the bidding of Heiser's class, if not of Heiser himself.

In this novel of historical echoes, Heiser is, as noted, a latter-day Robert Moses. With this observation I wish to end our consideration of *Red Hook*, bringing as it does Cohen's text full circle once more. Historically, the American narrative of immigration, assimilation, and acculturation entailed leaving the neighborhood of one's first arrival for greener pastures. Moving on up meant moving on out, which in New York often meant traveling on Moses's freeways out to the suburbs, the midcentury exodus that Larry Cosenza laments. When he asked earlier who is going to "buy a house here," the dream of homeownership and upward mobility echoes back to Jack's own tragic family history. Cohen divulges that Jack's parents' newly purchased house in Red Hook was destroyed by none other than Moses, who, in his unbending commitment to building highways and armed with the power of eminent domain to make it happen, left Jack's parents stranded, distressed, disoriented, and suffering from an enormous loss of capital. Moses's massive "highway ripped the heart out of Red Hook," destroying "a boulevard of little mom-and-pop stores, of newsstands, and family restaurants," Cohen writes (46). Jack's father, who had saved up to buy the house, was emotionally devastated. A divide that never healed as wide as the highway opened up between the father and the son. Moses "smashed right through the dream" (97). "He was always kind of hard," Jack's mother explains, "But he turned *mean* after Robert Moses tore down our home" (47). Added to the list of Jack's familial dysfunctions is Jack's estrangement from his own son, a budding documentary filmmaker who in one of the novel's minor storylines wants to make a movie about "the history of Red Hook" but soon realizes "that he was searching for his father's history" (238). As threats to Red Hook's current gentrification are exposed, the traumas of the neighborhood's earlier decline and destruction resurface in this other way, a legacy rippling through generations.

The opening pages of Cohen's follow-up *The Graving Dock* are set on a pier in Red Hook, with the Statue of Liberty looming in the background, along with the empty space in the skyline where the World Trade Center once stood. Taking place in December 2001, on the eve of Bloomberg's inauguration, the novel's Red Hook is still "a humble neighborhood of warehouses and machine shops."[25] "The shipping industry had drifted away from Brooklyn," writes Cohen, but there are signs of redevelopment blooming here and there, signs of what the mayor would claim is "new life." But something else drifts toward Jack's old neighborhood that will call him back again. On a "cold, blustery" day, a small, homemade coffin washes up, bringing death to Red Hook yet again.[26] The case of Red Hook continues.

MAKING A KILLING WITH REGGIE NADELSON

Three years after Bloomberg proposed a redeveloped New York City waterfront teeming with "new life," Reggie Nadelson opened her latest installment in her Artie Cohen series with the image of a murdered home-less man, his head bashed in, his Black body "spreadeagled, legs drifting in the water" under a rotting pier in Red Hook (5). His body is so tangled and trapped that the police resort to sawing off his limbs to free him, placing each one in a different body bag. This is a gruesome beginning to a crime novel of the low-crime era. "Our crime rate continues to fall," Bloomberg had intoned in 2002.[27] The NYPD detective Artie Cohen remarks in Nadelson's 2005 novel, "There's not much crime around here anymore" (14). Yet Nadelson's *Red Hook*, with its two murders, one suspicious sui-cide, and Russian mafia dealings, which the novel never brings into the light, has enough crime to sustain its 330 pages and to keep Artie busy. As we will see, Nadelson's Red Hook is soaked in blood but also in memories of the old neighborhood, whose recent gentrification gives rise to attempts to claim the story of its past at any cost.

Nadelson ties all crime in the novel to real estate development in the neighborhood. Whereas Detective Jack Leightner was compelled to ask, "What's been going on around here, real estatewise," for Nadelson's detec-tive the answer is obvious. In her novel, the New York waterfront is now in the midst of a full-blown revival: "People were coming back; all over the city, people were buying into the waterfront, the last big land grab. . . . You could see Red Hook was changing: fancy little signs that hung out front of warehouses proclaimed that artists and film people had moved in" (77). "We're getting a supermarket," says Sid, undoubtedly a reference to the upmarket Fairway in the converted cotton warehouse on Van Brunt Street (29). Red Hook is a "pot of gold" in the text (96). "Lots of real-estate. Lots of money," Nadelson writes (26). As the character Tolya puts it, his hands gesturing wide over "the Red Hook waterfront": "Imagine new buildings, imagine marinas and boats, imagine a brand new city" (96, 97). Tolya, who has his fingers in every real estate pot and plot in the city and who "wants to buy and make houses for rich people," proposes a boosterish narrative that could have been lifted from a politician's speech (162). Yet what Nadel-son offers is nothing so cheery. Hers is a narrative of real estate speculation as class conflict and a kind of capital-induced fever. Urban development drives people to violence in her novel, and all the new housing apparently still leaves poor people homeless and dead. "We're killing each other for a place to live," remarks a security guard protecting Tolya's neighborhood properties (131).

The parallels and overlaps between Cohen's *Red Hook* and Nadelson's *Red Hook* on the face of it are many. The two crime novels published four years apart share the same title, cover the same terrain, and follow recondite plotlines that link real estate and violence. But the books diverge in significant ways, viewing as they do the old neighborhood from opposing racial perspectives. While Detective Cohen leads the investigation into the Red Hook murders, the novel really belongs to the African American character, Sid McKay. He is obsessed with Red Hook's white, working-class past, whose racial borders the young Jack Leightner once tried to patrol to keep out African American teenagers like Sid. Whereas Jack was trying to forget Red Hook's painful history, Sid is desperately trying to recall and write about it. As Red Hook gentrifies all around Sid, he pens a book about its fast-disappearing midcentury industrial period. Research for the book sends him on an obsessive and murderous quest to recover its past.

Since the crimes in Nadelson's Red Hook only make sense in the context of its history, we have to dive for a few moments into the book's murky backstory. The murdered African American man, Earl, found floating early in the text was killed by his half-brother Sid, who brained him with a baseball bat. Driving home that this is a novel about nostalgia for the old neighborhood, Nadelson mordantly notes that the bat bore the logo of Sid's beloved Dodgers championship in 1955, two years before the team departed for Los Angeles, leaving behind a generation of inconsolable Brooklynites. A retired writer and editor, Sid spends his golden years in his waterfront studio trying to draft a book about the neighborhood he knew but was "forbidden" from really knowing as "a little black kid" who would draw queer looks from the locals (70). Nadelson's Red Hook, like Cohen's, is a largely extinct world of white, working-class masculinity, except in Sid's case he was on the outside peering in. The reader learns through Nadelson's exposition that Sid hails from a wealthy African American family in Brooklyn's Bedford-Stuyvesant neighborhood, and as a teenager he would bicycle with Earl to Red Hook, violating the orders of his father, "a proud Negro man" (69). Sid's transgression into the forbidden world of the waterfront was fueled by his voyeuristic fascination with the supposed vitality of the white ethnic life he found there, an implied contrast to the cultured society of his Black father. The pivotal moment in the backstory occurs in 1953, when a Soviet freighter ran aground and, as Sid looked on in wonder, Russian sailors jumped ship and vanished in Brooklyn. Sid befriended one of them,

Meler, who eventually fell off Sid's radar as he integrated himself into a new life in Brooklyn. "I spent years looking for him . . . I was obsessed," Sid admits, a pursuit that "connects me with everything in my life" (72). His fascination with the neighborhood, his profession as a reporter, his desire to write a book about Red Hook, all stem from it.

In the novel, tracking down Meler amounts to tracking down Red Hook's history, a history that will be subsequently converted into "information," a key term in the novel and one that I will argue is freighted with socioeconomic significance. Fifty years later, when Sid finally finds Meler, he relentlessly pesters him for the firsthand details that will bring midcentury Red Hook back alive. As Meler recounts in a broken-English paraphrase, Sid demands, "Tell me about smells, sights, sounds, name ships you noticed" (324). "He says is all there is, history," remarks Meler (324). Meler begs him, "Don't write, please, don't, leave history alone. Nothing comes from history except shit" (324). The undocumented Russian wants nothing more than to be left alone, fearing Sid's book will expose him and lead to his deportation to Putin's Russia, likely a death sentence. When Earl intervenes on Meler's behalf, Sid ends up whacking Earl with the bat, and Meler, in turn, takes revenge. Sid soon ends up floating in Red Hook's waters. All of this intrigue and action happens offstage (an important point that I will return to) and remains opaque until cleared up at the last minute. As Meler and Artie are on a boat in New York Harbor, tossing about in a storm, Meler reveals the whole backstory and confesses to the murder. Then he jumps ship for the second time, not for a new life but presumably to die in the choppy surf, "disappear[ing] with his history" and, in effect, taking Sid's history of Red Hook with him to a watery grave (329). In Nadelson's novel, people are "killing each other for a place to live" in early twenty-first-century Red Hook. But they are dying over its midcentury past too, which is enough to send them into murderous rage and suicidal despair.

In Nadelson's novel, the dramas of crime are a way of gathering together the manifold problems confronting Red Hook. At the start, the pressing question of who killed Earl expands into the question of who killed Sid. Yet by the end of the novel, both questions effectively expand into: Why are people killing one another over this neighborhood? The background is the foreground: the characters move through Red Hook, but Red Hook, richly described and historicized, is the main character. Like Larry Cosenza in Cohen's novel, Sid is "the historian, the philosopher, the poet of Red Hook," who is trying to keep its past alive but who is also acutely attuned to what is happening in the area in the present day (9). When Artie interviews Sid, all he wants to talk about is the community, not the murder. Artie tries to cut him off in the middle of his digressive monologue, but Sid responds, "Can you spare me half an hour more," as he wanders farther down memory lane (23). In trying to hurry Sid to the point at hand (who killed Earl), he misses that the whole point of the conversation—and one might even say, the whole point of the novel—is not to talk about crime but to talk about the neighborhood. As is often the case in crime fiction, the digressions lead to the center.

Nadelson mobilizes Sid's monologue as a vehicle for recreating Red Hook's industrial past on the page, which the novel ends up comparing to its postindustrial present and future in unexpected ways. As Sid gazes out over the waterfront, he waxes poetic about Red Hook's "docks loaded with tea, cashews, mahogany, lumber, sugar, grain," its "warehouses bursting" at the seams, and its streets bustling with "men from Italy, Ireland, Syria, Sweden, Russia, working these ports," a vibrant mix of mostly white, blue-collar immigrants (26). "I feel I can smell it when I'm out here, and I can hear them. . . . Can you imagine it, Artie? It was still here, some of it, when I was a boy," he says (26). Sid fetishizes manly Whitmanesque labor so much that he can almost smell the sweat. "There were rackets here, and gangsters, longshoremen who were really tough, but I loved it," he reminisces, reveling further in the romanticized world of white ethnic organized crime and organized labor (26). Yet now when Sid looks out at its "old docks and shipyards, the warehouses and factories, the inlets and canals," what he says he sees is "a whole square mile, most of it empty" (25).

But this is a limited view, I would suggest, as Sid himself knows. Look more closely and one espies a Red Hook buzzing with what Sid describes as "a lot of artists, crafts people, writers" (22). They are "people who couldn't afford Manhattan, or got priced out of Williamsburg and DUMBO and the hipper parts of Brooklyn," who have found their "way to the fringes, the old industrial city," wanting a piece of it "before it's all gone," Sid says (23). Nadelson peppers her book with young homeowners and hipsters engaged in high-end artisan craft making. Every few pages contain yet another reference to loft-living sculptors, painters, glassblowers. The epitome of these new arrivals is a woman whose handmade kites sell for "five hundred bucks a pop" within spitting distance of the impoverished Red Hook Houses (246).

She is a transplant from suburban Westchester, the novel's way of exempli-
fying the migration back to the city after the mass midcentury white
exodus.

It would be easy enough to view these "artists, crafts people, writers" with
weary derision, as Richard Price does in *Lush Life*. It would be easy to see
them as pale and effete compared to the sunburned dockworkers Sid loved
from a time of America's material abundance, signified in Red Hook's over-
flowing warehouses. It would be easy enough, too, to blame them for ruining the neighborhood by driving up rents and changing its culture, while
turning a blind eye to the area's entrenched poverty and racial divisions.
That would be one narrative of gentrification in which demographic and
class succession is understood as invasion followed by loss. Yet this is not
the story Sid tells himself. As a writer, he earnestly aligns with the newcomers, even at sixty-five, and sees in them evidence of Red Hook's renewed
vitality. "Urban Pioneers, we call ourselves," he says, evoking gentrification's
tropes of Manifest Destiny, in which the South Brooklyn neighborhood
epitomizes a frontier, a place where homesteading comes in the form of lofts
(23). "I like the idea of the place coming to life," he adds, insinuating it was
dead in the 1970s and 1980s (30). The latter claim drips with unintentional
irony, given the fact Earl has just been fished from Red Hook's waters, but
Sid appears to mean it.

How are we to understand this inconsistency in a character who celebrates the new Red Hook yet spends his day literally staring out the window, perhaps like Nadelson herself, trying to imagine Red Hook's past so
he can recreate it for readers? In the answer lies the complexity of how
Nadelson's novel, Sid's unpublished history, and narratives of gentrification
more generally make use of urban history. In the teleological narrative of
urban development, the emptied-out spaces of the city—that "whole square
mile" of Red Hook—lie fallow until their future purpose is realized when
the pioneers arrive and start repainting old houses, turning vacant lots into
farmers' markets, and rehabbing old factories into new stores. In Nadelson's
narrative, the remnants and residues of "the old industrial city," the creaky
"industrial bones" of an older mode of capitalism, are not bulldozed or
buried as they would have been by the ground-clearing ethos of midcentury urban renewal. In the context of the postindustrial economics of entrepreneurial ingenuity and resource scarcity, the remnants of "the old industrial city" are salvaged, repurposed, recycled, and upcycled. These pieces

of Red Hook's industrial urbanism serve an aesthetic purpose (atmospheric historical detail for memoirs like Sid's and novels like Nadelson's) and a practical one (retrofitted lofts, studios, and live-work spaces for producing knowledge and goods, including writing books). *Red Hook* is filled with references to these "industrial bones." The novel notes the "rotting docks and grain docks and container ports and rusty warehouses and cast-iron buildings and meat packing plants and places that made car parts, and printing presses" (93, 94). Hardly a scene goes by without mention of a dilapidated pier in the background or a note that these scraps of the industrial city are now what "people are fighting over" to reuse (93). In Nadelson's text, as in Richard Florida's theorizations of the creative class, the "Urban Pioneers" are the vanguard of development, innovation, and resourcefulness, repurposing the spaces of hollowed-out industrialism and the cultures of the folks who lived in its midst. This appears to be why Sid admires them as he once did the hardworking stevedores of yore. They too are industrious workers, only in a postindustrial way. The problem is they are ultimately only transitional figures laying the groundwork, intentionally or not, for those with deeper pockets and wider designs, the next wave of truly "rich people" Tolya wants to lure to the neighborhood (162).

Narratives of place by urban planners, historians, and writers (like Sid and Nadelson) are essential for place making. They market and prescribe how a place is to be imagined and how it is to be used, inhabited, and reused. They help shape the social boundaries of a place, help shape who belongs and who does not, who is part of the past and who is part of the future. These thoughts bring us to how the story Sid is trying to write about Red Hook's past fits into the story of Red Hook's redeveloped future. What Nadelson calls the "industrial bones" of the neighborhood are material signifiers of an older way of life that help writers like Sid, like Nadelson herself, reimagine the old neighborhood while writing in its newly converted spaces, such as Sid's own studio. For his history of Red Hook, Sid also needs the stories contained inside the neighborhood's architecture and infrastructure. Sid knows that history is not about buildings but about the social life that turns a *space* into a *place*: a place of memories, the imagination, the body, and struggle. For those stories he needs Meler. "God [is] in the details," Sid says (324). He needs to squeeze from Meler any vivid remembrance—all the sights, sounds, and smells emanating from those "rotting docks"—that Meler can remember, to help Sid rebuild midcentury Red Hook in the reader's mind.

Nadelson never elaborates on the deeper meaning of Sid's book, apart from it as an embodiment of his personal obsessions. To understand it, we have to step back and consider that its wider social function is to recall Red Hook's storied industrial history so it can be preserved in time but also built upon. This is what I alluded to earlier as the unexpected ways history is used in the novel. Narratives like Sid's about the historic neighborhood are what draw gentrifiers seeking a certain style of urban authenticity. They are what draw developers, too, who leverage it for additional urban growth.[28] "I'm in favor of development," Sid admits (30). Though he presumably does not want to gentrify himself out of the neighborhood, the kinds of development that his book might be used for will be out of his hands—repurposed by urban planners, real estate marketers, and politicians—much like how the recycled waterfront is reimagined in ways inconceivable to those who originally built it. To quote the novel's visionary developer Tolya once more: "Imagine new buildings, imagine marinas and boats, imagine a brand new city" (96, 97). In recreating the stories of Red Hook's industrial history, Sid's book will sell the neighborhood as a storied place central to the history of the city and nation and a place currently buzzing with excitement, a place where those with "lots of money" might want to live or, if not live, at least invest (26). This is not just speculation. We know this because the additional publicity that Sid's book will bring is what the undocumented Meler fears will lead to his deportation. In the end Sid's book never makes it into circulation. Its history sinks dead in New York's waters. What circulates instead is the other neighborhood story, not Sid's book but Nadelson's *Red Hook*, her story of the neighborhood's past and violently contested present that belies the boosterish narrative written by politicians and urban planners about its future.

But to end the story here is to miss one of *Red Hook*'s important but easily overlooked "clues" about the emerging postindustrial city of the early 2000s.

Like Cohen's novel, Nadelson's narrates the gentrification of the "old industrial city" through a story of conflicts over real estate. Yet she tells it in a different way, as the circulation and acquisition of "information," a signifier appearing nearly as often as Red Hook's rotting docks. In this way, I see Nadelson's text alluding to the new postindustrial information economy, in which the production, circulation, and consumption of information is a source of value as much as real estate. In fact, in the novel, they are almost indistinguishable. In working to discover who murdered Earl and Sid, Artie not only observes but also accumulates what Nadelson refers to time and again as "information." The developers who skulk Red Hook looking to make a killing, Nadelson writes, frequently called Sid to "plead for information" because "he kn[e]w his way around" the neighborhood (9). "I think he was murdered because he had information that people wanted, or didn't want him to have, or didn't want him spreading around," Artie speculates to Sid's son (216). He responds, "Information was all that mattered to him" (216). Nadelson hints the shadowy figure of Tolya may have knocked off Sid, because he was desperate for his secret documents about neighborhood real estate. Tolya tells Artie that when he first approached Sid about buying property in Red Hook, Sid told him, "I know this place, I know the people, the history. I keep notes. I have information" (111). Red Hook is as much Tolya's idée fixe as it was Sid's: "he wanted Red Hook like an object. . . . He was willing to do anything to get it" (193). "I want his files," says Tolya, who wants "Information" (185), specifically, "Who has rights, who owns what, who in the city makes promises," thus raising Artie's suspicions (97). Sid's frequently referenced folders are a knowledge commodity everyone wants and that some may have been willing to kill to get.

In *Red Hook*, these plots and subplots for "information" reflect upon the contemporary conditions of the genre's production and the kind of labor performed by the narrative itself. Consider, for a moment, that virtually all of the action—what we might call the labor of narrative motion—in *Red Hook* unfolds offstage, including the murder of Earl and Sid, and is conveyed through diegesis. We rarely see it in its raw form. Instead, we receive it as already processed information. This is to say, the action isn't so much exercised or executed, like the highly visible, muscular labor of industrialism, as it is summarized, processed, and distributed information packaged and repackaged as stories by Sid, Meler, and Artie, the invisible labor of postindustrial information production. Consider, too, that the labor that Artie performs is almost completely composed of interviewing people— immigrants at the soccer field, residents in the public housing projects, and white homeowners and business owners by the waterfront—each person providing more information about the neighborhood. In the traditional hardboiled novel, the corporeality of the tough detective signifies his working-class roots. The legwork and action in these books includes physically beating people up (a kind of manual labor) to solve crimes. Artie's work, however, is listening to and writing down information. What he does with this knowledge is assess its value and reliability, speculate on what it means, control its flow, and process it into an explanatory narrative. "I built a scenario. I made connections," he says (240). In short, he is an information manager.

Ultimately, information and real estate in Nadelson's novel are two commodities in the same economy transforming Red Hook. Sid murders Earl because he refuses to help him obtain the information he desperately wants for this book. And Meler murders Sid to prevent the information in his would-be history of Red Hook from becoming public. But perhaps the most damning piece of information of all is the misinformation that will circulate in the wake of Sid's murder. All surviving parties in the novel recognize one truth: it is better to lie about these deaths. Sid's and Earl's murders would be bad for business, a sign Red Hook is backsliding to the bad old days of the 1970s and 1980s, when it was "a bucket-of-blood kind of place," says Clara Fuentes, a cop who flirtatiously chats up Artie as Earl is gaffed out of the drink (14). She remembers "crack deals on every block, people squatting in abandoned buildings, using them as toilets, gunfire all night" in the years "after the shipping moved out" (14). To prevent the fear of those days from returning, Sid's death will be treated as an unfortunate slip on a rotten pier and a banged head. "People here are happy if this is an accident," Tolya cynically says. "Better for real estate" (305). Artie agrees: "unless I made a fuss, it would all be over. . . . Everyone in the city wanted a few quiet days; anyways there wasn't much crime in New York" (310). The novel concludes with the truth kept out of public circulation for the benefit of Red Hook's ongoing revitalization, underscoring how policing and development work in concert. The neighborhood has seen enough bloodshed for now.

FIGHTING TO STAY AFLOAT IN IVY POCHODA'S RED HOOK

Ivy Pochoda's literary thriller *Visitation Street*, published eight years after Nadelson's novel, also tells the story of the dismantling of the industrial waterfront. The old "industrial bones" that people murdered one another over in Nadelson's *Red Hook* are in Pochoda's novel piled in a "former truck loading zone" that locals call "Bones Manor."[29] Here the corrugated shipping containers formerly filled with mass-produced commodities provide makeshift housing to the growing population of the homeless, the human flotsam and jetsam of the new economy living in an industrial graveyard. Not far away, a small unseaworthy motorboat that the African American character Cree James owns sits parked in a weedy lot, waterlogged with dreams of Black flight from the rundown neighborhood of postwar liberalism. Elsewhere in the novel, a speedboat accident replays in the mind of one of the neighborhood's new gentrifying residents, James Sprouse, a traumatizing memory that has sent his life off course. When in the final pages of *Visitation Street* the colossal luxury cruise liner *Queen Mary* docks near where unionized stevedores once unloaded breakbulk cargo, it is a sign that the post-Fordist economy fueled, in part, by tourism has at last arrived. A struggling Lebanese convenience store owner named Fadi believes the cruise ships will revive his flagging fortunes. But when its passengers disembark and immediately speed off to Manhattan in taxis, we see that the new economy will leave Red Hook in its wake.

Pochoda's story starts one hot summer night when two teenage white girls, Val Marino and June Giatto, feeling "stir-crazy" and wanting to "cool off," paddle into the powerful currents of the harbor on a pink inflatable raft (5). Only Val returns, after nearly drowning. She falsely claims to have no memory of what transpired. Because the eighteen-year-old Cree was on the pier that night, the police immediately tag him as a suspect, though his "only crime is being in the wrong place at the wrong time" (215). Put another way, his only crime is being a young Black man around young white girls in Red Hook (215). "The cops can't wait to slap their cuffs on some black kid for this sort of crime. Even if there was no crime," Pochoda writes (253). The exact circumstances of June's vanishing form a blank spot in the narrative, the one place where the novel goes dark. This black hole is a rupture between the past and the present, a break that launches Pochoda's narrative that as it works its way forward will also work its way back to this moment. Soon every character's storyline in this garrulous text wraps around the mystery of the missing girl. Her disappearance galvanizes the community and tests its tense amalgamation of races, ethnicities, and classes. Because she is Italian-American and working class, her disappearance signifies the loss of that older community, its future dying away, unfairly and incorrectly blamed on Red Hook's Black residents.

Pochoda treads the same ground as Cohen and Nadelson, but she brings a different perspective that opens up new stories and makes available new voices. In doing so, she tells a different story of Red Hook in the early twenty-first century. *Visitation Street* is not a detective novel. There's no formal PI or police investigation driving the plot and no single governing point of view (usually of the white male enforcer of law) that filters and controls the story. In a typical hardboiled police procedural, June's whereabouts would be the story told by the police, or, at the very least, it would be the story organized around their procedures and operations. In *Visitation Street* the two police detectives, Coover and Hughes, play minor roles, popping in and out of the novel periodically to sweep the neighborhood and interrogate residents. *Visitation Street* is not their story. Pochoda shoves to the margins the voices of the NYPD and from the margins moves to center stage the voices of a diverse community. Her polyphonic novel belongs to Cree James living in the Red Hook projects and dreaming of attending a community college's "maritime technology program" (66); to the white working-class family of Val hanging on in a modest rowhouse; to the washed-up Broadway actor and trust-fund high-school music teacher James Sprouse seeking to reinvent himself by living on the fringe; to the small, ethnic business owner Fadi dreaming the American Dream; to a homeless man named Estaban living in a "jerry-rigged" shipping container; and even to the ghost of June who roams the neighborhood (81).

Pochoda mobilizes the dialogic form of *Visitation Street* by staging and restaging key scenes from several angles, each lens offering another point of view. For instance, on their way to the water with their raft, Val and June "turn and see Cree James" (8), who "watches the girls disappear up the dark street" (9). Later, Cree is fishing from the Beard Street pier when he sees their raft "crossing in front of him—the girls, two dark silhouettes against the distant Jersey docks" (15). Pochoda reveals at another point that this fateful moment, the last time the two girls are seen before "they are gone" (15), is witnessed from two additional perspectives: the young Renton Davis, a graffiti artist recently released from "juvee" for accidentally murdering Cree's father, Marcus, six years before, and Estaban, who skulks the waterfront and eventually leads Fadi to Bones Manor, where June's body is

interred (248). In another chapter that takes place days after June's mysterious disappearance, Cree and Val undress on the pier before diving into
the water to kiss. The subsequent chapter replays that same scene from the
perspective of the white gentrifier Jonathan. Years of racial bias organize
his visual field, though he seems unaware of it. Through his eyes, Cree is
unnamed and reduced to a type—"a young black man" whom Jonathan
"sees" and runs toward down the pier, "unsure whether [he] . . . intends to
harm or help" Val (100). By repeatedly shifting perspectives in this manner, Pochoda steers clear of a single colonizing gaze in a neighborhood as
complex and heterogeneous as Red Hook. Rather than a top-down perspective one might associate with a master planner's godlike view of the neighborhood, the novel offers a community-based, bottom-up portrait of the
area. Regardless of age, ethnicity, race, class, or housing status, everyone
participates in *Visitation Street*'s verbal construction of Red Hook. No single person's perspective can see the whole truth. Each adds another sight
line, another voice, and another source of knowledge (and misinformation)
about what happened to June and, more broadly, what is happening to the
neighborhood.

But perhaps this is to see things too positively.

Viewed from another angle, Pochoda's neighborhood is too cacophonous, too divided to ever be unified in the first place. When one character
says, "It's all one neighborhood" (148), the immediate rejoinder is "The hell
it is." Whites "come to our neighborhood, thinking they can steal what they
want" (149). The feeling that the neighborhood is balkanized is shared by
whites in Red Hook, too. "*It's about boundaries*," asserts Val's father, "Fire-
man Paulie." His racial animus is exercised by his policing of Val's sexuality
by trying to keep her away from Cree (177, 59). These class and racial divisions
map onto each other in the careful partitioning of the neighborhood. The
white working-class families "have their church, their VFW clubhouse,
their own block parties" and "act as if the Houses are in a different neighborhood with a different set of problems" (88). "*There's the projects and there's
the neighborhood*," Paulie claims, denying the former the status of a community (177). In Pochoda's text, geography is a determinant of identity:
where you live in Red Hook means everything. There are "waterside girls" (9)
like Val and June, and there are "kid[s] from the projects" like Cree (8).
The prepositional phrasing of the latter is revelatory. Cree does not just live
in the projects; he is *from* there. No matter where else in life he might go,

this racialization of space will trail after him, a point Pochoda underscores: the "association with crime and drugs . . . tainted all the project kids" (69).

Page after page, the novel maps a geography of long-standing tensions that gentrification exacerbates. The neighborhood is carved up and fought over: "At one end of the park is the old luggage factory, now converted into lofts, at the other, the first of the project high-rises, and in between a battleground of basketball and barbecues" (5). Also smack dab in the middle stands Fadi's bodega: at "ground zero, where the front meets the back . . . one of the only places patronized by both sides of Red Hook" (115). At the start of the novel, the Lebanese-American small business owner "believes in Red Hook" (31). In a neighborhood of Black and white tensions, he embodies the ethnic outsider, the mediating third position whose purpose in the novel is to heal racial and class divisions. Hoping his bodega can be the town square, he posts newspaper clippings about the community on his walls and prints a newsletter filled with anonymous suggestions, rumors, and complaints that residents submit. "He'd meant his pamphlet to unite the neighborhood," a place where the divided community could come together to speak freely (281). But it backfires: "all it has done," writes Pochoda, "is fracture his vision of the neighborhood. It's made him aware of the pointless grievances, the petty arguments, the irrational hatreds" (281). By the end of the novel, on the day the *Queen Mary* docks in Red Hook, Fadi scraps the newsletter, replacing it with an advertising flyer, "The Daily Visitation," to attract disembarking tourists and their dollars, but this too fails (284). The novel's racial, ethnic, and class tensions are seemingly irresolvable. They are baked into the red soil. They are also baked into the novel's form. Pochoda's narrational design—its "fracture[s]"—keeps characters apart even as it brings them together in one highly contested and deeply divided space.

The urbanist Lewis Mumford once observed that "in the city, time becomes visible," materialized in architectures that concretize prior modes of daily living and periods of urban transformation.[30] A closer examination of Pochoda's portrayal of the two halves—the back and the front—of Red Hook reveals not just two distinct spaces but two distinct urban temporalities, the remnants of midcentury industrialism and the present-day ruins of the late twentieth-century liberal state existing side by side.

The first impression *Visitation Street* conveys of the area around the water, the neighborhood's "back," is that it is "abandoned," a signifier that

Pochoda repeats so often in the opening pages that it sounds like a haunting echo. The old Red Hook is a place of "burned-out streetlights and abandoned warehouses" (7), "abandoned doorways and broken windows" (7), an "abandoned sugar refinery" (8) that lay in "ruins" not far from an "abandoned shipyard" (10). Filling out the initial view of this part of the neighborhood stands a "rotting factory where a two-masted sailboat is taking its time sinking into the murky basin" (11). Implying something more than the mere "emptiness" of Red Hook's waterfront, Pochoda's language of abandonment connotes a state of being—of desolation or loss—a mournful landscape historically left behind. What one finds in her depictions of the neighborhood are not the sudden traumas of urban renewal, as we saw in the bulldozing of Jack's family home in Cohen's novel, but the inexorable erosions of urban neglect, the gradual hollowing out of a way of life, life as an empty shell of its former self, much like a shipping container. The decades-long process of deindustrialization and the flight of capital are materialized in the rotting piers, rusted machines, and crumbling warehouses.

However, despite its forlornness, Pochoda's waterfront is indeed changing as the new economy "cannibaliz[es]" the past (167). In the novel, new homeowners in "the back" snap up "concrete bunkers being passed off as luxury living" or settle into "lofts overtaking the factories" that stand next door to "the skeletons of forgotten buildings" (167). The raffish "artists, chefs, and odd craftsmen" (20) who circulate in the background of the novel and hang out in its "new bars" creatively repurpose the neighborhood's castoff industrial architecture with the help of capital (167). It is given an afterlife in the postindustrial era and given new use values that increase the future exchange values of the area's real estate.

In contrast, the novel's other distinctive architecture, the forbidding Red Hook projects that have warehoused Blacks and Latinos since the 1960s and are the novel's red-brick embodiment of the dying welfare state, are seemingly incapable of revitalization. This is not because its residents are not similarly creative, if you will, but because the state has siphoned resources from low-income housing. Sprawling through the middle of Red Hook like a small city, the Houses represent a different kind of "abandoned" architecture and "abandoned" citizenry. Rather than picturesque period detail, like Red Hook's desolate piers and rusted cranes, the Houses are the living history of ongoing discrimination. They remain frozen in time precisely because the structural racism undergirding their decline remains unaddressed and unabated and thus unchanging. When it comes to the projects, the more things change, the more they stay the same. Referencing the 1970s and 1980s, Pochoda writes: "Back when, the Hook only made the news for criminality and such" (115). It was the "crack capital of America" (142), and "gunfire back then" was "background noise" (250). But "back then" is not that different from now for the novel's characters of color: "Looks like the same old decrepitness to me. Poor's still poor," asserts Renton (115). In an appropriation and inversion of the language of urban planning, he calls his graffiti and murals examples of "neighborhood beautification," not blight (119). He signs them "RunDown" (121). It is a verbal play on the pathologizing trope of urban degradation that sanctioned policies of disinvestment from Black neighborhoods in the first place. "Rundown is also this place, this hood. It's run-down. It's run me down," he tells Fadi (121).

In sum, one part of Red Hook feels like it is fast improving, and another part feels like it is going nowhere fast. However, the whole of the neighborhood feels unfamiliar because no part of community is immune from the effects of gentrification. In Pochoda's novel, the struggles over gentrification loosen memories from the silt of the unconscious of all residents. "The layers that form the Hook," its buried social and personal histories, are disturbed by gentrification, transforming it into "a neighborhood of ghosts" (167). Seemingly every apartment, street corner, courtyard, and park bench in *Visitation Street* is saturated with memories by residents banged up by violence and gentrification. Even as the neighborhood is divided and its boundaries policed, memories of the dead, dispossessed, and dislocated waft through the streets and along the piers. Cree's mother, Gloria, believes her murdered husband's "spirit lingers at the spot in the courtyard where he fell" (9). His cousin Monique hears voices in her head, snippets of language that turn out to be June communicating from beyond the grave. Cree himself spends much of his time repairing a boat that he had hoped to sail with his father to Florida. Though he does not believe in ghosts, "on certain nights Cree tricks himself," Pochoda discloses, "into seeing his father's shadow moving through the weeds and climbing aboard" (10). For his part, Jonathan, the novel's wealthy hipster, is drowning in the memory of his mother's death in a speedboating accident off Fishers Island, where he watched her "disappear . . . into the inky sound" (197). And June, the last generation of white working-class Red Hook, is revealed in the closing pages to be wandering as a spirit, "cataloging the days of her life in obsessive detail," uttering the words "*bridge, wind, rocks, expressway*" as though trying to connect herself back to a neighborhood fading away (298).

The question *Visitation Street* implicitly asks is: What should one make of these memories of life in the gentrifying neighborhood? In Cohen's novel, Jack wants to forget Red Hook but cannot; conversely, in Nadelson's, Sid wants to remember it but is unable. The overwhelming sense Pochoda's novel leaves one with is that everyone needs to let go of the past and move on. In *Visitation Street*, the problem is less that the past demands to be remembered than that the living refuse to forget it. In the final pages, several of the storylines reach a climax and resolution that comes in the guise of sudden revelations, followed by expiations of guilt. Val confesses that in anger over the prospect that June would abandon her ("She didn't like hanging out with me anymore"), she "pushed her off the raft," then tried to save her but could not (271). "I killed her," Val, on the verge of a breakdown, confides to Jonathan (271). He immediately counsels her, "You have to forgive yourself" (272), knowing, "This is how it starts, this guilt that grabs you like a vise, that grips and squeezes tighter every year" (271). If this narrative sets in, Val will wind up yet another one of Red Hook's "broken people," shattered and left behind (271). Jonathan knows this because his own guilt over not diving into the water to rescue his mother years ago has frozen him in place: "Part of him has never left the dock in Fishers Island and still stands there" (272). The reader also soon learns that Renton secretly carried June's lifeless body to Bones Manor, hiding it away to protect Cree, who was spotted on the docks and thus would likely be charged with her murder. Renton's purpose in the novel is both to save Cree from a fate like his own in the criminal justice system and to free him from his father's shadow, the lingering memories of his death that Renton himself caused. "You're going to spend your life in the Houses?" he asks, challenging Cree (217). Later, he tells him, "Ghosts aren't the dead. They're those the dead left behind. Stay here long enough, you'll become one of them—another ghost haunting the Hook" (252). In the end, Renton absconds with Cree's boat, leaving him to find another escape route from the neighborhood. It comes in the form of the $15,000 reward that Fadi collects for finding June's body and that he promptly gives to Cree. He is going to use it, Pochoda tellingly states, "to get moving . . . to go to college" and restart his life, which has been stuck in place since the death of his father (302).

What we find in Pochoda's novel are people "fighting to stay afloat" as economic forces sink their community (294). No one in *Visitation Street*, whether white working class, African American, or immigrant American, is safe from these effects. As this chapter of *The Gentrification Plot* draws to a close, let us note two images that bear this out. The first is the black hole surrounding June's disappearance in *Visitation Street*, the empty spot in the narrative that Pochoda finally fills in. Pochoda describes how "the tide pull[s]" her characters out in the harbor, how one wave after another batters the raft, and how when Renton tries to rescue Val, he wades into the water "until the bottom gave out" and how he soon feels "the current grip him" (294). The unrelenting tide, one's footing dropping away, the current tossing the body this way and that; these should be understood not simply as the forces of nature but as the forces of the market, the economic flows of the waterfront—immersive, uncontrollable, and deadly—that both buoy and drown, keep you afloat and pull you under. They are Pochoda's way of materializing what is difficult to figure, what is felt but cannot always be seen.[31] The other final image is the long-rumored arrival of the *Queen Mary* cruise liner. With its "massive hull and looming prow," it is the material instantiation of the new postindustrial economy dominating Red Hook as it finally eases into the dock (285). What had been anticipated as a sign of promise arrives as a threat. In this novel told from different perspectives, the ship is a monolith one cannot see past, a literal and metaphorical blockage. It "block[s] all the beyond that comes at the end of the street, the light bouncing off the water and the distant promise of the skyscrapers," "bring[ing] a sense of claustrophobia to the neighborhood," leading Fadi, in particular, to feel "trapped" (285). "He thought the ship would expand his world. . . . But now it's just sitting there, blocking the view" (285). The new economy, with its hopes and dreams of limitless opportunity, actually shrinks the possibilities of his future.

Pochoda's novel does not imagine any alternative options, and in the end, her other characters who cannot see past the ship join, in one way or another, what it represents. The music teacher Jonathan literally steps aboard, sailing off to sing on the ship after reconciling with his past and putting it behind him. For his part, Cree's future college degree in "maritime technology" will also make him a worker, and maybe a winner, in the new economy (302). Detective Jack Leightner's stevedore father in Cohen's series could not "fight something as abstract as technology."[32] Cree will not try to fight the change but harness it.

Just as Bloomberg was imagining New York City's waterfront filling up with "new life," Cohen, Nadelson, and Pochoda envisioned a waterfront from the perspective of those who were dogpaddling to keep their heads above water. One leaves their novels with a sinking feeling about Red Hook, a neighborhood that with climate change will one day be literally and economically under water. As we turn in the next chapter to Grace Edwards's *If I Should Die* (1997) and Ernesto Quiñonez's *Bodega Dreams* (2000) and *Chango's Fire* (2004), set, respectively, in Central and East Harlem, we will see how narratives of crime and gentrification take shape in stories about the lengths people will go to in order to protect a neighborhood reeling from racist policing, the exploitation and erasure of local culture, and a real estate market that places the American dream of homeownership further and further out of reach.

Chapter Four

HARLEM

Uptown Dead Zones

A year after announcing his revitalization plans for the waterfront, Mayor Bloomberg, the richest man in the most expensive city in America, declared to a gathering of business leaders that New York needed to rethink the image that it projected around the world. Bloomberg's vision of the city in his 2003 speech at Rockefeller University was not one of social democracy or greater equity; it was not one of a city that was diverse or affordable. It was not even really of a city that was a public space with a public sphere. What he imagined was a city remade in the image of a corporation. New York, he said, needed to sell itself as a "luxury product." "If New York City is a business, it isn't Walmart—it isn't trying to be the lowest-priced product in the market," he contended, dismissing the idea that the city, a haven for the global elite, would put first the needs of its working-class residents. Though the multinational corporation Walmart can hardly be said to have the best interests of the working class in mind, in Bloomberg's speech the low-cost retailer was a metonym for a certain kind of urban citizen reimagined as a kind of struggling consumer. New York, he said in his sales pitch, needed "to think like a private company" and target and attract the types of people and businesses willing to pay extra for the privilege of living and conducting business in the city.[1] What would drive people and companies out of New York or prevent them from relocating there in the first place was not the price tag that came in the form of high taxes, Bloomberg argued, but a deterioration in the quality of life in the city. He noted in particular "higher crime," a threat he used to mobilize and advance his neoliberal vision of New York. In the State of the City speech less than a month later, the mayor revealed that New York, with the guidance of the consulting firm McKinsey & Company, was hiring "its first chief marketing officer" to lure new companies and new professionals.[2] But Bloomberg did not want to merely rebrand the city; he wanted to remake it from east to west, north to south. The primary technology for accomplishing this was rezoning. Nearly 40 percent of the entire city would be rezoned by the time Bloomberg left office. No street, no neighborhood, even those putatively left for dead after years of disinvestment, even those hitherto thought ungentrifiable, was off-limits to rezoning. Building on Giuliani's crackdown on quality-of-life violations as a means to pacify unruly neighborhoods, Bloomberg rezoned 109 blocks in Manhattan in 2003, mostly in Harlem's central and eastern sections, long considered gentrification's frontier on the island.[3] Then five years later, his City Planning Commission steamrolled fierce community opposition to push through a river-to-river rezoning of 125th Street, the low-rise, bustling thoroughfare of America's storied Black neighborhood.

Among New York City neighborhoods, Harlem remains poorer and more crime-ridden than most. According to NYU's Furman Center, the poverty rate in Central and East Harlem in 2000 was 29 and 37 percent, respectively. It has declined in the subsequent decade and a half, largely because of gentrification, but is still significantly higher than the citywide average. The crime rate in these two parts of the neighborhood has also fallen over the years but in 2019 was still double the citywide average. In that year, the rate of reported major felonies—defined as assault, murder, rape, and robbery—was 8.9 and 8.1 per thousand people, respectively, whereas across the city it was 4.3.[4] Decades of high crime and entrenched poverty have been worsened by both the slow erosions of urban decline and the fast-spreading fires that ravaged the neighborhood in the 1970s and 1980s, the latter leaving the neighborhood littered with charred buildings and vacant lots. These crumbling structures and rubble fields have been unmistakable signs of urban blight but also "opportunities" for future investment, and, as this chapter will show, fertile ground for the literary imagination. Even in this neighborhood, or maybe especially in this neighborhood, poor as it is, and struggling with crime as it is, the neoliberal thinking espoused by Bloomberg has taken root. In fact, nearly a decade before Bloomberg, such thinking was central to the creation of the Upper Manhattan Empowerment Zone (UMEZ) in 1994 during Giuliani's mayoralty. The UMEZ, which I will return to momentarily, advocated for rebranding and remarketing of embattled neighborhoods through commercial development and culturally led revitalization. The Empowerment Zone's stated goal was (and still is) to attract private capital to northern Manhattan, lend money for mixed-use real estate at low rates, and make grants in communities to market their local culture in ways that attract tourists. This neoliberal logic, as this chapter will also show, has subtly wormed its way into the literature of the gentrifying neighborhood, too.

In this chapter I follow the story of the city's narratives of crime and gentrification to Central and East Harlem, the city's most famous Black and Latinx communities, respectively, and to the work of two writers, Grace Edwards and Ernesto Quiñonez. Edwards's *If I Should Die* (1997) and Quiñonez's *Bodega Dreams* (2000) and *Chango's Fire* (2004) are neighborhood novels of murder, drug smuggling, arson, and real estate and insurance fraud that unfold in the local context of the UMEZ's neighborhood rehabilitation efforts (alluded to by both writers) and in the wider context of the neighborhood's gentrification by new residents and new capital from outside the neighborhood. To truly comprehend their work and the granular attention they give to Central and East Harlem, we have to appreciate how their writing is deeply embedded both in the recent sociospatial transformation of the neighborhood and how their novels mobilize, in quite different ways, the earlier history of urban crisis and decline whose scars are still visible in the community. Edwards and Quiñonez add to *The Gentrification Plot* a Black and Latinx perspective on rezoning, gentrification, and crime; the neighborhood they write about, moreover, brings to this book a history that we do not find in the Lower East Side, Chinatown, or Red Hook, even as it shares with them a history of marginalization and gentrification.

The Blackness of Edwards's Central Harlem, in particular, sets it apart from the other neighborhoods we have considered so far. While the Lower East Side, Chinatown, or Red Hook have been historically synonymous with one ethnic group or another, these neighborhoods have been a mix of people often without a single group obtaining a majority and have never approached the extreme levels of ethnic or racial homogeneity that characterized Central Harlem for much of the twentieth century. The Black population in these neighborhoods, moreover, has often been small or, if not small, then largely isolated on the geographical edge, such as the perimeter blocks of NYCHA housing in the Lower East Side and Chinatown or the densely concentrated Red Hook Houses in "the front" of that neighborhood. The spatial isolation of African Americans in these areas has made these neighborhoods more susceptible to first-wave gentrification. In contrast, African American neighborhoods—whether Central Harlem or, as we will see in the next chapter, Bedford-Stuyvesant—are always the hardest and last to gentrify. To understand this dynamic, we have to see Central Harlem and Bedford-Stuyvesant as racialized spaces, which means something more than that they are simply neighborhoods where Blacks "live in proximity to each other based on similar identity, experiences, and cultural affinity." Decades of "de jure and de facto policies of racial segregation and discrimination" have racially homogenized and impoverished African-American neighborhoods.[5] This racialization of Black communities in the United States is the result of structural forces, not of the choices of individual renters and homeowners who have chosen to live in a particular racial or ethnic neighborhood. The political economy of recent gentrification, as this chapter will detail, seizes upon the historically undervalued geographies of these racialized spaces for profiteering, an exploitation that Edwards and Quiñonez address in different ways.

Born and raised in Central Harlem, Edwards published *If I Should Die* at sixty-four, the book launching her Mali Anderson Mystery series, which she would stretch across four novels. As a secretary and then later executive director (2007–2016) of the Harlem Writers Guild, Edwards was until her death in 2020 an important figure in supporting Black writing in New York. As such, she was deeply conversant with how Harlem had been portrayed in literature. Her own writing has been compared to Chester Himes's detective novels set in the same neighborhood decades earlier, yet they have little in common stylistically. Edwards's books have none of the surreal and oftentimes gothically violent Blaxploitation humor of Himes's fiction or its supercharged libidinality. More important still is Himes's and Edwards's radically divergent relation to the neighborhood, a fact attributable at least in part to their historical difference. Written during the depths of Harlem's decline and when representations of inner-city pathology were commonplace, Himes's work depicts the neighborhood as grotesquely squalid, rundown, and hyperviolent. In a 1963 essay, he likened Harlem to "a cancer on the body of a nation" and concluded that "the most important thing to many Harlem Negroes is how to escape from it."[6] Though Edwards lived through Harlem's midcentury decades of blight, slum clearance, and urban renewal, her novels from the 1990s and early 2000s depict a neighborhood that is gentrifying, a phenomenon that surely Himes would have found absurd, if not unimaginable.

As we will see, for Edwards the gentrification of Harlem poses an imminent threat, but it is also an opportunity for her to access a wider white readership that is curious, yet still unsure, about a neighborhood that has so often been thought of as a separate world, one that is off-limits, irredeemably different, or dangerous. "I take readers on a virtual tour of Harlem," she said of her novels, going on to state, "I aim to bring them in so close that they can see and get a real sense of the lives we live here."[7] Edwards invites outsiders in where Himes urged residents to flee. With no small amount of neighborhood pride, she speaks to the pedagogical aspect of her novels that show readers a "real" Harlem of everyday, ordinary residents: owners of small shops, street vendors, teachers, local jazz musicians, kids trying to stay out of trouble. "Ordinary," I will argue, is a badge of honor in *If I Should Die*. Hence, at the same time that the UMEZ was incentivizing Harlemites to market their neighborhood to outsiders, we can see Edwards was offering a warm welcome to white readers to her gentrifying neighborhood. It is a welcome that stands in sharp contrast to Himes, the pathologizing portraits of social scientists, and the Blacks-only aesthetic and politics of the Harlem-based Black Arts Movement from two decades earlier. Yet there is also an unmistakable sense in her work that Edwards wants to protect her Harlem from both outside influence (for example, developers and corrupt cops) and bad actors in the neighborhood (for example, drug dealers). This sensibility is reaffirmed when we recognize that the investigatory work of her protagonist Mali Anderson—who is neither a cop nor a detective but an amateur sleuth—amounts to an unpaid labor of love.

The Harlem that we find in her writing is a far cry from either the sensationalistic discursive portrayals of Harlem in the 1960s and 1970s as plagued by uncontrollable crime and deviancy or the more recent overheated real estate and urban development rhetoric of Harlem as a new frontier for profiteering. This point is incontrovertible. Yet it is equally true that Edwards's warm portrait of the Harlem community in *If I Should Die* is not without its problems, not without its crimes. *If I Should Die* is, after all, a crime novel. The bodies pile up by the novel's end, as is the case in all of the books in the Mali Anderson Mystery series, each with "Die" in the title. On its surface, *If I Should Die* has many of the qualities of a traditionally structured detective novel: a homicide launches an investigation that uncovers a wider criminal conspiracy of drug smuggling and attempted kidnapping, which is aided and abetted by the police, a plot that is ultimately undone when the perpetrators are either killed or arrested by the end. However, its narrational perspective through the eyes of a female ex-NYPD officer now in graduate school for sociology offers a markedly different point of view on the overpoliced and underprotected Black neighborhood. As this chapter will argue, in Edwards's text everyday, street-level crime (as opposed to the elaborate conspiracy Mali exposes) is presented as the tragic legacy of slum clearance and urban renewal. Reminders of Harlem's decades of decline are found in the novel's dilapidated public housing projects, a highly racialized and criminalized geography. This architecture shares space in Edwards's Harlem with newly constructed rowhouses and a rehabbed section of 125th Street (underwritten with UMEZ money) that Mali notes has displaced Black working-class vendors. These early indicators of gentrification during Giuliani's time in office, I will contend, are not seen by Edwards as encouraging signs of life in Harlem but rather as further instances of racial exploitation that affects ordinary residents and the culture of the community that Edwards's work quietly celebrates. However, if in the text encroaching gentrification provides a threatening backdrop to the crime at the novel's center, it is one that stays in the background, as though the novel does not quite know how to rein it in as much as it might wish. Edwards's Harlem is a highly racialized space, and as we will see, policing is a racist practice for managing it. This fact, Edwards makes clear, informed her protagonist's decision to join the force *and* her expulsion from it. Mali signed up to be a cop to prevent acts of racist policing in Harlem and was fired for protesting an act of racism directed at her. Ultimately, in *If I Should Die* systemic racism in the NYPD emanates from the very top in the guise of Giuliani, a vile and monstrous figure Edwards alludes to but whose name she refuses to even utter. It was Giuliani who tasked the police with enforcing the racialized strategy of broken-windows policing that disproportionately targeted Black neighborhoods, Harlem especially, as disorderly in advance of their gentrification. The racism of broken-windows policing has been the subject of other novels in *The Gentrification Plot*, but nowhere is it as explicitly exposed and critiqued as it is in Edwards's crime novel.

In contrast to *If I Should Die*, Quiñonez's *Bodega Dreams* and *Chango's Fire* are not typically read as novels in the genre of crime fiction. This is an oversight largely attributable to a narrow conception of crime fiction as narratively organized around a criminal investigation led by a police officer, private detective, or amateur sleuth. However, as Alfred Bendixen contends, crime fiction has a "remarkably wide range of narrative possibilities." If we think broadly about the genre as "the exploration of a crime—its causes, its consequences, and its social, moral, and political implications," one that "enables, and perhaps even requires, the deeper inquiry into the nature of democratic society," then crime fiction "marks many of the finest American novels and stories," Quiñonez's included.[8] Quiñonez's books are about everyday East Harlem residents leading their lives and struggling to keep a roof over their heads as the city becomes more and more unequal and as prices skyrocket in their own neighborhood. Arguably even more so than Edwards's work, these are novels about ordinary people doing anything to make do, including resorting to crime, in a city where every day it is a little harder to make the rent or the mortgage. From corruption to arson, from tax and insurance fraud to murder, crime is central to both of Quiñonez's novels. Reading for crime in these literary, but crime-filled, narratives reveals things we would not be able to see otherwise, or at least not see as clearly. In particular, it reveals the feelings of Latinx precarity and desperation engendered by neoliberal urbanism but also the feelings of opportunity and possibility that it produces in people. At the center of both texts are young, Latino protagonists—Julio Mercado and Julio Santana—who are the ethnic personifications of the neoliberal values of self-improvement, personal responsibility, hard work, and homeownership as the pathway up for one's self and one's family. The problem that Quiñonez stages is that hard work and playing by the rules are not enough to get by, or perhaps a little bit ahead, in a neighborhood that is, on the one hand, still struggling with the discriminatory legacy of decades of urban neglect and, on the other hand, now targeted for gentrification. To close the gap between what Quiñonez's protagonists earn at their low-wage jobs and what they need to survive in El Barrio as it becomes more expensive, they turn to crime, only to see their dreams go up in flames.

There is fire in Quiñonez's books: a lot of it. There are the fires that swept East Harlem in the 1970s and 1980s, and there are the fires of the FIRE industries (finance, insurance, and real estate) that came after, sweeping the neighborhood in the 1990s and early 2000s. One of the things we will see is that Quiñonez's writing underscores that the metaphorical "burning" of East Harlem by the FIRE industries reenacts the same logic and ironically results in many of the same outcomes as the literal burning of the barrio in decades past. As we will also see, the images of urban ruins in Quiñonez's work—vacant lots, charred bricks, the empty shells of buildings—are synecdoches for entire decades of Harlem's redlining and depopulation and the usual suspects that fill in what's been hollowed out: poverty, gangs, crime, and drugs. Conversely, the images of salsa museums, art galleries, cocktail lounges, and condos in these books are architectural materializations of the processes of gentrification and neoliberal urban development. Quiñonez's protagonists are caught in the middle of both kinds of spaces and the forces that produce them.

So what does Quiñonez give his two Julios to replace the semblances of the good life—a home, a family, close friends—that he snatches away? The answer is culture. If Spanish Harlem's culture was enlisted in the gentrification of the neighborhood off the page through the Empowerment Zone, on Quiñonez's pages culture is what is bestowed on you when your gentrified neighborhood is taken from you by FIRE in ways hauntingly recalling the displacements and fires of 1970s urban renewal. Arlene Dávila pointedly calls *Bodega Dreams* "the ultimate neoliberal novel" for the way it endorses entrepreneurial self-empowerment, often through culture, as a solution to structural inequalities.[9] *Bodega Dreams* ends with a literal dream sequence in which Julio—displaced out of his apartment and his personal relationships in tatters—optimistically imagines a future Spanish Harlem where Spanish and English mix in a new tongue that he will one day learn to use as a writer to celebrate the neighborhood. For his part, Julio in *Chango's Fire* is reimbursed for his many losses with the prospect of personal and spiritual transformations through his immersion in his community's "stories" of "survival, of diversity, of color and magic," stories that he will be the bearer of into the future (76). The empowering hopes and dreams at the end of Quiñonez's two books are not symbolic resolutions of the structural tensions, conflicts, and contradictions of urban political economy in East Harlem. Rather, they are expressions of structural inequalities that remain unresolved in symbolic form. *Bodega Dreams* and *Chango's Fire* are novels of downward Latino mobility, novels of being kicked down the class ladder in a rezoned neighborhood on the upswing. When you lose your home in these books, what you gain is a textual home housing a community in words.

(DIS)EMPOWERMENT ZONES AND
THE REMAKING OF 125TH STREET

As we have with previous neighborhoods, it helps to orient ourselves geographically, historically, and discursively before navigating deeper into this chapter's literature. Edwards's and Quiñonez's novels are neighborhood novels firmly anchored in the terrain of Central and East Harlem. Without a sense of these parts of the neighborhood, it is harder to make sense of the work.

At approximately 3.5 square miles, Harlem is an expansive neighborhood. Its south-central border is 110th Street at the northern edge of Central Park; from there it stretches to 155th Street, with a sizeable cutout on the west side lorded over by Columbia University, a development juggernaut that has used eminent domain to acquire more and more acreage in recent years to construct what is in effect a moat around itself. In the central blocks of the neighborhood in the 130s and 140s between St. Nicholas Ave and Adam Clayton Powell Jr. Boulevard is a historic district of elegant townhomes. The most famous among them are the Italian Renaissance, Federal Renaissance, and Georgian-style red brick and brownstone houses on Strivers' Row (138th and 139th Streets), which in the 1920s were home to Harlem's Talented Tenth of educators, composers, and doctors. Tellingly, here Grace Edwards has Mali Anderson live with her father, a noted jazz musician, while she completes her MA in sociology at the City University of New York. Mali's residential location signals she is a member of the Black bourgeoisie and effectively aligns Edwards's novels with the historical heart of the Harlem Renaissance. These picturesque houses—described in other Harlem novels and used as the settings for films in the neighborhood—serve as reminders of Harlem's storied past, when it was the vital center of Black culture in the country. They are also signs of Harlem's contemporary gentrification. Since the early 2000s, the neighborhood's rowhouses and brownstones have been fiercely coveted by new residents and investors, many of whom buy them precisely because of their rich historical associations and the aura of authenticity emanating from their nineteenth-century architectural details.

As Brian Goldstein has noted, "Harlem's variegated residential fabric" contains not only rows and rows of brownstones but also "vast complexes of public housing towers," much of it built under the aegis of Title III of the Housing Act of 1949.[10] Rather than horizontally integrated into the fabric of the neighborhood, Harlem's housing projects were constructed on super-blocks created by bulldozing New York's distinctive low-rise street wall of tenements and shops and breaking up the city's grid laid in 1811. Though these projects are scattered throughout Harlem, many of them are clustered on the east side of the neighborhood, which has the second-highest concentration of public housing in the United States.[11] Cordoned off by fencing, green space, and parking lots, such towers became in time what Goldstein characterizes as "vast centers of concentrated poverty" and racial isolation. It is in one of these complexes—Schomburg Plaza on Fifth

FIGURE 4.1. Strivers' Row, at 245–219 West 139th Street, Harlem, New York City. *Source:* Beyond My Ken, CC BY-SA 4.0 (https://creativecommons.org/licenses/by-sa/4.0), via Wikimedia Commons.

Avenue near 110th Street—that Ernesto Quiñonez spent his teenage years in the 1970s, the decade during which the historian David Levering Lewis pronounced the neighborhood as having suffered a "slow, sleazy death." In his *New York Times* essay "The Fires Last Time," Quiñonez described his home as a "crime-infested" tower in a neighborhood filled with vacant lots, scorched buildings, and "piles and piles of uncollected trash."[12] Schomburg Plaza is where his protagonist also lives, and wants to escape from, in *Bodega Dreams*, Quiñonez's novel of social activism, crime, and housing at the dawn of the new millennium.

If Harlem's brownstones call to mind its glorious Renaissance period, its housing towers—the enduring architecture of racial liberalism—call to mind the period of postwar urban crisis when "Harlem" was effectively shorthand for all the ills of America's so-called Black inner cities. This other narrative of the neighborhood, this narrative of poverty, violence, and urban decline in the 1960s and 1970s, supplanted in the urban imaginary the narrative of its cultural flowering and independence in the 1920s, when Harlem, though not without its problems, was the most famous neighborhood in America for diametrically different reasons. In these two images of housing—which we will also find in Edwards's novel—we can see two different temporalities and two radically different stories of the neighborhood and what it has stood for in the minds of residents and Americans at large. We can see here, as well, what Monique Taylor calls "the architecture and space of class," where two different "productions of race" are at play in the neighborhood, the Black bourgeoisie and those that punitive-minded urban policy often referred to as the undeserving poor. Late twentieth- and early twenty-first-century gentrification is a third temporality that transforms how Harlem is interpreted. "Formerly America's best-known 'ghetto,' by the end of the century Harlem stood," Goldstein argues, "as a symbol that even the most forsaken urban neighborhoods could again become sought-after destinations for a middle-class that had largely deserted them."[13] If gentrification could succeed here, it could succeed anywhere, the thinking went. As gentrification plays out as a racial and class struggle over space in Harlem, it brings these two forms of housing—brownstones and housing projects—and the ways of life they contain into opposition.

The central portions of Harlem that are Edwards's turf and the eastern portions that are Quiñonez's have been subjected to many of the same problems and pressures, from gang violence to gentrification, but they also have distinctive geographies, histories, and demographic patterns. The central and western sections of Harlem are the historic home of Black culture and the site of many of its most famous landmarks, like the Abyssinian Baptist Church, the Apollo Theater, and the Schomburg Center for Research on Black Culture. This part of the neighborhood was originally conceived in the nineteenth century as a middle- and upper-middle-class area for whites seeking a residential idyll away from, but connected to, downtown. It was rapidly built up in anticipation of the opening of subway lines that would link home and work. However, as subway construction was repeatedly delayed, the speculative housing bubble that had been expanding for years finally burst in 1904. Developers and real estate brokers eventually turned for renters to the city's burgeoning African American population arriving from the South as part of the Great Migration in the 1910s, often charging them above-market rates in the segregated city, leading to the untenable situation in which those who could least afford it paid more for their housing. Almost overnight and for much of the rest of the twentieth century, Central Harlem was nearly exclusively Black and impoverished, a condition that resulted from a confluence of forces that affected American cities generally but that disproportionately affected African American areas in particular. These included deindustrialization and disinvestment, federally subsidized white flight to the suburbs through FHA loans, and urban renewal. Other policies and tactics were deliberately targeted at keeping Black neighborhoods spatially contained and economically isolated, such as white violence in the form of mob attacks and fire bombings of Black-owned houses, restrictive housing covenants to prevent resale of property to Black would-be homeowners, and the Home Owners' Loan Corporation's residential security maps that redlined Black neighborhoods. These practices and policies produced unprecedented concentrations of racial poverty and "a new spatial order" bearing "little resemblance to the American city of the past." As Douglas Massey and Nancy Denton argue, "racial segregation became a permanent structural feature of the spatial organization of American cities in the years after World War II." And it was effective. In the north, "the average level of black spatial isolation more than doubled between 1930 and 1970, going from 32% to nearly 74%."[14] By 1980, Central Harlem's Black population counted for 96 percent of its residents.

If earlier redevelopment tactics and housing policies kept Central Harlem Black, gentrification in recent years has made it whiter, creating what some community activists, such as members of the Harlem Tenants Council, see as a new wave of Jim Crowism displacing Black residents from the very neighborhood to which they had been relegated. Two sections of the neighborhood—the streets that hug the northern edge of Central Park and the streets around Marcus Garvey Park—saw signs of gentrification as early as the mid-1980s, in the guise of new condo construction and the city's silent auction of a dozen foreclosed brownstone houses to seed revitalization.[15] The year 1993 saw the establishment of a Business Improvement District in Harlem, and a year later the Upper Manhattan Empowerment Zone legislation, spearheaded by Harlem's long-serving congressperson Charles Rangel, was passed, which led to a flood of new development in the decades that followed. Significantly, the Abyssinian Development Corporation, "the real estate wing" of the famed church, with UMEZ underwriting, led the construction of Harlem USA, a 275,000-square-foot "suburban-style strip mall" located between Saint Nicholas and Eighth Avenue on 125th Street, the most important commercial artery in the neighborhood.[16] When she alludes to the UMEZ's transformation of 125th Street, Edwards's Mali feels nothing but loss. Gentrification of Central Harlem was later hastened by the Bloomberg administration's aggressive rezoning of the same thoroughfare in 2008. The plan, which also encompassed streets around 125th, used the sweetener of more culture to entice neighborhood development to those resistant to additional luxury housing and corporate retail. To this end, the rezoning plan included "a 'special arts and entertainment district,'" which mandated that new developments with "60,000 square feet or more [of] floor space" must set aside "five percent of their total floor area to arts- and entertainment-related uses such as museums, performance venues and restaurants."[17] But what the redevelopment of the most distinctive commercial corridor in Black America has actually wrought is the abstract spatiality of Whole Foods, H&M, Old Navy, and the like, spaces shorn of any historical texture or neighborhood history. The kinds of locally owned and highly textured social spaces, such as the beauty salons, barber shops, and bars that are the heart of Edwards's fiction, are increasingly imperiled by gentrification. With the creation of Business Improvement Districts, Empowerment Zones, and new zoning plans, Harlem's inflationary housing prices have ballooned 250 percent in the decade between 1996 and 2006.[18] In the meantime, its Black population has dramatically fallen. By 2000, the Black population of Central Harlem was 77 percent; by 2018 it was a little more than half.[19] "Are we witnessing a second Harlem Renaissance?" a real estate advertising supplement in the *New York Times* asked in 2010.[20] The unasked question, however, was what was meant by "renaissance" if the reborn and revived Harlem was no longer Black.

Nearly to the extent that Central Harlem is the home of Black culture in New York, East Harlem has been the home of Latinx culture, especially Puerto Rican, in the city. The east side of Harlem—which starts at Ninety-Sixth Street and extends north to 143rd and stretches east from Fifth Avenue to the river—was, like Central Harlem, also synonymous with urban decline in the 1960s and 1970s and has been transformed in the new millennium by privatization and rampant commercial development. Its southernmost parts near Central Park are more or less indistinguishable from the rarified, blue-blooded environs of the Upper East Side. But once one crosses under the grimy tracks of the elevated train line clanging up Park Avenue—a shadowy warren of parked garbage trucks and pushcarts, low-rent bodegas, and homeless people—one emerges on the other side into what feels like an altogether different city. The neighborhood has an average life expectancy a full nine years shorter than the Upper East Side, has more than double the rates of childhood asthma hospitalizations than the rest of New York, and is a great deal poorer.[21]

The scars of slum clearance, disinvestment, and the widespread abandonment of the eastern section of Harlem in the postwar period are still visible in the neighborhood today in the guise of vacant lots and boarded-up buildings. But this is less and less so with recent gentrification, which has maximized the profitability of every available space. The empty lots and buildings that do remain also serve, in Quiñonez's fiction, as a haunting history of the neighborhood's roughest years. Goldstein remarks that New York City was "the major laboratory for the practice of slum clearance, exceeding all other American cities in both the scale and scope of midcentury urban redevelopment."[22] Among the city's many neighborhoods subjected to slum clearance, Harlem was experimented on the most. Large swaths of the east side in particular, such as the tracts around 106th Street near Fifth Avenue and 110th and 111th Streets between Park and Madison Avenues, were declared blighted, then bulldozed under the authority of the Housing Act of 1949.[23] The towers that were subsequently erected in the area housed over 62,000 residents in the 1950s and 1960s.[24] As large as it was, the number was still less than the number of East Harlem residents who had been displaced by the wrecking ball. Of all of the people displaced by urban renewal in New York City between 1959 and 1961, 76 percent were Puerto Rican.[25] The problem with massive midcentury urban renewal efforts in East Harlem (and in the surrounding areas) was that they did not work as a strategy of urban revitalization—and they were expensive. Most so-called blighted neighborhoods slated for renewal fell into precipitous decline *after* they were torn up. Not surprisingly, "by the mid-1960s, urban renewal had received widespread condemnation from all corners" as a failure.[26] Libertarians, liberals, and New Left radicals opposed it for different reasons: it cost too much money; its social costs were too high; its top-down, bureaucratic administration cost residents their self-determination. Whichever cost one singled out, by the fiscal crisis of the mid-1970s, the city felt it was too broke to finance the large-scale spatial reorganization of neighborhoods that experts and politicians had deemed to be disorderly sites of crime and poverty. Property abandonment by landlords and a

FIGURE 4.2. Aerial view of East Harlem, including Carver Houses. *Source:* Museum of the City of New York. Photo Archives. X2010.11.2521.

sharp reduction in city services (including police, firefighters, and building inspectors) soon followed, and what came after, predictably enough, was the burning of East Harlem, along with the South Bronx, Bedford-Stuyvesant, and other racialized neighborhoods in New York.

Whereas Harlem's central section was racially homogenous for nearly a hundred years before its recent gentrification, its eastern portion has had more mixed demographics. East Harlem or Spanish Harlem has not always been "Spanish," nor is it exclusively so today. Labeling it Spanish Harlem is to linguistically and ethnically claim it from others who also live there. In terms of East Harlem's history of ethnic succession, Puerto Ricans who dominate the area are relatively late arrivals, not coming in large numbers until the 1940s and 1950s, with the advent of cheaper air travel and the lure of work in the industrial and service sectors as the sugar industry back on the island dried up.[27] Not coincidentally, the area was first targeted for slum clearance at the same time Puerto Ricans arrived en masse. Their arrival also hastened the displacement of Italians, but not without a fight. At mid-century, East Harlem was the largest Italian-American neighborhood in the country, with upward of a hundred thousand residents. Remnants of the community are still found along Pleasant Avenue. The bare-knuckle struggle between Puerto Ricans and Italians is repeatedly alluded to in Quiñonez's work and dramatized directly in Piri Thomas's memoir *Down These Mean Streets* (1967), the most famous book to come out of the east side before *Bodega Dreams* and *Chango's Fire*. Steven Bender documents in *Tierra y Libertad: Land, Liberty, and Latino Housing* (2010) that "in 1945, only about 13,000 Puerto Ricans resided in New York City; by the following year, it was more than 50,000."[28] Despite the urban crises of the 1960s, 1970s, and 1980s, the influx of Puerto Ricans to New York continued in subsequent decades. By 2010 their numbers had soared to 800,000. Yet despite these gains overall, the number of Puerto Ricans in East Harlem itself has decreased as the area has gentrified. Today Spanish Harlem is less than half Hispanic, and among those who identify as such, only about 35 percent are Puerto Rican. The rest mostly hail from the Hispanophone Caribbean Basin, in particular from the Dominican Republic, and from Mexico and countries in Central and South America. The remainder of the neighborhood is African American, white (16 percent and growing), and Asian, in that order, with the Black population falling off year by year. Between 2000 and 2010, the white population in the northern part of the neighborhood increased almost

118 percent; in the southern, more gentrified section, it increased roughly 55 percent.[29] The fact that East Harlem is well serviced by transportation has been one of its selling points. The completion of the first phase of the Second Avenue subway line in 2017 has caused rents and property values to surge higher. As we will see, when Julio in *Chango's Fire* laments "El Barrio was no longer my barrio," these are the demographic trends fueling the resentment (16). Year by year it is less anyone's barrio.

Debates over what to call a neighborhood—East Harlem, Spanish Harlem, El Barrio—underscore struggles over who has the right to live in it and how that right is established, whether by property ownership, income status, racial or ethnic designation, the length of time one has resided in the area, or some other criterion. Part of the gentrification of the east side of Harlem has been its rebranding as "Upper Manhattan," "Upper Yorkville," and "Upper Carnegie Hill," geographical designators that "de-race the neighborhood" and align it with more prosperous areas.[30] The portmanteau "SpaHa"—adopted by a smattering of eager real estate companies (and Julio's white girlfriend in *Chango's Fire*)—is of all of the proposed names the one that most efficiently severs the neighborhood's ethnic and racial heritage in one fell swoop. None of these alternatives has truly caught on, and it is fair to say most New Yorkers still refer to the area as East Harlem. Upper Manhattan is too geographically vague to be meaningful. It could refer to a number of places: Harlem, Washington Heights, or Inwood. Yorkville is a residual, rarely used name for the nineteenth-century German community in the Upper East Side. If you ask for directions to "Upper Carnegie Hill" or "SpaHa," it is guaranteed to earn you quizzical looks and raise suspicions that you yourself arrived in the city just yesterday, from someplace like Dubuque, wherever that might be.

The UMEZ has been one of the mechanisms for undoing the damage wrought by decades of capital flight in Harlem. At first glance, the UMEZ may look like government support in the form of free money, but this is incorrect. Since the 1990s, the government's role in urban policy has been focused not on expanding public housing but on outsourcing redevelopment to the private market. "Stimulating private investment in high-poverty neighborhoods" has been the goal, and to this end, "the designation of Empowerment Zones [has] symbolized the national ascent of the market approach to urban development." The UMEZ's mandate is to "revitalize the country's most economically distressed areas by using public funds to spur private investment and ultimately restore economic vitality to those areas."[31] One of the pillars of the Empowerment Zone's development initiative was, and still is, its Cultural Investment Fund, which seeks to jumpstart economic revitalization through the arts. The fund encourages entrepreneurial self-empowerment in communities like Harlem, using money as a lure to change. In order to access its grants or loans, Harlem arts organizations are tasked with finding innovative ways to sell themselves to outsiders. As Arlene Dávila has shown, on the east side this has meant using the area's local culture—Latin jazz, cuisine, colorful street festivals, parades, and museums—as an advantage in a crowded urban marketplace of gentrifying neighborhoods. The neighborhood is, in essence, asked to think like a company and to think of visitors and new residents as customers. Harlem's culture is explicitly called on through the Empowerment Zone to help "create jobs," create and market "products and services" for "patrons and consumers," and boost "tourist traffic." "The EZ and its Cultural Industry Investment Fund," Dávila writes, "marked the first time in East Harlem's history that the community had been directly encouraged to sell itself and to think about how best to attract people into the area strictly in business and entrepreneurial ways."[32] To this end, the culture of Spanish Harlem has been put to work resignifying what the neighborhood stands for in the minds of investors and potential residents. When Dávila calls Quiñonez's *Bodega Dreams* a neoliberal novel, she is remarking on the market logic that structures the book. As I will argue, the novel softens the image of Spanish Harlem by discrediting a utopian dream of radical political change predicated on its socioeconomic autonomy and replacing it with a more palatable, depoliticized image of the neighborhood as culturally inclusive, an image more inviting to outsiders.

At the local level, culturally led development efforts, such as envisioned by the Empowerment Zone, fuel gentrification, which, to simplify somewhat to Bloomberg's marketing vision of New York, is about attracting the right people to one particular neighborhood over another based on what it has to offer. In effect, the UMEZ has asked Harlem to harness "The Competitive Advantage of the Inner City," as the Harvard economist Michael Porter put it in the title to his landmark 1995 article that urged poor urban neighborhoods to leverage the power of their location, labor pool, underserved markets, and, I would add, local culture for profit making. As I have been arguing, such efforts should be understood as emblematic of the

waning of the welfare state, the foisting of responsibility for urban revitalization onto poor communities themselves, and the increasing ability of
contemporary capitalism to incorporate marginal cultures and ethnic and
racial identities into spheres of profit making. Reflecting on the UMEZ's
Cultural Investment Fund also helps us see Harlem's new place in a postindustrial economy that favors locally made, niche products so long as they
are "safe, comfortable, and entertaining," their sharp edges and points of
resistance sanded off.[33] In exacerbating gentrification, such efforts speed
up the erasure of the very cultures they endeavor to sell. Walking around
the east side of Harlem today, one can see the effects: soulless chain stores
like Starbucks, Walgreens, Target, and Costco and luxury condos with
rooftop gardens. The east side of the neighborhood is starting to look a lot
like the other side on 125th Street, which is to say, it is starting to look not
like Harlem but like Anywhere USA.

RACE AND RENEWAL IN GRACE EDWARDS'S HARLEM

One of the truisms about Harlem since its formation as a Black neighborhood in the 1910s is that it is a city-within-a-city, a designation that has been
a point of local pride, if also one that implied the neighborhood was closed
off, even insular. The extent that this truism is true has its basis in the historical practices of segregation and redlining that drew a firewall around
the neighborhood to keep it from expanding. In doing so, it fostered Harlem's inner resourcefulness and independence. This is the Harlem readers
find in Edwards's intensely local novel *If I Should Die*. What Fredric Jameson has said about Baltimore in *The Wire* holds true for Harlem in
Edwards's book: it "conveys the conviction that nothing exists outside of
it."[34] This impression is an effect of the novel's precise geographical realism
conveyed in multiple ways—including representations of Harlem's historical and cultural landmarks; descriptions of the local, everyday culture of
the neighborhood found in its beauty salons, barbershops, and restaurants
(some of which exist off the page); and the mapping of streets and avenues
as Edwards's protagonist walks the neighborhood to admire its vibrant
social life. The novel alludes to other geographical points beyond Harlem,
some as close by as Wall Street and City Hall and others as far away as
France, but it never actually breaks the seal, never ventures past the neighborhood's boundaries, as if to suggest what lies beyond could never be as

interesting. One of the common plotlines of crime fiction set in the so-called ghetto or ethnic enclave is the struggle to get out, put the neighborhood and the past behind oneself and start over somewhere, anywhere, else. This thought never occurs to Edwards's Mali. Harlem, with its jazz clubs, basketball courts, and brownstones, is life. Yet the feeling one comes away with by the novel's end is not only the vitality of the neighborhood but also its sheer fragility, as if it might die tomorrow.

The threats to life in Harlem in *If I Should Die* are the forces and structures that open the neighborhood outward and corrupt it from within. As this chapter will show, they come in three guises: first, urban redevelopment and gentrification, which are displacing the local culture that has built up over years and reversing the seemingly self-contained quality of the neighborhood; second, racist cops, a colonizing force in Harlem acting as brutal enforcers of white supremacy; and third, a cocaine-smuggling ring led by a murderous drug kingpin, Johnnie Harding, that Mali's investigation exposes. The second and third of these merge in the novel; Harding, an African American Harlem resident, is able to do business in the neighborhood because of the grifter NYPD officers Danny Williams and Terry Keenan, the latter a dyed-in-the-wool racist. The threat that urban development poses, however, is unintegrated into the plot; yet rather than this fact reducing it to a secondary concern, it has the opposite effect. Always humming in the background of the story, urban development is a menace that the novel and its sleuth have no answer for. This point is key. The flow of capital into the neighborhood is a corrosive force that *If I Should Die* suggests cannot be held at bay.

The narrative lens through which Edwards explores the neighborhood in this first-person point-of-view novel is her female protagonist. With her close-cropped hair and willingness to throw a punch, thirty-one-year-old Mali is the hard-charging, risk-taking, take-no-bullshit detective figure typically found in the genre's male heroes. As Edwards shows better than any other writer in *The Gentrification Plot*, these traits need not be gendered. Yet as she makes clear through repeated references to Mali's high heels, dresses, manicures, and facials, Mali's femininity is an important part of her self-presentation. Her gender difference is also one of the book's selling points; the jacket copy describes her as "young" and "stunning." If her outward appearance is an aspect of her character that is commented upon, so too is her so-called feminine intuition, which makes her a better detective than her hyperrational male counterparts, who have been a part of American crime fiction from at least Poe's mid-nineteenth-century stories. "Feelings, however vague and unscientific, do count for something," Mali says to herself.[35] In the world of Edwards's Harlem, her gender is both a liability that puts her at risk of sexual assault and an asset that gives her access to female spaces, specifically to beauty salons, where information about the criminal conspiracy circulates as gossip among the neighborhood's female residents. But arguably what most distinguishes Mali is not that she is Black and female but that she is a graduate student in sociology with an interest in social work, like her creator, who worked in New York's social services department as a disability analyst. This key detail about Mali's education in sociology is disclosed at the outset and informs the way that the novel looks at the Black neighborhood and what it sees. Rare in the genre of crime fiction, Edwards's protagonist combines a police detective's investigatory knowhow with a sociologist's eye for examining crime, drug abuse, and poverty as symptoms of underlying structural conditions that cannot be solved through broken-windows policing and mass incarceration.

Edwards's *If I Should Die* harnesses the investigation of a murder as an opening into a criminal conspiracy to uncover the deeper processes and structures that ail a neighborhood. However, it briefly delays the discovery of that murder, so that it can begin mapping the neighborhood from the perspective of a lifelong resident who is also professionally trained to read it through the lens of class, culture, and historical preservation, the concerns of an urban sociologist rather than a cop. In the novel's first scene, Mali stands on Strivers' Row, proudly "gaz[ing] down the block" at the "three- and four-story brownstones with iron filigree balconies and narrow, French-curtained windows," a street of "black professionals," she says (2). Here she was born, raised, and still lives with her father. Though the scene takes place in a wintry April, the blooming forsythia on the balconies are not only a sign that upper-middle-class Black homeowners are beautifying the neighborhood but a sign of Harlem coming back to life after years of disinvestment and decline. These are historic homes rehabbed by Black residents committed to the community and will stand in contrast to "the new construction" referenced periodically in the novel (180). As we will see, like most early signs of life in crime fiction, they are ironic. While admiring Strivers' Row, Mali remembers her father walking her around Harlem "where all the old neighborhood dance halls, nightclubs, and after-hours spots used to be"—"The Savoy," "Minton's Playhouse," "the old Cotton Club," "Smalls Paradise"—places that housed the social life of the Harlem Renaissance period, the 1950s, and beyond (3). "Those times and all of those places gone," Mali reflects (4). With its opening chapter, the novel thus constructs a spatial context that is layered with history and that points toward Harlem's future, which might destroy more culture than it preserves. Both urban decline and urban revitalization, Edwards contends, come with the threat of cultural loss. Set in 1995, gentrification is not yet a full-fledged problem in Edwards's Harlem, but its green shoots are detectable in the text. With its street-level view and intimate knowledge of the community, the novel is prescient about what is in the offing, the gentrification of the neighborhood, which within a few short years would threaten working-class Harlemites with displacement and threaten to erase the last vestiges of Harlem as the historic and historical home of Black culture.

The opening pages linger on one place in particular that we would do well to pause over to see how it embodies the sedimented layers of Harlem's twentieth-century history. The site is "the old Renaissance Casino dance hall near 138th Street" that Mali reflects on in her trip down memory lane. Once a Black-owned business in the 1920s, the Renaissance Casino was a prominent social center in Harlem, a place that hosted mass meetings,

FIGURE 4.3. Renaissance Casino and Ballroom, located at 2341–2359 Adam Clayton Powell Jr. Boulevard. *Source:* Beyond My Ken, CC BY-SA 4.0 (https://creativecommons.org/licenses/by-sa/4.0), via Wikimedia Commons.

wedding receptions, sporting events, and ballroom dances (2). By the early 1990s, after multiple owners and bankruptcies, the block-long, Moorish-style building was in such disrepair that it served as the setting for a crack den in Spike Lee's *Jungle Fever* (1991). Edwards does not note this filmic representation but rather notes that though it has been "boarded up for years" (2), the space in front of the building has been pragmatically repurposed as a farmers' market for southern Black specialties: "smoked hams, pig tails, collards, yams, and jars of honey" driven up from "Georgia and South Carolina" (3). The market breathes new life into the space, but "still, it was depressing," Mali remarks (3). The site is a haunting reminder of the rise and fall of the neighborhood, its history condensed in one resonant architectural space. Yet her reflection soon becomes more sanguine: "Lately, I had begun to feel differently. When David Dinkins and Charles Rangel arranged to have the Abyssinian Baptist Church buy the hall, my depression lifted. 'That grand old ballroom will be renovated, it's going to reopen,' I said. 'Harlem's coming back'" (3). The references are to the hall's 1993 purchase by the Abyssinian Development Corporation (ADC), a major real estate player in the community, a transaction orchestrated by New York's first Black mayor and the congressperson who led the UMEZ legislation and steered tens of millions of its dollars to Harlem. Millions of these UMEZ dollars have also flowed through the ADC, which has rehabbed buildings through the neighborhood, revitalizing Harlem in the minds of some residents but also hastening gentrification. During her reminiscence, however, Mali recalls her father's skepticism about the casino's rehabilitation: he "had raised one eye and smiled. . . .'[T]hey gotta get the deed in the hands; gotta get [the] title to the place'" (3). Her father's skepticism about the Renaissance Casino reopening proved prophetic, as though attuned to the probable future that would be brought to fruition a decade and a half later by economic pressures gathering steam in Harlem. The ADC purchased the building but never renovated it. Abyssinian instead resold the Renaissance Casino in the 2010s to new owners, who demolished it and erected on the plot the Rennie, a luxury condo whose cutesy name is a diminutive version of the casino and the Harlem Renaissance itself. In sum, what we see in this one site is Harlem at its cultural zenith in the 1920s, its deterioration from economic disinvestment that after years of urban decline reached its nadir during the crack-cocaine epidemic, its potential rebirth as a Black social space backed by Black capital, and its eventual erasure and transformation into upscale housing in an increasingly white and gentrified neighborhood.

Edwards's extended reflections on the spaces of Harlem's past and present establish at the novel's start a historical and spatial context shaped by flows of disinvestment and development. The murder and investigation that soon follow is thus situated within this context. Mali's meditation abruptly ends when she discovers her friend "Erskin Harding, the tour director of the Uptown Children's Chorus" lying dead on Strivers' Row next to a crying child as a Cadillac speeds away (5). The child was the target in an attempted kidnapping by Johnnie's men, who wanted to hold him for ransom as part of an elaborate plot to unwittingly enlist the young members of the Uptown Children's Chorus as mules to smuggle cocaine from France to Harlem. Edwards's decision to use the traveling chorus for this crime is significant. For one, it creates a "spatial opening" that links Harlem to the global drug trade for a regional customer base predominantly from out of state.[36] Thus, the novel undermines the notion that drugs and drug-related violence are a problem exclusive to the Black neighborhood. (The cars in the "carriage trade" in Harlem have "mostly Connecticut and Jersey plates" [232].) The decision to stage the conspiracy around the chorus is significant for another reason, too. In the novel, the renowned choir is a source of great pride for the neighborhood, its mere existence an unspoken counterargument to long-standing associations of Harlem with familial dysfunction and cultural pathology. Its mission is to "convinc[e] children that it was all right to want to be a choir kid instead of a gangster" (213). To corrupt the choir is to strike at the heart of Harlem. To save the choir, as Mali does by exposing the smuggling scheme, is to save the neighborhood in a not insignificant way.

"What's Happenin' wid Yo' Geography, Ma'am?"

As Edwards's novel unfolds, Mali's investigation expands from Strivers' Row to poorer parts of the neighborhood, underscoring Harlem's ongoing struggles with crime and poverty, its variegated social geography, and the disinvestment that was a precursor to gentrification. In the course of solving Erskin's murder, Mali visits a sprawling housing project—"eight buildings of twenty-one stories with ten apartments on every floor"—where the teenager Clarence lives, a choir member and one of the suspects in the killing (93). When she first remembers responding to "sixteen calls in one month" from this complex during the days she worked for the NYPD, we might think Mali will read this space through the predictable lens of law-and-order policing, as we saw Henry Chang do in his Jack Yu series. Yet she does not. Clarence is indeed arrested, though not by Mali, who has no legal authority. His arrest indeed is evidence that the rundown public housing complex, a legacy of midcentury urban renewal, is a criminalized geography through and through. Clarence, though, is innocent and later proves instrumental in saving Mali from Johnnie's men. What is guilty, however, of a crime—the social crime of urban neglect, racial isolation, and disinvestment—are the projects littered with "crack vials," reeking of "dried urine," their "cinder-block walls scarred with . . . graffiti" (94). Repeated endlessly in policy studies, essays, and popular media, images like these of slummy, deteriorating high-rises infested with gangs and deviancy became the standard template by the mid-1960s for depicting Harlem's despair and degradation, making the neighborhood a universal symbol of the American ghetto in crisis. If such images once worked to raise awareness of living conditions in Black neighborhoods and thus argued explicitly or implicitly for intervention of the state in the form of more federal money to ameliorate the problem, then by the antiwelfarist Reaganite 1980s, images like these were marshaled in a "blame-the-poor" discourse in which the residents themselves were solely at fault and unworthy of help. Edwards takes neither position. She lays the blame for the architectural and social deterioration squarely on the original sin of the state's programs of slum clearance and urban renewal that destroyed Black communities. The problem is not the people but the space itself, brought into existence by a policy that bulldozed existing communities to build isolating towers in the sky. "*Urban planning said pack them in, contain them. Ignore the pressures and pathology that builds in confined space*," Edwards writes (94). The public housing towers erected around Harlem are not designed for living, she implies, but as containers, really little more than holding pens for Black and brown bodies that are already othered ("pack them in"). Mass incarceration in public housing, Edwards suggests, breeds crime that leads to arrest and imprisonment.

Edwards's critique and demystification of the etiology of crime that we hear in her reflections on public housing are found throughout the novel. We see as much in another scene, when reporters storm Harlem in the days after Erskin's death. As news crews are out in full force, Edwards notes they run sensationalistic "stock footage of graffiti-scarred walls and burned-out tenements" alongside fresh video of "baggy-pants teenager[s]" looking "bewildered" (61). The "stock footage" underscores the press's lack of real interest in the neighborhood apart from the spectacle it offers. When they combine it with video of young, drug-addled delinquents, the images create a seamless, if highly selective and ideologically freighted, impression that confirms the worst stereotypes in the minds of white viewers. The locals who are interviewed, however, pop this racist illusion. One turns the questioning back on the reporter, asking why "every time somethin' bad happens" the news says it is in Harlem but "when somethin' okay happens, y'all say Upper West Side," referencing the adjacent wealthy white neighborhood. "What's happenin' wid yo' geography, ma'am?" the Harlem resident asks (61). *If I Should Die* never turns a blind eye to Harlem's poverty and crime, but it is also well aware of the material origins of these conditions and of how they are discursively and spatially constructed and mediated to reinforce racial inequality.

Interlaced with the novel's representations of Harlem's dilapidated housing are contrasting images of gentrification. We should keep in mind, however, that beneath the superficial contrast runs the seesawing logic of uneven geographical development. Its processes of slum clearance, benign neglect, and redlining lead to urban decline, but this decline is the precursor, not the antithesis, of gentrification. The deterioration of a neighborhood lays the groundwork for its eventual renewal and rehabilitation with a new infusion of capital. As Dennis Broe remarks in a brief assessment of Edwards's fiction, "new is not always nicer."[37] The first signs of gentrification in *If I Should Die* suggest not the improvement of the neighborhood for its Black residents but the exploitation of them by another means under the guise of neighborhood improvement. These images include the construction of "a four-block-long row of two-family houses" with freshly planted trees and new sidewalks, a sign of the arrival of new upper-middle-class homeowners (69). They include, too, the "grinding noise of bulldozers" in the background of several scenes (135) and a "community garden" uprooted by development, an act signaling that the repurposed space is for those who are not from the community (133). The novel's most pointed sign of gentrification is the relocation of the "African market on Lenox and 116th," with its small-time vendors selling "fabric, sandals, incense, and hats," not unlike the Afrocentric clothing store selling dashikis and caftans Edwards herself ran in Harlem in the 1960s (128). Mali notes that the "city administration had forced" the market from its "original location on 125th Street," an allusion to the Giuliani administration's deployment of excessive force in October 1994 when "more than five hundred police officers in riot gear swept 125th Street," cleared out the African vendors, and barricaded off the sidewalks.[38] It was an initial step to the UMEZ's remaking of the commercial corridor to create room for the corporate retailers of the Harlem USA mall, Disney first among them (128). With the African market gone, "Harlem's main thoroughfare now seemed drained of life," Mali comments (128). It is a dead zone. In the novel, urban revitalization vampirically sucks the vitality out of the neighborhood, destroying local culture in the process.

Even parts of the neighborhood that appear yet untouched by gentrification are suffused with the melancholic feeling that they are living on borrowed time. In one extended passage, Mali strolls through Harlem on foot, taking readers up Adam Clayton Powell Jr. Boulevard, across 145th Street, over to St. Nicholas Avenue, and farther west to Amsterdam Avenue, observing as she goes along the neighborhood's "numbers runners," locally famous characters like "TooHot," "a wedding party pulling up in block-long, silver limos," "the old Brown Bomber bar," "the Rock Tavern," and a crowd in a takeout line for the best "chicken and chips place" in the area (108–9). This passage and others like it of Mali walking through Harlem and waving to "bow-tied brothers" as she passes a mosque or feeling like she wants to "recapture some of [her] innocence" as she watches girls play double Dutch, "skipping into the ropes, spinning around with braids flying," are woven with memories and anecdotes that suggest her personal attachment to the neighborhood sedimented in its temporal layers that she knows intimately (216). These are more than streets and buildings; they are the sites of stories, memory, and local culture. When Edwards spoke of "tak[ing] readers on a virtual tour of Harlem," by which she obviously meant white readers who were not residents of the neighborhood, so they "can see and get a real sense of the lives we live here," these are the kinds of passages she references. This is the world of "ordinary people . . . going about ordinary business," Edwards writes, the dailiness of Harlem that is nearly invisible to outsiders (47). However vibrant these vignettes are, the impression the novel leaves is that this part of Harlem's life might fade into memory altogether, under threat as it is by development eating around Harlem's perimeter and through its central commercial strip.

As Mali's investigation into Erskin's murder weaves her through these local spaces of "ordinary people" and past the incipient signs of gentrification in Harlem, we have to pause and recognize something important. Tellingly, the novel does not appear to weave these signs of gentrification into the criminal conspiracy at the heart of the text, as we have seen in the work of Richard Price, Henry Chang, and Gabriel Cohen, whose cops hasten gentrification by suppressing crime and disrupting criminal plots that threaten a neighborhood's renewal. Though the NYPD as a whole is doing the bidding of the UMEZ in the novel, Johnnie Harding's drug-dealing operation, which is also aided and abetted by NYPD detectives, actually threatens to undermine the neighborhood's redevelopment by reinforcing Harlem's reputation as a haven of crime and substance abuse. Crime is bad for business, and in Mali's Harlem, "there's a murder every week" and multiple murders and attempted homicides related to Johnnie's scheme before *If I Should Die* reaches its final page (136). Given that the murderous conspiracy and the investigation into it unfold in the context of Harlem's early-stage gentrification without the two (Harding's scheme and Harlem's development) being directly connected, how should we understand this apparent gap between plot and setting? First we must recognize that undergirding the "ordinary" life in the neighborhood, the whole social milieu that Mali passes through and that the novel presents as a series of vignettes, is another structure of flows (urban development, the global traffic of drugs and money, and racist policing) that is always present, if not always visible. Second, this apparent disconnection between plot and setting in fact ironically signifies a deeper, unacknowledged relation between the two, which we can intuit when we recognize how Edwards's protagonist observes and comments on Harlem's losing its spirit, but is unable to counteract it either as a sociologist in training or as an ex-cop. Put more pointedly, she never even thinks to do anything about gentrification. This is not the result of some shortcoming of Edwards's smart and driven heroine but rather the byproduct of the universalization of capitalism, whose processes have become so deeply aligned with human nature that it is almost impossible to imagine a different future for the neighborhood. Even if "new is not always nicer," it nevertheless seems unstoppable in Edwards's novel.[39] All Mali can do is look wistfully at how Harlem is changing, feel the loss of innocence, mourn that it is "drained of life" (128), and regretfully comment, "Those times and all of those places [are] gone" (4).

Keeping the Natives in Check

If urban development reverberating in the background of Edwards's Harlem poses an implicit threat to the neighborhood's local culture and street life, the explicit threat in the foreground to the entire community is not just Johnnie Harding but the police who make his operation possible. In *If I Should Die* corrupt cops receive payment for providing protection for Johnnie, who is flooding the neighborhood with drugs and whose noisome crack den is filled not only with addicts but child prostitutes as young as eight and nine. Thus in Edwards's novel the bad cops—Terry Keenan and Danny Williams—threaten to undo the work that the UMEZ and gentrification more generally are doing to change the neighborhood's lingering reputation as a tangle of pathologies and crime.

However, if the corruption of cops in Edwards's book appears to work against the cleaning up of the neighborhood, in another sense they hasten it. In the work of other writers in this study, we have seen how the highly racialized practice of broken-windows policing facilitates gentrification by pacifying so-called disorderly neighborhoods—ridding them of homeless people and cracking down on quality-of-life violations—to make urban space amenable to urban redevelopment. In Edwards's text, this takes the form of the NYPD violently enforcing the existing racial order. While the racism undergirding broken-windows policing has been dramatized in the novels of other crime writers in *The Gentrification Plot*, nowhere is it as explicit and systemic as it is in *If I Should Die*. The incident that led Mali to join the NYPD was witnessing three cops beating a handcuffed Black man against a chain-link fence in Harlem when she was a student, a scene that gave her "nightmares for years" (52, 53). "Remember how he looked . . . his face a crisscross of swollen welts," she asks her friend Deborah over lunch, the memory pressed into her mind (52). Recalling the scene unsettles Mali, who finds the anger churning up in her throat "so hot and thick" it causes her to choke (52). "I joined the force because I thought I could work to make sure nothing like that happened again—at least not on my watch," she says after regaining her composure (53). Drawing on the language of colonial oppression, Deborah's response, accusing her of being both naïve and complicit, upsets Mali further, largely because its point lands: "What you really joined was a force dedicated to one thing: keeping the natives in check" (53). Mali is one of these unruly "natives" herself. The

NYPD's racial policing in the book extends to policing the racial hierarchy within its own ranks and forcing out those who refuse to stay in check. As the reader learns early in the text, Mali was fired after two years on the job for punching Terry as he was taping to her locker a "picture of two apes copulating" with her name written across the top, a filthy act of putting her in her place (12). To be a Black woman and a cop is untenable, the novel suggests.

Edwards's critique of racist cops is a critique of Giuliani, who implemented broken-windows policing and relentlessly enforced it for eight years. Giuliani is referenced twice in the novel, near the beginning and once again at the very end, suggesting that his ominous presence is felt throughout. The first reference is to the police riot in 1992 when Giuliani, then a prosecutor, was running a law-and-order campaign against Dinkins with barely disguised racist undertones. "The high point of his [Terry Keenan's] career," Edwards writes, "happened when he, in a mob of a thousand other officers of the law, egged on by a prosecutor who bore a striking resemblance to Frankenstein's monster, stormed City Hall, threatening and cursing Mayor Dinkins" (43). Long before Giuliani would warm up the crowd that invaded the U.S. Capitol on January 6, 2021, he had used a bullhorn to rile up ten thousand cops who had congregated at City Hall to protest Dinkins's police reforms, including his call for a Civilian Complaint Review Board and his creation of the Mollen Commission a year earlier to investigate NYPD misconduct. Off-duty police officers rushed City Hall, and thousands of others shouting "Rudy!" spilled out onto Brooklyn Bridge while chugging beer and wearing their firearms. The iconic New York journalist Jimmy Breslin reported in *Newsday* a complete portrait of the riot that made plain it was a white uprising against Black political power. "The cops held up several of the most crude drawings of Dinkins, black, performing perverted sex acts," not unlike Terry's picture on Mali's locker, shouting, "Now you got a nigger right inside City Hall. How do you like that? A nigger mayor," Breslin wrote, who went on to detail that NYPD officers also harassed two African American city councilwomen, one with a racial slur and the other by rocking her car as she was trapped on the Brooklyn Bridge.[40] What we should underscore here is that if Edwards's protagonist joined the NYPD to put an end to a modern-day lynching such as this, her antagonist Terry, the racist cop who works with Johnnie Harding, signed up in order to join in the fray. The riot is the "high point" of his service as an NYPD officer. One notes that in the days after the insurrection Giuliani refused to denounce the police's actions and language. His campaign, nevertheless, commissioned a "vulnerability study" six months later. Its first section was titled "RACIST" in all caps, followed by a thirty-two-page analysis of his involvement in and reaction to the riot. The vulnerability turned out not to be one at all. Giuliani would victoriously ride white grievance—which manifested itself most pointedly over complaints about high crime—to the mayor's office in 1994. Edwards's novel keeps the memory of this historical wrong alive for readers and enacts a measure of poetic justice by calling out Giuliani's racism and the structural racism of the NYPD at large.

In the last pages of *If I Should Die*, after Terry and Danny are killed in Johnnie's crack den, Edwards alludes to Giuliani once more. "The mayor—the same man who had encouraged thousands of policemen to riot, to storm City Hall—this mayor would be on the six o'clock news trying to explain this latest betrayal of the public trust," Edwards writes (255). It is perhaps easy enough to contextualize Edwards's novel with the cop riot of 1992, an insurrection that has largely passed from public memory. What is more imperative is to see what Edwards makes of it in her narrative, the way it frames the entire book and informs the motivations of characters within it. Revealingly, Edwards never utters Giuliani's name (Dinkins's appears multiple times), as though "Giuliani" is a slur that she refuses to let into her textual space, refuses to let into her Harlem, even if his cops are everywhere on Harlem's streets.

In 2000 in *Essence* magazine, Edwards reflected on how her heroine is an "ordinary citizen" who finds herself "pulled into situations" that she has to solve. The description clearly echoes the warm portrait in *If I Should Die* of "ordinary people . . . going about ordinary business," whose way of life Mali wants to protect (47). "The one constant," Edwards remarked, "is Mali's belief that crime disturbs the social order, and order must be restored."[41] Surprisingly, Edwards here aligns her protagonist with what some scholars, such as Ernest Mandel and Stephen Knight, see as crime fiction's conservative disposition. They argue that the genre's strong narrative push toward resolution offers readers a reassuring worldview in which crime can be controlled, justice served, and the legitimacy of the state reaffirmed.[42] The genre returns the world to what it was before the ruptures and traumas of a crime. I cannot help but notice two painful ironies when it comes to Edwards's comment regarding crime and the restoration of social order, ironies that weigh heavily not only on her novel but on all of the novels in this study. The first is that what helped usher Giuliani into office was a violent act of civil *disorder* by beer-swilling officers of the law, the same cops who supported his *order-maintenance*, broken-windows policing. What also cannot pass without comment is the other fact that by far the most common criminal summons issued by the NYPD enforcing quality-of-life violations in putatively disorderly neighborhoods during the eight years of the Giuliani administration was for holding an open container of alcohol, a policy that netted up hundreds of thousands of New Yorkers of color. In the early pages of *If I Should Die*, Mali comments that she and Tad, her love interest, "were acutely aware of the ever-present undercurrent of racism that infected everything in our daily lives" (11). This undercurrent runs throughout the entire book like a live wire. In its reflections on the NYPD's racism and the racism of the state's housing policies, the latter seen in Edwards's critique of urban planning, the novel thus opens up the questions: What is criminal even if it is technically legal? What is a social crime, even if it is perpetrated by the state and its enforcers? To me, this is the far-ranging and radical social and political critique I detect in Edwards's novel. Thus the second irony is that the "social order" that "must be restored" in *If I Should Die*, according to Edwards, is the one that sadly never went away in the first place but should be dismantled, the one where "racism . . . infected everything in our daily lives."

At the novel's end, Johnnie Harding's drug operation is brought down, but Giuliani is still mayor, of course; 125th Street is still on its way to becoming a UMEZ-sponsored mall; and gentrification is still encroaching on Harlem's local culture. As Mali's friend Deborah tells her, "sometimes you have to change the world before you can change the neighborhood" (53). That's a scale of change that Edwards's novel, and crime fiction more generally, has trouble imagining.

THE FIRES OF ERNESTO QUIÑONEZ

When we shift our attention several blocks east from Edwards's territory in her Mali Anderson series, we find ourselves in the terrain of Quiñonez's work. In his first two novels, *Bodega Dreams* and *Chango's Fire*, the haunting legacy of the 1970s, when the neighborhood was regularly on fire (a tragic if foreseeable consequence of closing firehouses) meets the new crisis of the late 1990s and early 2000s, when it was, and still is, being rapidly consumed by the FIRE industries fueling gentrification. Quiñonez's novels deploy the trope of fire as a figure that connects Harlem's history across decades to underscore that urban abandonment and new development are two expressions of a single economics of exploitation. What at first might appear to be polar-opposite economic processes, the latter a corrective to the former, are in actuality part of a cycle of disinvestment, decline, reinvestment, and rehabilitation that damages the neighborhood at each turn. In *Chango's Fire*, Quiñonez notes "a new policy" for twenty-first-century urban neighborhoods that "is going into effect soon," but he remarks that it is really an old policy with a depressingly familiar set of strategies: "they can call it Planned Shrinkage, Benign Neglect, Model Cities, Urban Renewal, or whatever they want. It means one thing: slum-clearing for industry and expensive housing, the burning of ghettoes."[43] Dávila makes a related point when arguing that "after all, gentrification—whether called renewal, revitalization, upgrading, or uplifting—always involves the expansion and transformation of neighborhoods through rapid economic investment and population shifts, and yet it is equally implicated with social inequalities."[44] The original burning of Spanish Harlem in the 1970s is a history woven into Quiñonez's texts in extended passages of backstory meant to educate the reader. The postindustrial city's FIRE sectors that have spread through the fallow terrain in the years since form the foreground for his narratives of young Puerto Rican men entangled in real estate and insurance fraud, men who turn to crime to make ends meet, only to find themselves burned in a neighborhood rising from the ashes.

Both *Bodega Dreams* and *Chango's Fire* are autos-da-fé that test each man's mettle as a price for his crimes. In both novels, Quiñonez's protagonists are burned out of their apartments in the present-day gentrifying neighborhood, conflagrations signifying a traumatic return of history that Quiñonez knows personally. In his essay "The Fires Last Time," he recounts one Saturday morning as he watched cartoons "black smoke" billowing "underneath the front door" of his family's six-story walk-up apartment "like a genie out of a bottle." As he tells it, he roused his parents and together they hurried onto the fire escape and climbed down to the wintry street. The family spent two weeks in a "welfare hotel in Midtown," with prostitutes in makeshift rooms separated only by curtains, before relocating to

Schomburg Plaza, which, though riddled with crime, was at least "fireproof."
He concludes "The Fires Last Time" by directing his attention to the FIREs
this time that are transforming East Harlem into the latest hotspot in a
feverish housing market. "The building I used to live in sat there and sat
there, empty and broken, for decades," Quiñonez writes. "Then the better
days its landlord was waiting for arrived," he comments, adding, "In 1994,
Spanish Harlem became part of the Upper Manhattan Empowerment
Zone." Quiñonez describes his old neighborhood from that point forward
as gentrifying beyond recognition. With its "renovated buildings with their
outrageous rents, its co-ops, its trendy bars and cafes," it is less Spanish, less
Harlem, and more "SpaHa."[45] "Those who are profiting in today's age of gentrification," he notes, "would like to forget the burning of the ghettos."
Quiñonez's novels ask readers to remember.

Drugs, Development, Displacement

In the opening pages of *Bodega Dreams*, Quiñonez's narrator Julio Mercado
remembers Spanish Harlem's public housing complexes in the 1970s and
1980s, the "projects with pissed-up elevators, junkies on the stairs, posters
of the rapist of the month, and whores you never knew were whores until
you saw men go in and out of their apartments like through revolving
doors."[46] It is a portrait of an ugly place where "your life meant shit from
the start" and where it was often short (4). As a teenager, Julio earns extra
cash painting R.I.P. murals. The neighborhood surrounding the projects
was no better, as Julio recalls. "One day a block would have people, the next
day it would be erased by fire" (5). Images of urban ruins litter his memory: the rubble of "burned-down buildings" that would "house junkies,"
"gutted tenements" that were eventually toppled when "the City of New
York would send a crane," and "graveyard[s] [of] stolen cars" with their
"doors, tires, windows," and anything salvageable removed (5). What Julio
as a young boy does with these spaces is key: he uses them as "playgrounds"
and as places "to explore," transfiguring them into spaces of the imagination, thus foreshadowing his future as a writer at the book's end (5). Julio
will use his formative experience in this urban wasteland, Quiñonez hints,
to one day *symbolically* transform and redeem Spanish Harlem in words.
The foil to Julio is Willie Bodega, a Young Lord radical turned drug lord
and intent on "becoming the second-biggest slumlord" in the city (37). As

a social activist and criminal housing developer, he rehabilitates the neighborhood's ruined spaces *materially* to make them livable again, an endeavor that violently fails. What replaces Bodega's material project is the home that Quiñonez builds in the world of fiction.

Bodega Dreams begins as a novel about a social crime, the decimation of a Latinx neighborhood by the forces of redlining, legislated urban renewal in the 1960s and 1970s, and systemic discrimination. The novel proposes to correct for this crime with a solution that is also criminal. To repair the damage from the past and also to prevent the neighborhood in the present from being destroyed a second time by gentrification, Bodega embarks on a scheme to bribe city officials so he can acquire crumbling buildings, renovate them, and rent them out at below-market rates to Latinos in return for their loyalty. The buildings are technically owned by a shell company that Bodega uses to conceal his identity and skirt taxes. He directly likens his social engineering project to Johnson's "Great Society," but with critical differences: he designs it for people who were excluded from the original vision of midcentury liberalism, and he does so in the neoliberal era, that is, without any government support. Also, Bodega pays for it through the sale of heroin and crack to his fellow Harlemites (31).

In effect, Bodega wants to construct a closed economy in which he extracts money from the community to rebuild the community as a stronghold for its current residents, a project urgently needed because of the neighborhood's impending gentrification. One would think, as in Edwards's novel, additional drug dealing and the social catastrophe wrought by addiction—attributable at least in part to Bodega—would stymie gentrification, too, but Quiñonez does not entertain this idea. "This neighborhood will be lost unless we make it ours. Look at Loisaida, that's gone," Bodega's partner-in-crime Edwin Nazario tells Julio, using the Nuyorican pronunciation of the Lower East Side (106). "All those white yuppies want to live in Manhattan, and they think Spanish Harlem is next for the taking," he explains (106–7). Bodega's utopian dream is of a neighborhood radically independent and decolonized, an island-state unto itself on the island of Manhattan. Rather than have it sell itself to outsiders as the UMEZ proposed, he aims to seal off Harlem as a self-empowered and self-contained ethnic redoubt. To attain this dream, he is willing to poison the neighborhood in order to save it, repairing its broken windows with one hand and creating crack houses with the other. Edwards's *If I Should Die* takes us inside Harding's noisome crack den, a hellish space where faces appear and disappear in the dark when "lighters flickered like fireflies" and where men stand in a line with "their pants open" as "girls' cries filled the room" (233–35). We never see such spaces in *Bodega Dreams*, largely because Quiñonez wants his title character to remain a community hero, if a fatally flawed one.

But as with Edwards's book, what is and is not a crime is a core issue of *Bodega Dreams*. "Everyone's a thief. Crime is a matter of access," Quiñonez writes (103). In one scene, as Nazario and Julio walk through the neighborhood, Nazario points out the James Weldon Johnson Houses and imagines a future when he and Bodega could "knock those projects down" (107). "We're trying to do things here," he boasts (159). "Through crime," Julio asks, an accusation more than a question. "Through whatever means are at our disposal," he counters (159). In Julio's mind, these criminal methods are enticing because they might accelerate his own traditional, by-the-bootstraps upward mobility, but he remains leery: "I had enrolled at school thinking about other ways to come out on top," he says (160). As the novel goes on, he gets in deeper with Bodega, at one point storing drugs for his crew and at another moving into one of Bodega's larger renovated apartments in exchange for a favor. "Graduate, get a good job, save, buy a house—but those ways were slow," he laments, realizing he has a wife, Blanca, and baby on the way to care for (160). In a time of worsening economic precarity in a neoliberal city that is gutting help to the poor, Julio recognizes these liberal pathways are no longer "guarantees of success" (160). "Social services were being cut," he notes, adding, "Financial aid for people like me and Blanca who were trying to better themselves was practically nonexistent" (38). The novel thus reflects the truth of its late 1990s moment, the inability of traditional institutions to provide the makings of a better life. For Julio, who has a clean sheet, apart from quality-of-life violations ("hopp[ing] a few turnstiles"), crime becomes an alluring alternative not for social justice reasons, as Bodega dreams, but for getting ahead in the marketplace, a point underscored by his surname Mercado (178). When the novel starts, Julio's dream is to "get out of here," leave the neighborhood for good (11).

Upon closer scrutiny, we can see that the radical autonomy Quiñonez ascribes to East Harlem and to Bodega is also mobilized by the traditional American ethic of self-reliance spurred on by governmental neglect and discrimination. America's vaunted ethos of self-improvement is effectuated by impoverishment, ruination, and scarcity, which are the conditions of life in Bodega's neighborhood and which in theory light a proverbial fire under one's ass. It is one of the novel's many ironies. "No one but one of its own residents was going to improve Spanish Harlem," Julio states emphatically, reflecting Bodega's own assessment (171). "Housing. . . . Thass how I'm going to do it. Thass the vision," declares Bodega (28), boasting, "Where the city sees burned buildings I see opportunity" (37). It is about more than housing, though: "It's about upward mobility. It's about education and making yourself better. It's about sacrifice" (106). Providing decent, inexpensive housing marks the first step in his grander dream of creating a "professional class . . . born and bred in Spanish Harlem" (106). He plans to build a home-grown, brown Talented Tenth who, with his financing, will go "to college to study law, medicine, education, business, political science, anything useful" (106). Thus, Bodega's project is not solely to improve the neighborhood but also to keep Spanish Harlem from becoming whiter by ensuring Latinos will not be displaced by gentrification and by ensuring they can obtain material success and social mobility without having to leave the neighborhood, as historically has been the case.

The dream of the novel is the dream of a neighborhood resisting the forces of gentrification by unifying around a common identity and a shared goal of radical economic self-sufficiency. Quiñonez, however, cannot imagine this dream actualized. Bodega's vision is "something out of the sixties," Julio says dismissively (31). In a flurry of action in the novel's closing pages, this dream collapses like a house of cards on fire. The apartment building Julio lives in as a reward for helping Bodega is torched by Nazario, who risks killing everyone inside so he can appear on the scene as a savior reassuring the traumatized residents. Julio and his wife are "displaced. Disoriented. No insurance, no new place, everything lost" (144). Bodega then takes the fall for his ex-lover Vera's murder of her husband, only to be gunned down by Nazario, who secretly loved Vera all along and conspired with her. Realizing his own life is in danger, Julio rats out Nazario and Vera to NYPD detectives, who swoop in at Bodega's funeral and arrest the couple. "Bodega's dreams were dead," Quiñonez states perfunctorily (197). For much of the novel, Quiñonez entertains the revolutionary idea of Bodega's criminality as an antistatist critique and an exercise of radical praxis with socially liberatory potential. Yet the novel forecloses this possibility with the thud of a coffin lid. As crime fiction often does, *Bodega*

Dreams "reimpose[s] the law and return[s] society to what it had been before."[47]

The novel, however, refuses to conclude on this sour note. If the project of Bodega was to build and manage a Latino "Great Society" in Spanish Harlem, the project of the book, I would argue, is to incinerate this dream and replace it with another one. Put another way, Quiñonez kills off Bodega and his radical politics so he can clear the field for what turns out to be a novel about writing. In the last page and a half, the text offers Julio, as well as readers, a compensatory dream to replace the one that goes up in smoke. This new dream marks a jarring shift in the text, one that feels tacked on: it's an ending that makes the novel more hopeful and marketable to readers of literary fiction who demand some redemption in a character after a life of hardship and who seek, more broadly, an affirmation of the healing power of art.

On the night of Bodega's funeral, Julio dreams Bodega returns to visit, and the two of them step onto a fire escape, where they hear residents in the neighborhood conversing in a mix of Spanish and English, a blending Bodega aestheticizes as "a poem," claiming, "It's a beautiful new language" and that a "new language means a new race" (212). "Spanglish is the future," Bodega tells Julio (212). It is a curious claim, not the least because to conflate language and race, while evoking hybridity, erases the very differences within East Harlem's already existing diverse (and competing) communities of Puerto Ricans, Mexicans, and Dominicans. This "new language being born out of the ashes of two cultures clashing with each other" is presented to Julio as a gift bestowed with strings attached. "You will use a new language," Bodega says, imagining that Julio will become a writer (212).

What can we possibly call this moment except a kind of primal scene: the writer Quiñonez, who is half-Ecuadorian and half–Puerto Rican, like Julio, and shares his nickname Chino, witnessing the instance of his own conception as an artist in the presence of a father figure. Notably, Quiñonez positions Julio not quite *in* the street but rather slightly *above* it—the position of the writer surveying his territory. The clear implication is Julio will continue Bodega's work but in a different vein; he will use this "new language" to do something "like what I was trying to do," Bodega says (212). Like but not the same. Julio will create a house of words filled with the voices of Spanish Harlem's residents, rather than a house of bricks to hold them. Or as Quiñonez himself disclosed, studying writing and literature in City

College "taught me" that "Spanish Harlem was as valid material for literature as Joyce's Dublin. The world was not just filled with whiteness but rather it was a swirl of flavors and people, and it was my mission to add more color and spice to the wonderful but pale pages of American letters."[48] This is what takes shape in the final paragraphs. From the fire escape—a poignant pun in a neighborhood prone to burning—Julio offers a lengthy description of a neighborhood "alive" with "music and people" who are "shaking with love and desire for each other," children playing in the stream of fire hydrants, elderly women gossiping on "project benches," people "jumping, shaking, and jamming," "stereos playing at full blast," the active gerunds piling up sentence by sentence (212, 213). This concluding scene, flitting from one imagined street vignette to another, a harmonic rhapsody found in the closing credits of so many films, is a portrait of what the urban neighborhood is now and what it might continue to be in the future. Julio pointedly says it is "my dream," not Bodega's (213).

To appreciate the novel's ending, we have to notice what is newly absent in the scene, as well as what is newly present. First, we note that this active scene is not a scene of activism. It is a scene of everyday pleasure, which from one angle can be understood as a political act to imbue with life a space that had been discursively rendered by urban sociologists as a deadly stew of pathologies or that has been rendered by urban planners and politicians as an abstract, geometrical space to be rationally and soullessly mapped and partitioned. Quiñonez's discursive or textual activism thus is his resignification of Spanish Harlem into what Edward Soja calls a "fully *lived space*, a simultaneously real-and-imagined, actual-and-virtual, locus of structured individual and collective experience and agency."[49] From another angle, one notes that the kind of action in the final scene and the kind of discursive activism it presupposes signals exactly how much those dreams of 1960s activism are in the ash heap of history. So much so that they cannot really be imagined anymore except as good ideas that failed.

In the end, Julio takes ownership of a new "dream" of cultural and linguistic hybridity, which replaces the older militant dream of ethnic homogeny. But in embracing this new dream, Julio also appears to reject not just the radical dream but also part of the liberal dream he once believed in. This dream of upward mobility has historically necessitated that the ethnic American not only leave the enclave for a "better" neighborhood but also leave his or her ethnicity behind. If Julio has gained the neighborhood—a Spanish Harlem of hybrid, pluralistic identities rather than assimilated ones—the cost has been the loss of his wife, who leaves him because of his involvement with Bodega. This loss of Blanca is a loss of his own whiteness, the loss of the dream that would require him to shed his ethnicity and his past. In earlier decades of expanding opportunities and a growing middle class, this requirement, this "choice," if you will, was willingly made. But in the era of neoliberal gentrification, geographical mobility is no longer an exercise of freedom and social mobility for many Latinos like Julio so much as it is a reality of geographical displacement and deterritorialization by the forces of the market that Bodega's dream was designed to guard against. With Bodega gone, one cannot help but think Julio is more likely, not less, to leave Spanish Harlem, only now not by his own choice. This prospect of displacement poignantly enters the novel at the moment Julio commits himself to the neighborhood. His new dream of staying in the neighborhood might be an illusion. The final scene of celebration is redolent of a bitter sweetness that one cannot escape.

The Crimes of the FIRE Industries

"It seemed like a good place to start" (213). The final sentence of *Bodega Dreams*, this is Julio's observation as he looks out over Spanish Harlem in the aftermath of Bodega's murder and in the wake of his own pregnant wife having left their marriage. Quiñonez's follow-up *Chango's Fire* is also a novel about starting over. By the time the novel concludes, the twenty-nine-year-old Julio Santana, an upwardly mobile striver, has been burned out of the apartment he owns because of his involvement in a criminal real estate insurance plot, much like his doppelgänger in *Bodega Dreams*. He and his family are forced back into the public housing they had struggled to escape from, his achievements and aspirations in smoking ruins in a Harlem that is haunted, as it was in Quiñonez's debut, by a historical geography of burned blocks and rubble. At the end of the book, even his love life with a white woman is in shambles because of his criminal activities. In the final pages of *Chango's Fire*, we see Julio preparing to rebuild his life in a neighborhood that has been built, burned down, and rebuilt repeatedly. The rewards for this work of rebuilding a life are somewhere off in the future, as they seemingly always are in American fiction, never arriving by the last sentence. As in his first book, Quiñonez symbolically offsets Julio's losses with the promise of personal reinvention and a deeper immersion in a community's "stories" of survival.

Readers can be forgiven for wondering whether they've read this story before. One might chalk up the numerous parallels to a writer's sophomore slump. Seeking to capitalize on a successful debut, the writer recycles what worked the first time around. One might even see Quiñonez, a writer with high literary ambitions, as writing a kind of formula fiction or genre fiction—the ethnic gentrification novel, if you will—with a repeated set of character types (even repeated names), repeated settings, repeated scenarios, and repeated resolutions. That's one way to look at it, but it does not get us very far. And it misses the larger thematics across the two books: the cycles of uneven development of the urban neighborhood, its spaces tilled and retilled to extract profit, and the seemingly irresolvable political and personal problems this causes. So the other way to look at it is to see Quiñonez's revisiting of the familiar territory of *Bodega Dream*'s Spanish Harlem as an enactment of this logic of return, a plot structure across two books that mimics the circular flow of money and people and the rise and fall and rise again of the urban neighborhood. The fact that each novel ends with the promise, but not the actuality, of a new beginning suggests, on the one hand, a hope for a different urban future and, on the other hand, a recognition that it will not be that different, that the same issues and the same problems will repeat themselves. We see as much in the final sentence of *Chango's Fire*: "And so, full of hope and light, I went back inside my apartment and closed the door behind me" (273). In the very moment that it posits a new beginning, a new door opening, the book ends with the protagonist literally turning his back, returning to his apartment in the projects, and closing "the door behind" him (273). So much for "hope." So much for "light."

But some things have changed since *Bodega Dreams*. Or a more honest way of putting it is that things have gotten worse. The Spanish Harlem of *Bodega Dreams* is caught betwixt and between the ever-shrinking liberal welfare state, which has largely abandoned the neighborhood, and the first wave of gentrifiers who are about to move in but have not yet arrived in large numbers. By the time of *Chango's Fire*, Bodega's barricades are gone, and gentrification is spreading through the neighborhood. Indeed, the subtle if ominous threat of displacement that I hear in the closing notes of *Bodega Dreams* is borne out four years later, only it is a different Julio who is forced from his home. Quiñonez does not broach the dream of rehabilitating apartments to house a new professional class of Puerto Ricans in *Chango's Fire*. There is no radical political imaginary in the book, no collective dream to inspire the neighborhood. The work of restoring tenements in Spanish Harlem does go on, only now it is managed by a low-level Italian mobster named Eddie Naglioni, whose construction crews rehabilitate "beautiful buildings" that were "set afire years ago" (26) and rent them out to those who can afford "absurdly high" prices (7). There is no hint of altruism to this work, only tragic irony and a great deal of profit earned at the start and the end of the cycle of burning and rebuilding. Eddie rebuilds the neighborhood for the gentrifying inflow in the early 2000s; in the 1970s, his work was the inverse: he "burned down half of El Barrio and most of the South Bronx," which led to the earlier outflow (6). Julio comments that back then "he got a cut of the insurance money from the property owners, including the city" (6).

Chango's Fire transforms the sociological realities of gentrification by the FIRE industries into a narrative about crime and complicity and the hell you have to pay for it in the end. The central drama of the text inheres in the impossible situations, choices, and double binds that an unequal urban political economy demands of the poor and people of color. Throughout the novel, Julio is committed to Spanish Harlem as an ethnic fortress on an island getting richer and whiter by the day. To survive in the neighborhood, you have to "claim your territory," he declares (51). One might think that he would be repelled by Eddie, but he is not, or at least he cannot afford to be. Julio burns the candle at both ends for him. He works for Eddie's crews during the day, work that gentrifies the neighborhood and threatens his place and the place of other Puerto Ricans in it. At night he still works for Eddie, this time as an arsonist in his fraud racket, which involves burning down houses at their owner's request. Crime does pay, for Julio. It pays the mortgage. The "crumbs" he gets from his illicit earnings are enough to meet the payments on his modest apartment, which he otherwise could not afford with the money from his day job (5). So here's the rub. The economy of the novel, much like the economy outside of it, demands private-property ownership as the ticket for entry into the middle class yet provides strivers like Julio with only low-status work that pays wages woefully inadequate for buying a home of one's own, especially in a gentrifying neighborhood. To solve the conundrum, Julio seeks out additional money through crime, sells a piece of his soul, as he puts it, and in doing so he winds up compounding the problem in a way that claims his own home in an act of arson (52).

Quiñonez bookends the novel with two fires. In the first, Julio torches a house in the wealthy suburb of Westchester, pointedly described as "an American house new immigrants dream of . . . the type of house America promises can be yours if you work hard, save your pennies and salute the flag" (3). In the second, he watches the Harlem apartment he has struggled to buy go up in flames. It is an "old battered, three-story walk-up," Julio says early in the novel, but it is his dream house: "I'm happy there. At times and for no reason, I go outside and cross the street and stare at my building. I smile. See the third floor? I own it, I tell myself" (5). Near the end, he stands back out in the street looking up at a "shell of bricks and towering clouds of smoke" (254). In between its two conflagrations, Quiñonez's text follows Julio's trials and tribulations. These include his vexed romance with the novel's resident creative-class gentrifier, a white woman named Helen who lives in his building at 103rd Street and Lexington and owns Spa Ha Gallery. They include, too, his mentorship by Felix, affectionately called Papelito, an older gay man who runs a botanica and educates him about Chango, a god of Santeria represented by "fire and lightning" (34). And they include, as noted, his entanglement with Eddie, who demands Julio burn down his own house when he botches the arson job in Westchester in a manner that denies Eddie the fraudulent insurance claim. If Julio refuses to do it, Eddie says he will have it done anyways, and those living in the building will not receive advance warning. When Julio refuses to torch his own building and fork over the insurance money, Trompo, Eddie's unacknowledged autistic son, does the job. The beloved Felix dies rescuing those inside, the novel's queer of color character sacrificed on the pyre in a manner that sets the stage for Julio's future rebirth from the ashes.

Even more so than *Bodega Dreams*, Quiñonez's second novel is about the crimes of fire and the FIRE industries in the gentrifying ethnic enclave. As in *Bodega Dreams*, the Spanish Harlem of the follow-up book suffers the lingering traumas of the arson of the 1970s that left much of the neighborhood littered with "worthless property" (6). But unlike *Bodega Dreams*, the FIRE industries of the early 2000s that are reclaiming these ruins are now in full blaze. The novel embodies these forces in Eddie, who works for a sprawling, shadowy real estate network that stretches to DC and profits by burning buildings as a means of "slum-clearing for industry," reinvesting the fraudulent insurance claims to build "expensive housing" (117). The work that Eddie does is Quiñonez's way of giving narrative shape to the economic processes that restructure the economy and reconstruct the city to suit the needs of capital, capitalists, and the creative class.

We find evidence of this restructuring on nearly every street in the novel. Julio's Harlem is crawling with "yuppies" and "greedy real estate brokers" and crowded with art galleries and luxury apartments (16). In a scene that is a little too on point, Helen's hip white friends play Monopoly; the guy who wins is the one who owns the slum properties, "the cheap places that are worth investing in" (144). "I just bought an old townhouse in Harlem," he says, proud of the fact that he plays the real estate game in real life, too (144). Increasingly, Julio feels like a stranger in the only neighborhood he has ever known. Huge tour buses "full of white people" (99) park in front of the Salsa Museum, trendy lounges that "are alien to Spanish Harlem" are popping up on corners where residents are used to "paper-bagging their cans of Budweisers" (140), and the commercial avenues are lined with the earliest arrivals of the nonplaces of late-stage gentrification: "Gap. Starbucks. Blockbuster Video. Old Navy" (7).

The signifiers of gentrification's upscaling of the neighborhood in Chango's Fire are familiar ones. So too are the signifiers of urban disinvestment and decline that the novel offers up: "The burned buildings, the vacant lots, the graffitied trains, the broken elevators, the heaps of garbage, the many buildings and places that no longer exist in a fading neighborhood" (83). I hear in perfunctory lists like this not the shock of urban devastation but a kind of narrative exhaustion. This is a paratactic prose of a writer tired of explaining yet again the underlying causes that led a community to be burned, broken, and tossed in a heap. Even still, Quiñonez provides this historical education for readers to reveal the brutalizing processes behind the euphemistic jargon of urban planning in phrases like "Benign Neglect." Quiñonez writes: "You keep burning a neighborhood down, you keep cutting services. With all the unhappiness, crime will rise. Now you can blame the people who live there for the decay of the neighborhood. The landlords will sit on the burned buildings, vacant lots, waiting it out, because sooner or later the government will have to declare it an empowered zone and throw money their way" (117). Quiñonez here nods to the UMEZ, which has helped gentrify the neighborhood. In time, those "burned out buildings" will be "gold mines" (7). But at a cost. "El Barrio was no longer my barrio, and the past seemed irretrievable," says Julio (16). For Quiñonez, what is lost in the gentrification process is not only the neighborhood's lived spaces of ethnic identity but also ethnic history, the "spiritual landmarks," the "holy places that speak to your soul, vibrant streets that tell you about those who came before you" (53).

The sentiment expressed here for the old neighborhood often animates the literature of gentrification. When identity and place are equated and the latter starts to change, this is what results. There is a politics effectuated in Quiñonez's interpellative grammar of "you," the shift to the second person that some persons might welcome but others might second guess and ultimately resist. Concealed beneath the affect generated by this "you" is the political question of to whom it refers. Like many New York City neighborhoods, the history of East Harlem is a history of different groups laying claim to it. The novel acknowledges as much: "Spanish Harlem had always been a springboard. A place where immigrants came to better themselves and, when they had reached the next plateau, they'd leave traces of their culture, a bit of themselves behind, and move on. A melting pot of past success stories—Dutch, Jews, Irish, Italians" (7). Left out of this thumbnail history is the blood that Julio knows soaks the sidewalk. "The Italians beat the shit out of us," he reveals later in the novel (51), adding, "The history of all countries is the battle over land" (117). Julio's preference is to keep Spanish Harlem Hispanic, though his own work rehabilitating apartments is counterproductive to this wish. The story Chango's Fire tells of the gentrifying ethnic enclave is of the ethnic resident who does not want to "leave," does not want to "move on," and who, candidly, does not want to live next to "white people" (7, 16). "White people" is Julio's shorthand for everything wrong with gentrification. For him, Puerto Ricans purchasing property in Spanish Harlem is a way of putting down roots but also a way of keeping the neighborhood out of other people's hands. The novel equates gentrification with integration and equates integration with the loss of ethnic history and space when the integrated neighborhood becomes homogeneous, which is to say, when it becomes white.

The other problem Quiñonez creates for Julio is having him fall in love with Helen, the white woman living downstairs. The economic contradictions around work and property that structure the novel are thus complemented with another set of contradictions between individual libidinal desires that exceed one's political commitments and the desire to commit to the collective politics of ethnic solidarity. No matter how much Julio might resent gentrification, it is what makes his romance of racial integration possible. "Is she an intruder in Spanish Harlem" or "is she not," he asks himself (179–80). The frank question is not so much resolved as dismissed by the urgency of the heart's desire: "The fact is, she's here. Right now. And I want her here, with me" (180).

The ending of *Chango's Fire* sees the fraying of numerous narrative threads as the contradictions that structure the text can no longer be sustained. Julio's relationship with Helen flames out when she, not unreasonably, breaks up with him after he reveals his criminal activity, which leads to her own apartment going up in smoke. "I'm going to call the police," she says (251). The whole building is gutted, but the biggest casualty is Felix, the sixty-eight-year-old, "black as tar," gay high priest of Santeria who rushes into the conflagration, saving Julio's family and dying in the process (33). As a favor, Felix had secretly held the mortgage to Julio's apartment because Julio would never have been approved for a sizeable loan when much of his income is from illegal earnings. The result is that there is no insurance claim Julio can use to buy a new apartment or fork over to Eddie. The disaster sends Julio and his parents back to the projects. Eventually, in the space where his apartment once stood is a "new building" where some "white guys" live (261). To add insult to injury, Quiñonez replaces Julio's manual-labor construction work—"a real job, with benefits and union"—with a dead-end job slinging pizza (for another Italian, one presumes), thus forcing him into the growing minimum-wage service sector, the part of the labor market disproportionally represented by people of color in the postindustrial city (29).

Quiñonez compensates Julio for putting him through this hell with what he gave the other Julio in *Bodega Dreams*: culture, more specifically, stories, which in this novel are more important than work and housing. Quiñonez informs the reader that on nights when Julio was not committing arson, he attended night school, earning "a BA in management" despite finding the classes boring: just "a bunch of information. A series of technologies for a new and supposedly improved job market" (80). At the novel's end, the logical next step would be for Julio to take an entry-level position in management in the FIRE sectors after years of hammering nails, but a move up the employment ladder by this route has no appeal. "I'm not learning stories to guide me," he had said of his business classes, "But stories interest me" (80). The lesson Quiñonez beats into his struggling protagonist—by way of Helen and Papelito—is to be less materialistic and to see the spaces of the neighborhood less as literal material and more as material for the imagination. Kindling for stories, if you will. What Quiñonez teaches him is to imaginatively transform Harlem, even if he cannot transform it materially. Or, to read the admonition more generously: to imaginatively transform the neighborhood as a first step to materially changing it. This is the earnest advice Helen offers Julio in a letter initiating their reconciliation:

> What I'm trying to tell you, Julio, is that you are obsessed with the material: your building, demolition, and fire. What you have lost is the beauty and imagination your culture gave you as a child that made living in vacant lots and streets of fire bearable, even exciting and pleasurable. . . . You go around talking all this history of your neighborhood and trying to fix everything partly because you are somewhat responsible for its demise.
> (264)

It is a bit rich for a rich white person to tell a poor person of color to stop "trying to fix everything" and instead embrace the cultural beauty and color that emerges out of the economics of extreme scarcity. But Julio does not read it this way; he calls the letter "authentic, genuine and true" (273).

Rather than critique this view, the novel doubles down on it through Felix, who sees "beauty in anything" (35). At one point he becomes transfixed by the iridescence of oil dripping from a car into the gutter, the colors "coiling around each other . . . all that beauty flowing in that filthy water" (35). What we see in this small moment is a strained effort to locate meaning in a domain other than one valorized by work and consumption, even if this space, with its car, oil, and degraded urban setting, is fashioned out of what capital creates. Quiñonez writes that Felix finds "the meaning of life . . . contained in all our throwaways,"; in what has been reduced to use value and then used up, he can extract another kind of value—beauty, wonder, attentiveness (35). It is Felix who sees in Julio "a son of Chango," a fiery god burning with passion (34). This is the novel's third kind of fire, the one replacing all others. In his frequent visits to Felix's botanica, Julio learns about Santeria's stories of "survival, of diversity, of color and magic" that have flowered from the horrors of slavery and the persecutions of Catholicism (76). Its "powerful stories," Felix says, "teach me how to experience life, my life. How to live my life within nature and my community" (78). With this comment, one hears Quiñonez positing an edificatory function for his own novel and its place in contemporary Latinx literature as a repository for empowering stories of East Harlem's survival, vibrancy, and difference, which are at risk of being lost to the erosions and erasure of gentrification. In a strange and discomfiting logic of equivalency, the deceased Felix is replaced in the closing pages by the sudden, almost magical appearance of another santero in the novel named Manny, who offers to train Julio, teaching him to burn with the stories and rituals that will lead to "saintliness" and "to love [himself] and all living things" (271). Helen, who in the meantime has upgraded to an entire brownstone on 120th Street and First Avenue, also shows up at the last second at Julio's door in the projects, in a scene suggesting a rekindling of love.

All of this is too little, too late. At least, that's how I see it. The gap between what has been lost and what has been gained remains too wide. Yet this is not to suggest fiction needs to balance out the ledger at the end but to suggest that in *Bodega Dreams* and *Chango's Fire* the magnitude of the losses—personal displacement, the death of loved ones, the traumas of fire, the destruction of wealth, the ruining of intimate relationships—are not acknowledged as such and that the paucity of the gains are made to seem larger than they are. Susan Méndez argues that "love, education, stories, and storytelling can all work together within Santeria to provide Julio with a viable future" and that "this faith . . . holds legitimate promises for him, as long as he works hard and is truthful and dedicated."[50] She maintains that "on a grander scale, Santeria can offer agency so as to enable a community's fight against gentrification." It is hard to see how this can be true, hard to see this statement as anything other than a reaffirmation of the novel's own rhetoric of uplift, which at every turn the novel reveals as bankrupt while still redeploying as an inspiration and motivator for personal change. The note that *Chango's Fire* ends on is Julio's commitment to his own bootstrap entrepreneurialism, combined with his newfound immersion in the community's stories. Thus his own personal and cultural empowerment will be his way to fight for success in a system that a more radical political position would argue requires top-to-bottom restructuring, if not outright replacement. "I got knocked back down a few notches. I've been in the projects before and I got out. And I'll get out again. This time, I'll do it right," he says, intimating that he will scratch his way up the American ladder of social mobility by owning a home again someday, by playing by the rules, by doing it the legal way (273). Julio's hope is a yet-to-be-realized American dream coated in the ashes of a material reality.

When Harlem was designated as an Empowerment Zone, it was called upon to harness the power of the market, to think like a company or like a community of entrepreneurs selling their distinctive culture in a gentrifying, postindustrial city where culture is one of the drivers of urban development. This was the mandate handed down in the context of a state that had severely curtailed its role in securing sociospatial justice in urban neighborhoods. In Edwards's *If I Should Die*, we saw ordinary working-class Black residents struggling to make do when caught between, on the one hand, urban development tearing up community gardens and displacing the African market on 125th Street and, on the other, racist cops and corrupt community members whose drug conspiracy undermined the neighborhood's efforts to emerge from the dark days of the 1970s and 1980s. If Edwards's fiction is about fighting such crimes, Quiñonez's fiction is about the crimes Harlemites commit to fill in the irresolvable gaps created by gentrification and the economy at large in which low-wage work, the lack of affordable housing, and widespread discrimination are realities that structure, shatter, and restructure dreams.

In *Bodega Dreams*, Nazario had promised to take a wrecking ball to the projects. By the end of *Chango's Fire*, these vestiges of the state are still standing, even if the state's investment in public housing has greatly waned. What we will see next in Bedford-Stuyvesant in Wil Medearis's *Restoration Heights* and Brian Platzer's *Bed-Stuy Is Burning* is neoliberal urbanism running rampant and individuals fending for themselves. What results in these books is not a dream of community empowerment or racial and ethnic solidarity. Rather, what results is the painful unraveling and rebuilding of white identity in the Black neighborhood.

Chapter Five

BEDFORD-STUYVESANT

White Boys in the Hood

When the character Buggin Out in Spike Lee's *Do the Right Thing* (1989) runs into Mookie on the streets of Bedford-Stuyvesant, he tells him, "Stay Black." The admonition is not so much directed at Mookie but at the Brooklyn neighborhood where both characters live. The advice is seemingly unnecessary—according to the then most recent census in 1980, the neighborhood was 98 percent Black—but Lee's film, with its precocious sense that gentrification is coming and the neighborhood is whitening, is able to detect the earliest signs years, even decades in advance. In this chapter, I turn to this sprawling central Brooklyn neighborhood, better known as Bed-Stuy, to try to understand what it and the stories that are emerging from it can tell us about gentrification and perhaps surprisingly, about white identity. "You thought Bed-Stuy was too black to change," says the African American money manager Derek in Wil Medearis's debut, *Restoration Heights* (2019), to the white protagonist, Reddick.[1] Derek implies that Bed-Stuy's segregating wall of color, to say nothing of its reputation for crime and poverty, putatively meant the neighborhood was too Black to ever gentrify. That was the commonly held belief—the story, if you will—about Bed-Stuy for years. But a succession of new novels and memoirs that I will consider in this chapter—Medearis's thriller, Brian Platzer's novel *Bed-Stuy Is Burning* (2017), and, briefly, Brandon Harris's memoir *Making Rent in Bed-Stuy*

(2017)—suggests new stories are emerging from the neighborhood in the 2010s as its demography and physical environment have rapidly changed.

The racial difference that has defined Bed-Stuy in the urban imaginary cannot be properly understood apart from the racialization of space that has produced it. The fact that Bed-Stuy was 98 percent Black in 1980 is neither an accident nor a result of the individual choices of its residents. Understandably, Buggin Out wants the neighborhood to "Stay Black" as a point of pride. From a policy perspective, what made it and other neighborhoods Black in the first place were "discriminatory practices including isolated public housing, urban renewal, redlining, discriminatory mortgage lending, exclusionary zoning, and empowerment zone designation." In full effect in the postwar decades, these policies have "isolate[d] and contain[ed] Blacks to the social and economic benefit of Whites," Paula Johnson has argued.[2] The gentrification of Bed-Stuy since the early 2000s, which has seen its Black population literally cut in half, has been the result of another set of policies, including the rezoning of the neighborhood by the Bloomberg administration, stepped-up policing, the availability of easy credit through subprime loans, and a spate of luxury condo building. Gentrification has followed, and its fallout has been a new literature of crime and gentrification set in Bed-Stuy.

If Bed-Stuy's gentrification once seemed impossible, in retrospect, it seems inevitable. This is not attributable solely to a marked shift in urban policies but to two other factors unique to Bed-Stuy. First is its proximity to Williamsburg, Brooklyn. As that trendy neighborhood—the epicenter of a global brand of Brooklyn cool—became increasingly expensive in the late 1990s, its hipster diaspora poured into Bed-Stuy and nearby Bushwick. Second is Bed-Stuy's status as the last affordable brownstone neighborhood in Brooklyn within convenient commuting distance to Manhattan. As other parts of brownstone Brooklyn—Boerum Hill, Fort Greene, Cobble Hill, and Clinton Hill—fully gentrified, Bed-Stuy, as a large neighborhood with the largest collection of highly coveted brownstones in the borough, was on every real estate broker's radar. This reputational transformation, evident in the hardscrabble informal motto of "Bed-Stuy Do or Die" giving way to the real estate boosterism of "Bed-Stuy Rent or Buy," may seem like a welcome reversal of fortunes. The problem is that the fortunes have stayed in the same hands. With the notable exception of Black homeowners who have held on through Bed-Stuy's decades of crisis, the neighborhood's gentrification, to borrow from Johnson, has also largely been for the "social and economic benefit of Whites."

In what follows, I turn in detail to the work of two white writers, Medearis and Platzer, to interrogate how they have given novelistic shape to the sociospatial transformations of the neighborhood since the early 2000s. At first glance, there are significant similarities between Medearis's *Restoration Heights* and Platzer's *Bed-Stuy Is Burning*. Both novels focus on housing and development as a way of aggregating gentrification's often unruly and sometimes invisible flows of capital. Both novels also cast their white protagonists as putative heroes in the neighborhood. In doing so, both texts underscore how the processual nature of gentrification provides narratives or scripts for how whiteness is constructed and reinforced, how whiteness is built (and also how it falls apart) around homeownership and the right to the neighborhood. More than any other chapter in *The Gentrification Plot*, this one lays bare that construction.

But the differences between *Restoration Heights* and *Bed-Stuy Is Burning* are more pronounced than their similarities. The superficial commonalities soon give way to novels that are inversions of each other. In Medearis's noirish tale, the well-meaning white protagonist Reddick's efforts to save Bed-Stuy from villainous (and possibly murderous) white developers lead to the dissolution of his benevolent white fantasies about the Black neighborhood and ultimately to Reddick's shocking awareness of his complicity, as a white person, in the "crime" of Bed-Stuy's gentrification. What we will see in Medearis's text is a redescription of Bed-Stuy as a "community" to Bed-Stuy as a "territory," which is to say, its redefinition as a place of racial affinity and racial cohesiveness to a place of pure mercenary interest for Blacks as well as whites who are willing to exploit the neighborhood for cold cash (322). To redefine a place is an attempt to control and profit from it. Medearis dramatizes this redescription by harnessing the crime genre's familiar search for a missing white woman, in this case Reddick's search for Hannah Granger, who disappears one night in Bed-Stuy in front of his building, a search that leads to a corrupt real estate development and finally to an unspooling of his own sense of self. What gentrification makes clear by the novel's end is that whiteness is a social structure with far-reaching deleterious social effects that are in excess of any one person's good or bad intentions.

If Medearis's white protagonist fights to save the neighborhood for Black residents, the wealthy white family at the center of Platzer's novel fights to save themselves from Blacks who lay siege to their million-dollar brownstone in a violent uprising against police brutality and gentrification. *Bed-Stuy Is Burning* casts its protagonists Aaron, a Wall Street trader, and Amelia, a fledging journalist, as victims of a gentrification backlash, only to recast them as heroes who survive it. They do more than survive, though. The couple comes out the better for it by seizing upon their trials and tribulations as an opportunity to reinvent themselves, launch new careers, and reformulate their intimate relations with each other around heterosexual love and the nuclear family. In Platzer's hands, the narrative of a neighborhood's social and physical transformation is leveraged for the spiritual and ethical enrichment (and monetary enrichment too) of whites, at great cost to the Black residents of Bed-Stuy, whose material property and neighborhood stories are expropriated. What we will see is that in Platzer's novel gentrification induces feelings of white guilt, something true of *Restoration Heights*, too. But in Platzer's text, unlike Medearis's, white guilt is something that you can pay to go away through charity that makes you feel better about yourself. One other difference—a formal one—distinguishes these two texts as well and their place in the genre of crime fiction. Unlike the narrative structure of Medearis's thriller, whose point of view is organized around one man's dogged hunt for the truth as an amateur private eye, Platzer's novel does not deploy an investigatory plot to drive it forward. Rather, *Bed-Stuy Is Burning* is a literary novel with multiple crimes at its heart—three murders to be exact—that endeavors to give a dialogic portrait of a neighborhood experiencing the traumas of broken-windows policing and gentrification. However, this dialogic structure, in which many voices and points of view are ostensibly invited to participate in a conversation about race, class, gentrification, and policing, is exposed as a ruse and a tool for the furtherance of white privilege. Ultimately, what *Bed-Stuy Is Burning* seems to long for is a neighborhood that can put the political and social upheavals of gentrification once and for all behind it, to cleanse itself of such matters and turn to the subjects of personal fulfillment and family life, in other words, the subjects not of genre fiction but of literary fiction that one might argue takes life in the fully gentrified neighborhood as its precondition.

If Platzer's narrative gestures toward this future for Bed-Stuy—a Bed-Stuy that is comfortably white—Brandon Harris's peripatetic memoir dramatizes his personal experience of trying to find a place to stay in the neighborhood that cannot "Stay Black." To Harris's *Making Rent in Bed-Stuy*—a narrative of Black precarity in a whitening neighborhood—I now momentarily turn to get a lay of Bed-Stuy's land and its history.

"THIS IS BED-STUY, BITCH"

The opening scene of *Making Rent in Bed-Stuy: A Memoir of Trying to Make It in New York City* is of the self-described two-hundred-plus-pound "high yellow Negro" author running with his new laptop through the neighborhood early in the morning of July 4, 2006, while being chased by a man wielding a "sawed-off bike handle."[3] After slipping into his building, Harris "proceeded to smash" the guy's arm as hard as possible "several times" with the building's "very heavy glass-and-metal door," until he pulled back "shuddering" in "great pain" (2). "This is Bed-Stuy, bitch," the assailant yelled, threatening, "I gonna get y'all," with "tears in his eyes," his arm no doubt broken in multiple places (2, 3). Harris then quickly retreated upstairs to his "loft," "smoked a spliff," and "got ready to face the phony celebration of national independence that the day to come promised to offer" (2, 3). It is with this toxic collision of gentrification, violent assault, and national sentimentality that Harris's memoir begins. Welcome to my neighborhood, Harris says in so many words.

Making Rent in Bed-Stuy follows Harris from one rundown, roommate-filled apartment to another (after he can no longer afford his shared loft) in the neighborhood as he tries to launch his career as a young filmmaker fresh out of a BFA program at SUNY Purchase. For much of the memoir, Harris "scrap[es] by" on food stamps, "my welfare money," he sardonically calls it, freely spending his government largesse on "newfound delicacies" like "duck breast and lamb chops" at the recently gentrified "ghetto grocer" (146, 147). "I had become the stuff of Grover Norquist's nightmares," he quips (146). As Harris tells it, he hails from a prosperous Black family in Cincinnati, with an Ivy League–educated mother, a property developer who named a street—Brandonburg Lane—after him (7). But Bed-Stuy with its own rapid development in the early 2000s has no such place he can afford to call his own. Harris titles his chapters by the street addresses, eleven in all, where he lived over the better part of a decade.

Harris remarks that when he first arrived, Bed-Stuy was still pockmarked by crime, good blocks and bad ones, streets with "reminders of the past," "corridors where one felt unwelcome at worst and uneasy at best" (55). But by the end of the memoir, those days are gone, and the neighborhood where Harris cannot get a foothold or a leg up is swarming with "young upwardly mobile professionals" with "strollers and expensive jackets, designer bags, running lycra" (144). Such running for leisure by the "pale hordes" contrasts with Harris running for his life at the book's start and running to stay in place for most of its middle (259). "A great social experiment was suddenly unfolding in our midst," he writes, though throughout the memoir it is an experiment that is failing him (144). "I still didn't have a stable home," he comments (143). Near the end of *Making Rent*, the line "This is Bed-Stuy, bitch" is reprised, without the expletive, by a realty company for the tagline and title of a "deeply offensive" promotional video (267). Featuring "smiling blond twentysomethings" discussing "the neighborhood's amenities" over "brunch cocktails," "This Is Bed-Stuy" makes zero mention of its Black history or its Black-owned establishments (267). This is the real crime, the crime of displacement and erasure, Harris suggests.

I pause over Harris's memoir because it, along with Medearis's and Platzer's novels, all published within the same two-year stretch, suggests an emerging effort to make sense of a historically Black neighborhood in flux. Both on and off the pages of these texts, Bed-Stuy is a neighborhood undergoing massive redevelopment and rehabilitation even while many of the structural issues contributing to the neighborhood's problems with poverty and crime remain unaddressed. Bed-Stuy is a large neighborhood with a long history and sharp contrasts. At approximately three square miles, it is about twice the size of the Lower East Side and Manhattan's Chinatown combined. Two busy commercial arteries frame it, Broadway to the north and Fulton to the south, which nearly converge on each other where the neighborhood tapers deep into Brooklyn by Evergreens Cemetery and East New York. Most of the neighborhood is residential with a mix of retail, some warehouses, and a church on nearly every other block. The wider western section along Classon Avenue and Flushing borders the upscale neighborhoods of Clinton Hill and South Williamsburg, whose spillover into Bed-Stuy has pushed up rents. Parts of Nostrand, Bedford, and Lewis that run longitudinally through the neighborhood are increasingly gentrified, as evident by the cafés, wine bars, and restaurants with chalkboard menus. In contrast, the neighborhood's sprawling central stretch remains a food desert, with high rates of poverty. Walk these streets and you will find bare-brick apartment buildings wrapped in bars and graffiti, a lot of bodegas, liquor stores, neon nail salons, Chinese takeout joints ensconced in bulletproof glass, the low-rent retail typical of New York's poorer neighborhoods. All of Bed-Stuy is starved for green space, but especially streets in this part of the neighborhood are treeless; in the summer it can get piping hot, even with the fire hydrants open.

Before it was built up in the late nineteenth century, Bed-Stuy was farmland, with a village named Bedford Corners, which featured an inn you might stop at overnight or pause to feed and water your horse on the trail to Jamaica, Queens, or farther to eastern Long Island. Some two hundred people resided in the area by the late 1700s, a third of them slaves, "marking a continuous black presence in Bedford-Stuyvesant extending back likely to its earliest settlement."[4] The neighborhood's status as a safe haven for African Americans continued into the early nineteenth century, when James Weeks founded the free Black community of Weeksville in 1838 on the southeastern edge of Bed-Stuy, where the neighborhood blurs into Crown Heights. As Weeksville's African American population reached five hundred, the population of the neighborhood at large remained more European. In the fifty-year period from 1870 to 1920, the majority of Bed-Stuy's picturesque and now highly desirable and expensive three-and-four-story brownstones were constructed with upper-middle- and upper-class Germans, Italians, Irish, and Eastern European Jews in mind. With "roughly 8,800 buildings built before 1900," the neighborhood has "perhaps the largest collection of intact and largely untouched Victorian architecture in the country."[5] Many of the most luxurious rowhouses are clustered along Decatur, Lewis, Chauncey, and Stuyvesant, in a subsection known as Stuyvesant Heights (where Platzer's protagonists live), a desirable patch in this expansive neighborhood that the Landmarks Preservation Committee designated as a Historic District in 1971.

Beginning in the 1930s, the demographics of the neighborhood shifted markedly, with in-migration locally from Harlem, thanks largely to the extension of the A subway line to Bed-Stuy in 1936, and migrations from farther away, especially Blacks from southern parts of the United States and the Caribbean. Bed-Stuy's Bajan community, for instance, is reflected in Paule Marshall's *Brown Girl, Brownstones* (1959), about a transplanted family from Barbados. During the war years, when many African Americans were employed in the nearby Navy Yard, Bed-Stuy became the second-largest Black community in New York City, earning it the moniker "Little Harlem," and by the 1960s it was the largest in the nation. Its population swelled to over 400,000 by midcentury, more than Detroit today. "Between 1940 and 1960 Bed-Stuy became 85 percent African American and Latino," Devorah Heitner remarks, adding that "prior to this it had been 75 percent white."[6] As the neighborhood's demographics changed, it was stamped with a D rating by banks, which redlined it into poverty for decades. As a consequence, between 1970 and 1980 Bed-Stuy's population plummeted. Approximately sixty thousand residents, many of them white, moved out as real estate agents blockbusted the area, furthering Bed-Stuy's economic decline but also leading to some opportunities for residents with savings.[7] In 1980—when, as noted, the neighborhood was 98 percent Black—entire brownstones on even the nicest streets in Bed-Stuy could be snapped up for ten to fifteen thousand dollars. Today, they would fetch two million, if not more.

Since 2000 the demography of the neighborhood has profoundly changed once again. While parts of the neighborhood are more Latinx and Afro-Caribbean, given the ongoing influx of immigrants from the Dominican Republic, Mexico, and Barbados, the most dramatic change has come with the arrival of whites, whose presence in Bed-Stuy has ballooned 600 percent between 2000 and 2012. On average, the newcomers have nearly twice the household income as long-term residents.[8] Data from NYU's Furman Center show the racial turnover—perhaps racial inversion, is more apt—has continued apace since 2012. Bed-Stuy was 75 percent African American in 2000, but by 2018 that number had plummeted to 46 percent, and within the same timeframe the share of the white population jumped from 2.4 percent to 30 percent. Housing prices during the same period have appreciated a mind-boggling 466 percent. In the midst of these changes, the Bloomberg administration aggressively rezoned Bed-Stuy. In 2007, two hundred blocks were rezoned; in 2012, another 140 were.[9] The rezoning, however, was not to hasten the construction of more market-rate high-rise condos, which had been cropping up for years. Quite the opposite. The area was newly "downzoned" in a bid to preserve the scale and the character of the neighborhood as it existed in the early 2000s. In other words, it was an effort to lock in economic gains for newer white residents in the old brownstones by preventing a glut of additional development. Yet even as Bed-Stuy has become significantly whiter, it contains many neighborhoods in one, stratified by class, national origin, and race. Of the many communities in this large neighborhood, one is in the brownstone blocks and another resides in its acres of public housing. The housing projects, fifteen in total scattered throughout the neighborhood, are home to some twenty thousand residents, "the highest number in any community district in Brooklyn."[10]

As we will see next, the violent tensions over territory and money in Bed-Stuy animates Wil Medearis's *Restoration Heights*, which in the end demystifies its well-meaning white protagonist's romanticized ideals of organic, urban "community" in ways that reveal its internal divisions.

THE WHITENESS OF WIL MEDEARIS

Like any good mystery, *Restoration Heights* is a novel of layers. On its surface, it is a story about the whereabouts (and presumed murder) of a young white woman named Hannah, who is last seen by the novel's protagonist, a freelance art handler and failed artist named Reddick, one night outside his apartment building in Bedford-Stuyvesant. Reddick's amateur investigation into her vanishing—an investigation aided by a reluctant cop, Clint, and an eager friend, Derek, well versed in financial accounting—turns *Restoration Heights* into a novel about gentrification, real estate, and banking fraud. In time, Reddick's obsessional search for Hannah reveals her to have been involved with a luxury housing development in Bed-Stuy through her fiancé, Buckley Seward, the scion of an extraordinarily wealthy family. As crime fiction follows the money, its narratives often weave together disparate urban geographies and social spaces. This one connects Bed-Stuy and the Upper East Side, two neighborhoods that on the face of it could not be more different but that are linked by the siphoning of money out of the former and into the latter, one of the whitest and richest neighborhoods in New York. Buckley is an investor in the housing project, called Restoration Heights, through his friends Franky Dutton, a "shitbag developer," and Mitchell Yang, a shady banker who takes kickbacks for approving Dutton's highly leveraged loans to finance the construction (123). It quickly becomes clear that Reddick's sense of personal responsibility for finding Hannah, dead or alive, is a conduit for his desire to rescue Bed-Stuy from the developers, bankers, and wealthy investors of the world who are ruining the neighborhood. But under this layer of intrigue about the skullduggery of real estate development lurk two other stories. Revealed at the end, the first is the extortion and blackmail of Buckley, Franky, and Mitchell by a behind-the-scenes Black powerbroker and money launderer in Bed-Stuy named Jeannie Tucker (aka "the Genie"). The second, which follows from the first, is the complete and utter disillusionment of Reddick's idealization of Bed-Stuy as an imperiled but unified community that he fights to save. When Reddick finally stands face to face with the illusive Jeannie in the concluding pages, she immediately sizes him up as "earnest and lost, desperate to attach [him]self to something that matters" (328). She schools him about the neighborhood before dismissing him with a flick of her finger. "I've got some sorry news. There is no *people*," she says. "That's the hard lesson this country taught me. It is the heart of my success. You want this to be a community but it's only a territory" (322). This is the "hard lesson" of the novel too; it is what *Restoration Heights* is really about.

If *Restoration Heights* is a novel about the illusions of community, it is also a novel about the delusions of white privilege. The novel exposes the social and economic structures that perpetuate white privilege even by white subjects who do not wish to exercise their racial advantage or who feel, as Reddick does, that because of their own marginal class position the benefits of whiteness do not amount to much. As we will see, in *Restoration Heights* the loss of one's romanticized notion of the urban community and the gaining of awareness of one's racial privilege cannot be disentangled. Reddick's idealization of the Black residents of Bed-Stuy as a *"people"* turns out to be an expression of his white point of view. Yet in the end, one cannot help think that the novel's reduction of all human motivation to economic self-interest, a view forcefully expressed as the secret of the Genie's "success," disempowers Bed-Stuy in a manner that advantages it for those who would exploit the neighborhood for their material gain.

People Versus Systems

To understand these assertions, we have to understand how Medearis, on the one hand, individuates Reddick as a character and, on the other, strips away his sense of individuality in an effort to expose him as merely another gentrifier in a neighborhood overrun with them. If you happened to brush shoulders with Reddick walking down Fulton Street or be seated across from him on the A train, you would not be blamed, Medearis acknowledges, for not remembering his face. The novel opens with exactly this sentiment: "You know Reddick. He's that white guy on the subway, past thirty and showing it, jeans and boots splattered by work that was never intended to be permanent. . . . He has claimed a space, found a comfort that lies somewhere between habit and ritual. You barely notice him. These guys are all over the city" (11). It seems like an inauspicious way for Medearis to start his novel, relegating his protagonist to a type, indistinguishable from the rest of the white thirtysomethings, someone you would not notice among all the others. We might note here in passing that the novel also imagines its reader as a New Yorker, someone familiar with gentrification and the urban types it produces, including not just Reddick (the artist-gentrifier) but also the type of blasé New Yorker who evinces a seen-it-all, urban indifference. In other words, the text assumes its reader is a kind of New Yorker produced by gentrification, thus aligning the reader and the protagonist at the same moment it appears to distinguish them. Medearis enjoins "you" to pass your eyes quickly over Reddick and move on to more interesting things, but when you pause and look closer, there is a lot you can see. We can detect the operations of racial privilege in this description, a major theme of the novel. To be "that white guy" is to "claim . . . a space," Medearis writes, which is to say, it is to appropriate a territory. It is the very ubiquity of this action and sense of white entitlement—so common it is "barely notice[d]," though it is "all over the city"—that is the actual problem. In a novel about the gentrification of the Black neighborhood, the phrase about a white guy claiming a space cannot pass without comment. *Restoration Heights*, one might say, commits to making whiteness visible, even if it means making its protagonist unremarkable.

It will turn out that the one person who is most shocked to see his whiteness made manifest is Reddick himself. This is what everyone around him remarks upon. That the novel pledges itself to this logic of exposure is evident in the way it comes full circle, ending almost exactly on the same note with which it began. After his dressing down by the Genie, a frustrated and enraged Reddick "repeatedly hammer[s]" the bell on the counter of her dry cleaners, its "panicked ringing" silenced only when he throws it against the wall (329). He then, in the final scene, storms out onto the streets of Bed-Stuy, where he watches "white, young" gentrifiers stream up from the subway station into "their new neighborhood, the spoils of their bloodless conquest . . . faces like his, skin like his" (330). "You can look and look but you'll never see the difference," writes Medearis in the novel's last sentence. While there are some "difference[s]" you cannot see, which make Reddick an individual, in the final analysis they do not mean that much. That seems to be the point of the whole novel.

Stated another way, the point of *Restoration Heights* is to deploy the gentrification plot to dramatize the tension between "the social structure we live in. *Systems*," as the Asian-American character Beth puts it, and "one individual. . . . a person, not a system," as Reddick retorts during a heated exchange with her (172). Or as the novel rephrases it later, the tension between "the impersonal tug of social patterns" and "individuals making decisions," real people who were not simply "placeholders for theories about justice or history" (311). Reddick's mere presence as a white guy in Bed-Stuy is emblematic of structural privilege and the flows of capital and labor across the city in the early 2000s. This is a fact he realizes at some level yet is unwilling to accept as a meaningful determinate or meaningful frame for understanding individual daily experience. "I *am* an individual," Reddick insists, while failing to understand that his insistence on his individuality is itself a marker of his white privilege. Beth, who is well versed in the language of critical theory, conversely interprets the world through the frames of "gender," "age," "ethnicity," and "skin color" (175). "Maybe your labels are worth it," he tells her. "Maybe in the end they do more good than harm. But that does not mean much to the people you stick them to" (175). "You think you're so fucking unique," Beth counters, adding, "but you're not, no one is" (175).

Despite all of this typifying, Medearis attempts to individuate Reddick to create the well-rounded, three-dimensional character that readers expect. This effort to satisfy the demands of realist fiction and its readers carries ideological weight. In creating Reddick, Medearis complicates his positionality both so that it exceeds the kinds of labels that Beth tries to affix to everyone and so that in Reddick's own mind he inhabits a truly singular subject position. For instance, Reddick has been in Bed-Stuy for eight years, much longer than the newcomers he is indistinguishable from. As a painter, he is an urban type, the gentrifying white artist, one of thousands in Bed-Stuy and nearby Bushwick who populate almost every page of the novel.

But he is different from these artists too. Unlike his roommate, Dean, and Dean's girlfriend Beth, both artists from upper-class families who went to "good fucking schools and tutors and after-school programs" and who can afford to scrape by just painting while waiting to be discovered, Reddick grew up "fucking poor" in the South, the son of a mill worker who abandoned the family. "*Success . . .* That's your heritage," he says to Beth when she tries to claim to her own marginal status (174). While she paints, he spends his working day installing art in Upper East Side townhouses of the rich, including Buckley Seward's, rather than creating art of his own (174). Moreover, and most importantly, he is white, like many of Bed-Stuy's new residents, but does not feel it, having grown up around African American kids in Gastonia, North Carolina. "Racial awareness had come in fits and starts, in isolated episodes," writes Medearis, who describes how when Reddick "walked into an all-white class for the first time," he "felt such crushing loneliness," a sense of "displacement," the "middle class" kids appearing to have "descended from another planet" (100). "*You talk like a nigger,* they said," Reddick recalls (100). "He learned that he was white," concludes Medearis: whiteness does not come naturally to him (101). As an adult, he chooses to live in Bed-Stuy because "there was something of Gastonia in it" (182). That "something" is Black life, which makes him comfortable, makes him feel like he is home. Throughout the novel, Reddick is more at home on the basketball court of the Bed-Stuy YMCA than any other place. One of the few "white guys" who dare to play there, he can jump higher and shoot more accurately than his Black teammates.

Reddick's heartfelt feeling of racial belonging as a white guy in a Black neighborhood is a white fantasy of Blackness. We see evidence of this in Reddick's long list of Bed-Stuy's qualities that have drawn him to the neighborhood: the "uncomplicated . . . pace of life" (182), "the commitment to simple courtesies," "the easy familiarity of strangers," "the Caribbean women on folding chairs on the sidewalk," "the hyperbolic earnestness of the children's sidewalk games," "the perfumed women in pretty dresses" on "Sunday mornings," "hymns seeping from the churches" (183). This is a warm, sentimental portrait of a Black urban village, a white imaginary of Black coherence, wholeness, and unity. Reddick's attachment to Bed-Stuy exemplifies what David Harvey characterizes as a "utopian longing" for "a simpler, less volatile . . . localized life" that is "materially embedded" in a community, a place where "affective and direct interpersonal relations established on a local basis" act as a counterweight to the "abstract and impersonal forces of globalization," neoliberalism, and gentrification.[11] Reddick is just scraping by, overeducated and underemployed, without prospects or a path forward in life. He even loses his freelance work because of his pursuit of Hannah. Of course he cares deeply about Bed-Stuy: the neighborhood is what he knows and all he has.

In the moment, the novel does not critique Reddick's list or the point of view it implies but simply lets it linger as a kind of dreamy atmosphere. But as readers we can see it for what it is or for what it is missing. Absent here is any recognition of the real internal divisions within the neighborhood, for example, between wealthy Black residents and poorer ones, or African Americans and Caribbean immigrants, or Black Christians and Black Muslims. Reddick's vision is of a Bed-Stuy free of conflicts. This is an ideological illusion of an organic and harmonious community of face-to-face relations and easy sociability uncomplicated and unmediated by politics, economics, or religion. Reddick says as much: Bed-Stuy is where he can look "people in the face" and "actually connect with the people," "regular people" as friends, not as a "white liberal" "ally" who has done his "duty" (173, 174). What he grooves to in Bed-Stuy is "a vibe, a rhythm you picked up in your bones," some kind of ineffable soul to the Black neighborhood (183). The only villains are outsiders trying to force their way in, such as the Restoration Heights development, which members of the community protest. Their intrusion into Bed-Stuy makes Reddick conscious of the fact that "he was afraid he would lose" the quality of small-town life (184)—"the same families on the same stoops in the summer, telling you good morning" (161)—which "formed an obligation" in him to protect (184). "I want to keep things from changing," he says, expressing a desire to preserve Bed-Stuy "in the moment" (125) and prevent the neighborhood from morphing into yet another "gluten-free, au pair, hip white wasteland" (170). This feeling of Blackness in his "bones" signifies Reddick's whiteness. That's Beth withering rebuke when she says, "It's just so *white male*, as though this is all your responsibility somehow. Like you're the neighborhood steward, and if you don't look out for it, no one will" (171).

The truth that Reddick does not want to acknowledge is that his move to Bed-Stuy eight years ago helped prime the neighborhood for the white influx that followed. Reddick's mere presence, Medearis implies, signaled the area was safe for investors and other white residents. Despite his desire to "keep things from changing," he has changed Bed-Stuy (125). This is a bitter white pill to swallow. In what might be the novel's keenest insight, Sensei, a neighborhood resident who chats with Reddick at the YMCA, rebuts the commonly held notion that those who resist gentrification, like Sensei himself, are nostalgic and resistant to change, like Reddick. "We're not fighting Restoration Heights because we want to preserve a moment," he explains, adding, "That's just another kind of conservatism, another kind of looking backward, and we can't look backward, there is too much ugliness in our history. Too much despair. We're fighting because we want to control our own change. We want to *direct* it" (126). At the moment, however, the reins are in the hands of whites. "By being here you helped it happen . . . you helped" the "developers," says Sensei (125). He then asks, "How many condos have gone up in the eight years you have been here" (125). What Sensei tries to impart to Reddick is that whiteness is a structure, not an identity. "I know the truth about myself," claims Reddick defensively,

FIGURE 5.1. Condos in Bedford-Stuyvesant, Brooklyn. *Source:* Mark Hogan, CC BY-SA 2.0 (https://creativecommons.org/licenses/by-sa/2.0), via Wikimedia Commons.

which is his way of stating that he might "look like one of them [the gentri-fiers]," but he is different (125). "It's about the effects," Sensei remarks (125), adding later, "It's not about you. You're missing my point" (126).

The route by which Reddick gets to the "missing . . . point" is through his hunt for the missing "girl." To achieve this, Medearis harnesses the conventional narrative structure of the detective genre's investigation into the perennial questions of what happened to someone and why it happened and redeploys them into an investigation of what is happening to a neighborhood and who or what is responsible. To say that the crime at the center of the novel is the crime of whiteness is a bit too pat, but there is truth to it: Reddick might not be the culprit, but he contributes to the problem, as he eventually learns. Though not a detective, he plays one in his fantasy. His obsessional pursuit of Hannah leads him to break into her apartment, skulk through the Restoration Heights's construction site, ask pointed questions around Bed-Stuy, and snap photos of financial records at the Seward's townhouse. The narrative that he pieces together is "a web of connected actions" (317). The novel features multiple scenes of Reddick staring at his case map, where he has pinned together names, locations, and bits of information in an effort to see what "he couldn't see" but "could sense" (158), looking desperately for "the connective tissue . . . meaning in the contours, the outlines, a unity of shape and intent, facts that could be shimmied into being by proximity" (201). The moment is familiar in recent crime fiction: the commission of a crime against a person launches an investigation that culminates in a retrospective narration about a place that is being economically exploited, murdered in its own way.

Yet each of the various narratives Reddick writes and revises along the way winds up being incorrect. Unlike the typical literary detective who in the genre's big reveal triumphantly discloses at the end a truth that has escaped most readers, Reddick keeps spinning out stories of Hannah's disappearance that are flat-out wrong. They are wrong because he lacks vital pieces of information or is willingly blind about what is there. This is not because he is necessarily a bad detective. It is because he is wedded to certain racial scripts of gentrification. Reddick's reluctance, for instance, to blame Ju'waun and Tyler for Hannah's disappearance, even though the two were with her the night she vanished, is because he worries about confirming racial stereotypes that "all young black men [are] criminals" (214). On this matter, Derek accuses him of "white guilt" (163). Thus, even as Reddick repeatedly claims he sees everyone as individuals, in the case of Ju'waun and Tyler, as well as other Black kids from his "old neighborhood," he actually sees them as "consequences . . . of the war on drugs . . . the wreckage that mass incarceration laid on certain communities," as "victims of a virus," the virus of racism that "he was born immune to" (214). Later Reddick posits that the duo might have been hired by Franky to murder Hannah, laying the blame at the top, but this too is proven to be untrue. Throughout *Restoration Heights*, Reddick struggles and struggles to connect what look like "two separate incidents—on the one hand a missing girl, on the other a real estate fraud" (308). Is he investigating a "crime of passion or of finance" or "both," he asks himself (179). What he cannot figure out is the reason that would lead the white developers and financiers, Franky or Buckley, to want to kill Hannah and to actually go through with it. As he "traces the lines radiating out from her name" on his case map, he murmurs "a list of possible motivations. *Jealousy, revenge, secrecy, fear, entitlement, rage. Jealousy, revenge, secrecy. Jealousy revenge. Revenge*" (311). Revenge becomes his answer.

Stepping back for a moment, we can see the hidden logic of race that emerges in Reddick's thinking, a logic where "neighborhood guys," which is to say poor people of color, like Ju'waun and Tyler, are largely without agency, subject to impersonal forces that affect their lives and their neighborhood, whereas Franky and Buckley, which is to say people who are wealthy and white, are individualized and able to control and shape their own lives and the lives of others. But Reddick's list of motivations for Franky and Buckley also ends up being wrong, wrong because the list presupposes the mystery has something to do with personal motivation, has something to do with "individuals making decisions," as he insists nearly until the end (311). Individuals do not matter much in the novel. But, surprisingly, neither does, as we will see, racial identity or the other categories or labels that Beth uses to explain the world. What matters is "cold business." It is the only thing that matters.

The Cold Business of Gentrification

Perhaps the most interesting character in *Restoration Heights* is the most mysterious: Jeannie Tucker, the mid-sixties African American woman who grants wishes and fixes problems, earning her the nickname the Genie. Her favors, though, are not free. Her brief backstory is that she bought up buildings on the cheap during the days of the crack wars and gang violence and used them to "run drugs" and "run girls" (323). As the neighborhood gentrified, the buildings became valuable in their own right. In the climactic scene of the novel between Jeannie and Reddick, we find the crime genre's trademark information dump that solves the urban mystery. It is Jeannie who delivers the big reveal, and most of what she says is head-spinning news to Reddick. We learn that Jeannie sold her buildings on Tompkins Avenue to Buckley and Franky only to watch a state senator, Anthony Leland, announce the next day the groundbreaking of Restoration Heights on the blocks where her property stood, immediately sending its market value skyrocketing. Learning that she has been duped and exploited, Jeannie hatches a plan using one of her "girls," Hannah (who was never missing or in danger), as a mole to record Buckley's confession that the properties were purchased with insider knowledge from Anthony, his secret lover. Armed with this information and the threat of a gay sex scandal that would end a Republican senator's career and ruin the Seward family's reputation, she blackmails Buckley, Franky, and Mitchell until she feels she has been paid the money due to her.

The novel's plot twist is standard fare for crime fiction, the surprise that we know is coming around the bend even if we do not know what it is. The true twist, however, is the way Reddick's pieties about himself and Bed-Stuy come crashing down with Jeannie's revelation. As Hannah watches, Jeannie taunts him, tells him she will not give him the "moral clarity that [he] want[s] so badly" (318). When he pleads with her, "Why did you sell? Why do you all sell to these arrogant developers when you know they don't care about the neighborhood," she rejects the question (322). "You all," she says accusingly, "The mysteries of the black heart, right? You want me to speak for my people" (322). A second later she delivers her line: "There is no *people*" (322). "I'm a businesswoman," she declares (329). It is an explanation as much as an affirmation, and it is a rejection of the idea she might be "a poor old black woman" who's been ripped off (329). She cashed out of her property because the "clean-ass white money" appeared too good to pass up at the time. "I sold," she says, "because it was rational" (322, 323). Only afterward did she understand that the deal was corrupt. Jeannie is neither out to get the white developer because he is white; nor is she trying to save

Bed-Stuy because it is Black. She does not hatch her plan because she is personally angry; she is not. She simply wants the money owed to her. There is not even an individual decision to make: if you are a "businesswoman," you do what you must do. "He had thought it was revenge, but revenge is always personal. . . . There as nothing like that here," Reddick learns at last as the wind is knocked out of him (328). As he feels his "body sink," he realizes all of this has been merely "cold business": "He had uncovered a plot without villains. . . . There was nothing to expose, no one who needed saving, who needed justice" (328).

It should go without saying that capitalism is racialized. The exploitation of Bed-Stuy for economic gain both in Medearis's novel and outside its pages is possible because of the racist practices of redlining and urban renewal that sent the neighborhood into decline for decades, making it ripe for later profiteering. For Jeannie, however, to think about space and capital through race is to think about them in the wrong way. The cynical question she asks is "Why should I care what happens to this neighborhood" (323). This is followed immediately by her even more cynical answer: "This is just a place where I earn a living" (323). In her eyes, Bed-Stuy is a "territory," not a people but a geography to be ruled over, divided up, and, when the time comes, sold off. Whereas a people connotes an authentic racial community bonded by a spirit that makes them greater than their mere numbers, what Jeannie sees are "individuals stuck in the same place" (322). In light of Jeannie's revelation regarding the real operations of power, Reddick's earlier idyllic images of Bed-Stuy as a Black community where he could feel at home may look like a naïve fantasy. However, we must note too that Jeannie's belief that "There is no *people*" is also a fantasy. This is not because there really is a "people" that preexist their political constitution or interpellation as such as a subject; there are not. Rather it is a fantasy because the belief that there is not "a people" is an ideological phantasmatic that deracializes capitalist exploitation in ways that legitimize the "rational" accumulation of wealth through ongoing practices that are indeed racialized. In other words, it is easier to exploit a "people" if you believe they do not exist. Jeannie infers this when she says the disavowal of a "people" has been "the heart of my success" (322), one that freed her from making ethical choices by reducing all relations to that of "cold business" (328). When poor Reddick wanders dazed out onto the streets of Bed-Stuy, he sees he is just another white gentrifier. But unlike him, they have bought into a fantasy that has paid handsomely. The unemployed Reddick watches them returning from their jobs and notes they are "speaking a language he never learned," which is the language of "success," the language of "cold business," the language where there is "no *people*" and no "home" but just another territory to add to "the spoils of their bloodless conquest" (330).

As we turn next to Brian Platzer's *Bed-Stuy Is Burning*, we will encounter another version of this logic of rationalized self-interest through the eyes of a white family that feels under siege in the gentrifying neighborhood where they make their home.

BRIAN PLATZER'S BROKEN WINDOWS

If Quiñonez's *Chango's Fire* told the story of Helen and the Spanish Harlem brownstone that she buys at the end, and if it had been told by a white author, it might read something like *Bed-Stuy Is Burning*. In an early moment in the novel, Aaron and Amelia—the wealthy, unmarried couple who are the focus of the story—sit back and admire their new purchase, an 1890s brownstone at 383 Stuyvesant Avenue. They'd bought it from an African American family who held on through the difficult decades in Bed-Stuy and then cashed out when the market got hot, relocating to suburban New Jersey. Aaron and Amelia's eyes linger lovingly over the house's mahogany woodwork, "carved to look like columns holding up a frieze, with little torches surrounded by wreaths carved into the corners," and its window-panes decorated with "orange teardrops emanat[ing] from a central sky-blue whirl surrounded by golden diamonds."[12] Platzer's novel is plainspoken; the moments of lyricism are few. So when it comes to describing this house, the suddenly effusive prose catches your attention. A baroque nonfunctional splendor, this semiotic excess is only nominally about the house itself. It is really a marker of so much accumulated wealth that its purpose is simply to be beautiful, to be contemplated as such as a reflection of one's own status. The house's beauty is useless but not worthless. We "bought the house because it was beautiful," Platzer's couple says (39). "They owned the stained-glass windows and the original woodwork surrounding them," Platzer writes, and he repeats nearly exactly the sentiment two sentences later: "Aaron and Amelia owned this woodwork" (36). The clunky repetition also calls attention to itself, and not just as a moment of unevenness in the wooden prose. It is evidence of the novel's larger unspoken theme.

Houses have use values, of course, even this one. And for this couple, the house is a place to raise their child Simon, a place to grow their white, heterosexual family. Houses, of course, are also ways of building wealth to pass down to one's children, reduplicating privilege generationally. Aaron and Amelia's brownstone on the best block in a Black neighborhood is an "investment" that, in a sense, naturally repeats itself: their capital nested inside this 1890s egg grows without them needing to do much of anything but sit back and watch it hatch (39). The house's pecuniary potential, as well as its beauty, is what makes it an attractive investment to Aaron and Amelia. Purchased for "$1.3 million," the house is "a steal" (37), having already appreciated "35 percent . . . in just a year" (39).

In Platzer's novel, money begets money. Wealth reduplicating itself without labor: the ultimate sign of privilege. "It took guts to be surrounded by people who didn't look like him," thinks Aaron, for whom living among African Americans is a sign of bravery and risk taking (39). He is actually addicted to risk—overcoming a gambling habit is part of his character's

FIGURE 5.2. Brownstones in Bedford-Stuyvesant, Brooklyn. *Source:* Newyork10r at English Wikipedia, public domain.

arc—but this one risk "was worth it" (39). Questions of "worth"—how much a piece of property is worth and whose stories are worth telling—are at the heart of the text. The only way they could "lose was a spike in crime to scare off new gentrifiers," Platzer remarks (39). However, this is not quite true. As we will see, even when Aaron and Amelia "lose" in this novel, they still win big. The social and economic relations in the text are configured so the upper-class, white gentrifiers always come out on top, even when their investment is attacked in a fiery conflagration at the center of the novel that costs the Black community dearly. To put it bluntly but accurately, Platzer depicts gentrification as a means of asserting racial and class power, acknowledges the inescapable ethical problems this poses, and then engineers the machinery of his plot so that a critique of gentrification is self-consciously incorporated and neutralized by his protagonists. Aaron and Amelia in effect "own" the critique while continuing to reap the rewards that gentrification affords them.

When Platzer's novel opens, racial tensions in Bed-Stuy that have been inflamed for years by gentrification and the humiliations of quality-of-life policing explode into a violent uprising. The catalyst is the killing of Jason Blau, a twelve-year-old African American boy whom cops shot ten times after mistaking the video-game controller in his hand for a weapon. In Platzer's novel, it is not "a dark kid with a gun," to quote Richard Price, but trigger-happy cops who are the problem, at least at the beginning. The police murders of Eric Garner, Michael Brown, and especially the twelve-year-old Tamir Rice, who was shot while playing with a toy gun in a Cleveland park in 2014, hang over this text. "This must end! By any means necessary" demands a protest flyer that Platzer pastes in the preface, along with the hashtags "#12yearsold10shots" and "#bedstuyrising." Taken together, the flyer and hashtags are meant to be dispositive of the novel's sociological authenticity, as though the story is one Platzer, a Bed-Stuy resident and brownstone owner himself, witnessed firsthand rather than invented. "I had a real neighborhood and a real city and a real police force . . . real restaurants, real streets, and real subway stations," Platzer has remarked when addressing his material for the book.[13] One notes, however, that Jason is not so much a real character in the novel as a plot device to instigate outrage. The ensuing uprising reaches its climax when an "angry mob" circles Aaron and Amelia's brownstone (232). Damien, a young African American man in the crowd, shoots and kills Derek Jupiter Sr., an African American neighbor who was at the house flirting with the nanny Antoinette and who had tried to deescalate the situation. In the mayhem that follows, Damien is killed by a shotgun-wielding Daniel, a white hipster and bitter adjunct professor who rents the brownstone's bottom floor. I will return to this scene of a Black siege on a white house, the novel's set piece, but here what I would note is the criminally high Black death toll—two young men and a boy—in what turns out to be a tale of upper-class white uplift. The lives of three other African Americans, Derek Jupiter's son, also named Derek, Sarah, a young woman in NYCHA housing, and her hospitalized brother Andy, are also shattered, to say nothing of the many nameless residents placed in handcuffs in the book. "The important thing is that we survived," Aaron sighs (301). As Mychal Denzel Smith commented in a review for the *New York Times*, "This is ultimately a novel about black people happening to white people."[14]

Fort Apache, Bed-Stuy

Bed-Stuy Is Burning's omniscient point of view dutifully assembles diverse urban voices, as if a textual town square where everyone has a chance to speak about gentrification and police violence. At first glance, it is a cacophonous, dialogic novel, a large social canvas characteristic of a prominent kind of urban realism. But it quickly becomes apparent that the space on the social canvas is unequally apportioned. Scenes are told from the perspective of the Jamaican immigrant Antoinette, who out of curiosity is "becoming Muslim" but is "still Christian" and whose role in the racial conflict unfolding is to safeguard Aaron and Amelia's cherished son Simon at all costs (189). Along with this immigrant voice, the novel includes the voice of the aforementioned Sara, the angry lesbian—"a girl who looked like a boy" (60)—who "embodied the repercussions of gentrification," more a materialization of social forces than a character (214). In the novel, most of the other Black characters residing in Bed-Stuy's projects are a faceless and nameless mass either being frisked by police at the Utica Avenue subway station or agitating to throw a brick through a window. They are depicted as caught in unbreakable cycles of underclass rage and defeat. They contrast with the well-meaning and hardworking Derek Jupiter, "a forty-year-old single father" and homeowner who is a fleshed-out presence in the novel before he is shot twice in the chest. He has bought his rowhouse on an electrician's income and by, as he says, "working my ass off . . . no drink, waking up early, no gambling, nothing . . . working and putting money way" (72). Property status is one way that Platzer's text morally differentiates its African American characters. Among Platzer's Black characters, Derek Jupiter is "the good one" (136). He serves as a coercive counterexample to the African Americans in public housing, embodying as he does the idea that if one only strives harder, denies oneself any vices, and saves more, one can rise up, rather than, well, rise up in the other sense of the phrase. The novel also gives William Bratton his own chapter, the police commissioner who first implemented New York's head-cracking broken-windows tactics under Giuliani in 1994. He returned for a second stint as commissioner under Bill de Blasio from 2014 to 2016 and has a significant presence in the novel. In early drafts, he was merely a voice on a police radio, a kind of puppet-master figure controlling the scene, but his role grew in later revisions: "I wanted to humanize him as much as I could," Platzer has revealed.[15]

Platzer's novel seeks to include everyone in the urban neighborhood. It does so because the novel subscribes to a liberal, pluralist politics of dialogue in which the conflicts of urban gentrification can be hashed out by talking, rather than through racial and class struggle. Consider, for a moment, the scene where Aaron sees the cops harassing African American teenagers each morning on his way to his Wall Street office. He pauses to think how he'd like to "sit and listen to both sides" so "at the very least, the police officers and the kids from the neighborhood would feel as though they'd been heard" (60). The novel starts from the premise that open and honest dialogue, in which everyone has an equal voice, erases racial and class privilege, leveling the proverbial playing field. But this is, of course, neither how it works in reality nor how it even works in the novel. In Platzer's novel, dialogue is the means by which the racial and class struggle of gentrification is defused in the interest of those who not only control the debate but insist debate is the only solution. This is the privilege that the novel dramatizes. The ones who want to talk things out and solve the problems of the gentrifying neighborhood are Aaron and Amelia. For all of the novel's dialogism, and for all of Aaron and Amelia's paeans to listening, their voices dominate the text. It is their story that we are meant to care about. And in their story, they are both the victims and, as they themselves say, the "hero[es]" (324).

Platzer's novel dramatizes the costs of broken-windows policing to African Americans in the city's gentrifying neighborhoods. But it also dramatizes the seeming benefits of it for whites. Early in the text, Platzer transcribes a morning interview segment on the local NPR station WNYC in which Bratton explains the rationale behind the policing method, borrowing liberally from Wilson and Kelling's seminal 1982 article on policing as he does so: *"'Broken windows' . . . asserts that in communities contending with high levels of disruption, maintaining order not only improves the quality of life for residents, it also reduces opportunities for more serious crimes. . . . A neighborhood where minor offenses go unchallenged soon becomes a breeding ground for more serious criminal activity"* (18). Amelia then switches off the radio and gets out of bed. A couple of things are going on here. Most obviously, Platzer is educating the reader on a subject that is essential for understanding the rest of the novel: the policing strategy that figured urban space in epidemiological terms ("breeding ground") where cultures of crime could multiply. More subtly, he is setting up the ambivalent feelings his white, upper-class protagonists have toward this method of policing. Amelia's NPR listening signals that she is a liberal and is, or should be, troubled by the violence and social injustice inherent in the NYPD's order-maintenance tactics. Her liberal credentials are further burnished when a page later we learn that she wants to move beyond penning articles about celebrities, such as the one she is writing on Jonah Hill, and begin addressing weightier issues. She is fortunate to be able to pay Antoinette $1,400 a month so she can "be free of" her baby, which allows her to retreat upstairs to write more articles like "The Paradox of Bed-Stuy" (158). Her piece on the neighborhood's history, gentrification, and rates of violent crime ("among New York City's worst") gets published on the real-estate blog Brownstoner.com (46). As a self-described "kindhearted white gentrifier" (170) and the co-owner of a 1.3-million-dollar brownstone herself, she seemingly has a lot to gain from the neighborhood's continuing gentrification and thus a lot to gain from Bratton's police preventing the unruly locals from breaking her expensive stained-glass windows. After the NPR segment, Amelia peeks outside to see if she can detect "any sign of protest or disruption" percolating (21). Her use of the word "disruption" as a corrective to the word "protest" speaks volumes: she is quoting Bratton's language.

Back at the earlier scene in the novel in the subway station, we see low-level, order-maintenance policing in action before the uprising breaks out.

Cops are "holding seven black boys" in handcuffs "for jumping the turn-stile," "talking back," and skipping school (41). The police are a perennial presence at the station, but they are out in larger-than-usual numbers in anticipation of the protest over Blau's murder. Rounding up kids in advance is the police's tactic for preventing things from getting out of hand later. "Do you need to be doing this," Aaron shouts at an officer, "treating them like this?" (43). In the scene, Aaron sports a $8,000 suit on his way to his $250,000-a-year job at Stifler & McDermott (43). He complains, "Almost every day I've got to see this on my way to work. It's not good for the com-munity" (43). The antecedent to "it's" may refer to police harassment itself, but it seems more likely to refer to the harassment's bad optics. The latter is a sign that the community is still gentrifying, not yet fully there. Neither the cops nor "them" take kindly to Aaron's meddling. "Do I need to be keep-ing your streets safe," a cop replies (43). "Fuck you, man," says "a kid in cuffs," then another threatens to rape his wife (43).

In *Bed-Stuy Is Burning*, broken-windows policing fails to maintain the neighborhood's order. In fact, it immediately precipitates the uprising, a claim Amelia ends up making later when she confronts Bratton at a con-ference: "Broken-windows policing is why the riots happened," she says (310), but Bratton will not "revisit the police methodology" (312) and "won't apologize for keeping New York safe" (244). During the increasingly tense scene in the subway station, Bratton's cops round up more and more peo-ple until there are "more than a hundred . . . kids mostly" lined up on the sidewalk under a baking sun (108). Among their ranks are Sara, her brother Andy, and Derek Jupiter's son, who begins reciting the addresses of white-owned businesses and homes. When Andy jumps a cop, he is brutally beaten, and all hell breaks loose. Soon enough the crowd sets the high school on fire, loots stores along Fulton Street, and gathers at the doorstep of Aaron and Amelia's brownstone "to take the neighborhood back" (214), yelling "No justice! No peace!" (199).

Since Aaron and Amelia's house is where the disparate plot lines con-verge, it is worth pausing over this lengthy scene in which their home is attacked. The language Platzer uses to describe the assault marries the imag-ery of broken-windows theory with the imagery of gentrification as a modern example of nineteenth-century homesteading. Living on gentrifi-cation's urban fringe, Amelia likens herself to a rugged "pioneer woman" (15) and Bed-Stuy's African American residents to "the Indians the white people hadn't killed" and who now "lived in poverty in glorified ghettos" (16). The faceless mob of six hundred protestors from the housing projects who encircle the brownstone are meant to be seen as Native Americans attacking a fort, an outpost of civilization on the frontier. Earlier on the radio segment, Bratton had explained that broken windows is a "metaphor"; Platzer makes it literal. While Amelia and Antoinette are bunkered inside and Aaron is racing back home, the "Indians" hurl bricks "through the window glass" (196). By the time Aaron arrives, Derek and his assailant Damien are both dead, and glass shards are everywhere. Damien "shot Jupiter through the glass of the decorative inner door . . . then stepped up toward the interior door where the glass had all been shattered" and shot him again (135). Meanwhile, "kids" are climbing "on trees to reach at Amelia's windows" (149), and the white renter Daniel is "pac[ing] back and forth on the parlor floor looking through the cracks in the wooden shutters deciding whether or not to aim his shotgun," like a character in a John Ford western squinting to get a good sightline on an Apache (150). Following the logic of broken-windows theory, Platzer's novel implies that if this white house falls, the entire neighborhood will be overrun with violence, the civilizing work of gentrification wasted.

So how does Platzer prevent this from happening? The answer is through talking. Talk backed up by firepower. *Bed-Stuy Is Burning* is deeply invested in the politics of dialogue between whites and Blacks to adjudicate gentrification's racial and class inequalities and to discredit and defuse the mass protest that threatens white property in the Black neighborhood. This much is clear in the strange scenes that unfold inside the house between Amelia and Sara and outside the house between Aaron and the crowd. In the unfolding chaos Sara charges inside, barricades herself upstairs, and refuses to vacate the premises. While Amelia clumsily wields her ex-husband's pistol, she confronts her intruder. Amelia wants "to get the girl out of her house as quickly as possible," but she also senses a story in the making that might bolster her fledgling career (217). Amelia thinks she could interview Sara at gunpoint, thinks "she could write it as a first-person account. . . . No one else had a story like this one" (214). In effect, she wants to kill two birds with one stone: calm the situation down by talking to Sara and in talking to Sara pry out of her a story she can write up and sell. "Tell me about yourself," she says. "Let's tell each other about ourselves" (216). After briefly making small talk, she proceeds to coax information out of the sobbing Sara about her participation in the mass protest, asking, "Why did you come here" and "What do you want, Sara?" (215, 220). The conversation soon descends into shouting and threats until Amelia closes her eyes and pulls the trigger, missing Sara by a foot.

The parallel situation outside the home is one in which dialogue is again a means of deescalating the threat of Black-on-white violence. As we will see, what's most important in this novel is not that you are actually heard (and something is done about what you say) but that you "feel as though [you've] been heard" whether or not you actually have been (60). After threading his way to the front of the crowd, then drawing upon his training as a rabbi, Aaron delivers an impromptu sermon on the doorstep. It is not much of a mount, but the steps are enough to elevate him above the protestors as he tries to placate them and save his family and his house. He does so, oddly enough, by retelling the story from the book of Genesis in which a mob clamors to drag Lot's houseguests outside and sodomize them. Given the circumstances (protecting Amelia and Simon inside), it is a curious choice for a sermon, since to save his houseguests, whom Lot has just met, Lot thoughtfully offers up his virgin daughters instead to the rabid Sodomites. The "flesh-hungry crowd," however, is in no mood to bargain: they want the houseguests, who are angels in disguise (237). Lot fails, as we say, to read the room. But Aaron succeeds.

The part of the story that Aaron focuses on is God's agreement with Abraham to not smite the city if anyone righteous can be found living there. The rush to judgment that God made, Aaron says to his audience, was that "He saw Sodom as a single mass of people. But then Abraham initiated the conversation. He acted. Just as you are acting today. He broke up the mass into individuals. Abraham got God to focus on his people. On the individuals" (237, 238). When the crowd shouts Aaron down, "a female voice call[s] out" "Let him talk" (234). "Just by talking to God . . . Abraham made God see that there were in fact good people in Sodom," says Aaron (237). "That's right!" the crowd shouts out in affirmation (237). It is this part of the story that Aaron spins in a new way as he preaches that each person in the crowd should act ethically as an individual. The irony is lost on him, since Aaron does not see individuals, only an "angry mob" referred to repeatedly as "them," "the crowd," "a female voice," and, vaguely, as "someone" (233, 234). "The lesson," from Genesis, Aaron explains, "is that you must not become the mob," adding that "you are doing the right thing here. . . . You are drawing attention to yourself. You are making people see you as individuals" by drawing "attention to the right grievances" (238). "Things will change now," he predicts. "Police will think twice before shooting. But don't become the mob. . . . Stop now. You've done your job. Don't hurt the women and the children" (238). "This hooked them," writes Platzer. "Aaron would save his own life, and the lives of Simon and Amelia" (233). A hearty "Amen!" is shouted by "one woman in the crowd," followed by an exclamation of "God's love!" from an unnamed "someone" (238). On cue, Amelia steps outside, and in a feel-good moment the couple "hugged out there in front of the crowd" as the "mob applauded" and "broke out in cheers" (239). Having "vented their anger, and had their release," the crowd "turned into individuals again," writes Platzer (240). The people eventually disperse, apparently convinced that the "desire to burn this city down" is not in their self-interest (239).

There is a lot to unpack here, but what intrigues me most is how collective political action in *Bed-Stuy Is Burning* is immediately atomized into more liberal individual subject positions that are easier for whites to control. The radicalism of Platzer's text, if one can call it that, is in how it exposes the most liberal of shibboleths, "dialogue" and "debate"—the sharing of opinions, airing of grievances, the building of empathy—as merely pro forma gestures that conceal the operations of entrenched power. Aaron's sermon is a confusing muddle of overlapping and contrasting subject positions, but the clear purpose of the speech is to convince the angry Black crowd that Aaron and his family are "good people" and to convince them that they are better off, and Aaron and Amelia are better off, if they see themselves not as a radical collective protesting police violence and gentrification but as individuals. If liberal oratory does not work, well, there is always Amelia's pistol and Daniel's shotgun.

Messed-Up Stories

Are Aaron and Amelia "good people"? Or are they, as Daniel thinks of them, entitled "asshole[s]" (58)? Aaron and Amelia, I would suggest, are the kind of "asshole[s]" who do not want to be seen as such, the kind who really do want to be viewed as "kindhearted . . . good people," (170) and not as "douchey . . . one percenter[s]" (58). Antoinette sees the couple as the real victims, describing them as "good people" who "deserved better" than what happened to them (307). In this way, Platzer enlists the perspective of the working-class immigrant of color to convey sympathy on the novel's two wealthy, white protagonists. Being "good" and being an "asshole" turn out to be two sides of the same coin. This is the underlying logic of the novel. The affective relation Aaron and Amelia have to the conditions of their existence—having so much economic privilege when so many people around them have so little—is a combination of guilt and self-interest. Aaron, in particular, ameliorates his guilt by giving away his money so he can stop feeling bad for having so much of it. He plans on donating 20 percent of his salary each year, "fifty grand, a lot of money," because, as he says, "I want to help people who are suffering" (60). "Charity *was* good. Noble. Especially given what he was doing for a living," Platzer writes, referring to Aaron's guilt-inducing job of "betting on the right stocks," which pays him handsomely for doing almost nothing (61). Freeing himself of some of this economic privilege improves his sense of self-worth, which in this novel really is something money can buy.

For her part, Amelia is less charitable to strangers but still invested in being seen as good, especially if it advances her self-interest. "Good people look after their own," she says (62). She chooses to do her do-gooding closer to home. Amelia wants to be the kind of good liberal woman who can "lean in" Sheryl Sandberg–style and "be present for those she loved" (19). Using money to do good will also help Amelia do better. In the aftermath of the attack, she knows she sits on a "potentially career-making story" (273) about "Gentrification. Poverty. The riots" in Bed-Stuy (278). To gain access to a part of the neighborhood that is off-limits to her, she hires Sara as her research assistant. Interviewing Sara at gunpoint is less efficient than just paying her $2,000 a week to let Amelia see up close her dirty apartment in the projects, with its litter of chicken wings and soda bottles, and let her talk with her Black friends in the neighborhood. "You show me your world. Explain why it's messed up," Amelia says, and Sara agrees (279). It is patronizing, to say the least, but it seems at first like a win-win-win situation. Amelia gets her story, Sara gets money she needs, and Bed-Stuy gets needed attention to systemic issues of inequality (278). Platzer concludes, "It would be an investment in the neighborhood. In the community. In both their careers"—though one notes that Sara does not have a "career" (279). Amelia's story about gentrification and the Black underclass ends up published in the *New York Times* and serves as the basis of her first book. When Sara reveals to the press that Amelia paid her as a source, the journalistic scandal redounds in Amelia's favor. Amelia's agent tells her, "We couldn't have planned it better. . . . This will be all the publicity we need" (323). Apparently, there's always a market for stories of Black pathology.

If Platzer's novel is any indication, there is always a market for stories of white redemption, too. The arc of his two white protagonists bends not toward justice but toward personal and spiritual renewal. Out of the fires of gentrification, Aaron is reborn a better man. In the denouement, he enters Gamblers Anonymous for his addiction, which has led him to take risky, high-stakes bets his whole life. He reconnects to Judaism and though an atheist, he decides to pursue a more meaningful life by becoming "a rabbi again" (300). Once "utterly lost," he has found a new path (267). "We're going to start over. Here. In Bed-Stuy," he declares (300). For her part, Amelia falls in love all over again with Aaron after watching him deliver his stirring sermon on the stoop and finally agrees to marriage. "Their life could be about truth," thinks Amelia. "Honesty with each other, and a greater honesty where she could try to begin to better understand the trajectory of her own life" (302). In contrast, "the trajectory" of the African American characters in the gentrifying neighborhood is a downward slope or not even a slope but a dead end for some and a circle for others. Derek Jupiter is murdered. His son remains caught in a cycle of rage and sorrow, screaming, "What the fuck am I supposed to do now" that his father is dead and so is his killer, which leaves him unable to enact revenge (292). Platzer reduces him to inarticulate anger: "Fuck! Fuck! Fuck! Fuck! Fuck!" yells Derek, whom we see carrying a pistol in the final pages (292). Sara is in nearly the same spiral of anger and despair, needing "to contain herself from screaming or getting violent" (287). The machinery of this gentrification plot should be seen for what it is: an engine for revitalizing and enriching the novel's white characters at the Black community's expense.

What are the ethics of writing the kind of story Amelia writes or the kind of novel Platzer does? The novel is self-conscious about the question, and so is the author, who in an essay in *Literary Hub* has called for more white writers to make the empathic leap and "inhabit . . . Black characters with a goal of better understanding and expressing their experience."[16] I cannot help but note Platzer's word choice and how it makes me uncomfortable, how it feels ill-fitting: *inhabit*, used in this context to mean fully possessing a Black character, owning him or her, living inside his or her body, taking on his or her habitus, living in his or her habitat in Bed-Stuy, as Aaron and Amelia do. To bridge the gap in racial experience between himself and some of his characters, Platzer finds the nonracial common denominator, the lowest common denominator, really: self-interest. "I think that's how I kept myself honest. I wanted to keep in [the] forefront in my own imagination everyone's self-interest," he has admitted, a sentiment we hear in Medearis's Jeannie Tucker too. Steering clear of writing the "cringe-worthy," "classic white savior trope" and the "reverse-cliché" of the "incredibly sophisticated" "minority character," Platzer sees all of his characters as selfish people. "I tried to present people who are out for themselves as much as possible, as I think all human beings are," he says.[17] Rather than Black or white, in Platzer's novel we have *homo economicus*, the subjectivity of the neoliberal market that is out to get what it can.

Bed-Stuy Is Burning fulfills this vision. Amelia's news story is about Black victimization, poverty, and despair, which she profits from for her own advancement as a writer. The story is not exactly "a steal," like their brownstone, but it is pretty close to stolen, even though she paid for it. "She was the hero of the story," writes Platzer, "and she couldn't let herself forget it" (324). But more than a hero, "Amelia would be the appropriator" (273). The story "*was* hers," even though "really, it belonged to Sara" (273). "She knew there was something not fully decent about telling this story, but she equally knew that she was going to tell it," writes Platzer (273). This admission about Amelia's "not fully decent" story is perhaps an unintended comment by Platzer on his role in telling the story he tells. It is the inverse of the "stories" of the last chapter, the stories of "survival, of diversity, of color and magic" that Quiñonez's Julio in *Chango's Fire* hopes to someday tell (76).

Stories of gentrification have purchase in that they offer ways of imagining an urban past, present, and future and one's place in it. But not all these stories have equal purchasing power or cultural capital. Amelia's story is already sold, while Julio's stories, still to be related, are both mortgaged into the future and paid for in the present by the kind of losses, such as his home, his work, even his love life, that in Platzer's novel are Aaron and Amelia's gains.

Medearis's *Restoration Heights* ends with the fall from grace of Reddick's cherished individualism. We last see him standing on a street in Bed-Stuy silently screaming at his shocking commonality with the hated white gentrifiers whom he has defined himself against. *Bed-Stuy Is Burning* ends on the opposite note, with Aaron and Amelia affirming their difference from the neighborhood around them. At the end, what Aaron and Amelia seek is plainly a version of the good life. What that means for them is a life where they can focus their attention and energies on "truth" and "honesty," on the inner life of the spirit, on loving each other, and on raising their son (302). Sprinkled throughout the final pages are brief scenes of the couple exchanging "I love yous" and caring for Simon, feeding him, playing with him, and changing his diapers. It is cloying, and it is sincere. And it is family life in all of its undramatic, everyday beauty. Such a peaceful vision of life requires a space in which it can unfold.

Time and again, the novels in *The Gentrification Plot* have underscored the fundamentally political nature of space, the neighborhood as a space of shouts and shootings, a space of conflicts over the right to exist, the right to have a foothold on a patch of urban real estate, the right to freely plot one's course in life, the right not to be emplotted by others. The genre of crime fiction brings these conflicts to the fore and will not let you forget them for a moment.

The ending of *Bed-Stuy Is Burning* strongly suggests, however, a desire to move beyond this, beyond the stories of cops, broken-windows policing, racial conflict, and neighborhood struggle, to move to another kind of story, to the kind we find in literary fiction of the white middle class, to leave behind the genre of crime fiction, in effect, for the stories that we find in neighborhoods that are already gentrified rather than the ones going through the process. The end of Platzer's book is suffused with a longing to leave the fractious politics of race, ethnicity, and class in the past, a desire to treat them as settled so its white couple can move on without having to physically move on. The novel concludes by wanting to reorient life to the pleasures and challenges of domesticity and the stories that can emerge from it: stories of searching for personal fulfillment and self-discovery, growing one's wealth, tending to one's family. "Gentrification is dependent on telling us that things are better than they are—and this is supposed to make us feel happy," writes Sarah Schulman.[18] What Platzer's novel dreams of is a neighborhood that no longer burns with the fires of gentrification, one whose gentrification story is history.

ESCAPE FROM NEW YORK

In the spring of 2020, as COVID-19 was sweeping the city and I was holed up inside finishing this book, I found myself several times a day staring at an Instagram page dedicated to the furniture and household goods New Yorkers were tossing to the curb. Among the flotsam and jetsam were steamer trunks, benches of reclaimed lumber, numerous upright pianos, boxes upon boxes of books, a fainting couch with flower upholstery, glass vanities, bar stools, two Noguchi coffee tables, stand-up globes (I counted at least three) that hatched open at the meridian so you could store liquor inside, seemingly every fiddle-leaf fig tree in the five boroughs, and other bric-a-brac and impedimenta and whatever else could be quickly discarded in a desperate effort to get out of New York as fast as possible. When I moved to the city in 1999, knowing no one, I would wander around like a character in Paul Auster's *In the Country of Last Things* looking for items to salvage for my mostly empty apartment. It was a way of getting to know my new neighborhood and a way of filling the hours in my day when I was not reading for graduate school. Had the city in the spring of 2020 not been the world epicenter of coronavirus, had ten thousand New Yorkers not already perished in the first six weeks, had I not had a wife eight and a half months pregnant (both of us terrified of us and the baby becoming infected during delivery), had these things not been true, I would have taken the subway to Williamsburg to see if that midcentury sideboard or that replica Philippe Starck Ghost chair was still waiting to be rescued from the piles of trash.

It was always Williamsburg. Or if it was not, then it was Gowanus or Bushwick or Bed-Stuy. In other words, it was always one of the recently upscaled neighborhoods in the city. That's the pattern I discerned from the Instagram page. What I was witnessing was the discarded cargo of gentrification, the process that had defined life in New York for more than two decades seemingly rolled up like a carpet by the virus in a matter of weeks and heaved to the side. Economic processes are hard to see, but here was gentrification materialized. Here was its interior décor, the stuff that those who were last to arrive and first to leave could not take with them or did not care to when they packed up their laptops and headed out of the city to work remotely. The ship was sinking; it was time to go, and they went fast.

It was only the year before, in 2019, that Hudson Yards had opened to much fanfare and much criticism on the far west side of Manhattan. The largest private-public urban redevelopment project in American history, the twenty-eight-acre site is a sign, like none other, of the excesses of neoliberal urbanism that are killing New York. If gentrification had once been thought of as a process unfolding over years, even decades, as artists, musicians, writers, and the like moved into rough-and-tumble neighborhoods of working-class ethnics whom they displaced, only to be priced out and replaced themselves by the next wave of upper-middle-class newcomers seeking a place with a bit of atmospheric grime and proximity to work, and if gentrification had once been thought of as unfolding in stages that we could see in the shifting retail landscape as low-rent shops catering to the local ethnic community gave way to artisanal cafés and bespoke haberdasheries that soon enough found themselves fighting for space alongside the bland familiarity of Starbucks and Walgreens, if all of this happened slowly and then rapidly, like a time-lapse film of a flower budding, blooming, and dying, Hudson Yards proved finally that one no longer need wait. Hudson Yards, with its half-dozen, brand-spanking-new skyscrapers sheathed in prophylactic glass, as if they were truly something new under the sun, with its apartments ranging from $3 million to $32 million, and with its luxury mall anchored by Neiman Marcus, in effect said that a new uber-wealthy neighborhood could shoot up instantly if the plinth of capital plunked down was heavy enough. It even has its art to lure in the tourists. At the center of the site stands *The Vessel*, a two-hundred-million-dollar

FIGURE E.1. *The Vessel* in Hudson Yards, Manhattan, New York. *Source:* Epicgenius, CC BY-SA 4.0 (https://creativecommons.org/licenses/by-sa/4.0), via Wikimedia Commons.

sculpture resembling a giant wastebasket. It is composed of stairs that tellingly lead nowhere.

Success may be about location, location, location, but it also depends on timing. If Hudson Yards is emblematic of New York's neoliberal urbanism on steroids, it might still be a victim of the pandemic. Living in New York in the early 2000s, I had come to believe that gentrification was an unstoppable and irreversible process. Now I'm not so sure. Hudson Yards' retail anchor has filed for bankruptcy. Many of the exorbitantly expensive restaurants that grace upper floors of the mall have permanently shuttered after being open only a few months, their life sucked out by the virus. *The Vessel* is closed, after three people during the pandemic have climbed up its stairs and leaped 150 feet to their deaths. As the city has retreated inward and emptied out, shootings by the end of 2020 almost doubled, and murders spiked nearly 40 percent, the largest year-over-year increases after twenty years of nearly continuous decline.

It is possible money will rush back in once the all-clear signal has sounded and we can remove our masks, but it is possible, too, that the city will be a smaller place for a while. What is almost certain, however, is that a new literature of crime will emerge in the years to come. Perhaps it will be a crime literature of degentrification and decline, reminiscent of the mid-1970s, when President Gerald Ford was famously quoted as telling the bankrupt city to "drop dead." Reports of Ford's death wish, whether actually uttered or not (he claimed he did not), came in the context of his administration initially refusing the financially distressed city any additional federal aid. The forced neoliberalization of New York in the mid-1970s left the city at the mercy of banks, which hacked away at its social welfare infrastructure as a condition of debt financing, a move that almost certainly produced more desperate people and more crimes of desperation. If this is what awaits New York in the 2020s as it teeters on insolvency and struggles with rising crime, its future will look an awful lot like its past. I began this book with the crime writer Reggie Nadelson calling New York a "welcoming" city in 2009 and George Dawes Green labeling it a "sweet city." If history repeats itself, both of these labels will be ill-fitting. Perhaps New York will once again be "Fear City," as the NYPD called it in 1975. That was the year cops circulated the pamphlet "Welcome to Fear City: A Survival Guide for Visitors to the City of New York" to startled tourists disembarking at LaGuardia and JFK. Staring hollow-eyed from its cover was a memento mori Grim Reaper meant, one supposes, as an avatar for the city and as a memento of one's visit, should one make it out alive. Whatever we call New York years from now, this much is certain: it will be a sweet time to be a crime writer.

ACKNOWLEDGMENTS

My interest in crime fiction as a subject of literary study began when I was a student in an undergraduate course on the genre; the whole semester, I was in a state of continuous disbelief I was getting credit for reading this stuff. But my fascination as a lay reader started earlier, when I was a teenager, and it must have had something to do with the fact that my now late father, whom I did not know well, bore an uncanny resemblance to Humphrey Bogart. Watching Bogart play Dashiell Hammett's and Raymond Chandler's detectives was akin to watching my father's face.

I owe an enormous debt of gratitude to my editor, Philip Leventhal, and to Matt Hart and everyone working on the Literature Now series who believed in this book from its early pages. Philip and Matt expertly steered it through all of the publication wickets to bring it into print. For that, I am grateful beyond words. I also am truly thankful to have had the wisdom and insights of two generous anonymous reviewers for Columbia University Press. Their comments made me rethink and restructure parts of this book, making it immeasurably better. For years, I have been fortunate to work with the Ruhr Center for American Studies on issues related to urban transformation, city culture, and narratives of place. I have benefited enormously from conversations on these issues with Jens Gurr, Barbara Buchenau, Julia Sattler, Maria Sulimma, and Selma Bidlingmaier. Friends, colleagues, and fellow academics, including John Beckman, Andrew

Strombeck, Monica Popescu, Carlo Rotella, Andrew Pepper, Ross Posnock, Ugo Rubeo, Jon Hegglund, and Theodore Martin, have left their indelible imprint on this book as well. While writing and revising *The Gentrification Plot*, I taught seminars on crime fiction to students at McGill University and Penn State–Abington and have benefited from their insights, arguments, and enthusiasms. I want to thank the Chancellor's Office at Penn State–Abington for supporting this project with a grant that made some of my research possible.

Three parts of this book were published previously, though in substantially different forms. Portions of chapter 2 have been adapted from "Richard Price's Lower East Side: Cops, Culture, and Gentrification," *Journal of Urban Cultural Studies* 1, no. 2 (2014): 235–54. Portions of chapter 3 have been adapted from "Detecting Chinatown: New York, Crime Fiction, and the Politics of Urban Inscrutability," in *Spaces—Communities— Representations: Urban Transformations in the U.S.A.*, ed. Julia Sattler (Bielefeld: Transcript-Verlag, 2015): 229–53. Parts of the epilogue originally appeared as "My Beautiful City," published in the March 2021 issue of *The Brooklyn Rail: Critical Perspectives on Art, Politics and Culture*.

The person who kept me sane and laughing while writing much of this book is still much too young to even read: Margaux Emi Hiroto-Heise. Little One, I hope your New York City is as magical as mine. More than anyone, this book is dedicated to and made possible by Allison Akiko Hiroto, my partner in crime and my dearest love. Without your grace, intelligence, and determination, my life would be immeasurably smaller. All of these words are for you.

NOTES

INTRODUCTION: DEATH AND LIFE IN POSTINDUSTRIAL NEW YORK

1. Reggie Nadelson, Lee Child, and George Dawes Green, "New York City Thrillers," interview by Leonard Lopate, *The Leonard Lopate Show*, WNYC, December 24, 2009, https://www.wnyc.org/story/59750-new-york-city-thrillers.
2. Reggie Nadelson, "Artie Cohen's Harlem Whodunit," interview by Salman Rushdie, *Vanity Fair*, October 2010, https://www.vanityfair.com/culture/2010/10/reggie-nadelson-201010.
3. Diane Cardwell, "Mayor Says New York Is Worth the Cost," *New York Times*, January 8, 2003.
4. Andrew Karmen, *New York Murder Mystery: The True Story Behind the Crime Crash of the 1990s* (New York: NYU Press, 2006), 1.
5. Franklin E. Zimring, *The City That Became Safe: New York's Lessons for Urban Crime and Its Control* (Oxford: Oxford University Press, 2012), 6.
6. Karmen, *New York Murder Mystery*, 1–2.
7. Zimring, *The City*, 5.
8. Quoted in Karmen, *New York Murder Mystery*, 7.
9. Julian Brash, *Bloomberg's New York: Class and Governance in the Luxury City* (Athens: University of Georgia Press, 2011), 19, 120.
10. Michael Bloomberg, "State of the City Address," *Gotham Gazette*, January 23, 2003.
11. Susanna Schaller and Johannes Novy, "New York City's Waterfronts as Strategic Sites for Analyzing Neoliberalism and Its Contestations," in *Transforming Urban Waterfronts: Fixity and Flow*, ed. Gene Desfor et al. (New York: Routledge, 2011), 171.

12. Jeremiah Moss, *Vanishing New York: How a Great City Lost Its Soul* (New York: Dey St., 2017), 161.

13. Kevin Baker, "The Death of a Once Great City: The Fall of New York and the Urban Crisis of Affluence," *Harper's*, July 2018, https://harpers.org/archive/2018/07/the -death-of-new-york-city-gentrification.

14. Rent Guidelines Board's 2013 Housing Supply Report, qtd. in Moss, *Vanishing New York*, 162.

15. Ingrid Gould Ellen, Keren Mertens Horn, and David Reed, "Has Falling Crime Invited Gentrification?," *Journal of Housing Economics* 46 (December 2019): 1.

16. Dennis Porter, *The Pursuit of Crime: Art and Ideology in Detective Fiction* (New Haven, CT: Yale University Press, 1981), 190.

17. See "Welcome to Fear City: A Survival Guide for Visitors to the City of New York," Council for Public Safety, 1975; Reggie Nadelson, *Red Hook* (New York: Walker, 2005), 23, 97.

18. Nadelson et al., "New York City Thrillers."

19. Baker, "Death."

20. Quoted in Karmen, *New York Murder Mystery*, 7.

21. Richard Price, *Lush Life* (New York: Picador, 2008), 433.

22. Wil Medearis, *Restoration Heights* (Toronto: Hanover Square, 2019), 173.

23. Henry Chang, *Year of the Dog* (New York: Soho, 2008), 161.

24. Michael Katz, "Reframing the Underclass Debate" in *The "Underclass" Debate: Views from History*, ed. Michael Katz (Princeton, NJ: Princeton University Press, 1994), 444, 443–44.

25. Paula C. Johnson, "Beyond Displacement: Gentrification of Racialized Spaces as Violence—Harlem, New York, and New Orleans, Louisiana," in *Accumulating Insecurity: Violence and Dispossession in the Making of Everyday Life*, ed. Shelley Feldman, Charles Geisler, and Gayatri A. Menon (Athens: University of Georgia Press), 84.

26. Moss, *Vanishing New York*, 64.

27. Stewart King, "Place," in *The Routledge Companion to Crime Fiction*, ed. Janice Allan et al. (New York: Routledge, 2020), 211; Alfred Bendixen, "Researching the Premises: The Centrality of Crime Fiction in American Literary Culture," in *The Centrality of Crime Fiction in American Literary Culture*, ed. Alfred Bendixen and Olivia Carr Edenfield (New York: Routledge, 2017), 5; Eva Erdmann, "Nationality International: Detective Fiction in the Late Twentieth Century," in *Investigating Identities: Questions of Identity in Contemporary International Crime Fiction*, ed. Kate M. Quinn and Marieke Krajenbrink (Amsterdam: Rodopi, 2009), 12; David Harvey, "Uneven Geographical Developments and Universal Rights," in *Readings in Urban Theory*, ed. Susan S. Fainstein and Scott Campbell (Chichester: Blackwell-Wiley, 2011), 367.

28. Bendixen, "Researching," 2.

29. Charles J. Rzepka, "Introduction: What Is Crime Fiction," in *A Companion to Crime Fiction*, ed. Charles J. Rzepka and Lee Horsley (Chichester: Blackwell-Wiley, 2010), 1, 2.

30. Andrew Pepper, *The Contemporary American Crime Novel: Race, Ethnicity, Gender, Class* (Edinburgh: Edinburgh University Press, 2000), 13, 31.

31. Jesper Gulddal and Steward King, "Genre," in *The Routledge Companion to Crime Fiction*, ed. Janice Allan et al. (New York: Routledge, 2020), 13, 14.

32. Gulddal and King, "Genre," 15.

33. Bendixen, "Researching," 2.

34. Bendixen, "Researching," 2.

35. Jeremy Rosen, "Literary Fiction and the Genres of Genre Fiction," *Post45*, August 7, 2018, https://post45.org/2018/08/literary-fiction-and-the-genres-of-genre-fiction.

36. Rosen, "Literary Fiction."

37. Theodore Martin, *Contemporary Drift: Genre, Historicism, and the Problem of the Present* (New York: Columbia University Press, 2017), 6, 7, 14.

38. Lucy Andrew and Catherine Phelps, introduction to *Capital Crimes: Crime Fiction in the City*, ed. Lucy Andrew and Catherine Phelps (Cardiff: University of Wales Press, 2013), 3; Catalina Neculai, *Urban Space and Late Twentieth-Century New York Literature* (New York: Palgrave, 2014), 12; David Schmid, "Imagining Safe Urban Space: The Contribution of Detective Fiction to Radical Geography," *Antipode* 27, no. 3 (1995): 243; Carlo Rotella, *The World Is Always Coming to an End: Pulling Together and Apart in a Chicago Neighborhood* (Chicago: University of Chicago Press, 2019), 69, 68; Andrew Pepper, "Black Crime Fiction," in *The Cambridge Companion to Crime Fiction*, ed. Martin Priestman (Cambridge: Cambridge University Press, 2003), 220 (here, Pepper speaks of Walter Mosley's work specifically, but the claim is true for much crime fiction); Clayton Moore, "Richard Price and the Lush Life," *Bookslut*, January 2008, http://www.bookslut.com/mystery_strumpet/2008_01_012356.php.

39. Andrew Pepper, *Unwilling Executioner: Crime Fiction and the State* (Oxford: Oxford University Press, 2016), 17.

40. Peter Brooks, *Reading for the Plot: Design and Intention in Narrative* (Cambridge, MA: Harvard University Press, 1984), 18, xiii.

41. Raymond Chandler, *Selected Letters of Raymond Chandler*, ed. Frank MacShane (London: Jonathan Cape, 1981), 129–30.

42. Martin, *Contemporary Drift*, 103, 105.

43. Fredric Jameson, *Raymond Chandler: The Detections of Totality* (London: Verso, 2016), 3.

44. Ernesto Quiñonez, *Bodega Dreams* (New York: Vintage, 2000), 38; Schmid, "Imagining Safe Urban Space," 246.

45. Dashiell Hammett, *Red Harvest* (New York: Vintage, 1992), 3, 6.

46. Paul Auster, *The New York Trilogy: City of Glass, Ghosts, The Locked Room* (New York: Penguin, 2006), 106–7.

47. Medearis, *Restoration Heights*, 317.

48. Brooks, *Reading*, 5.

49. Franco Moretti, *Signs Taken for Wonders: Essays in the Sociology of Literary Forms* (London: Verso, 2005), 136.

50. Pepper, *Unwilling*, 12.

51. Porter, *Pursuit of Crime*, 120.

52. Gabriel Cohen, *Red Hook* (New York: Thomas Dunne, 2001), 96; Cohen, *The Graving Dock* (New York: Thomas Dunne, 2007), 86.

53. Porter, *Pursuit of Crime*, 29, 30.

54. Nadelson, *Red Hook*, 240.
55. Carlo Rotella, "Urban Literature: A User's Guide," *Journal of Urban History* 44, no. 4 (2018): 804.
56. Ernesto Quiñonez, *Chango's Fire: A Novel* (New York: Rayo, 2004), 16; Medearis, *Restoration Heights*, 126; Price, *Lush Life*, 196.
57. Steve Herbert, *Policing Space: Territoriality and the Los Angeles Police Department* (Minneapolis: University of Minnesota Press, 1997) 22, 10.
58. Brash, *Bloomberg's New York*, 28.
59. See Richard Lloyd, *Neo-Bohemia: Art and Commerce in the Postindustrial City* (New York: Routledge, 2006); Christopher Mele, *Selling the Lower East Side: Culture, Real Estate, and Resistance in New York City* (Minneapolis: University of Minnesota Press, 2000); Sarah Schulman, *The Gentrification of the Mind: Witness to a Lost Imagination* (Berkeley: University of California Press, 2012); Sharon Zukin, *Naked City: The Death and Life of Authentic Urban Places* (Oxford: Oxford University Press, 2009).
60. Henri Lefebvre, *The Production of Space*, trans. Donald Nicholson-Smith (Oxford: Blackwell, 1991), 1, 27; Manuel Castells, *The City and the Grassroots* (Berkeley: University of California Press, 1983), 311.
61. Henri Lefebvre, *The Urban Revolution*, trans. Robert Bononno (Minneapolis: University of Minnesota Press, 2003), 15; Edward Soja, *Postmodern Geographies: The Reassertion of Space in Critical Social Theory* (London: Verso, 1989), 81.
62. Soja, *Postmodern Geographies*, 184; David Harvey, "The Urban Process Under Capitalism: A Framework for Analysis," *International Journal of Urban and Regional Research* 2 (1978): 124.
63. Soja, *Postmodern Geographies*, 170.
64. Ruth Glass, *London: Aspects of Change* (London: MacGibbon & Kee, 1964), xviii.
65. Neil Smith, *The New Urban Frontier: Gentrification and the Revanchist City* (New York: Routledge, 1996), 32; Martha Rosler, "Fragments of a Metropolitan Viewpoint," in *If You Lived Here: The City in Art, Theory, and Social Activism*, ed. Brian Wallis (Seattle: Bay Press, 1991), 25.
66. Moss, *Vanishing*, 415; Richard Florida, *The New Urban Crisis* (New York: Basic Books, 2017), 61.
67. Smith, *Urban Frontier*, 39.
68. Johnson, "Beyond Displacement," 83.
69. In Florida's 2017 book *The New Urban Crisis*, he offers something of a mea culpa for his unbridled enthusiasm for urban development led by the creative class. "Seemingly overnight, the much-hoped for urban revival turned into a new kind of urban crisis," he writes, addressing specifically gentrification and inequality (3). Yet he goes on to dismiss gentrification as largely "the media's obsession" (58).
70. Richard Florida, *Cities and the Creative Class* (New York: Routledge, 2005), 1, 3, 166, 7.
71. Florida, *Cities*, 166.
72. Florida, *Cities*, 114, 132.
73. Florida, *Cities*, 132, 167.
74. Florida, *Cities*, 7, 6.
75. Brash, *Bloomberg's New York*, 7.

76. Brash, *Bloomberg's New York*, 48.

77. Smith, *Urban Frontier*, 61, 32, 41.

78. Schulman, *The Gentrification of the Mind*, 27.

79. Neil Smith, "Gentrification and Uneven Development," *Economic Geography* 58, no. 2 (April 1982): 151.

80. Roger Starr, "Making New York Smaller," *New York Times*, November 14, 1976.

81. Richard Price, "Richard Price—Living a Lush Life in Some Small Dive," interview by Ronald Sklar, *Popentertainment.com*, March 2, 2008, https://www.popen tertainmentarchives.com/post/richard-price-living-a-lush-life-in-some-small-dive.

82. Quiñonez, *Chango's Fire*, 117.

83. Brash, *Bloomberg's New York*, 28.

84. Michel de Certeau, *The Practice of Everyday Life*, trans. Steven Rendall (Berkeley: University of California Press, 1984), 92.

85. C. R. Sridhar, "Broken Windows and Zero Tolerance: Policing Urban Crimes," *Economic and Political Weekly* 41, no. 19 (May 13–19, 2006): 1842; Karmen, *New York Murder Mystery*, 121.

86. James Q. Wilson and George L. Kelling, "Broken Windows: The Police and Neighborhood Safety," *The Atlantic*, March 1982, 31.

87. For a critique of Wilson and Kelling's "less-than-faithful reading" of Zimbardo's study, see Bench Ansfield's "The Broken Windows of the Bronx: Putting the Theory in Its Place," *American Quarterly* 72, no. 1 (March 2020): 117.

88. Wilson and Kelling, "Broken Windows," 31.

89. Wilson and Kelling, "Broken Windows," 31–32.

90. William Bratton, "Police Strategy No. 5: Reclaiming the Public Spaces of New York," New York City Police Department, 1994, 5, 7.

91. James Q. Wilson, *Varieties of Police Behavior* (Cambridge, MA: Harvard University Press, 1968), 40.

92. Wilson, *Varieties*, 39–40.

93. Wilson and Kelling, "Broken Windows," 31.

94. Wilson and Kelling, "Broken Windows," 34–35.

95. Themis Chronopoulos, *Spatial Regulation in New York City: From Urban Renewal to Zero Tolerance* (New York: Routledge, 2011), 2.

96. Chronopoulos, *Spatial Regulation*, 2.

97. Wilson and Kelling, "Broken Windows," 34.

98. Marianne Maeckelbergh, "Mobilizing to Stay Put: Housing Struggles in New York City," *International Journal of Urban and Regional Research* 36, no. 4 (July 2012): 661.

99. Chronopoulos, *Spatial Regulation*, 1.

100. Sridhar, "Broken," 1842.

101. Brad Lander and Laura Wolf-Powers, "Remaking New York City: Can Prosperity Be Shared and Sustainable," Pratt Institute Center for Community and Environmental Development, November 2004, 11, https://repository.upenn.edu/cgi/view content.cgi?article=1042&context=cplan_papers.

102. Philip K. Eure, "An Analysis of Quality-of-Summonses, Quality-of-Life Misdemeanor Arrests, and Felony Crime in New York City, 2019–2015," New York Office of Investigation, Office of the Inspector General for the NYPD, June 22, 2016, 3.

103. Carlo Rotella, *October Cities: The Redevelopment of Urban Literature* (Berkeley: University of California Press, 1998), 125.

104. Bart Keunen and Bart Eeckhout, "Whatever Happened to the Urban Novel? New Perspectives for Literary Urban Studies in the Era of Postmodern Culture," in *Postmodern New York City: Transfiguring Spaces*, ed. Günter Lenz and Utz Reise (Heidelberg: Heidelberg University Press, 2003), 58.

105. Jan Lin, *The Power of Urban Ethnic Places: Cultural Heritage and Community Life* (New York: Routledge, 2011), 46.

106. Lara Belkind, "Stealth Gentrification: Camouflage and Commerce on the Lower East Side," *Traditional Dwellings and Settlements Review* 21, no. 1 (Fall 2009): 28.

107. Arlene Dávila, *Barrio Dreams: Puerto Ricans, Latinos, and the Neoliberal City* (Berkeley: University of California Press, 2004), 23.

108. Robert Smi, "Red Hook: A Mystery Writer's Guide to the Brick and Bodies of the Neighborhood," *North Country Public Radio*, July 28, 2009, http://www.northcountrypublicradio.org/news/npr/131009145/red-hook-a-mystery-writer-s-guide-to-the-bricks-and-the-bodies-of-the-neighborhood.

109. Price, "Living a Lush Life."

110. Gabriel Cohen, email message to author, October 27, 2020.

111. Quiñonez, *Chango's Fire*, 13.

112. Soja, *Postmodern Geographies*, 6.

113. Howard Silver, "Richard Price Reads from and Discusses *Lush Life*," March 23, 2009, YouTube video, 4:40, http://www.youtube.com/watch?v=YFVgV4mXFAA.

114. Silver, "Richard Price Reads."

115. Marisa Solomon, "'The Ghetto is a Gold Mine': The Racialized Temporality of Betterment," *International Labor and Working-Class History* 95 (Spring 2019): 78; Peter Kwong, "Answers About the Gentrification of Chinatown," *New York Times*, September 16, 2009.

1. THE LOWER EAST SIDE: COPS, CULTURE, AND THE CREATIVE CLASS

1. Neil Smith, *The New Urban Frontier: Gentrification and the Revanchist City* (New York: Routledge, 1996), 20, 21; "'A Divided Community': A Study of the Gentrification of the Lower East Side Community, New York," Two Bridges Neighborhood Council, Inc., June 2004, 3, https://twobridges.org/publications/a-divided-community-a-study-of-gentrification-of-the-lower-east-side-community-new-york-2004.

2. Richard Price, *Lush Life* (New York: Picador, 2008), 210.

3. Richard Price, "Richard Price—Living a Lush Life in Some Small Dive," interview by Ronald Sklar, *Popentertainment.com*, March 2, 2008, https://www.popentertainmentarchives.com/post/richard-price-living-a-lush-life-in-some-small-dive.

4. Price, "Living a Lush Life."

5. Richard Price, "For Crime Novelist Richard Price, Life is 'Lush,'" interview by Terry Gross, *Fresh Air*, NPR, March 5, 2008, https://www.npr.org/transcripts/101238934?storyId=101238934?storyId=101238934.

6. Howard Silver, "Richard Price Reads from and Discusses *Lush Life*," March 23, 2009, YouTube video, 4:40, http://www.youtube.com/watch?v=YFVgV4mXFAA.

7. Suleiman Osman, *The Invention of Brownstone Brooklyn: Gentrification and the Search for Authenticity in Postwar New York* (New York: Oxford University Press, 2011), 15.

8. Lara Belkind, "Stealth Gentrification: Camouflage and Commerce on the Lower East Side," *Traditional Dwellings and Settlements Review* 21, no. 1 (Fall 2009): 21.

9. Smith, *Urban Frontier*, 7.

10. Luc Sante, *Low Life: Lures and Snares of Old New York* (New York: Vintage, 1991), 32.

11. Belkind, "Stealth," 24.

12. Smith, *Urban Frontier*, 20, 21, 22.

13. "'A Divided Community,'" 1, 2.

14. Victor Papa, foreword to "'A Divided Community.'"

15. "'A Divided Community,'" 11.

16. Papa, foreword to "'A Divided Community.'"

17. Jeremy Rosen, "Literary Fiction and the Genres of Genre Fiction," *Post45*, August 7, 2018, https://post45.org/2018/08/literary-fiction-and-the-genres-of-genre-fiction.

18. Rosen, "Literary Fiction."

19. Clayton Moore, "Richard Price and the Lush Life," *Bookslut*, January 2008, http://www.bookslut.com/mystery_strumpet/2008_01_012356.php.

20. Moore, "Richard Price."

21. Price, "Living a Lush Life."

22. Liz Bondi, "Gender Divisions and Gentrification: A Critique," *Transactions of the Institute of British Geographers* 16, no. 2 (1991): 196.

23. Silver, "Richard Price Reads."

24. David Schmid, "Imagining Safe Urban Space: The Contribution of Detective Fiction to Radical Geography," *Antipode* 27, no. 3 (1995): 246.

25. Smith, *Urban Frontier*, 20.

26. Richard Florida, *Cities and the Creative Class* (New York: Routledge, 2005), 4.

27. Nicholas Wroe, "Excavation of the Lower East Side," *The Guardian*, August 15, 2008, https://www.theguardian.com/books/2008/aug/16/fiction1.

28. Jacob Riis, *How the Other Half Lives* (New York: Norton, 2010), 5, 166.

29. Riis, *How the Other Half Lives*, 5, 17.

30. Elizabeth Gumport, "Gentrified Fictions," *n+1*, November 2, 2009, http://nplusonemag.com/online-only/book-review/gentrified-fiction.

31. Christopher Mele, *Selling the Lower East Side: Culture, Real Estate, and Resistance in New York City* (Minneapolis: University of Minnesota Press, 2000), 288.

32. "Why the Ludlow?," Edison Properties, http://www.theludlownyc.com/neighborhood.

33. Andreas Huyssen, *Present Pasts: Urban Palimpsests and the Politics of Memory* (Stanford, CA: Stanford University Press, 2003), 87.

34. Mele, *Selling the Lower East Side*, 284.

35. Smith, *Urban Frontier*, 22.

36. Silver, "Richard Price Reads."

37. Smith, *Urban Frontier*, 12; the quotation from Barthes comes from the same source.

38. Jane Harris, "The Lush History of the Lower East Side," *Art in America*, August 3, 2010, https://www.artnews.com/art-in-america/features/lush-life-franklin-evans -omar-lopez-chahoud-58028/.
39. Media Farzin, "Lush Life: An Exhibition in Nine Chapters, New York," *Art Agenda*, August 11, 2010, http://www.art-agenda.com/features/232273/lush-life-an-exhibition -in-nine-chapters-new-york.
40. Harris, "Lush History."
41. Price, "Living a Lush Life."

2. CHINATOWN: POLICING THE ETHNIC ENCLAVE

1. Marisa Solomon, " 'The Ghetto Is a Gold Mine': The Racialized Temporality of Betterment," *International Labor and Working-Class History* 95 (Spring 2019): 78.
2. Richard Price, "Richard Price—Living a Lush Life in Some Small Dive," interview by Ronald Sklar, *Popentertainment.com*, March 2, 2008, https://www.popenter tainmentarchives.com/post/richard-price-living-a-lush-life-in-some-small -dive.
3. Peter Kwong, "Answers About the Gentrification of Chinatown," *New York Times*, September 16, 2009.
4. Bethany Y. Li et al., "Chinatown Then and Now: Gentrification in Boston, New York, and Philadelphia," Asian American Legal Defense and Education Fund, 2013, 2–3, 29, 41.
5. Li, "Chinatown," 41.
6. Henry Chang, *Year of the Dog* (New York: Soho Press, 2008), 161.
7. Carlo Rotella, "Urban Literature: A User's Guide," *Journal of Urban History* 44, no. 4 (2018), 804.
8. Steven Kurutz, "Murder on Mott Street," *New York Times*, October 24, 2008; Henry Chang, "Henry Chang Interview with Tomie Arai," video, February 21, 2013, Portraits of Chinatown, Museum of Chinese in America, New York.
9. Henry Chang, *Chinatown Beat* (New York: Soho Press, 2006), 11.
10. Chang, "Interview with Tomie Arai."
11. "Race/Ethnic Change by Neighborhood," May 23, 2011, distributed by the Center for Urban Research, Graduate Center, CUNY, http://www.urbanresearchmaps .org/plurality/files/RaceEthnic%20Change%20by%20Neighborhood%205- 23-11.xls.
12. Ching Yeh Chen, interview by Lena Sze, Archaeology of Change Archives, Museum of Chinese in America, New York, AOC_Ching Yeh Chen_Nov_9_2007.WMA; Dirk Westphal, interview by Lena Sze and Tomie Arai, Archaeology of Change Archives, Museum of Chinese in America, New York, AOC_Dirk Westphal_8 Jan 08.WMA.
13. Jan Lee, interview by Lena Sze and Tomie Arai, Archaeology of Change Archives, Museum of Chinese in America, New York, AOC_Jane Lee_18 Jun 2008.WMA.
14. Lee, interview.
15. Spring Wang, interview by Lena Sze and Tomie Arai, Archaeology of Change Archives, Museum of Chinese in America, New York, AOC_Spring Wang_18 March 2008.WMA; Kam Mak, interview by Lena Sze and Tomie Arai, Archaeology of

of Change Archives, Museum of Chinese in America, New York, AOC_Kim Mak_6 March 2008.WMA.

16. "175 East Broadway #5D," StreetEasy, Zillow, Inc., https://streeteasy.com/property /784296-the-forward-building-5d.

17. Henry Chang, "Henry Chang: A Chinatown Walking Tour with the Mystery Writer," *AsiaPacific Forum*, April 21, 2009, https://www.asiapacificforum.org /show-detail.php?show_id=148#394.

18. Kurutz, "Murder."

19. Chang, "Walking Tour"; Chang, "Interview with Tomie Arai."

20. Lee, interview.

21. Kayo Ong, interview by Lena Sze and Tomie Arai, AOC_Kayo Ong_Feb_19 2008. WMA. Archaeology of Change Archives, Museum of Chinese in America, New York.

22. Henry Chang, *Year of the Dog* (New York: Soho Press, 2008), 174.

23. Kurutz, "Murder."

24. Solomon, "Ghetto," 82, 78.

25. Henry Chang, *Red Jade* (New York: Soho Press, 2010), 10.

26. Roman Polanski, dir., *Chinatown* (Los Angeles: Paramount, 1974).

27. Jacob Riis, *How the Other Half Lives* (New York: Norton, 2010), 56, 58, 60.

28. Quoted in Robert McClellan, *The Heathen Chinee: A Study of American Attitudes Toward China, 1890–1905* (Athens: Ohio State University Press, 1971), 32.

29. James D. Phelan, "Why the Chinese Should Be Excluded," *North American Review* 173, no. 540 (1901): 673.

30. Quoted in McClellan, *Heathen Chinee*, 35.

31. K. Scott Wong, "Chinatown: Conflicting Images, Contested Terrain," *MELUS* 20, no. 1 (1995): 4.

32. Jan Lin, *Reconstructing Chinatown: Ethnic Enclave, Global Change* (Minneapolis: University of Minnesota Press, 1998), 3.

33. Michael Cimino, dir., *Year of the Dragon* (Beverly Hills, CA: Metro-Goldwyn-Mayer, 1985).

34. Frank Chin and Jeffery Paul Chan, "Racist Love," in *Seeing Through Shuck*, ed. Richard Kostelanetz (New York: Ballantine, 1972), 65; Elaine H. Kim, *Asian American Literature: An Introduction to the Writings and Their Social Context* (Philadelphia: Temple University Press, 1982), 18.

35. Dolores Hayden, *The Power of Place: Urban Landscapes as Public History* (Cambridge, MA: MIT Press, 1995), 9.

36. Sau-Ling Cynthia Wong, "Ethnic Subject, Ethnic Sign, and the Difficulty of Rehabilitative Representation: Chinatown in Some Works of Chinese American Fiction," *Yearbook of English Studies* 24 (1994): 257.

37. The correct reference is to the late 1980s and early 1990s hip-hop group Niggaz Wit Attitudes. The mistake may be a sign that Chang is reaching for the first available image of "thug culture" (*Year*, 164).

38. Julian Brash, *Bloomberg's New York: Class and Governance in the Luxury City* (Athens: University of Georgia Press, 2011), 28.

39. Lin, *Reconstructing Chinatown*, 15.

40. Cover copy, *China Trade*, by S. J. Rozan (New York: Minotaur, 1994).

41. Li, "Chinatown," 3.

42. Mak, interview.
43. James Q. Wilson and George L. Kelling, "Broken Windows: The Police and Neighborhood Safety," *The Atlantic*, March 1982, 31.
44. Chang, "Walking Tour."
45. Kurutz, "Murder."
46. On January 23, 2020, a five-alarm fire tore through 70 Mulberry, the building housing MOCA's archives. Only about half of its 85,000 items were digitized at the time of the fire. Now the museum has embarked on a rescue effort to salvage the waterlogged ephemera of Chinatown's collective life, such as old newspapers, paper fans, suitcases, and posters, that are dissolving away, taking their memories with them.

3. RED HOOK: BLOOD ON THE INDUSTRIAL WATERFRONT

1. Gabriel Cohen, *Red Hook* (New York: Thomas Dunne, 2001), 29; Ivy Pochoda, *Visitation Street* (New York: Harper Perennial, 2013), 80; "Mayor Michael Bloomberg's State of the City Address," *New York Times*, January 30, 2002.
2. Mitchell Moss, qtd. in Susanna Schaller and Johannes Novy, "New York City's Waterfronts as Strategic Sites for Analyzing Neoliberalism and Its Contestations," in *Transforming Urban Waterfronts: Fixity and Flow*, ed. Gene Desfor et al. (New York: Routledge, 2011), 170.
3. Robert Smi, "Red Hook: A Mystery Writer's Guide to the Brick and Bodies of the Neighborhood," *North Country Public Radio*, July 28, 2009, http://www.northcountrypublicradio.org/news/npr/131009145/red-hook-a-mystery-writer-s-guide-to-the-bricks-and-the-bodies-of-the-neighborhood.
4. Reggie Nadelson, *Red Hook* (New York: Walker & Company, 2005), 23, 97, 9.
5. New York City Department of City Planning, *Red Hook: A Plan for Community Regeneration* (New York: Department of City Planning, 1996), https://www1.nyc.gov/assets/brooklyncb6/downloads/pdf/bkcb6-197a-plan.pdf, 8, 45.
6. Molly Ivins, "Red Hook Survives Hard Times Into New Era," *New York Times*, November 16, 1981.
7. Rebecca Salima Krisel, "Gentrifying a Superfund Site: Why Gowanus, Brooklyn Is Becoming a Real Estate Hot Spot," *Consilience* 14 (2015): 223.
8. H. P. Lovecraft, "The Horror at Red Hook" (1927), in *The Tomb and Other Tales* (New York: Ballantine, 1965), 72, 71, 73, 77.
9. Arthur Miller, *A View from the Bridge* (New York: Penguin, 1955), 2, xiv.
10. NYC DCP, *The New Waterfront Revitalization Program* (New York: Department of City Planning, 2002), https://www1.nyc.gov/assets/planning/download/pdf/applicants/wrp/wrp_full.pdf; NYC DCP, *Vision 2020: New York Comprehensive Waterfront Plan* (New York: Department of City Planning, 2011), https://www1.nyc.gov/assets/planning/download/pdf/plans-studies/vision-2020-cwp/vision2020/vision2020_nyc_cwp.pdf; NY Rising Community Reconstruction Red Hook Planning Committee, *Red Hook: NY Rising Community Reconstruction Plan* (New York: NY Rising Community Reconstruction Red Hook Planning Committee, 2014), https://stormrecovery.ny.gov/sites/default/files/crp/community/documents/redhook_nyrcr_plan_20mb_0.pdf.

11. James Throgmorton, "Planning as Persuasive Storytelling in a Global-Scale Web of Relationships," *Planning Theory* 2, no. 2 (2003): 127, 128.

12. NY Rising, *Red Hook*, 9, 18.

13. Quentin Stevens, "Conclusion: Patterns of Persistence, Trajectories of Change," in *Transforming Urban Waterfronts: Fixity and Flow*, ed. Gene Desfor et al. (New York: Routledge, 2011), 302; Schaller and Novy, "New York City's Waterfronts," 174; see photographs in NY Rising, *Red Hook*, 22, 16, 19.

14. Throgmorton, "Planning," 143; NY Rising, *Red Hook*, 21.

15. "This Ex-NYC Drug Cop Has Amassed a $400M Real Estate Portfolio," *Real Deal*, June 17, 2019, https://therealdeal.com/2019/06/17/this-ex-nyc-drug-cop-has-amassed -a-400m-real-estate-portfolio.

16. Jonathan Bowles, "Q&A with Red Hook Developer Greg O'Connell," Center for an Urban Future, March 2005, https://nycfuture.org/research/qa-with-red-hook -developer-greg-oconnell-the-importance-of-balanced-growth.

17. Gabriel Cohen, email message to author, October 27, 2020.

18. Robert Caro, *The Power Broker: Robert Moses and the Fall of New York* (New York: Vintage, 1975), 19.

19. Gabriel Cohen, *The Ninth Step* (New York: Thomas Dunne, 2010), 273.

20. Dennis Porter, *The Pursuit of Crime: Art and Ideology in Detective Fiction* (New Haven, CT: Yale University Press, 1981), 190.

21. John Scaggs, *Crime Fiction* (London: Routledge, 2005), 22.

22. Porter, *Pursuit of Crime*, 29; Scaggs, *Crime*, 47.

23. Gabriel Cohen, *The Graving Dock* (New York: Thomas Dunne, 2007), 86.

24. Cohen, *Graving Dock*, 232.

25. Cohen, *Graving Dock*, 1.

26. Cohen, *Graving Dock*, 1.

27. "Mayor Michael Bloomberg's State of the City Address."

28. For more on this point, see Sharon Zukin, *Naked City: The Death and Life of Authentic Urban Places* (Oxford: Oxford University Press, 2009), 27.

29. Ivy Pochoda, *Visitation Street* (New York: Harper Perennial, 2013), 80.

30. Lewis Mumford, *The Culture of Cities* (New York: Secker & Warburg, 1940), 4.

31. One might see, too, Pochoda subtly alluding to the climatological (and political) disaster of Superstorm Sandy in 2012 that washed over Red Hook and as the waters receded left behind rising rents.

32. Cohen, *Graving Dock*, 232.

4. HARLEM: UPTOWN DEAD ZONES

1. Diane Cardwell, "Mayor Says New York Is Worth the Cost," *New York Times*, January 8, 2003.

2. Nicole M. Christian, "Sales Pitch: New York Worth the Cost," *New York Times*, January 24, 2003.

3. Jeremiah Moss, *Vanishing New York: How a Great City Lost Its Soul* (New York: Dey St., 2017), 161.

4. NYU Furman Center for Real Estate and Urban Policy, "Central Harlem, MN10," https://furmancenter.org/neighborhoods/view/central-harlem; NYU Furman

Center for Real Estate and Urban Policy, "East Harlem, MN11," https://furmancenter
.org/neighborhoods/view/east-harlem.

5. Paula C. Johnson, "Beyond Displacement: Gentrification of Racialized Spaces as
Violence—Harlem, New York, and New Orleans, Louisiana," in *Accumulating
Insecurity: Violence and Dispossession in the Making of Everyday Life*, ed. Shelley
Feldman et al. (Athens: University of Georgia Press, 2011), 82, 81.

6. Chester Himes, "Harlem, ou le cancer de l'Amerique," *Presence Africaine* 45, 1 Trimestre (1963): 78.

7. Quoted in Herb Boyd, "Noted Author Grace F. Edwards Dies at 87," *Amsterdam
News* (New York), April 9, 2020, http://amsterdamnews.com/news/2020/apr/09
/noted-author-grace-f-edwards-dies-87.

8. Alfred Bendixen, "Researching the Premises: The Centrality of Crime Fiction in
American Literary Culture," in *The Centrality of Crime Fiction in American Literary Culture*, ed. Alfred Bendixen and Olivia Carr Edenfield (New York: Routledge,
2017), 2.

9. Arlene Dávila, "Dreams of Place: Housing, Gentrification, and the Marketing of
Space in El Barrio," *Centro Journal* 15, no. 1 (2003): 114.

10. Brian Goldstein, *The Roots of Urban Renaissance: Gentrification and the Struggle
Over Harlem* (Cambridge, MA: Harvard University Press, 2017), 5.

11. Office of City Council Speaker Melissa Mark-Viverito, *East Harlem: A Neighborhood Plan*, facilitated by WXY with Hester Street Collaborative (New York: Office
of City Council Speaker, 2016), https://council.nyc.gov/land-use/wp-content
/uploads/sites/53/2017/11/EHNP_FINAL_FINAL_LORES.pdf, 118.

12. Goldstein, *Roots*, 7, 205; Ernesto Quiñonez, "The Fires Last Time," *New York Times*,
December 18, 2005.

13. Monique Taylor, *Harlem Between Heaven and Hell* (Minneapolis: University of
Minnesota Press, 2002), 175, 176; Goldstein, *Roots*, 16.

14. Thomas Sugrue, "The Structures of Urban Poverty: The Reorganization of Space
and Work in Three Periods of American History," in *The "Underclass" Debate:
Views from History*, ed. Michael Katz (Princeton, NJ: Princeton University Press,
1994), 11; Douglas S. Massey and Nancy A. Denton, *American Apartheid: Segregation
and the Making of the Underclass* (Cambridge, MA: Harvard University Press,
1993), 47.

15. Richard Schaffer and Neil Smith, "The Gentrification of Harlem?," *Annals of the
Association of American Geographers* 76, no. 3 (1986): 356–57.

16. Moss, *Vanishing*, 295.

17. Alessandro Busà, "After the 125th Street Rezoning: The Gentrification of
Harlem's Main Street in the Bloomberg Years," *Urbanities* 4, no. 2 (November
2014): 56.

18. Busà, "125th Street Rezoning," 60.

19. Schaffer and Smith, "Gentrification of Harlem?," 351; NYU Furman Center for Real
Estate and Urban Policy, "Central Harlem," https://furmancenter.org/neighborhoods
/view/central-harlem.

20. Quoted in Busà, "125th Street Rezoning," 51.

21. Office of City Council Speaker Melissa Mark-Viverito, *East Harlem: A Neighborhood Plan*, 118.

22. Goldstein, *Roots*, 20.
23. Arlene Dávila, *Barrio Dreams: Puerto Ricans, Latinos, and the Neoliberal City* (Berkeley: University of California Press, 2004), 29.
24. Goldstein, *Roots*, 21.
25. Dávila, *Barrio*, 29.
26. Goldstein, *Roots*, 7.
27. Steven Bender, *Tierra y Libertad: Land, Liberty, and Latino Housing* (New York: NYU Press, 2010), 113.
28. Bender, *Tierra y Libertad*, 114.
29. Center for Urban Research, "Race/Ethnic Change by Neighborhood," CUNY Graduate Center, May 23, 2011, http://www.urbanresearchmaps.org/plurality/files/RaceEthnic%20Change%20by%20Neighborhood%205-23-11.xls.
30. Bender, *Tierra y Libertad*, 116.
31. Goldstein, *Roots*, 241–42, 249; Upper Manhattan Empowerment Zone and Regional Plan Association, "Leveraging the Power of Cultural Investments: A Report on Cultural Capacity Building," March 2016, 2.
32. Dávila, *Barrio*, 72, 75.
33. Dávila, *Barrio*, 73.
34. Fredric Jameson, "Realism and Utopia in *The Wire*," *Criticism* 52, nos. 3–4 (2010): 369.
35. Grace F. Edwards, *If I Should Die* (New York: Doubleday, 1997), 58.
36. Jameson, "Realism," 369.
37. Dennis Broe, "Class, Labor, and the Home-Front Detective: Hammett, Chandler, Woolrich, and the Dissident Lawman (and Woman) in 1940s Hollywood and Beyond," *Social Justice* 32, no. 2 (2005), 179.
38. Moss, *Vanishing*, 294.
39. Broe, "Class," 179.
40. Quoted in Nat Hentoff and Nick Hentoff, "Rudy's Racist Rants: An NYPD History Lesson," Cato Institute, July 14, 2016, https://www.cato.org/commentary/rudys-racist-rants-nypd-history-lesson.
41. Denolyn Carroll, "First Person Singular," *Essence*, September 2000, 100.
42. For an overview of these arguments, see José V. Saval, "Crime Fiction and Politics," in *The Routledge Companion to Crime Fiction*, ed. Janice Allan et al. (New York: Routledge, 2020), 328.
43. Ernesto Quiñonez, *Chango's Fire: A Novel* (New York: Rayo, 2004), 116, 117.
44. Dávila, *Barrio*, 11.
45. Quiñonez, "Fires."
46. Ernesto Quiñonez, *Bodega Dreams* (New York: Vintage, 2000), 4–5.
47. Andrew Pepper, *Unwilling Executioner: Crime Fiction and the State* (Oxford: Oxford University Press, 2016), 16.
48. Ernesto Quiñonez, introduction to *Review: Literature and Arts of the Americas* 50, no. 1 (2017): 7.
49. Edward Soja, *Postmetropolis: Critical Studies of Cities and Regions* (Malden, MA: Routledge, 2000), 11.
50. Susan Méndez, "The Fire Between Them: Religion and Gentrification in Ernesto Quiñonez's *Chango's Fire*," *Centro Journal* 23, no. 1 (2011): 192.

5. BEDFORD-STUYVESANT: WHITE BOYS IN THE HOOD

1. Wil Medearis, *Restoration Heights* (Toronto: Hanover Square, 2019), 161.
2. Paula C. Johnson, "Beyond Displacement: Gentrification of Racialized Spaces as Violence—Harlem, New York, and New Orleans, Louisiana," in *Accumulating Insecurity: Violence and Dispossession in the Making of Everyday Life*, ed. Shelley Feldman et al. (Athens: University of Georgia Press, 2011), 84, 82.
3. Brandon Harris, *Making Rent in Bed-Stuy: A Memoir of Trying to Make It in New York City* (New York: Amistad, 2017), 2, 1.
4. Seth Kamil and Eric Wakin, *The Big Onion Guide to Brooklyn: Ten Historic Walking Tours* (New York: NYU Press, 2005), 61.
5. Alison Gregor, "Bedford-Stuyvesant: Diverse and Changing," *New York Times*, July 9, 2014.
6. Devorah Heitner, "The Good Side of the Ghetto: Visualizing Black Brooklyn, 1968–1971," *Velvet Trap* 62 (Fall 2008): 51.
7. Thomas P. DiNapoli and Kenneth B. Bleiwas, "An Economic Snapshot of the Bedford-Stuyvesant Neighborhood" (New York: Office of the New York State Controller, September 2017), 2, https://www.osc.state.ny.us/sites/default/files/reports/documents/pdf/2018-11/report-5-2018.pdf.
8. DiNapoli and Bleiwas, "Economic Snapshot," 3.
9. NYU Furman Center for Real Estate and Urban Policy, "Bedford-Stuyvesant," https://furmancenter.org/neighborhoods/view/bedford-stuyvesant; Jeremiah Moss, *Vanishing New York: How a Great City Lost Its Soul* (New York: Dey St., 2017), 344.
10. DiNapoli and Bleiwas, "An Economic Snapshot," 5.
11. David Harvey, "Uneven Geographical Developments and Universal Rights," in *Readings in Urban Theory*, ed. Susan S. Fainstein and Scott Campbell (Chichester: Blackwell, 2011), 367.
12. Brian Platzer, *Bed-Stuy Is Burning* (New York: Washington Square, 2017), 36.
13. Brian Platzer, "Bed-Stuy's Many Faces of Gentrification: Brian Platzer with Liz von Klemperer," interview by Liz von Klemperer, *Brooklyn Rail*, July–August 2017, https://brooklynrail.org/2017/07/books/Bed-Stuys-Many-Faces-of-Gentrification-Brian-Platzer-with-Liz-von-Klemperer.
14. Mychal Denzel Smith, "*Bed-Stuy Is Burning* Takes on Gentrification in Brooklyn," *New York Times*, August 11, 2017.
15. Platzer, "Bed-Stuy's Many Faces."
16. Brian Platzer, "When Are You Going to Write About Black People?" *Literary Hub*, July 11, 2017, https://lithub.com/when-are-you-going-to-write-about-black-people/.
17. Platzer, "Bed-Stuy's Many Faces."
18. Sarah Schulman, *The Gentrification of the Mind: Witness to a Lost Imagination* (Berkeley: University of California Press, 2012), 161.

BIBLIOGRAPHY

Andrew, Lucy, and Catherine Phelps. Introduction to *Capital Crimes: Crime Fiction in the City*, ed. Lucy Andrew and Catherine Phelps, 1–5. Cardiff: University of Wales Press, 2013.

Ansfield, Bench. "The Broken Windows of the Bronx: Putting the Theory in Its Place." *American Quarterly* 72, no. 1 (March 2020): 103–27.

Auster, Paul. *The New York Trilogy: City of Glass, Ghosts, The Locked Room*. New York: Penguin, 2006.

Baker, Kevin. "The Death of a Once Great City: The Fall of New York and the Urban Crisis of Affluence." *Harper's*, July 2018. https://harpers.org/archive/2018/07/the-death-of-new-york-city-gentrification.

Barajas, Elías Dominguez. "The Postmodern Ethnic Condition in Ernesto Quiñonez's *Bodega Dreams*." *Latino Studies* 12, no. 1 (2014): 7–26.

Belkind, Lara. "Stealth Gentrification: Camouflage and Commerce on the Lower East Side." *Traditional Dwellings and Settlements Review* 21, no. 1 (Fall 2009): 21–36.

Bender, Steven. *Tierra y Libertad: Land, Liberty, and Latino Housing*. New York: NYU Press, 2010.

Bendixen, Alfred. "Researching the Premises: The Centrality of Crime Fiction in American Literary Culture." In *The Centrality of Crime Fiction in American Literary Culture*, ed. Alfred Bendixen and Olivia Carr Edenfield, 1–7. New York: Routledge, 2017.

Black, Joel. "Crime Fiction and the Literary Canon." In *A Companion to Crime Fiction*, ed. Charles J. Rzepka and Lee Horsley, 76–89. Chichester: Blackwell-Wiley, 2010.

Bloomberg, Michael. "State of the City Address." *Gotham Gazette*, January 23, 2003.

Bondi, Liz. "Gender Divisions and Gentrification: A Critique." *Transactions of the Institute of British Geographers* 16, no. 2 (1991): 190–98.

Bowles, Jonathan. "Q&A with Red Hook Developer Greg O'Connell." Center for an Urban Future, March 2005. https://nycfuture.org/research/qa-with-red-hook -developer-greg-oconnell-the-importance-of-balanced-growth.

Boyd, Herb. "Noted Author Grace F. Edwards Dies at 87." *New York Amsterdam News*, April 9, 2020. http://amsterdamnews.com/news/2020/apr/09/noted-author-grace-f -edwards-dies-87.

Brash, Julian. *Bloomberg's New York: Class and Governance in the Luxury City*. Athens: University of Georgia Press, 2011.

Bratton, William. "Police Strategy No. 5: Reclaiming the Public Spaces of New York." New York City Police Department, 1994.

Broe, Dennis. "Class, Labor, and the Home-Front Detective: Hammett, Chandler, Woolrich, and the Dissident Lawman (and Woman) in 1940s Hollywood and Beyond." *Social Justice* 32, no. 2 (2005): 167–85.

Brooks, Peter. *Reading for the Plot: Design and Intention in Narrative*. Cambridge, MA: Harvard University Press, 1984.

Busà, Alessandro. "After the 125th Street Rezoning: The Gentrification of Harlem's Main Street in the Bloomberg Years." *Urbanities* 4, no. 2 (November 2014): 51–68.

Caro, Robert. *The Power Broker: Robert Moses and the Fall of New York*. New York: Vintage, 1975.

Carroll, Denolyn. "First Person Singular." *Essence*, September 2000.

Castells, Manuel. *The City and the Grassroots*. Berkeley: University of California Press, 1983.

Center for Urban Research, Graduate Center, CUNY. "Race/Ethnic Change by Neighborhood." May 23, 2011. http://www.urbanresearchmaps.org/plurality/files /RaceEthnic%20Change%20by%20Neighborhood%205-23-11.xls.

Certeau, Michel de. *The Practice of Everyday Life*. Trans. Steven Rendall. Berkeley: University of California Press, 1984.

Chandler, Raymond. *The Big Sleep*. New York: Vintage Crime, 1992.

——. *Farewell, My Lovely*. New York: Vintage Crime, 1940.

——. *Selected Letters of Raymond Chandler*. Ed. Frank MacShane. London: Jonathan Cape, 1981.

Chang, Henry. *Chinatown Beat*. New York: Soho, 2006.

——. "Henry Chang: A Chinatown Walking Tour with the Mystery Writer." *Asia Pacific Forum*, April 21, 2009. http://www.asiapacificforum.org/show-detail.php ?show_id=148#394.

——. "Henry Chang Interview with Tomie Arai." Portraits of Chinatown, Museum of Chinese in America, New York, February 21, 2013. Video.

——. *Red Jade*. New York: Soho, 2010.

——. *Year of the Dog*. New York: Soho, 2008.

Chen, Ching Yeh. Interview by Lena Sze. "AOC_Ching Yeh Chen_Nov_9_2007. WMA." Archaeology of Change Archives, Museum of Chinese in America, New York.

Chin, Frank, and Jeffery Paul Chan. "Racist Love." In *Seeing Through Shuck*, ed. Richard Kostelanetz, 65–79. New York: Ballantine, 1972.

Christian, Nicole M. "Sales Pitch: New York Worth the Cost." *New York Times*, January 24, 2003.

Chronopoulos, Themis. *Spatial Regulation in New York City: From Urban Renewal to Zero Tolerance*. New York: Routledge, 2011.

Cimino, Michael, dir. *Year of the Dragon*. Beverly Hills, CA: Metro-Goldwyn-Mayer, 1985. Film.

Cohen, Gabriel. *The Graving Dock*. New York: Thomas Dunne, 2007.

——. *The Ninth Step*. New York: Thomas Dunne, 2010.

——. *Red Hook*. New York: Thomas Dunne, 2001.

Council for Public Safety. "Welcome to Fear City: A Survival Guide for Visitors to the City of New York." 1975.

Dávila, Arlene. *Barrio Dreams: Puerto Ricans, Latinos, and the Neoliberal City*. Berkeley: University of California Press, 2004.

——. "Dreams of Place: Housing, Gentrification, and the Marketing of Space in El Barrio." *Centro Journal* 15, no. 1 (2003): 112–37.

Deutsche, Rosalind, and Cara Gendel Ryan. "The Fine Art of Gentrification." *October* 31 (1984): 91–111.

DiNapoli, Thomas P., and Kenneth B. Bleiwas. "An Economic Snapshot of the Bedford-Stuyvesant Neighborhood." New York: Office of the New York State Controller, September 2017. https://www.osc.state.ny.us/sites/default/files/reports/documents/pdf/2018–11/report-5–2018.pdf.

Edison Properties. "Why the Ludlow?" http://www.theludlownyc.com/neighborhood.

Edwards, Grace F. *If I Should Die*. New York: Doubleday, 1997.

Erdmann, Eva. "Nationality International: Detective Fiction in the Late Twentieth Century." In *Investigating Identities: Questions of Identity in Contemporary International Crime Fiction*, ed. Kate M. Quinn and Marieke Krajenbrink, 11–26. Amsterdam: Rodopi, 2009.

Eure, Philip K. "An Analysis of Quality-of-Summonses, Quality-of-Life Misdemeanor Arrests, and Felony Crime in New York City, 2019–2015." New York Office of Investigation, Office of the Inspector General for the NYPD, June 22, 2016.

Farzin, Media. "Lush Life: An Exhibition in Nine Chapters, New York." *Art Agenda*, August 11, 2010, http://www.art-agenda.com/features/232273/lush-life-an-exhibition-in-nine-chapters-new-york.

Florida, Richard. *Cities and the Creative Class*. New York: Routledge, 2005.

——. *The New Urban Crisis*. New York: Basic Books, 2017.

Glass, Ruth. *London: Aspects of Change*. London: MacGibbon & Kee, 1964.

Goldstein, Brian. *The Roots of Urban Renaissance: Gentrification and the Struggle over Harlem*. Cambridge, MA: Harvard University Press, 2017.

Gould Ellen, Ingrid, Keren Mertens Horn, and David Reed. "Has Falling Crime Invited Gentrification?" *Journal of Housing Economics* 46 (December 2019): 1–11.

Gregor, Alison. "Bedford-Stuyvesant: Diverse and Changing." *New York Times*, July 9, 2014.

Gulddal, Jesper, and Steward King. "Genre." In *The Routledge Companion to Crime Fiction*, ed. Janice Allan et al., 13–21. New York: Routledge, 2020.

Gumport, Elizabeth. "Gentrified Fictions." *n+1*, November 2, 2009. http://nplusonemag.com/online-only/book-review/gentrified-fiction.

Hammett, Dashiell. *Red Harvest*. New York: Vintage Crime, 1992.

Harris, Brandon. *Making Rent in Bed-Stuy: A Memoir of Trying to Make It in New York City*. New York: Amistad, 2017.

Harris, Jane. "The Lush History of the Lower East Side." *Art in America*, August 3, 2010. http://www.artinamericamagazine.com/news-features/news/lush-life-franklin-evans -omar-lopez-chahoud.

Harvey, David. "Uneven Geographical Developments and Universal Rights." In *Readings in Urban Theory*, ed. Susan S. Fainstein and Scott Campbell, 357–76. Chichester: Blackwells, 2011.

——. "The Urban Process Under Capitalism: A Framework for Analysis." *International Journal of Urban and Regional Research* 2 (1978): 101–31.

Hayden, Dolores. *The Power of Place: Urban Landscapes as Public History*. Cambridge, MA: MIT Press, 1995.

Heitner, Devorah. "The Good Side of the Ghetto: Visualizing Black Brooklyn, 1968–1971." *Velvet Trap* 62 (Fall 2008): 48–61.

Hentoff, Nat, and Nick Hentoff. "Rudy's Racist Rants: An NYPD History Lesson." Cato Institute, July 14, 2016. https://www.cato.org/commentary/rudys-racist-rants-nypd -history-lesson.

Herbert, Steve. *Policing Space: Territoriality and the Los Angeles Police Department*. Minneapolis: University of Minnesota Press, 1997.

Himes, Chester. "Harlem, ou le cancer de l'Amerique." *Presence Africaine* 45, 1er Trimestre (1963): 46–81.

Huyssen, Andreas. *Present Pasts: Urban Palimpsests and the Politics of Memory*. Stanford, CA: Stanford University Press, 2003.

Ivins, Molly. "Red Hook Survives Hard Times Into New Era." *New York Times*. November 16, 1981.

Jameson, Fredric. *Raymond Chandler: The Detections of Totality*. London: Verso, 2016.

——. "Realism and Utopia in *The Wire*." *Criticism* 52, nos. 3–4 (2010): 359–72.

Johnson, Paula C. "Beyond Displacement: Gentrification of Racialized Spaces as Violence—Harlem, New York, and New Orleans, Louisiana." In *Accumulating Insecurity: Violence and Dispossession in the Making of Everyday Life*, ed. Shelley Feldman, Charles Geisler, and Gayatri A. Menon, 79–103. Athens: University of Georgia Press, 2011.

Karmen, Andrew. *New York Murder Mystery: The True Story Behind the Crime Crash of the 1990s*. New York: NYU Press, 2006.

Katz, Michael. "Reframing the Underclass Debate." In *The "Underclass" Debate: Views from History*, ed. Michael Katz, 440–78. Princeton, NJ: Princeton University Press, 1994.

Keunen, Bart, and Bart Eeckhout. "Whatever Happened to the Urban Novel? New Perspectives for Literary Urban Studies in the Era of Postmodern Culture." In *Postmodern New York City: Transfiguring Spaces*, ed. Günter Lenz and Utz Reise, 53–68. Heidelberg: Heidelberg University Press, 2003.

Kim, Elaine H. *Asian American Literature: An Introduction to the Writings and Their Social Context*. Philadelphia: Temple University Press, 1982.

King, Stewart. "Place." In *The Routledge Companion to Crime Fiction*, ed. Janice Allan et al., 211–18. New York: Routledge, 2020.

Krisel, Rebecca Salima. "Gentrifying a Superfund Site: Why Gowanus, Brooklyn Is Becoming a Real Estate Hot Spot." *Consilience* 14 (2015): 214–24.

Kurutz, Steven. "Murder on Mott Street." *New York Times*, October 24, 2008.

Kwong, Peter. "Answers About the Gentrification of Chinatown." *New York Times*, September 16, 2009.

Lander, Brad, and Laura Wolf-Powers. "Remaking New York City: Can Prosperity Be Shared and Sustainable." Pratt Institute Center for Community and Environmental Development, New York, November 2004. https://repository.upenn.edu/cgi/viewcontent.cgi?article=1042&context=cplan_papers.

Lee, Jan. Interview by Lena Sze and Tomie Arai. "AOC_Jane Lee_18 Jun 2008. WMA." Archaeology of Change Archives, Museum of Chinese in America, New York.

Lefebvre, Henri. *The Production of Space*. Trans. Donald Nicholson-Smith. Oxford: Blackwell, 1991.

——. *The Urban Revolution*. Trans. Robert Bononno. Minneapolis: University of Minnesota Press, 2003.

Lewis, Oscar. *A Study of Slum Culture: Backgrounds for La Vida*. New York: Random House, 1968.

Li, Bethany Y., Andrew Leong, Domenic Vitiello, and Arthur Acoca. "Chinatown Then and Now: Gentrification in Boston, New York, and Philadelphia." Asian American Legal Defense and Education Fund, 2013.

Lin, Jan. *The Power of Urban Ethnic Places: Cultural Heritage and Community Life*. New York: Routledge, 2011.

——. *Reconstructing Chinatown: Ethnic Enclave, Global Change*. Minneapolis: University of Minnesota Press, 1998.

Lloyd, Richard. *Neo-Bohemia: Art and Commerce in the Postindustrial City*. New York: Routledge, 2006.

Lovecraft, H. P. "The Horror at Red Hook." In *The Tomb and Other Tales*, 70–93. New York: Ballantine, 1965.

Maeckelbergh, Marianne. "Mobilizing to Stay Put: Housing Struggles in New York City." *International Journal of Urban and Regional Research* 36, no. 4 (July 2012): 655–73.

Mak, Kam. Interview by Lena Sze and Tomie Arai. "AOC_Kim Mak_6 March 2008 WMA." Archaeology of Change Archives, Museum of Chinese in America, New York.

Marshall, Paule. *Brown Girl, Brownstones*. New York: Feminist Press, 1981.

Martin, Theodore. *Contemporary Drift: Genre, Historicism, and the Problem of the Present*. New York: Columbia University Press, 2017.

Massey, Douglas S., and Nancy A. Denton. *American Apartheid: Segregation and the Making of the Underclass*. Cambridge, MA: Harvard University Press, 1993.

"Mayor Michael Bloomberg's State of the City Address." *New York Times*, January 30, 2002.

McClellan, Robert, *The Heathen Chinee: A Study of American Attitudes Toward China, 1890–1905*. Athens: Ohio State University Press, 1971.

Medearis, Wil. *Restoration Heights*. Toronto: Hanover Square, 2019.

Mele, Christopher. *Selling the Lower East Side: Culture, Real Estate, and Resistance in New York City*. Minneapolis: University of Minnesota Press, 2000.

Méndez, Susan. "The Fire Between Them: Religion and Gentrification in Ernesto Quiñonez's *Chango's Fire*." *Centro Journal* 23, no. 1 (2011): 177–95.

Miller, Arthur. *A View from the Bridge*. New York: Penguin, 1955.

Moore, Clayton. "Richard Price and the Lush Life." *Bookslut*, January 2008. http://www
.bookslut.com/mystery_strumpet/2008_01_012356.php.

Moretti, Franco. *Signs Taken for Wonders: Essays in the Sociology of Literary Forms.*
London: Verso, 2005.

Moss, Jeremiah. *Vanishing New York: How a Great City Lost Its Soul.* New York: Dey
St., 2017.

Mumford, Lewis. *The Culture of Cities.* New York: Secker & Warburg, 1940.

Nadelson, Reggie. "Artie Cohen's Harlem Whodunit." Interview by Salman Rushdie.
Vanity Fair, October 2010. https://www.vanityfair.com/culture/2010/10/reggie
-nadelson-201010.

——. *Red Hook.* New York: Walker, 2005.

Nadelson, Reggie, Lee Child, and George Dawes Green. "New York City Thrillers."
Interview by Leonard Lopate. *The Leonard Lopate Show*, WNYC, December 24,
2009. https://www.wnyc.org/story/59750-new-york-city-thrillers.

Neculai, Catalina. *Urban Space and Late Twentieth-Century New York Literature.* New
York: Palgrave, 2014.

New York City Department of City Planning. *The New Waterfront Revitalization Program.* 2002. https://www1.nyc.gov/assets/planning/download/pdf/applicants/wrp
/wrp_full.pdf.

——. *Red Hook: A Plan for Community Regeneration.* 1996. https://www1.nyc.gov/assets
/brooklyncb6/downloads/pdf/bkcb6-197a-plan.pdf.

——. *Vision 2020: New York Comprehensive Waterfront Plan.* 2011. https://www1.nyc
.gov/assets/planning/download/pdf/plans-studies/vision-2020-cwp/vision2020
/vision2020_nyc_cwp.pdf.

NY Rising Community Reconstruction Red Hook Planning Committee. *Red Hook: NY
Rising Community Reconstruction Plan.* 2014. https://stormrecovery.ny.gov/sites
/default/files/crp/community/documents/redhook_nyrcr_plan_20mb_0.pdf.

Office of City Council Speaker Melissa Mark-Viverito. *East Harlem: A Neighborhood
Plan.* Facilitated by WXY with Hester Street Collaborative. https://council.nyc.gov
/land-use/wp-content/uploads/sites/53/2017/11/EHNP_FINAL_FINAL_LORES
.pdf.

Ong, Kayo. Interview by Lena Sze and Tomie Arai. "AOC_Kayo Ong_Feb_19 2008.
WMA." Archaeology of Change Archives, Museum of Chinese in America, New
York.

Osman, Suleiman. *The Invention of Brownstone Brooklyn: Gentrification and the Search
for Authenticity in Postwar New York.* New York: Oxford University Press, 2011.

Papa, Victor. Foreword to "'A Divided Community': A Study of the Gentrification of
the Lower East Side Community, New York." New York: Two Bridges Neighborhood
Council, Inc., June 2004. https://twobridges.org/publications/a-divided-community
-a-study-of-gentrification-of-the-lower-east-side-community-new-york-2004.

Pepper, Andrew. "Black Crime Fiction." In *The Cambridge Companion to Crime Fiction*, ed. Martin Priestman, 209–26. Cambridge: Cambridge University Press, 2003.

——. *The Contemporary American Crime Novel: Race, Ethnicity, Gender, Class.* Edinburgh: Edinburgh University Press, 2000.

——. *Unwilling Executioner: Crime Fiction and the State.* Oxford: Oxford University
Press, 2016.

Phelan, James D. "Why the Chinese Should Be Excluded." *North American Review* 173, no. 540 (1901): 663–76.

Platzer, Brian. *Bed-Stuy Is Burning*. New York: Washington Square, 2017.

——. "Bed-Stuy's Many Faces of Gentrification: Brian Platzer with Liz von Klemperer." *Brooklyn Rail*, July–August 2017. https://brooklynrail.org/2017/07/books/Bed-Stuys -Many-Faces-of-Gentrification-Brian-Platzer-with-Liz-von-Klemperer.

——. "When Are You Going to Write About Black People?" *Literary Hub*, July 11, 2017. https://lithub.com/when-are-you-going-to-write-about-black-people/.

Pochoda, Ivy. *Visitation Street*. New York: Harper Perennial, 2013.

Polanski, Roman, dir. *Chinatown*. Los Angeles: Paramount, 1974. Film.

Porter, Dennis. *The Pursuit of Crime: Art and Ideology in Detective Fiction*. New Haven, CT: Yale University Press, 1981.

Price, Richard. "For Crime Novelist Richard Price, Life is 'Lush.'" Interview by Terry Gross. *Fresh Air*, NPR, March 5, 2008. http://www.npr.org/templates/transcript /transcript.php?storyId=101238934.

——. *Lush Life*. New York: Picador, 2008.

——. "Richard Price Discusses *The Whites* with Editor John Sterling." YouTube video, February 3, 2015. http://www.youtube.com/watch?v=0FGxBK9NQ-0.

——. "Richard Price—Living a Lush Life in Some Small Dive." Interview by Ronald Sklar. *Popentertainment.com*, March 2, 2008. https://www.popentertainment archives/post/-price-living-a-lush-life-in-some-small-dive.

Quiñonez, Ernesto. *Bodega Dreams*. New York: Vintage Contemporaries, 2000.

——. *Chango's Fire: A Novel*. New York: Rayo, 2004.

——. "The Fires Last Time." *New York Times*, December 18, 2005.

——. Introduction to *Review: Literature and Arts of the Americas* 50, no. 1 (2017): 6–8.

Riis, Jacob. *How the Other Half Lives*. New York: Norton, 2010.

Rosen, Jeremy. "Literary Fiction and the Genres of Genre Fiction." *Post45*, August 7, 2018. https://post45.org/2018/08/literary-fiction-and-the-genres-of-genre-fiction.

Rosler, Martha. "Fragments of a Metropolitan Viewpoint." In *If You Lived Here: The City in Art, Theory, and Social Activism*, ed. Brian Wallis, 15–44. Seattle: Bay, 1991.

Rotella, Carlo. *October Cities: The Redevelopment of Urban Literature*. Berkeley: University of California Press, 1998.

——. "Urban Literature: A User's Guide." *Journal of Urban History* 44, no. 4 (2018): 797–805.

——. *The World Is Always Coming to an End: Pulling Together and Apart in a Chicago Neighborhood*. Chicago: University of Chicago Press, 2019.

Rozan, S. J. *China Trade*. New York: Minotaur, 1994.

Rzepka, Charles J. "Introduction: What is Crime Fiction." In *Companion to Crime Fiction*, ed. Charles J. Rzepka and Lee Horsley, 1–9, Chichester: Blackwell-Wiley, 2010.

Sante, Luc. *Low Life: Lures and Snares of Old New York*. New York: Vintage, 1991.

Saval, José V. "Crime Fiction and Politics." In *The Routledge Companion to Crime Fiction*, ed. Janice Allan et al., 327–34. New York: Routledge, 2020.

Scaggs, John. *Crime Fiction*. London: Routledge, 2005.

Schaffer, Richard, and Neil Smith. "The Gentrification of Harlem?" *Annals of the Association of American Geographers* 76, no. 3 (1986): 347–65.

Schaller, Susanna, and Johannes Novy. "New York City's Waterfronts as Strategic Sites for Analyzing Neoliberalism and Its Contestations." In *Transforming Urban Waterfronts: Fixity and Flow*, ed. Gene Desfor et al., 166–87. New York: Routledge, 2011.

Schmid, David. "Imagining Safe Urban Space: The Contribution of Detective Fiction to Radical Geography." *Antipode* 27, no. 3 (1995): 242–69.

Schulman, Sarah. *The Gentrification of the Mind: Witness to a Lost Imagination*. Berkeley: University of California Press, 2012.

Silver, Howard. "Richard Price Reads from and Discusses *Lush Life*." YouTube video, 4:40. March 23, 2009. http://www.youtube.com/watch?v=YFVgV4mXFAA.

Smi, Robert. "Red Hook: A Mystery Writer's Guide to the Brick and Bodies of the Neighborhood." *North Country Public Radio*. July 28, 2009. http://www.northcountrypublicradio.org/news/npr/131009145/red-hook-a-mystery-writer-s-guide-to-the-bricks-and-the-bodies-of-the-neighborhood.

Smith, Mychal Denzel. "*Bed-Stuy Is Burning* Takes on Gentrification in Brooklyn." *New York Times*, August 11, 2017.

Smith, Neil. "Gentrification and Uneven Development." *Economic Geography* 58, no. 2 (April 1982): 139–55.

——. "New Globalism, New Urbanism: Gentrification as Global Urban Strategy." *Antipode* 34, no. 3 (2002): 427–50.

——. *The New Urban Frontier: Gentrification and the Revanchist City*. New York: Routledge, 1996.

Soja, Edward. *Postmetropolis: Critical Studies of Cities and Regions*. Malden, MA: Routledge, 2000.

——. *Postmodern Geographies: The Reassertion of Space in Critical Social Theory*. London: Verso, 1989.

Solomon, Marisa. "'The Ghetto Is a Gold Mine': The Racialized Temporality of Betterment." *International Labor and Working-Class History* 95 (Spring 2019): 76–94.

Sridhar, C. R. "Broken Windows and Zero Tolerance: Policing Urban Crimes." *Economic and Political Weekly* 41, no. 19 (May 13–19, 2006): 1841–43.

Starr, Roger. "Making New York Smaller." *New York Times*, November 14, 1976.

Stevens, Quentin. "Conclusion: Patterns of Persistence, Trajectories of Change." In *Transforming Urban Waterfronts: Fixity and Flow*, ed. Gene Desfor et al., 295–315, New York: Routledge, 2011.

Sugrue, Thomas. "The Structures of Urban Poverty: The Reorganization of Space and Work in Three Periods of American History." In *The "Underclass" Debate: Views from History*, ed. Michael Katz, 85–117. Princeton, NJ: Princeton University Press, 1994.

Taylor, Monique. *Harlem Between Heaven and Hell*. Minneapolis: University of Minnesota Press, 2002.

Throgmorton, James. "Planning as Persuasive Storytelling in a Global-Scale Web of Relationships." *Planning Theory* 2, no. 2 (2003): 125–51.

Two Bridges Neighborhood Council. "'A Divided Community': A Study of the Gentrification of the Lower East Side Community, New York." June 2004. https://twobridges.org/publications/a-divided-community-a-study-of-gentrification-of-the-lower-east-side-community-new-york-2004.

Upper Manhattan Empowerment Zone and Regional Plan Association. "Leveraging the Power of Cultural Investments: A Report on Cultural Capacity Building." March 2016.

Wang, Spring. Interview by Lena Sze and Tomie Arai. "AOC_Spring Wang_18 March 2008 WMA." Archaeology of Change Archives, Museum of Chinese in America, New York.

Westphal, Dirk. Interview by Lena Sze and Tomie Arai. "AOC_Dirk Westphal_8 Jan 08.WMA." Archaeology of Change Archives, Museum of Chinese in America, New York.

Wilson, James Q. *Varieties of Police Behavior.* Cambridge, MA: Harvard University Press, 1968.

Wilson, James Q., and George L. Kelling. "Broken Windows: The Police and Neighborhood Safety." *The Atlantic*, March 1982.

Wong, K. Scott. "Chinatown: Conflicting Images, Contested Terrain." *MELUS* 20, no. 1 (1995): 3–15.

Wong, Sau-Ling Cynthia. "Ethnic Subject, Ethnic Sign, and the Difficulty of Rehabilitative Representation: Chinatown in Some Works of Chinese American Fiction." *Yearbook of English Studies* 24 (1994): 251–62.

Wroe, Nicholas. "Excavation of the Lower East Side." *The Guardian*, August 15, 2008. https://www.theguardian.com/books/2008/aug/16/fiction1.

Zimring, Franklin E. *The City That Became Safe: New York's Lessons for Urban Crime and Its Control.* Oxford: Oxford University Press, 2012.

Zukin, Sharon. *Naked City: The Death and Life of Authentic Urban Places.* Oxford: Oxford University Press, 2009.